Mathematics
In Our World
Third Edition

Robert E. Eicholz

Phares G. O'Daffer

Charles R. Fleenor

Contributing Writer
Randall I. Charles

Addison-Wesley Publishing Company

Menlo Park, California · Reading, Massachusetts · London · Amsterdam · Don Mills, Ontario · Sydney

Illustration Acknowledgments

Jane McCreary: 48–49, 50, 395–402

Masami Miyamoto: 10, 82, 102–103, 127, 180, 181, 187

Steve Osborne: 78–79

Wayne and Teresa Snyder: 34–35, 36, 44, 45, 100, 106–107, 116, 117, 128, 129, 163, 225, 243, 244, 261, 278, 285, 332

Thumbs Up Studio: 98–99

All other illustrations by Addison-Wesley Publishing Company.

Photograph Acknowledgments

Elihu Blotnick*: 189 top right, 212 right, 300 bottom left

John M. Burnley/Bruce Coleman Inc.: 94 left

Francisco Erize/Bruce Coleman Inc.: 193 right

Elliott Erwitt/Magnum Photos: 148

M. C. Escher—Escher Foundation—Haags Gemeentemuseum—The Hague: 304 center left, "Study of Regular Division of the Plane with Birds;" 304 center right, "Study of Regular Division of the Plane with Fish and Birds;" 304 bottom left, "Study of Regular Division of the Plane with Horsemen;" 304 bottom right, "Study of Regular Division of the Plane with Birds," 1955

© *Jeffrey Foxx/Woodfin Camp & Associates:* 1 top, 2–3

George B. Fry III: 1 bottom left, 14–15

George B. Fry III*: 1 bottom right, 6, 22, 24, 40, 52, 60, 69 bottom right, 76, 81, 84, 86, 87, 88, 90–91, 94 top right, 104, 112, 119, 127 center and top right, 138, 146–147, 152, 154, 157, 158–159, 161, 164 top and bottom, 165, 189 bottom center, 208, 212 left, 214, 216, 218, 219, 220, 222, 226, 243 bottom left, 300 top left, top right, center right and bottom right, 331, 336, 338, 344 top right, 364

Fritz Goro, courtesy SCIENTIFIC AMERICAN, July, 1976: 69 top left, 109

Clem Haagner/Bruce Coleman Inc.: 189 top left, 192, 193 left

George Hall*: 115, 145

Grant Heilman: 317 top right, 337

Wayland Lee*/Addison-Wesley Publishing Company: 42, 43, 110, 122, 130, 141, 150, 194, 195, 198, 201, 202, 241, 243 top right, 259, 265, 271, 272, 274, 276, 299, 301, 302, 305, 315, 317 bottom left, bottom center and center right, 335, 341, 342, 343, 344 bottom, 345, 346, 347, 349, 350, 351, 352, 353, 354, 356, 357, 372, 376, 379

Julie Lundquist/Van Cleve Photography: 257

Lee Lyon/Bruce Coleman Inc.: 196–197

Bruce McAllister: 32–33

Joe McDonald/Tom Stack & Associates: 69 top right, 94 bottom right

Burton McNeely/Van Cleve Photography: 207

NASA: 5, 69 bottom left, 72–73

National Bureau of Standards, U.S. Department of Commerce: 121

Charles E. Rotkin/Photography for Industry: 149

Wayne Scherr/Tom Stack & Associates: 94 center right

Harald Sund: 30–31

Tom Tracy: 246–247

Mark Tuschman*: 9, 164 bottom

Baron Wolman: 204–205

Nikolay Zurek*: cover

*Photographs provided expressly for the publisher.

ISBN 0-201-18180-0
DEFGHIJ-DO-87

Contents

Unit

The Decimal System
Operations and Expressions
Addition and Subtraction
Using Your Skills
Geometry—Construction and Measurement

The Decimal System

Suppose you had these five cards.

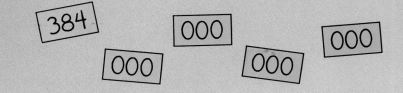

How many of the cards would you need to show each of these numbers?

1. three hundred eighty-four million

2. three hundred eighty-four thousand

3. three hundred eighty-four

4. three hundred eighty-four trillion

5. three hundred eighty-four billion

6. One of these numbers is very close to the average distance to the moon in kilometers. Two cards will give the number. Which number is it?

The age of the moon in years was recently estimated to be at least 4 600 000 000. The chart below shows how place value is used to help in reading and writing numbers of this size.

Place value names	hundred trillions	ten trillions	one trillions	hundred billions	ten billions	one billions	hundred millions	ten millions	one millions	hundred thousands	ten thousands	one thousands	hundreds	tens	ones
Numeral						4	6	0	0	0	0	0	0	0	0
Period names	Trillions			Billions			Millions			Thousands			Units		

Read each number.

1. Surface area of moon: 38 000 000 square kilometers (km²)

2. Part of moon's surface directly visible from earth: 22 420 000 km²

3. Closest moon gets to earth: 348 294 km

4. Orbital speed of moon: 3700 kilometers per hour (km/h)

Write the standard numeral.

5. thirty-five billion

6. two billion, eight hundred million

7. two hundred six trillion

8. four million, three hundred two thousand

9. five hundred thirty-seven thousand

10. three trillion, ninety-six billion, forty-six million

11. three billion seven hundred thousand

12. twenty-two million, sixty-five

13. sixty-eight thousand, thirty-four

14. ninety-seven billion, thirty-two million

Comparing and rounding whole numbers

At one place in its orbit the
moon is 384 763 km away from
the earth. At another place
in its orbit it is 384 298 km
away. Which of these distances
is greater?

384 763 is greater than 384 298
384 763 > 384 298

384 298 is less than 384 763
384 298 < 384 763

Round the greater distance to the nearest thousand.

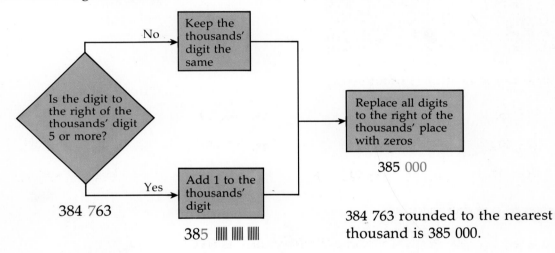

385 000

384 763 rounded to the nearest
thousand is 385 000.

Other examples

Round 9643 to the nearest hundred.

The tens' digit is less than 5.
9643 rounded to the nearest
hundred is 9600.

Round 8 365 632 to the nearest ten
thousand.

The thousands' digit is 5 or more.
8 365 632 rounded to the nearest
ten thousand is 8 370 000.

Round the greater of the two numbers to the nearest thousand.

1. 38 476 38000
   38 289

2. 536 496
   536 738

3. 3 942 865
   3 942 179

4. 49 532
   49 496

5. 36 043
   32 967

6. 56 947 568
   56 947 396

7. 9768
   9387

8. 372 498
   372 501

Round to the nearest hundred.

1. 859
2. 6578
3. 92 365
4. 8437
5. 436 976
6. 843 295
7. 7986
8. 4863
9. 57 985
10. 3 965 472
11. 83 752
12. 865 407

Round to the nearest ten thousand.

13. 576 385
14. 48 685
15. 763 942
16. 8 765 438
17. 836 594
18. 28 643
19. 97 658
20. 3 457 986
21. 945 387
22. 238 742
23. 6 957 387
24. 23 876 943

Round to one digit accuracy.

Example: 597   rounded to one digit accuracy is 600.
         674 392   rounded to one digit accuracy is 700 000.
            9365   rounded to one digit accuracy is 9000.

25. 538
26. 297
27. 3562
28. 8793
29. 46 518
30. 93 742
31. 837 965
32. 4 521 903

33. The diameter of the moon is 3476 km. Round this number to the nearest thousand.

34. A skylab crew once traveled 34 469 696 miles. Round this number to the nearest ten thousand.

How old, to the nearest year, would a person be who had lived 1 million hours?

Is this person older or younger than a person who has lived 6000 weeks?

Estimate first, then calculate.

Decimal notation

Machinists sometimes use a micrometer to make very accurate measurements.
The rod has a diameter of **one and six hundred fifty-eight thousandths** centimeters.
Give the number of tenths, hundredths, and thousandths for this number.

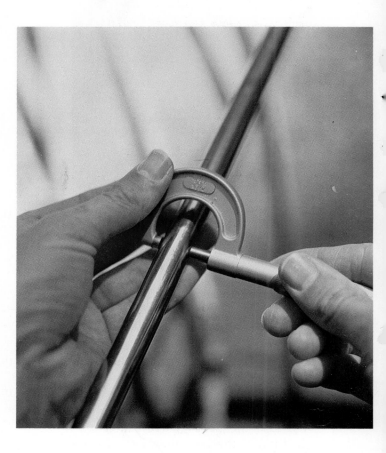

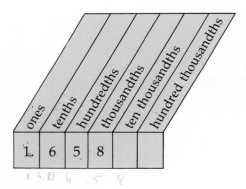

Other examples

3.724 ⟶ 7 tenths
  2 hundredths
  4 thousandths

75.4096 ⟶ 4 tenths
  0 hundredths
  9 thousandths
  6 ten thousandths

Give the number of tenths, hundredths, and thousandths for each decimal.

1. 36.281
2. 41.003
3. 4 738.075

4. 0.756
5. 672.040
6. 692.341

7. 8.032
8. 3.756
9. 2.084

10. 175.362
11. 0.008
12. 69.807

Tell what each red digit means.

1. 702.48
2. 6.5139
3. 53.48
4. 1.2179
5. 0.156
6. 0.615
7. 0.7651
8. 5.1460
9. 2.404
10. 5.354
11. 2.8706
12. 8.407
13. 82.46
14. 3.950
15. 5.9094
16. 9.318
17. 6.354
18. 6.272
19. 6.8825
20. 0.0213
21. 1.373
22. 27.0412
23. 4.9101
24. 1.1571
25. 7.265
26. 1.1809
27. 0.2982
28. 1.4681
29. 0.612
30. 4.7900
31. 3.001
32. 2.8754

33. Give a number that has
    4 in the tenths' place,
    2 in the tens' place,
    5 in the hundredths' place, and
    7 in the ones' place.

34. Give a number that has
    9 in the hundredths' place,
    4 in the ones' place,
    0 in the tenths' place, and
    6 in the thousandths' place.

Without measuring, tell which decimal is the best measure of each rod.

35.

?

A 21.34 cm
B 213.4 cm
C 2.134 cm

36.

?

A 33.24 cm
B 3.324 cm
C 332.4 cm

The large blocks have the same mass and the small blocks have the same mass. Each large block has a mass twice as large as the mass of a small block. All the blocks together have a mass of 35 kilograms. What is the mass of a large block?

Comparing decimals

Which of the two rods
has the greater diameter?

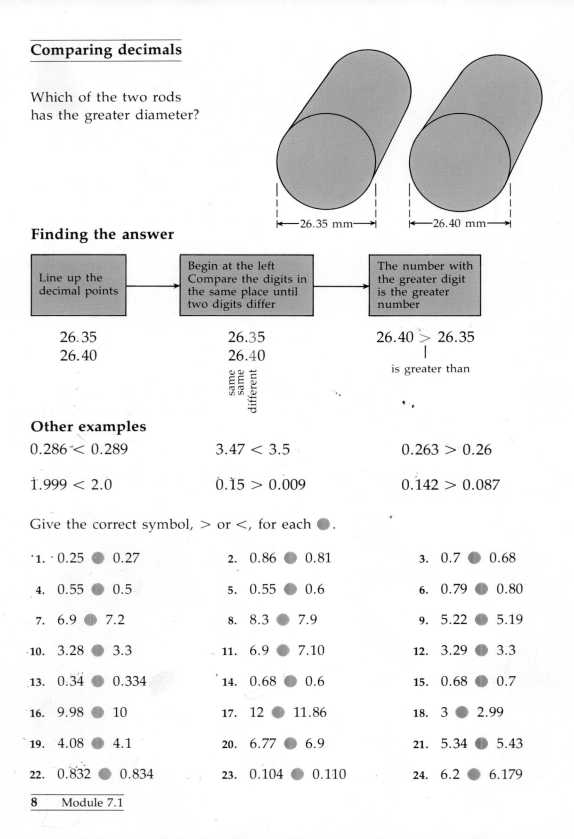

|←——26.35 mm——→| |←——26.40 mm——→|

Finding the answer

Line up the decimal points	Begin at the left Compare the digits in the same place until two digits differ	The number with the greater digit is the greater number

26.35
26.40

26.35
26.40

same
same
different

26.40 > 26.35
|
is greater than

Other examples

0.286 < 0.289   3.47 < 3.5   0.263 > 0.26

1.999 < 2.0   0.15 > 0.009   0.142 > 0.087

Give the correct symbol, > or <, for each ⬤.

1. 0.25 ⬤ 0.27   2. 0.86 ⬤ 0.81   3. 0.7 ⬤ 0.68

4. 0.55 ⬤ 0.5   5. 0.55 ⬤ 0.6   6. 0.79 ⬤ 0.80

7. 6.9 ⬤ 7.2   8. 8.3 ⬤ 7.9   9. 5.22 ⬤ 5.19

10. 3.28 ⬤ 3.3   11. 6.9 ⬤ 7.10   12. 3.29 ⬤ 3.3

13. 0.34 ⬤ 0.334   14. 0.68 ⬤ 0.6   15. 0.68 ⬤ 0.7

16. 9.98 ⬤ 10   17. 12 ⬤ 11.86   18. 3 ⬤ 2.99

19. 4.08 ⬤ 4.1   20. 6.77 ⬤ 6.9   21. 5.34 ⬤ 5.43

22. 0.832 ⬤ 0.834   23. 0.104 ⬤ 0.110   24. 6.2 ⬤ 6.179

Inspectors in machine shops sometimes use a gauge like the one below to check steel rods. Here are the rules they use:

A If the rod passes through one end of the gauge but not the other, it passes inspection.

B If the rod passes through both holes, it has been cut too small and must be scrapped.

C If the rod won't pass through either hole, it is returned to be cut smaller.

The rod must pass through this end. →

The rod must not pass through this end.

0.865

0.875

The decimals give the diameters in centimeters.

Tell whether each rod (**A**) passes inspection, (**B**) must be scrapped, or (**C**) should be returned for cutting down.

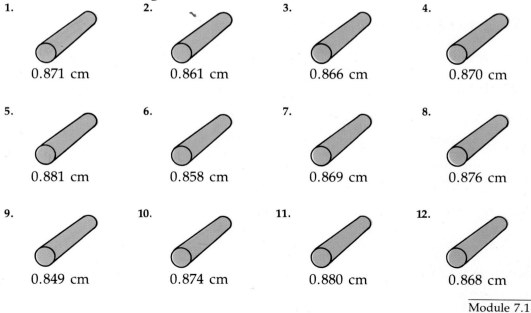

1. 0.871 cm

2. 0.861 cm

3. 0.866 cm

4. 0.870 cm

5. 0.881 cm

6. 0.858 cm

7. 0.869 cm

8. 0.876 cm

9. 0.849 cm

10. 0.874 cm

11. 0.880 cm

12. 0.868 cm

Rounding decimals

A study of the human hair shows that the average hair grows about 1.27 cm a month.

What is this length rounded to the nearest tenth?

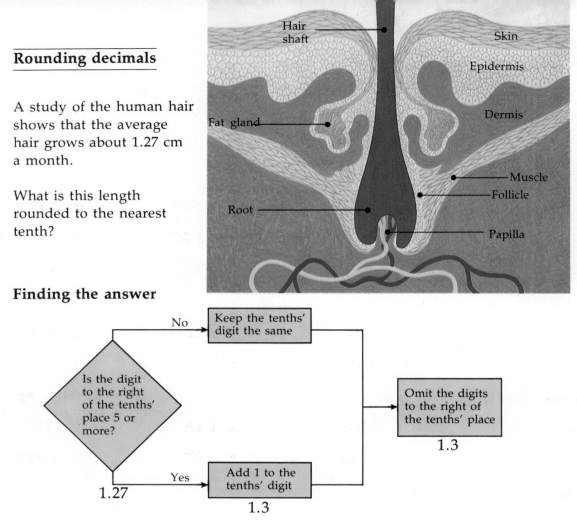

Hair shaft
Skin
Epidermis
Dermis
Fat gland
Muscle
Follicle
Root
Papilla

Finding the answer

Is the digit to the right of the tenths' place 5 or more?

No → Keep the tenths' digit the same

Yes → Add 1 to the tenths' digit

1.27

1.3

Omit the digits to the right of the tenths' place

1.3

The average hair grows about 1.3 cm per month, to the nearest tenth.

Other examples

6.24 rounded to the nearest tenth is 6.2.

15.387 rounded to the nearest hundredth is 15.39.

6.7425 rounded to the nearest thousandth is 6.743.

15.38 rounded to the nearest whole number is 15.

0.494 rounded to one digit accuracy is 0.5.

Round to the nearest tenth.

1. 13.28   2. 6.73   3. 5.89   4. 17.45

5. 386.11   6. 3.14   7. 16.07   8. 50.28

Round to the nearest hundredth.

1. 8.262
2. 645.728
3. 8.512
4. 1.409

5. 53.657
6. 0.561
7. 2.973
8. 27.140

9. 9.395
10. 714.473
11. 36.094
12. 0.803

Round to the nearest thousandth.

13. 9.1443
14. 8.5566
15. 5.0310
16. 2.4769

17. 1.9151
18. 0.1295
19. 7.3478
20. 0.8079

21. 4.2607
22. 3.6582
23. 1.7924
24. 6.8338

Round to the nearest whole number.

25. 27.95
26. 912.5
27. 88.27
28. 24.2

29. 356.3
30. 13.16
31. 906.6
32. 7.39

Round to one digit accuracy.

33. 7.375
34. 28.493
35. 0.429
36. 904.8

37. 372.93
38. 5.0703
39. 0.037
40. 0.0068

41. The average growth of a hair is 0.423 mm a day. Round this length to the nearest hundredth.

42. Find a way to check the growth rate of your own hair. Is your growth rate above or below average?

Find each of these interesting decimal quotients and round to the nearest thousandth.

1. $7 \div 9$
2. $7 \div 99$
3. $7 \div 999$
4. $8 \div 9$
5. $8 \div 99$
6. $8 \div 999$
7. $10 \div 81$
8. $10 \div 27$

Expanded notation using powers of ten

Powers of ten are often used to express large numbers.
The diagram below shows the power of ten for one million.

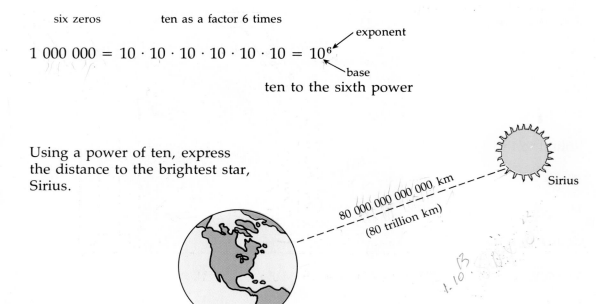

six zeros   ten as a factor 6 times

exponent

$$1\ 000\ 000 = 10 \cdot 10 \cdot 10 \cdot 10 \cdot 10 \cdot 10 = 10^6$$

base

ten to the sixth power

Using a power of ten, express
the distance to the brightest star,
Sirius.

Sirius

80 000 000 000 000 km
(80 trillion km)

$$80\ 000\ 000\ 000\ 000 = 8 \cdot 10\ 000\ 000\ 000\ 000 = 8 \cdot 10^{13}\ \text{km}$$

Using a power of ten, express each of these numbers.

1. 8 000 000
2. 4 000 000
3. 3 000 000 000

4. 3 000
5. 600 000 000
6. 200 000

7. 70 000 000 000
8. 7 000 000 000
9. 900 000 000 000

10. 60 000 000
11. 20 000 000 000 000
12. 10 000 000 000

13. 50 000 000 000
14. 8 000 000 000 000
15. 100 000 000 000 000

16. 20 000 000 000
17. 500 000 000 000
18. 400 000 000

19. 900 000 000
20. 60 000
21. 30 000 000 000

The average distance from the earth to the sun is about 149 500 000 km.

The chart shows how to express this number in expanded notation using powers of ten.

Period names				Billions			Millions			Thousands			Units		
Place-value names			hundred billions	ten billions	one billions	hundred millions	ten millions	one millions	hundred thousands	ten thousands	one thousands	hundreds	tens	ones
Numeral						1	4	9	5	0	0	0	0	0
Place-value names			100 000 000 000	10 000 000 000	1 000 000 000	100 000 000	10 000 000	1 000 000	100 000	10 000	1 000	100	10	1
Power of ten			10^{11}	10^{10}	10^{9}	10^{8}	10^{7}	10^{6}	10^{5}	10^{4}	10^{3}	10^{2}	10^{1}	10^{0}

$$149\ 500\ 000 = (1 \cdot 10^8) + (4 \cdot 10^7) + (9 \cdot 10^6) + (5 \cdot 10^5)$$

Other examples

$$3\ 247\ 000 = (3 \cdot 10^6) + (2 \cdot 10^5) + (4 \cdot 10^4) + (7 \cdot 10^3)$$
$$8\ 650\ 000\ 000 = (8 \cdot 10^9) + (6 \cdot 10^8) + (5 \cdot 10^7)$$

Express each number in expanded notation using powers of ten.

1. 36 000 000

2. 16 005 000

3. 520 000

4. 78 240 000 000

5. 1 907 420

6. 687 000 000

7. 452 190

8. 42 370 000 000

9. 7 243 000

10. 5 263 800

11. 21 045 000

12. 93 106 000

13. Distance from the planet Pluto to the sun: 5 880 000 000 km

14. Distance from the earth to the closest star, Alpha Centauri: 40 678 000 000 000 km

Scientific notation for large numbers

In 1961, an official altitude record was set for a manned balloon flight. The balloon soared to nearly $3.5 \cdot 10^4$ m over the Gulf of Mexico.

A number expressed as the product of a number between 1 and 10 and a power of ten is written in **scientific notation**.

The balloon's altitude was 35 000 m.

$3.5 \cdot 10^4 = 35\ 000$

Other examples

$485\ 000\ 000 = 4.85 \cdot 10^8$

$90\ 000\ 000 = 9 \cdot 10^7$

$7\ 640\ 000 = 7.64 \cdot 10^6$

$1\ 000\ 000 = 1 \cdot 10^6$

Give the missing numbers in the chart.

	Standard numeral	Scientific notation
1.	48 000	$4.8 \cdot 10^{\text{▨}}$
2.	370 000	$\text{▨} \cdot 10^5$
3.	▨	$6.43 \cdot 10^6$
4.	▨	$5.2 \cdot 10^4$
5.	6 300 000	▨
6.	780 000 000	▨
7.	▨	$7.86 \cdot 10^{10}$

Express each measurement in scientific notation.

1. In 1914, a distance record of nearly 3100 km was set for a manned balloon flight.

2. In 1966, an unofficial altitude of nearly 37 800 m was reached in a manned balloon.

3. In 1974, a hot-air balloon was flown a distance of 553 000 m.

4. In 1972, a toy balloon was released in California and recovered 20 days later in South Africa, a distance of 14 500 km.

5. The largest balloon ever flown had a volume of more than 736 000 m³.

6. The largest balloon had a circumference of about 35 200 cm.

7. Weather balloons sometimes reach altitudes of 45 700 m.

8. Echo I, a large plastic balloon with a thin metallic coating, was used as a communication satellite. It had a circumference of 25 100 cm.

Express each number in scientific notation.

9. 46 000 000

10. 710 000 000

11. 381 400 000

12. 513 000 000

13. 2 500 000 000

14. 9 000 000

15. 30 200 000

16. 4100

17. 800

18. 170 000 000

19. 3 090 000 000

20. 6 070 000

Answers for Self-check 1. million 2. 4 678 000 3. 2 tenths 4. 4 hundredths
5. 6 ten thousandths 6. 3 thousandths 7. 4 thousandths 8. 8 hundredths 9. $<$ 10. $<$
11. $>$ 12. 13.7 13. 3.8 14. 562.2 15. $(3 \cdot 10^7) + (6 \cdot 10^6) + (1 \cdot 10^5) + (7 \cdot 10^4)$
16. $(4 \cdot 10^5) + (8 \cdot 10^4) + (5 \cdot 10^3)$ 17. $8.05 \cdot 10^8$ 18. $9.14 \cdot 10^6$

Self-check

1. 62 000 000 means sixty-two ___?___ (thousand, million, billion).

2. Round 4 678 413 to the nearest thousand. _4 678 000_

Tell what each red digit means.

3. 38.24 _10_

4. 526.34 _100_

5. 0.7826 _tenthou_

6. 25.623 _1000_

7. 0.764 _1000_

8. 3.087 _100_

Give the correct symbol, > or <, for each ●.

9. 18.3 ● 19

10. 14.23 ● 14.26

11. 9.3 ● 9.28

Round to the nearest tenth.

12. 13.67 _= 13.7_

13. 3.824 _= 3.8_

14. 562.19
_562.2_

Express each number in expanded notation using powers of ten.

Express each number in scientific notation.

15. 36 170 000

16. 485 000

17. 805 000 000

18. 9 140 000

Answers for Self-check—page 15

Test

1. 53 000 000 000 means fifty-three ___?___ (thousand, million, billion).

2. Round 8 709 426 to the nearest thousand.

Tell what each red digit means.

3. 0.264

4. 3.825

5. 87.6404

6. 4.308

7. 0.629

8. 356.8

Give the correct symbol, > or <, for each ●.

9. 6.8 ● 7.0

10. 5.28 ● 5.25

11. 7.18 ● 7.2

Round to the nearest hundredth.

12. 56.281

13. 13.052

14. 0.776

Express each number in expanded notation using powers of ten.

Express each number in scientific notation.

15. 52 489 000

16. 312 000

17. 3 600 000

18. 472 000

Math lab

Ancient Numeration Systems

The tables show some of the ancient numerals used by the Egyptians, Greeks, and Romans. In the Egyptian and Greek systems, the values of the symbols were simply added to give the number. The Roman system used both addition and subtraction of the symbol values.

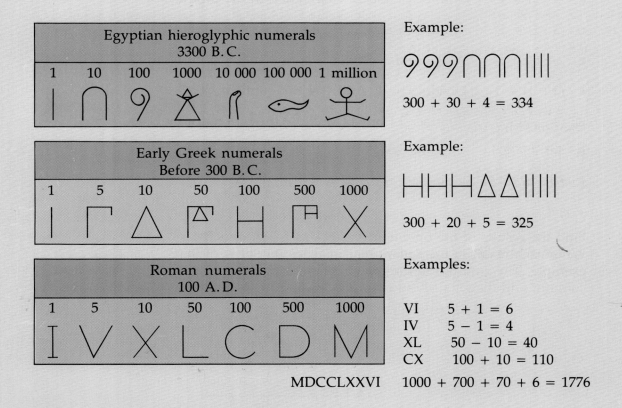

Egyptian hieroglyphic numerals 3300 B.C.						
1	10	100	1000	10 000	100 000	1 million

Example:

300 + 30 + 4 = 334

Early Greek numerals Before 300 B.C.						
1	5	10	50	100	500	1000

Example:

300 + 20 + 5 = 325

Roman numerals 100 A.D.						
1	5	10	50	100	500	1000

Examples:

VI 5 + 1 = 6
IV 5 − 1 = 4
XL 50 − 10 = 40
CX 100 + 10 = 110

MDCCLXXVI 1000 + 700 + 70 + 6 = 1776

Show these numbers with Egyptian, Greek, and Roman numerals.

1. Your age
2. Your year of birth
3. Number of students in your classroom
4. Number of students in your school
5. This year

Operations and Expressions

Parentheses ( ) are often used in mathematics to tell which operation to do first.

A $(9 - 2) + 1$ Subtract 2 from 9. Then add 1.

B $9 - (2 + 1)$ Add 2 and 1. Then subtract the sum from 9.

C $(3 \cdot 2) + 1$ Multiply 3 and 2. Then add 1 to the product.

D $(3 \cdot 2) - 1$ Multiply 3 and 2. Then subtract 1 from the product.

E $2 \div (1 + 1)$ Add 1 and 1. Divide 2 by the sum.

F $(2 \div 1) + 1$ Divide 2 by 1. Add 1 to the quotient.

G $(4 - 2) \cdot 2$ Subtract 2 from 4. Multiply the difference by 2.

H $4 - (2 \cdot 2)$ Multiply 2 and 2. Subtract the product from 4.

I $(10 - 7) - 1$ Subtract 7 from 10. Then subtract 1.

Find the results of the operations in examples **A** through **I**. Write each result in the square that matches the letter of that example. The sum of the three numbers in each row, column, and diagonal should be 12.

C	H	D
I	G	B
F	A	E

> Whenever parentheses are used with $+$, $-$, $\times$, or $\div$, do the computation inside the parentheses first.

> When there are no parentheses, first do all multiplications and divisions in order from left to right. Then do all additions and subtractions in order from left to right.

These rules can be used to **simplify an expression**, that is, to find a number for the expression.

Examples:

$$9 \cdot (24 \div 3)$$
$$9 \cdot 8$$
$$72$$

$$20 - 16 \div 2$$
$$20 - 8$$
$$12$$

$$10 + 6 \cdot 2$$
$$10 + 12$$
$$22$$

Simplify each expression.

1. $24 \div (4 \cdot 3)$

2. $(9 \cdot 6) + (4 \cdot 6)$

3. $(18 + 9) \div 3$

4. $8 \cdot (12 - 5)$

5. $84 - (4 \cdot 5)$

6. $(6 \cdot 9) - (8 \cdot 4)$

7. $6 \cdot (19 - 8)$

8. $(27 + 5) \div (4 + 4)$

9. $25 - 8 + 7$

10. $12 + 13 - 4$

11. $3 \cdot 4 \div 2$

12. $8 \cdot 5 \div 10$

13. $2 \cdot 8 - 5$

14. $25 - 7 \cdot 3$

15. $25 - 2 \cdot 10$

16. $9 + 2 \cdot 8$

17. $8 + 6 \div 2$

18. $18 \div 6 + 3$

Calculator problems

19. $1967 + (493 \cdot 526)$

20. $3946 + 837 \cdot 296$

21. $6693 \div (93 + 4)$

22. $48\ 563 - 43\ 992 \div 78$

Evaluating expressions

The expressions below contain letters and numbers.

$$m + 5 \qquad x - 5 \qquad \frac{c}{4} \left(\frac{c}{4} \text{ means } c \div 4\right) \qquad 3b \ (3b \text{ means } 3 \cdot b)$$

The letters m, x, c, and b are called variables.
To evaluate an expression, replace the variable with a number and simplify.

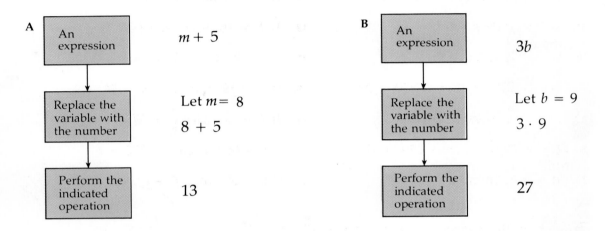

A

An expression	$m + 5$
Replace the variable with the number	Let $m = 8$ $8 + 5$
Perform the indicated operation	13

B

An expression	$3b$
Replace the variable with the number	Let $b = 9$ $3 \cdot 9$
Perform the indicated operation	27

Other examples

$14 - t$	$4a$	$\dfrac{x}{2}$	$\dfrac{12}{x}$
Let $t = 6$	Let $a = 7$	Let $x = 8$	Let $x = 3$
$14 - 6$	$4 \cdot 7$	$\dfrac{8}{2}$	$\dfrac{12}{3}$
8	28	4	4

Evaluate each expression. Replace each a with 7 and x with 4.

1. $8a$ 2. $x + 9$ 3. $\dfrac{14}{a}$ 4. $\dfrac{12}{x}$ 5. $\dfrac{x}{2}$

6. $7x$ 7. $9x$ 8. $a + 12$ 9. $9a$ 10. $21 - a$

Evaluate each expression. Replace each n with 8 and b with 6.

1. $n + 9$
2. $7b$
3. $\dfrac{56}{n}$
4. $13 - b$
5. $24 - n$

6. $32 - b$
7. $8b$
8. $16 + n$
9. $7n$
10. $9b$

11. $43 + n$
12. $b - 6$
13. $\dfrac{54}{b}$
14. $n + 17$
15. $\dfrac{b}{3}$

Evaluate each expression.

16. If $n = 8$, then $n + 12 = $ ▥

17. If $x = 9$, then $8 \cdot x = $ ▥

18. If $t = 5$, then $t + 7 = $ ▥

19. If $b = 16$, then $b - 9 = $ ▥

20. If $r = 36$, then $\dfrac{r}{9} = $ ▥

21. If $t = 7$, then $30t = $ ▥

22. If $n = 250$, then $n - 250 = $ ▥

23. If $x = 59$, then $x - 9 = $ ▥

24. If $p = 100$, then $9p = $ ▥

25. If $b = 64$, then $\dfrac{b}{8} = $ ▥

26. If $r = 200$, then $r + 299 = $ ▥

27. If $t = 650$, then $t - 250 = $ ▥

28. If $x = 8$, then $12 - x = $ ▥

29. If $y = 27$, then $6 + y = $ ▥

Evaluate each expression when the variable is replaced by the numbers given in the table.

	y	$15y$
30.	1	▥
31.	0	▥
32.	3	▥
33.	5	▥
34.	10	▥
35.	20	▥

	r	$\dfrac{r}{12}$
36.	12	▥
37.	0	▥
38.	24	▥
39.	144	▥
40.	96	▥
41.	108	▥

A truthful girl said, "I have the same number of sisters as I have brothers." Her truthful brother said, "I have twice as many sisters as brothers." How many boys and girls are in the family?

Evaluating expressions—combined operations

A mechanical engineer designs parts, tests materials, and must pay attention to small details. For example, to estimate the stress on a steel bar, an expression such as $\dfrac{6(b - 15)}{3}$ might be evaluated.

This expression means 6 times $(b - 15)$ divided by 3.

What is the value of the expression when the length of the bar (b) is replaced by 20?

Finding the answer

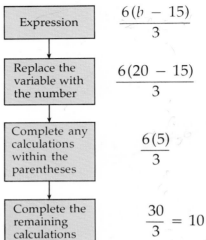

Expression	$\dfrac{6(b - 15)}{3}$
Replace the variable with the number	$\dfrac{6(20 - 15)}{3}$
Complete any calculations within the parentheses	$\dfrac{6(5)}{3}$
Complete the remaining calculations	$\dfrac{30}{3} = 10$

The value of the expression is 10.

Evaluate each expression for the replacements given.

$\dfrac{5(f - 12)}{4}$, when f is replaced by . . .	**1.** 20	**2.** 16	**3.** 24	**4.** 32
$4s + 10$, when s is replaced by . . .	**5.** 9	**6.** 25	**7.** 8	**8.** 12
$\dfrac{60}{2(x + 5)}$, when x is replaced by . . .	**9.** 5	**10.** 10	**11.** 25	**12.** 0

Evaluate each expression. Replace each n with 9 and a with 4.

1. $8(a + 5)$

2. $3(12 - n)$

3. $9a - 6$

4. $2n + 3$

5. $5a - 10$

6. $\dfrac{8a}{2}$

7. $17 - n$

8. $\dfrac{2n}{6}$

9. $12 - 2a$

10. $\dfrac{a}{2} + 18$

11. $5n - 6$

12. $3(a + 6)$

13. $3n - 7$

14. $\dfrac{36}{n} - 1$

15. $\dfrac{28}{a} + 6$

16. $\dfrac{16}{a} \cdot 5$

Evaluate.

17. If $s = 2$, then $8s + 3 = $ ▥

18. If $e = 7$, then $42 - 3e = $ ▥

19. If $x = 3$, then $\dfrac{24}{x} + 5 = $ ▥

20. If $c = 10$, then $3c + 2 = $ ▥

21. If $r = 9$, then $6r \div 27 = $ ▥

22. If $f = 4$, then $6f \div 3 = $ ▥

23. If $t = 7$, then $9t - 6 = $ ▥

24. If $d = 2$, then $9d \div 6 = $ ▥

25. If $a = 6$, then $\dfrac{12}{a} \cdot 5 = $ ▥

26. If $y = 5$, then $3y + 4 = $ ▥

27. If $z = 4$, then $9z \div 6 = $ ▥

28. If $b = 8$, then $\dfrac{32}{b} - 1 = $ ▥

Copy and complete each table by evaluating the expression for the numbers given.

	n	$3(n - 1)$
29.	2	▥
30.	5	▥
31.	25	▥
32.	75	▥
33.	301	▥
34.	1501	▥

	t	$\dfrac{5t}{3}$
35.	3	▥
36.	6	▥
37.	9	▥
38.	12	▥
39.	30	▥
40.	180	▥

	x	$2x + 3$
41.	4	▥
42.	7	▥
43.	11	▥
44.	15	▥
45.	25	▥
46.	200	▥

Evaluating formulas

A landscape gardener wants to
mark a rectangular plot with string.
The plot is 15 m long and 8 m wide.
What is the perimeter?

Finding the answer

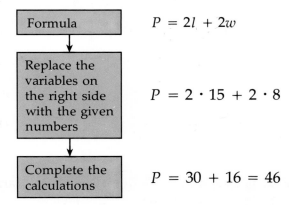

$P = 2l + 2w$

$P = 2 \cdot 15 + 2 \cdot 8$

$P = 30 + 16 = 46$

The perimeter of the rectangular plot
is 46 m.

Evaluate each formula for the replacements given.

1. $D = rt$, when $r = 50$, and $t = 6$ (rt means r times t)

2. $A = \dfrac{bh}{2}$, when $b = 5$ and $h = 8$

3. $I = \dfrac{pr}{100}$, when $p = 50$ and $r = 10$

4. $V = (E - F) + 2$, where $E = 13$ and $F = 6$

5. $C = \dfrac{5(F - 32)}{9}$, where $F = 41$

6. $A = \dfrac{h(a + b)}{2}$, where $h = 5$, $a = 6$, and $b = 2$

Evaluate each formula for the replacements given.

1. $R = \dfrac{E}{I}$; $E = 120, I = 2$ 60

2. $A = bh$; $b = 9, h = 7$

3. $P = 2(l + w)$; $l = 12, w = 8$ 40

4. $l = a + d(n - 1)$; $a = 2, d = 3, n = 6$

5. $S = 180(n - 2)$; $n = 12$ 1800

6. $D = rt$; $r = 40, t = 5$

7. $V = Bh$; $B = 20, h = 5$

8. $W = EI$; $E = 110, I = 2$

9. $A = hP$; $h = 6, P = 8$

10. $P = S - C$; $S = 6000, C = 5500$

11. $C = \dfrac{5(F - 32)}{9}$; $F = 41$

12. $A = \dfrac{h(a + b)}{2}$; $h = 4, a = 7, b = 3$

Evaluate each formula by replacing the variables
with the numbers given in the table.

	$A = \dfrac{bh}{2}$		
	b	h	A
13.	8	3	
14.	5	6	
15.	10	10	
16.	8	5	
17.	7	6	

	$P = 2(l + w)$		
	l	w	P
18.	9	6	
19.	12	8	
20.	30	20	
21.	18	6	
22.	9	4	

 The formula $N = 75\,lh$, where l and h are the desired length and height of a wall in meters, is sometimes used to estimate the number of bricks needed to build the wall.

A wall of a building is 25 m long and 8 m high. If bricks cost 28¢ each, about how much would be the total cost of the bricks needed?

Answers for Self-check 1. 14 2. 27 3. 70 4. 7 5. 63 6. 6 7. 2 8. 7 9. 4 10. 210 11. 48
12. 40 13. 45

Self-check

Simplify each expression.

1. $(8 - 3) + 9$

2. $7 + 5 \cdot 4$

3. $9(3 + 5) - 2$

Evaluate each expression for the replacement number given.

4. $15 - b, b = 8$

5. $9c, c = 7$

6. $\dfrac{54}{x}, x = 9$

7. $\dfrac{n + 6}{7}, n = 8$

8. $\dfrac{r}{9} + 5, r = 18$

9. $\dfrac{(4t + 4)}{9}, t = 8$

Evaluate each formula for the replacements given.

10. $D = rt; r = 30, t = 7$

11. $A = bh; b = 8, h = 6$

12. $P = 2(l + w); l = 16, w = 4$

13. $A = \dfrac{h(a + b)}{2}; h = 10, a = 5, b = 4$

Answers for Self-check—page 25

Test

Simplify.

1. $6 + (13 - 8)$

2. $17 - 4 \cdot 2$

3. $7(6 + 3) + 5$

Evaluate each expression for the replacement number given.

4. $8a, a = 9$

5. $16 - r, r = 7$

6. $\dfrac{42}{d}, d = 6$

7. $\dfrac{2x - 4}{3}, x = 8$

8. $\dfrac{r}{8} - 3, r = 64$

9. $\dfrac{3s + 2}{5}, s = 6$

Evaluate each formula for the replacements given.

10. $V = Bh; B = 30, h = 9$

11. $A = \dfrac{bh}{2}; b = 8, h = 6$

12. $P = 2l + 2w; l = 10, w = 9$

13. $A = \dfrac{h(a + b)}{2}; h = 2, a = 6, b = 2$

Math lab

Pick's Formula for Area

1. You can find the **area** of a
    polygon by counting squares. If
    the area of figure **A** is 1, what are
    the areas of **B**, **C**, and **D**?

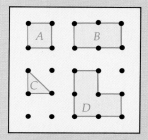

2. You can also find the area of a
    polygon by using Pick's Formula:

$$A = \frac{b}{2} + i - 1,$$

      where A = the area,
           b = the number of nails
             touched by the rubber band,
    and i = the number of nails inside
            the rubber band.

    Find the area of figures **A** through **F**
    using Pick's Formula.

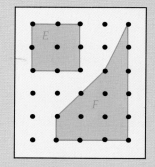

3. If the polygon has holes, you
    can find its area by using this
    formula:

$$A = \frac{b}{2} + i - 1 + H,$$

    where b = the number of nails
            touched by rubber bands,
        i = the number of nails
           inside the polygon,
  and H = the number of holes.

    Find the areas of figures **G**, **H**, **I**,
    and **J**. Check these areas by
    counting squares.

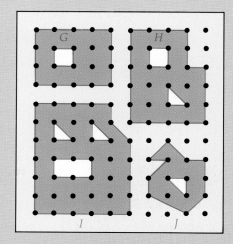

Addition and Subtraction

Basic principles

Commutative principle of addition
For any whole numbers a and b, $\qquad a + b = b + a \qquad$ Examples: $\quad 3 + 9 = 9 + 3$ $\qquad\qquad\qquad\qquad\qquad\qquad\qquad\qquad 47 + 56 = 56 + 47$

Which of these is true?

1. $4 + 8 = 8 + 4$
2. $72 + 34 = 34 + 72$
3. $53 + 35 = 35 + 53$
4. $596 + 247 = 247 + 596$
5. $7 - 5 = 5 - 7$
6. $97 - 43 = 43 - 97$

Associative principle of addition
For any whole numbers a, b, and c, $\quad (a + b) + c = a + (b + c) \qquad$ Examples: $\quad (2 + 5) + 4 = 2 + (5 + 4)$ $\qquad\qquad\qquad\qquad\qquad\qquad\qquad\qquad\quad 3 + (4 + 2) = (3 + 4) + 2$ $\qquad\qquad\qquad\qquad\qquad\qquad\qquad\qquad\quad (34 + 75) + 96 = 34 + (75 + 96)$ $\qquad\qquad\qquad\qquad\qquad\qquad\qquad\qquad\quad 82 + (17 + 39) = (82 + 17) + 39$

Which of these is true?

7. $(4 + 5) + 6 = 4 + (5 + 6)$
8. $24 + (32 + 108) = (24 + 32) + 108$
9. $8 - (3 - 1) = (8 - 3) - 1$
10. $(37 + 41) + 82 = 37 + (41 + 82)$
11. $52 + (79 + 86) = (52 + 79) + 86$
12. $(72 - 33) - 15 = 72 - (33 - 15)$

Zero principle of addition
For any whole number a, $\qquad a + 0 = a \qquad$ Examples: $\quad 7 + 0 = 7 \qquad 327 + 0 = 327$ $\qquad\qquad\qquad\qquad\qquad\qquad\qquad 0 + 3 = 3 \qquad 0 + 515 = 515$

Name the principle shown in each exercise.

13. $53 + 72 = 72 + 53$
14. $(87 + 2) + 74 = 87 + (2 + 74)$
15. $12 + (84 + 61) = (12 + 84) + 61$
16. $0 + 84 = 84$
17. $75 + 0 = 75$
18. $313 + 420 = 420 + 313$

Add.

Examples:

$$\begin{array}{r} 1 \\ 46 \\ +39 \\ \hline 85 \end{array}$$

$$\begin{array}{r} 1\ 1 \\ 387 \\ +996 \\ \hline 1383 \end{array}$$

$$\begin{array}{r} 1\ 2\ 2 \\ 8\ 475 \\ 1\ \ \ 397 \\ +56\ 948 \\ \hline 65\ 820 \end{array}$$

1.	59 + 68	2.	269 + 76	3.	578 + 243	4.	658 + 745
5.	239 + 984	6.	5342 + 868	7.	8762 + 3423	8.	9675 + 8547
9.	8364 + 2579	10.	5487 + 9658	11.	674 394 + 586	12.	964 387 + 532
13.	468 793 + 275	14.	3857 1296 + 7847	15.	5436 9274 + 3865	16.	4935 964 3985 + 4071
17.	986 79 4 568 + 18 765	18.	9436 47 684 + 5716	19.	79 864 3 716 + 51 923	20.	7524 389 8698 + 94
21.	594 386 + 69 476	22.	697 384 + 238 965	23.	683 728 + 9 654	24.	386 547 + 27 683

25. $5964 + 97 + 386$

26. $867 + 59 + 6436$

27. $237 + 596 + 84 + 3879$

28. $35\ 684 + 976 + 4832$

Find these sums.
  5 addends

$1 + 3 + 5 + 7 + 9 = n$
  10 addends

$1 + 3 + 5 + 7 + 9 + \ldots = n$
  20 addends

$1 + 3 + 5 + 7 + 9 + \ldots = n$

Can you guess the answers to these?
  100 addends

$1 + 3 + 5 + 7 + 9 + \ldots = n$
  1000 addends

$1 + 3 + 5 + 7 + 9 + \ldots = n$

Adding whole numbers and decimals

Yosemite Falls, located in California's Yosemite National Park, consists of three sections. In the upper falls, water drops 435.9 m. It then drops 205.7 m down the cascades known as the middle falls. At the lower falls, the water drops a final 97.5 m. How far does the water drop over all three sections of Yosemite Falls?

Finding the answer

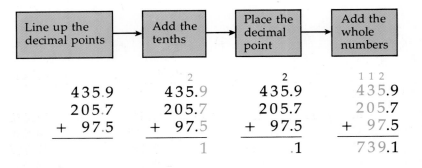

Line up the decimal points	Add the tenths	Place the decimal point	Add the whole numbers

```
              2              2          1 1 2
  435.9      435.9        435.9        435.9
  205.7      205.7        205.7        205.7
+  97.5    +  97.5      +  97.5      +  97.5
            _____       _____       _____
               1           .1         739.1
```

The water drops 739.1 m over all three sections of the Falls.

Other examples

```
   11 1                 1 2 2                 1 11
  36.572                62.78               ₁4.263
+ 58.964                 3.42               17.560
 _____               965.79            +  0.839
  95.536              + 42.75              _____
                      _____              22.662
                      1074.74
```

Find the sums.

	1.		2.		3.		4.	
	56.2		3.67		0.738		473.8	
	75.9		5.92		2.617		69.7	
	68.3		0.83		+ 0.566		562.3	
	+ 24.7		+ 1.56				+ 12.4	

Add.

1.	76.35 4.38 + 92.47	**2.**	562.3 8267.5 + 480.6	**3.**	67.234 56.780 + 70.036

4.	54.026 7.284 + 93.578	**5.**	56.73 + 87.46	**6.**	0.928 + 0.736

7.	92.7 + 86.8	**8.**	576.34 + 821.98	**9.**	67.2 88.7 + 54.3

10.	9.26 0.83 + 5.91	**11.**	6.834 7.693 + 5.998	**12.**	75.624 8.927 + 56.343

13.	5.76 8.93 7.98 + 6.77	**14.**	0.834 6.275 0.098 + 3.506	**15.**	9.842 7.665 0.560 + 2.934	**16.**	28.692 4.836 37.962 + 5.037

Add.

17. 39.6 + 48.36 + 9.56

18. 8.375 + 92.65 + 8.3

19. 14.62 + 8.375 + 24.68

20. 56.5 + 2.37 + 29.368

21. 57.25 + 8.34 + 9.365

22. 1.768 + 0.05 + 8.36

23. The water flowing over Bridalveil Falls at Yosemite drops 91.5 m farther than the 97.5 m of lower Yosemite Falls. What is the total drop at Bridalveil Falls?

24. The water at Ribbon Falls drops 55.4 m farther than the 435.9 m of upper Yosemite Falls. How far is this?

The magic sum for this magic square is 445.5. Find the missing numbers.

264.6	2.7	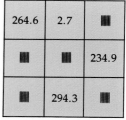
		234.9
	294.3	

More practice, page 382, Set A

Subtracting whole numbers

The city of Santa Fe, New Mexico, has an altitude of 2118 m. The altitude of Denver is 1609 m. How much greater is the altitude of Santa Fe?

Finding the answer

Trade a ten Subtract the ones	Subtract the tens (Trade only when necessary)	Trade a thousand Subtract the hundreds	Subtract the thousands

$$
\begin{array}{r}
{\scriptstyle 0\ 18} \\
21\cancel{1}\cancel{8} \\
-\ 1609 \\
\hline
9
\end{array}
\qquad
\begin{array}{r}
{\scriptstyle 0\ 18} \\
21\cancel{1}\cancel{8} \\
-\ 1609 \\
\hline
09
\end{array}
\qquad
\begin{array}{r}
{\scriptstyle 1\ 11\ 0\ 18} \\
\cancel{2}\cancel{1}\cancel{1}\cancel{8} \\
-\ 1609 \\
\hline
509
\end{array}
\qquad
\begin{array}{r}
{\scriptstyle 1\ 11\ 0\ 18} \\
\cancel{2}\cancel{1}\cancel{1}\cancel{8} \\
-\ 1609 \\
\hline
509
\end{array}
$$

Santa Fe is 509 m higher than Denver.

Other examples

$$
\begin{array}{r}
{\scriptstyle 5\ 12\ 14\ 17} \\
\cancel{6}\cancel{3}\cancel{5}\cancel{7} \\
-\ 3898 \\
\hline
2459
\end{array}
\qquad
\begin{array}{r}
{\scriptstyle 7\ 9\ 9\ 16} \\
\cancel{8}\cancel{0}\cancel{0}\cancel{6} \\
-\ 3568 \\
\hline
4438
\end{array}
\qquad
\begin{array}{r}
{\scriptstyle 7\ 15\ 9\ 10} \\
\cancel{8}\cancel{6}\cancel{0}\cancel{0} \\
-\ 3765 \\
\hline
4835
\end{array}
\qquad
\begin{array}{r}
{\scriptstyle 4\ 9\ 16\ 10} \\
\cancel{5}\cancel{0}\cancel{7}\cancel{0} \\
-\ 3697 \\
\hline
1373
\end{array}
$$

Subtract.

1.	636 − 278	2.	803 − 456	3.	593 − 185	4.	620 − 368	5.	3827 − 2489
6.	3125 − 1248	7.	8714 − 5396	8.	4231 − 2876	9.	5384 − 1467	10.	7003 − 2516

Subtract.

1.	5004 − 3487	**2.**	9324 − 4587
3.	8003 − 4021	**4.**	6008 − 3287
5.	4926 − 2687	**6.**	4000 − 1856
7.	6700 − 3458	**8.**	3825 − 1976
9.	9502 − 3453	**10.**	8206 − 4550

11.	6080 − 4738	**12.**	3640 − 1796	**13.**	9050 − 2593	**14.**	8030 − 5783	**15.**	7311 − 6744
16.	8000 − 4538	**17.**	5154 − 4796	**18.**	6957 − 1868	**19.**	8000 − 5274	**20.**	7792 − 3875
21.	35 434 − 2 048	**22.**	86 500 − 42 794	**23.**	31 040 − 11 845	**24.**	53 147 − 3 806	**25.**	94 340 − 84 857

26. The altitude of Reno, Nevada, is 1368 m. The altitude of Provo, Utah, is 1386 m. What is the difference in these two altitudes?

27. Grand Junction, Colorado, is 1399 m above sea level. Colorado Springs is 1822 m above sea level. How much higher is Colorado Springs?

 The capacity of a football stadium at the University of Michigan (the largest college stadium in the U.S.) is 101 701 people. Recently the population of the state of Michigan was 8 875 083 people. About how many times would this stadium need to be filled to hold all the people in the state? Guess. Then calculate to check your guess. (Use repeated subtraction or division.)

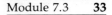

Subtracting decimals

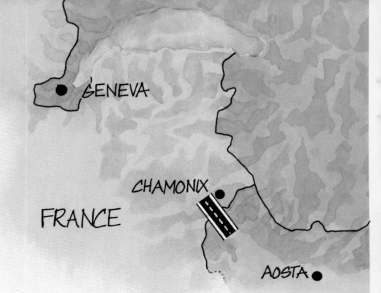

The world's longest railway
tunnel is 19.82 km long,
between Italy and Switzerland.
The longest highway tunnel is
11.66 km long, between Italy
and France. How much longer
is the railway tunnel?

Finding the answer

Line up the decimal points	Subtract the hundredths	Subtract the tenths Place the decimal point	Subtract the whole numbers

```
                    7 12              7 12              7 12
   19.82         19.8̶2̶           19.8̶2̶           19.8̶2̶
 − 11.66       − 11.6 6         − 11.66          − 11.66
                       6            .16             8.16
```

The railway tunnel is 8.16 km longer than the highway tunnel.

Other examples

```
   5 9 13            6 9 9 14          4 13 6 11 14
  7̶6̶0̶3̶            6.2̶0̶0̶4̶          5̶3̶7̶2̶4̶
 − 1385          − 2.3458          − 38 496
   6218            4.3546            15 228
```

Find the differences.

1.	6.23	2.	864.2	3.	74.06	4.	60.072
	− 1.47		− 598.3		− 38.29		− 25.683
5.	72.4	6.	38.76	7.	406.3	8.	6.302
	− 16.9		− 19.88		− 157.8		− 1.486

SWITZERLAND

ITALY

Find the differences.

1.	622 − 138	**2.**	507 − 239	**3.**	6.28 − 4.69
4.	37.2 − 19.5	**5.**	7604 − 2569	**6.**	8342 − 2897
7.	8149 − 5255	**8.**	6004 − 3578	**9.**	9005 − 1683
10.	6.007 − 2.589	**11.**	7.862 − 1.493	**12.**	632.4 − 251.6
13.	78.03 − 14.67	**14.**	38.009 − 9.664	**15.**	39.605 − 36.198	**16.**	563.03 − 176.95
17.	317.86 − 38.79	**18.**	56.700 − 12.764	**19.**	659.80 − 283.91	**20.**	652.00 − 337.66
21.	9.4826 − 0.8951	**22.**	7.04 − 3.594	**23.**	63.512 − 18.387	**24.**	0.2004 − 0.1875

Solve the equations.

25. 43.25 − 27.6   **26.** 5.396 − 0.47   **27.** 12.462 − 8.6

28. 32.467 − 19.82   **29.** 26.35 − 17.594   **30.** 3.6 − 1.87

31. One of the longest underwater highway tunnels is 2.78 km long. What is the difference in the length of this tunnel and the 11.66 km length of the longest highway tunnel?

32. The Holland Tunnel under the Hudson River consists of two separate tubes, 2.61 km long and 2.55 km long. What is the difference in the length of these tubes?

Think!

The sum of two numbers a and b is 6.2. Their difference is 0.6. Find the numbers.

$a + b = 6.2$
$a - b = 0.6$

More practice, page 382, Set B

Using addition and subtraction to solve equations

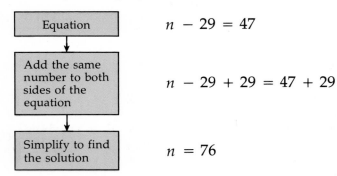

IF YOU SUBTRACT 29 FROM MY NUMBER, YOU WILL GET 47. WHAT'S MY NUMBER?

To solve the puzzle problem, we let n represent the unknown number. Then write the equation $n - 29 = 47$.

Solving the equation

| Equation | $n - 29 = 47$ |

| Add the same number to both sides of the equation | $n - 29 + 29 = 47 + 29$ |

| Simplify to find the solution | $n = 76$ |

To undo subtracting 29, we add 29. Adding 29 to both sides maintains the equality.

The number is 76.

Other examples

$$n - 13 = 42$$
$$n - 13 + 13 = 42 + 13$$
$$n = 55$$

$$a - 24.2 = 9.4$$
$$a - 24.2 + 24.2 = 9.4 + 24.2$$
$$a = 33.6$$

Solve these equations. Show each step.

1. $n - 13 = 23$
2. $a - 14 = 9$
3. $c - 54 = 15$
4. $x - 15 = 25$
5. $r - 36 = 48$
6. $n - 329 = 264$
7. $y - 567 = 89$
8. $t - 395 = 278$
9. $b - 200 = 800$
10. $d - 14.5 = 58.9$
11. $x - 6.24 = 23.56$
12. $n - 29.683 = 17.496$
13. $y - 2874 = 4196$
14. $s - 9 = 55$
15. $m - 35.4 = 26.57$

Solve the equation, $c + 26 = 93$.

Equation

$$c + 26 = 93$$

↓

Subtract the same number from each side of the equation

$$c + 26 - 26 = 93 - 26$$

To undo adding 26, we subtract 26. Subtracting 26 from both sides maintains the equality.

↓

Simplify to find the solution

$$c = 67$$

Other examples

$$x + 8 = 14$$
$$x + 8 - 8 = 14 - 8$$
$$x = 6$$

$$b + 2.15 = 3.04$$
$$b + 2.15 - 2.15 = 3.04 - 2.15$$
$$b = 0.89$$

Solve these equations. Show each step.

1. $c + 8 = 12$

2. $x + 9 = 18$

3. $y + 8.5 = 17.3$

4. $r + 75 = 93$

5. $t + 0.9 = 1.65$

6. $d + 6 = 14$

7. $b + 35 = 72$

8. $s + 29 = 100$

9. $n + 5.5 = 8.7$

10. $q + 29 = 36$

11. $x + 476 = 927$

12. $c + 70 = 100$

13. $d + 1468 = 5302$

14. $a + 3.276 = 6.514$

15. $n + 17 = 25$

Calculate the following:

$(1 \cdot 8) + 1 = n$
$(12 \cdot 8) + 2 = n$
$(123 \cdot 8) + 3 = n$
$(1234 \cdot 8) + 4 = n$

Continue this pattern.

Give, without calculating, the answer to:

$(123\ 456\ 789 \cdot 8) + 9 = n$

Answers for Self-check 1. zero principle 2. commutative principle 3. associative principle 4. 952 5. 142.57 6. 88.424 7. 1283.4 8. 534.05 9. 459 10. 756 11. 17.78 12. 32.93 13. 657.82 14. $c = 17$ 15. $n = 8$ 16. $t = 1470$ 17. $m = 6$ 18. $r = 6.1$ 19. $s = 8$

Self-check

Name the basic principle for addition, **commutative**, **associative**, or **zero**, that is illustrated by each equation.

1. $93 + 0 = 93$ 2. $37 + 95 = 95 + 37$ 3. $9 + (8 + 7) = (9 + 8) + 7$

Add or subtract.

4.
```
  763
+ 189
```

5.
```
  54.62
+ 87.95
```

6.
```
   3.486
  75.273
+  9.665
```

7.
```
  572.8
   34.9
+ 675.7
```

8.
```
  309.4
   27.85
+ 196.8
```

9.
```
  856
- 397
```

10.
```
  1403
-  647
```

11.
```
  35.62
- 17.84
```

12.
```
  60.28
- 27.35
```

13.
```
  713.4
-  55.58
```

Solve each equation.

14. $c - 9 = 8$ 15. $n - 3 = 5$ 16. $t - 596 = 874$

17. $m + 6 = 12$ 18. $r + 6.74 = 12.84$ 19. $s + 12 = 20$

Answers for Self-check—page 37

Test

Name the basic principle for addition, **commutative**, **associative**, or **zero**, that is illustrated by each equation.

1. $(3 + 4) + 7 = 3 + (4 + 7)$ 2. $76 + 0 = 76$ 3. $47 + 25 = 25 + 47$

Add or subtract.

4.
```
  582
+ 759
```

5.
```
  62.38
+ 19.81
```

6.
```
   6.384
  57.662
+  7.856
```

7.
```
  672.3
  761.0
+  39.9
```

8.
```
  84.67
  75.3
+ 91.34
```

9.
```
  726
- 248
```

10.
```
  1307
-  479
```

11.
```
  78.34
- 29.69
```

12.
```
  75.03
- 26.37
```

13.
```
  6.008
- 3.439
```

Solve each equation.

14. $p - 7 = 8$ 15. $k - 2.5 = 1.5$ 16. $x - 967 = 843$

17. $n + 9 = 18$ 18. $a + 4 = 12$ 19. $r + 278 = 1023$

Math lab

Computation Puzzles

1. Make cards with these digits on them.

1 2 3 4 5 8 7 9 6

Make as many different addition problems as you can using all the cards. Here is one example.

$$
\begin{array}{r}
2\ 3\ 5 \\
+\ 7\ 4\ 6 \\
\hline
9\ 8\ 1
\end{array}
$$

2. Match the letters A through Z with amounts of money 1¢ through 26¢. Here is a $1.00 word.

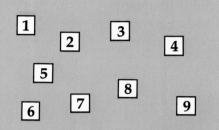

T	U	R	K	E	Y
20¢	21¢	18¢	11¢	5¢	25¢

How much is your name worth? Can you find another $1.00 word?

3. A problem like this is called an **alphametic** or sometimes a **cryptarithm**. Each different letter represents a different digit.

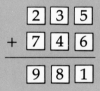

$$
\begin{array}{r}
F\ I\ V\ E \\
-\ F\ O\ U\ R \\
\hline
O\ N\ E
\end{array}
$$

Name some digits the letters could represent. There is more than one answer.

4. Write 58, reverse the digits to 85, and add. Continue this until the answer is a **palindrome** (a number that reads the same backwards and forwards).

$$
\begin{array}{r}
58 \\
+\ 85 \\
\hline
143 \\
+\ 341 \\
\hline
484
\end{array}
$$

Try to find some other numbers that produce palindromes.

Problem Solving
Using Your Skills

Medical assistants help doctors in a variety of ways. They
prepare patients for examinations, treatment, and even
surgery. Temperature, blood pressure, and pulse rate are
often taken by medical assistants. They sometimes prepare
the doctor's examination rooms and sterilize the instruments.
Besides working directly with patients, these assistants might
also keep medical records, file insurance forms, and make
out bills.

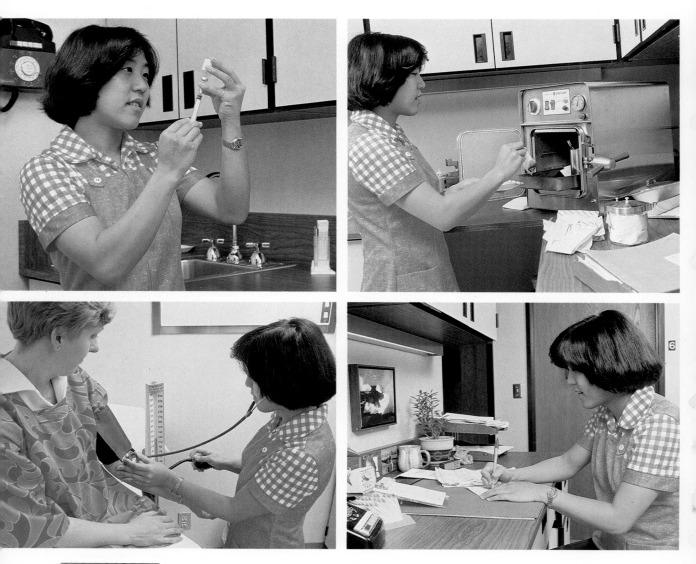

When working with a patient's records, the medical assistant must take care to record facts accurately.

Find the necessary facts and solve these problems.

1. Mr. Lorenzo's record:
   First visit: mass—72.9 kg
                    pulse rate—76
   Second visit: mass—74.7 kg
                    pulse rate—78
   How much had Mr. Lorenzo gained in mass?

2. Ms. Fetzer's bill:
   X-rays: $52.00
   Injection: 16.00
   Medicine: 24.50
   Office visits: ▥
   Ms. Fetzer's insurance paid for everything but the office visits. Her total bill was $220.50. How much did Ms. Fetzer have to pay?

3. Susan Sumo's record:
   First visit: height—137 cm
                    mass—43.2 kg
   Second visit: height—142 cm
                    mass—45.6 kg
   How much had Susan grown, in mass and height, between visits?

4. Dr. Hobart's appointments:
   Monday   29 patients
   Tuesday   26 patients
   Wednesday   19 patients
   Thursday   35 patients
   Friday   27 patients
   How many more patients did the doctor see on Thursday and Friday than on Monday and Tuesday?

5. July office expenses:
   Rent $790.00
   Cleaning   270.00
   Utilities   195.00
   Other   128.00
   What was the total office expense for July?

Estimation and problem solving

For each of these problems, estimate
the answer. Then find the exact answer.

Example: How much does Maria pay for
car payments and rent together?

	Estimate	Answer
$195.00 $\longrightarrow$	$200.00	$195.00
+ 325.00 $\longrightarrow$	300.00	325.00
	$500.00	$520.00

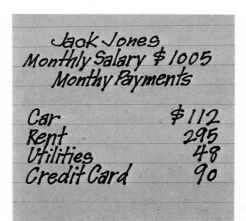

MARIA MONTEZ
MONTHLY BUDGET

CAR PAYMENT	$195
RENT	325
UTILITIES	50

1. How much remains after Jack makes
   his car payment?

2. How much remains after Jack makes
   his car payment and pays his rent?

3. How much does Jack pay for his car,
   rent, utilities, and credit card
   altogether?

4. How much remains after Jack pays the
   four items shown?

Jack Jones
Monthly Salary $1005
Monthy Payments

Car	$112
Rent	295
Utilities	48
Credit Card	90

5. How much remains after Sue makes her
   car payment?

6. How much remains after Sue pays for
   her car, rent, and credit cards?

7. Sue saves $100.00 each month.
   How much does she have for other
   expenses after the four
   items shown and her savings
   are subtracted?

Sue Smith
Monthly Salary $1210
Monthly Payments

Car	$189
Rent	390
Credit Cards	110
Furniture	95

8. How much does Betty pay for rent and extra help together?

9. How much more does Betty pay for rent than utilities?

10. How much does Betty pay per month on the rent, utilities, and loan?

11. How much more does Betty pay for rent and utilities than for extra help and the loan?

BETTY'S BIKE SHOP MONTHLY BUDGET

RENT	$685
EXTRA HELP	495
UTILITIES	189
LOAN	314

12. How much did Clint spend for rent and utilities?

13. How much did he spend for cleaning and part-time help?

14. How much more did Clint pay for rent and utilities than for the part-time help and repairs?

15. How much was spent for the five listed items?

CLINT'S CAMERA CORNER OCTOBER EXPENSES

RENT	$795
UTILITIES	210
CLEANING SERVICE	190
PART TIME HELP	385
REPAIRS	405

16. How much does Hazel spend for rent and utilities per year?

17. How much more does Hazel spend for rent than for interest?

18. How much more does Hazel spend for utilities than for insurance?

19. How much does Hazel spend for all five items?

20. How much more does Hazel spend for salaries than for the other four items?

HAZEL'S HARDWARE STORE YEARLY BUDGET

RENT	$9985
UTILITIES	3075
SALARIES	30200
INTEREST ON LOAN	3980
INSURANCE	988

Everyday uses of estimation

Estimation is often helpful in comparing prices of certain items. Estimating the total cost of an item is also useful.

Estimate first. Then find the exact answer.

Example: What is the total cost of a box of strawberries and a loaf of bread?

	Estimate		Answer
Strawberries ⟶	$0.80		$0.79
Bread ⟶	0.70		0.68
	$1.50		$1.47

$0.79
Strawberries

$0.52
Tomatoes

$0.68
Bread

1. What is the total cost of a jug of cider and a bunch of broccoli?

2. How much more is a jug of cider than a loaf of bread?

3. What is the total cost of a can of tomatoes and a bunch of broccoli?

4. How much more is a box of strawberries than a bunch of broccoli?

5. What is the total cost of a can of tomatoes, a jug of cider, and a bunch of broccoli?

6. How much more is a jug of cider than a loaf of bread and a bunch of broccoli?

7. What is the total cost of all the five items shown?

8. How much more are the tomatoes, cider, and broccoli than the strawberries and bread?

$1.49
Cider

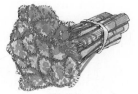
$0.45
Broccoli

First estimate the answer. Then find the exact answer.

1. What is the cost of a package of cheese, a box of crackers, and 3 cans of juice?

98¢ a pkg   79¢ a box   3 for 86¢

2. How much more is a package of cheese and a box of crackers than 3 cans of juice?

89¢ a box   2 for 75¢ $1.98 a pkg

3. How much more is the sugar than the cereal and 2 cartons of milk?

4. What is the total cost of 3 packages of meat, 2 packages of buns, and a jar of mustard?

$1.25 a pkg   6-pack 2 for $1.19   37¢ a jar

Estimate each total. Then find the exact total.

5.
```
      1.75
      0.37
      0.65
      2.89
      5.76
      0.30
 Tax  0.85
 Total ▨
```

6.
```
      0.65
      3.50
      4.95
      3.10
      0.95
 Tax  0.85
 Total ▨
```

7.
```
      5.49
      1.98
      0.50
      4.00
      1.39
      2.68
 Tax  1.26
 Total ▨
```

8.
```
      3.56
      1.49
      0.89
      4.20
      3.98
      2.79
 Tax  1.46
 Total ▨
```

Problem solving—reading a table

In many localities you are charged a sales tax when you buy certain items. The table shows the tax in places where the rate is 4%. The red shading shows the tax for a purchase of $15.95.

Purchase	$15.95
Tax	0.64
Total	$16.59

The total cost would be $16.59.

SALES TAX TABLE (4%)			
SALE	TAX	SALE	TAX
0.01– 0.12	0.00		
0.13– 0.37	0.01	10.13–10.37	0.41
0.38– 0.62	0.02	10.38–10.62	0.42
0.63– 0.87	0.03	10.63–10.87	0.43
0.88– 1.12	0.04	10.88–11.12	0.44
1.13– 1.37	0.05	11.13–11.37	0.45
1.38– 1.62	0.06	11.38–11.62	0.46
1.63– 1.87	0.07	11.63–11.87	0.47
1.88– 2.12	0.08	11.88–12.12	0.48
2.13– 2.37	0.09	12.13–12.37	0.49
2.38– 2.62	0.10	12.38–12.62	0.50
2.63– 2.87	0.11	12.63–12.87	0.51
2.88– 3.12	0.12	12.88–13.12	0.52
3.13– 3.37	0.13	13.13–13.37	0.53
3.38– 3.62	0.14	13.38–13.62	0.54
3.63– 3.87	0.15	13.63–13.87	0.55
3.88– 4.12	0.16	13.88–14.12	0.56
4.13– 4.37	0.17	14.13–14.37	0.57
4.38– 4.62	0.18	14.38–14.62	0.58
4.63– 4.87	0.19	14.63–14.87	0.59
4.88– 5.12	0.20	14.88–15.12	0.60
5.13– 5.37	0.21	15.13–15.37	0.61
5.38– 5.62	0.22	15.38–15.62	0.62
5.63– 5.87	0.23	15.63–15.87	0.63
5.88– 6.12	0.24	15.88–16.12	0.64
6.13– 6.37	0.25	16.13–16.37	0.65
6.38– 6.62	0.26	16.38–16.62	0.66
6.63– 6.87	0.27	16.63–16.87	0.67
6.88– 7.12	0.28	16.88–17.12	0.68
7.13– 7.37	0.29	17.13–17.37	0.69
7.38– 7.62	0.30	17.38–17.62	0.70
7.63– 7.87	0.31	17.63–17.87	0.71
7.88– 8.12	0.32	17.88–18.12	0.72
8.13– 8.37	0.33	18.13–18.37	0.73
8.38– 8.62	0.34	18.38–18.62	0.74
8.63– 8.87	0.35	18.63–18.87	0.75
8.88– 9.12	0.36	18.88–19.12	0.76
9.13– 9.37	0.37	19.13–19.37	0.77
9.38– 9.62	0.38	19.38–19.62	0.78
9.63– 9.87	0.39	19.63–19.87	0.79
9.88–10.12	0.40	19.88–20.12	0.80

Find the total cost with tax for each of the following purchases.

1. $5.00   2. $14.49   3. $10.95   4. $16.88   5. $4.39

6. $11.29   7. $13.40   8. $17.37   9. $7.95   10. $15.50

11. $6.49   12. $19.95   13. $2.25   14. $12.19   15. $9.20

Find the subtotal for each sales slip. Then find the tax
and the total cost.

Example:

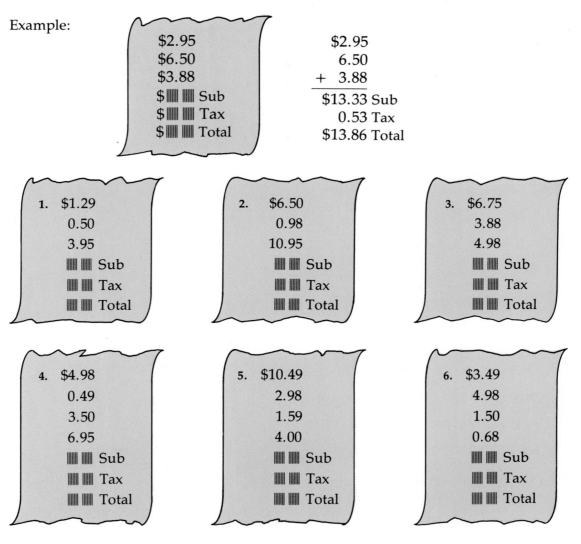

$2.95
$6.50
$3.88
$▐▐▐ Sub
$▐▐▐ Tax
$▐▐▐ Total

$2.95
6.50
+ 3.88
———————
$13.33 Sub
0.53 Tax
$13.86 Total

1. $1.29
    0.50
    3.95
    ▐▐▐ Sub
    ▐▐▐ Tax
    ▐▐▐ Total

2. $6.50
    0.98
    10.95
    ▐▐▐ Sub
    ▐▐▐ Tax
    ▐▐▐ Total

3. $6.75
    3.88
    4.98
    ▐▐▐ Sub
    ▐▐▐ Tax
    ▐▐▐ Total

4. $4.98
    0.49
    3.50
    6.95
    ▐▐▐ Sub
    ▐▐▐ Tax
    ▐▐▐ Total

5. $10.49
    2.98
    1.59
    4.00
    ▐▐▐ Sub
    ▐▐▐ Tax
    ▐▐▐ Total

6. $3.49
    4.98
    1.50
    0.68
    ▐▐▐ Sub
    ▐▐▐ Tax
    ▐▐▐ Total

7. Joan paid a total of $13.47 for
a pair of gloves. The tax was
54 cents. How much were
the gloves?

8. Tom bought a book and
paid a total of $16.38.
The tax was 66 cents. How
much did the book cost?

☆ 9. One T–shirt was priced
at $5.50. Another was priced
at $8.95. What is the difference
in the total costs with tax?

☆ 10. One record was priced at
$6.95. Another was on sale
for $4.49. What was the
difference in the total costs
with tax?

Problem solving—reading a map

The map shows some of the major roads between some of the cities in western Michigan. The roads shown in red are used more frequently than those shown in black.

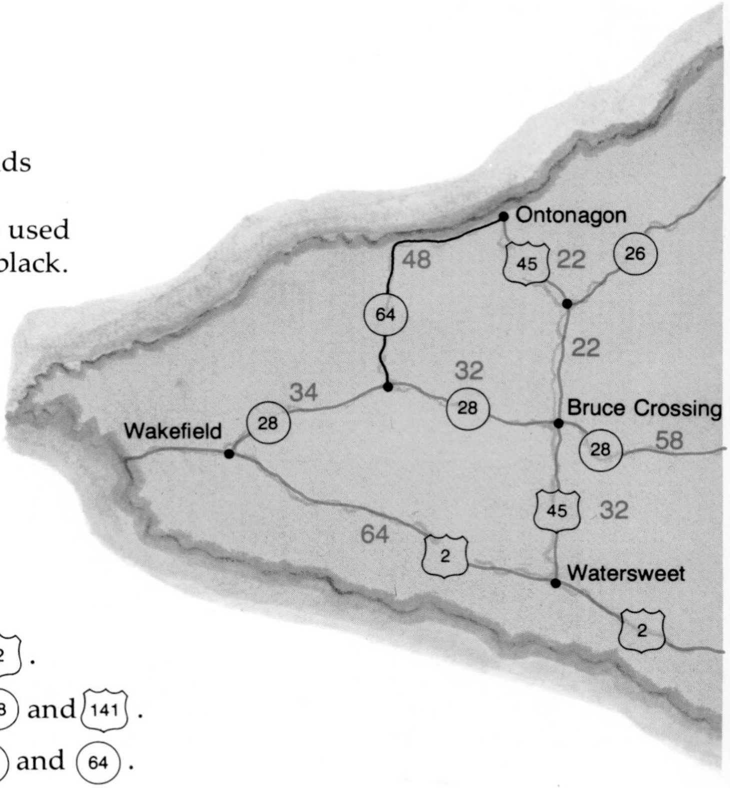

All distances (in blue) are in kilometers between cities or intersections marked with black dots.

Give the distance for each trip.

1. Wakefield to Crystal Falls along 2.
2. Wakefield to Crystal Falls along 28 and 141.
3. Wakefield to Ontonagon along 28 and 64.
4. Wakefield to Ontonagon along 28 to Bruce Crossing, then north on 45.
5. Menominee to Marquette on 41.
6. Iron Mountain to Covington on 141.
7. Iron Mountain to Covington on 95 to 41 and west to Covington.

First inspect each route. Guess which is shorter. Then calculate each distance to find the shortest route.

8. Bruce Crossing ⟶ Crystal Falls

   Route A
   Take 28 east to Covington. Then take 141 south to Crystals Falls.

   Route B
   Take 45 south to Watersweet. Then take 2 east to Crystal Falls.

9. Wakefield ⟶ Iron Mountain

   Route A
   Take 28 to Covington. Turn south on 141 to Iron Mountain.

   Route B
   Take 2 all the way to Iron Mountain.

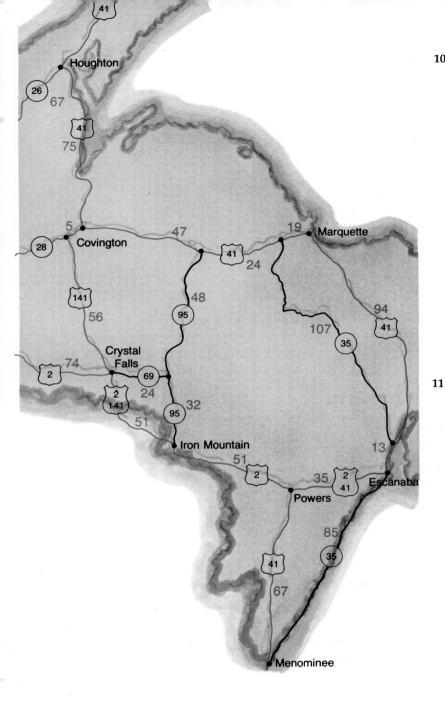

10. Covington ⟶ Escanaba
Route A
Take (28) to the intersection with [41] . Go east on [41] . Stay on [41] to Escanaba.

Route B
Take [141] south to Iron Mountain. Then take [2] to Powers and go east on [2] [141] to Escanaba.

Route C
Take (28) to [41] . Go east on [41] to (35) . Go south on (35) to Escanaba.

11. Menominee ⟶ Houghton
Route A
Take [41] to [2] and turn west to Crystal Falls. Go north on [141] to Covington. Then go east on (28) to [41] and north on [41] to Houghton.

Route B
Take (35) all the way north to [41] outside of Marquette. Turn west on [41] and continue on [41] all the way to Houghton.

Route C
Take [41] all the way to Houghton.

Answers for Self-check 1. About $350; $343 2. Subtotal: $12.83; tax: $0.51; total cost: $13.34 3. Route A: 146 km; Route B: 76 km; Route B is shorter.

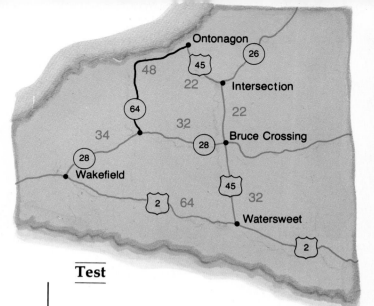

SALES TAX TABLE (4%)	
SALE	TAX
12.13–12.37	0.49
12.38–12.62	0.50
12.63–12.87	0.51
12.88–13.12	0.52
13.13–13.37	0.53
13.38–13.62	0.54
13.63–13.87	0.55
13.88–14.12	0.56

Self-check

1. Each month, Donna pays $190.00 for rent, $105.00 for car payments, and $48.00 on her credit card. Estimate the total of these 3 items. Then find the exact cost.

2. Find the subtotal for the sales slip. Then find the tax from the table and figure the total cost.

   $3.95
   $2.89
   $5.99
   ▓▓ ▓▓ Subtotal
   ▓▓ ▓▓ Tax
   ▓▓ ▓▓ Total

3. Find the distance for each trip. Then tell which trip is shorter.

   Route A Watersweet to Wakefield along ②. Then ㉘ to ㉔. Take ㉔ north to Ontonagon.

   Route B Watersweet north all the way to Ontonagon on ㊺.

Answers for Self-check—page 49

Test

1. Each month Dan pays $305.00 for rent, $198.00 for car payments, and $52.00 on his credit card. Estimate the total of these 3 items. Then find the exact cost.

2. Find the subtotal for the sales slip. Then find the tax and the total cost.

   $4.12
   $6.98
   $1.95
   ▓▓ ▓▓ Subtotal
   ▓▓ ▓▓ Tax
   ▓▓ ▓▓ Total

3. Find the distance for each trip. Then find the difference in the distances.

   Route A Wakefield to Ontonagon along ㉘ and ㉔. Then south on ㊺ to the Intersection.

   Route B Wakefield to Watersweet on ②. Then north on ㊺ to the Intersection.

Math lab

Ternary Coins

In the imaginary land of Ternary, there are five different values of coins.

It is a law in Ternary that no one can possess more than 2 coins of the same value at one time. If someone gets more than 2 coins of the same value, that person must immediately trade them in for a coin of larger value. Paper money is used for values of $2.43 or larger.

Copy and complete the table below showing the number of coins allowed for each amount of money. Remember, no more than 2 coins of the same value are allowed.

Amount	81¢	27¢	9¢	3¢	1¢
50¢	0	1	2	1	2
60¢	0	2	0	2	0
13¢	▓	▓	▓	▓	▓
36¢	▓	▓	▓	▓	▓
92¢	▓	▓	▓	▓	▓
$1.00	▓	▓	▓	▓	▓
$2.00	▓	▓	▓	▓	▓
$1.75	▓	▓	▓	▓	▓

Choose some amounts of money on your own. What coins could be used to make the amounts?

Geometry—
Construction and Measurement

What geometric figure is suggested by the red outline above?
Which of these other geometric figures can you find in the picture?

1. point

2. segment

3. triangle

4. square

5. right angle

6. acute angle

7. obtuse angle

8. isosceles triangle

9. parallel lines

Match each figure with its name and its symbol.

Example: **1.**, **B.**, **f.**

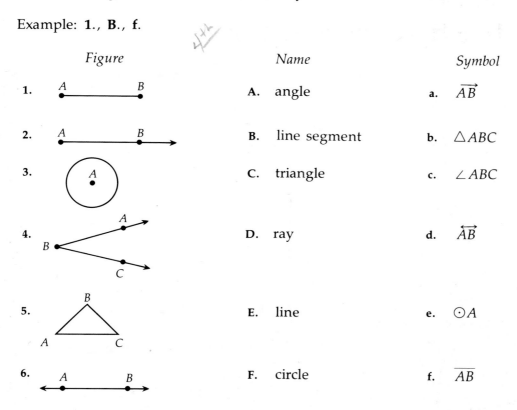

Figure	Name	Symbol
1. A ——— B	**A.** angle	**a.** $\overrightarrow{AB}$
2. A ——— B →	**B.** line segment	**b.** $\triangle ABC$
3. (circle with center A)	**C.** triangle	**c.** $\angle ABC$
4. (rays from B to A and C)	**D.** ray	**d.** $\overleftrightarrow{AB}$
5. (triangle A, B, C)	**E.** line	**e.** $\odot A$
6. ← A ——— B →	**F.** circle	**f.** $\overline{AB}$

Name each figure shown in red.

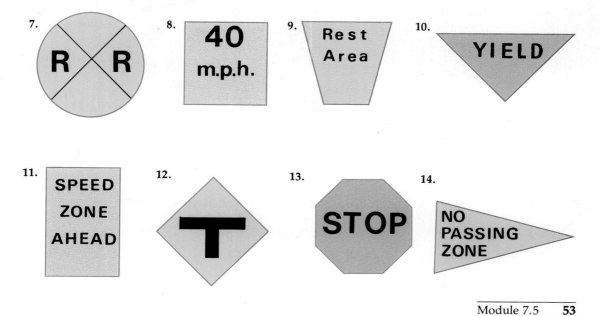

7.   8. **40 m.p.h.**   9. **Rest Area**   10. **YIELD**

11. **SPEED ZONE AHEAD**   12. **T**   13. **STOP**   14. **NO PASSING ZONE**

Constructing and measuring congruent segments

Try these constructions. Check the results by measuring
the segments with a ruler marked in millimeters (mm).

Copy a segment

Step 1

$A \qquad B$

given
segment

Step 2

$A \qquad B$

Open your
compass the
length of $\overline{AB}$.

Step 3

C

Draw a ray
from C.

Step 4

$C \qquad D$

Use the
opening from
A to B to
mark D.

Step 5

$C \qquad D$

$\overline{CD}$ is a copy
of $\overline{AB}$.

Segment CD **is congruent to**
segment AB. $\overline{CD} \cong \overline{AB}$

The length of segment CD equals the
length of segment AB. $l(\overline{CD}) = l(\overline{AB})$

Bisect a segment

Step 1

$A \qquad B$

given
segment

Step 2

$A \qquad B$

Draw an
arc.

Step 3

$A \qquad B$

Draw a second
intersecting
arc.

Step 4

$A \qquad M \quad B$

Draw the
bisecting
line.

Since $\overline{AM} \cong \overline{MB}$, we call M
the **midpoint** of $\overline{AB}$.

Use a ruler to draw each segment. Construct a copy of each segment and
bisect it.

1. $l(\overline{AB}) = 60$ mm

2. $l(\overline{CD}) = 45$ mm

3. $l(\overline{EF}) = 95$ mm

4. $l(\overline{GH}) = 30$ mm

5. $l(\overline{IJ}) = 72$ mm

6. $l(\overline{KL}) = 53$ mm

Copy each segment and bisect it.

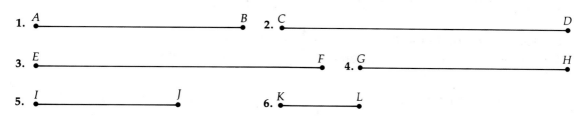

1. A ●————————————● B 2. C ●————————————————● D

3. E ●————————————● F 4. G ●————————————————● H

5. I ●————————● J 6. K ●————————● L

Trace each figure as necessary to complete the exercises.
Use your compass or ruler to check congruent segments.

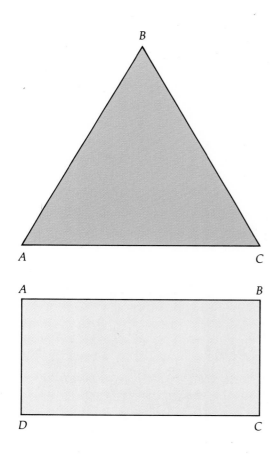

7. Are any of the segments in the triangle congruent? Name them.

8. Find the midpoint of each side of the triangle. Join these midpoints. What is the name of the interior figure?

9. The segment joining the midpoints of two sides of the triangle is __?__ the length of the third side. Use a ruler.

10. Name the pairs of congruent segments of the rectangle.

11. Find the midpoint of each side of the rectangle. Join these midpoints. What is the name of the interior figure?

 Using 16 toothpicks, make these 8 small triangles. Can you remove 4 toothpicks so only 4 triangles are left?

Constructing and measuring congruent angles

Try these constructions. Check the results by measuring the angles with a protractor.

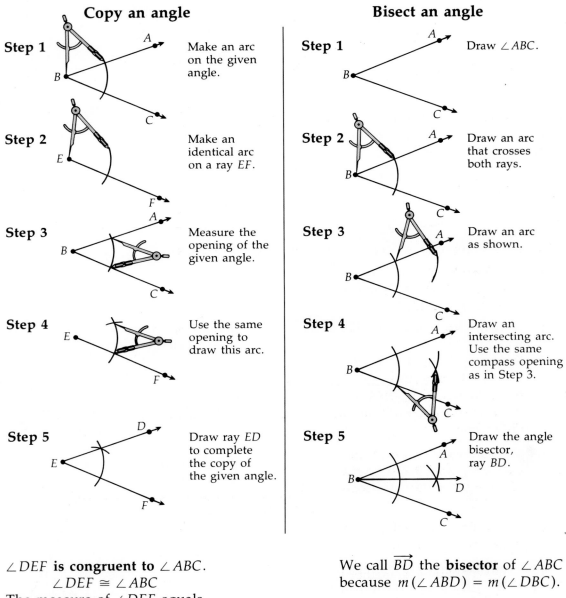

Copy an angle

Step 1 — Make an arc on the given angle.

Step 2 — Make an identical arc on a ray *EF*.

Step 3 — Measure the opening of the given angle.

Step 4 — Use the same opening to draw this arc.

Step 5 — Draw ray *ED* to complete the copy of the given angle.

Bisect an angle

Step 1 — Draw ∠*ABC*.

Step 2 — Draw an arc that crosses both rays.

Step 3 — Draw an arc as shown.

Step 4 — Draw an intersecting arc. Use the same compass opening as in Step 3.

Step 5 — Draw the angle bisector, ray *BD*.

∠*DEF* **is congruent to** ∠*ABC*.
  ∠*DEF* ≅ ∠*ABC*
The measure of ∠*DEF* equals
the measure of ∠*ABC*.
  $m(\angle DEF) = m(\angle ABC)$

We call $\overrightarrow{BD}$ the **bisector** of ∠*ABC* because $m(\angle ABD) = m(\angle DBC)$.

For which pairs of angles below is one angle a copy of the other?
Use your protractor to measure each angle.

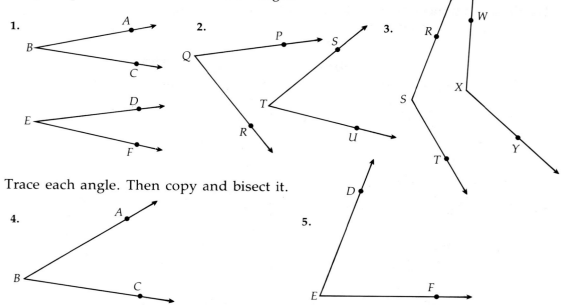

1. **2.** **3.**

Trace each angle. Then copy and bisect it.

4. **5.**

Trace these figures as necessary to complete the exercises.

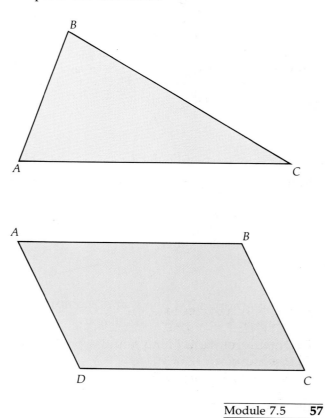

6. Bisect each angle of the triangle. Do the 3 bisectors meet in a point?

7. Measure each angle of the triangle. Find the sum of these measures. If it were possible to measure exactly, the sum would be 180°. By how much does your sum differ from 180°?

8. Measure each angle of the parallelogram. Which pairs of angles have a sum close to 180°?

9. Which pairs of angles do you think are congruent?

10. Find the sum of all 4 angles of the parallelogram. The sum should equal 360°. By how much does your sum differ from 360°?

Angles and intersecting lines

Try these constructions. Check the results by measuring the angles with a protractor.

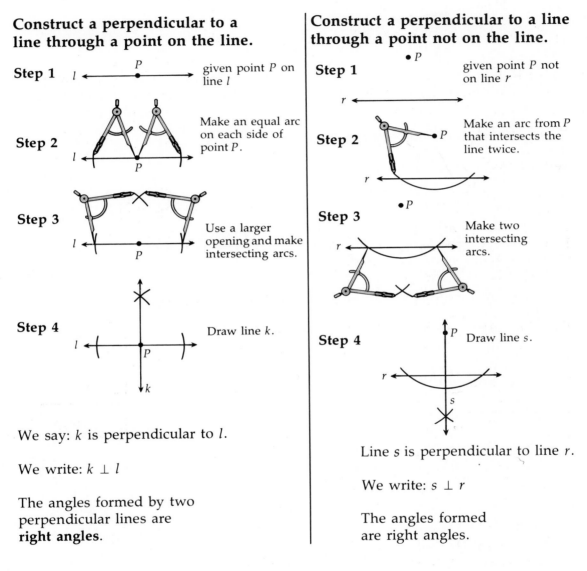

Construct a perpendicular to a line through a point on the line.

Step 1 l ←——●——→   given point P on line l

Step 2   Make an equal arc on each side of point P.

Step 3   Use a larger opening and make intersecting arcs.

Step 4   Draw line k.

We say: k is perpendicular to l.

We write: $k \perp l$

The angles formed by two perpendicular lines are **right angles**.

Construct a perpendicular to a line through a point not on the line.

Step 1   given point P not on line r

Step 2   Make an arc from P that intersects the line twice.

Step 3   Make two intersecting arcs.

Step 4   Draw line s.

Line s is perpendicular to line r.

We write: $s \perp r$

The angles formed are right angles.

---

1. Draw a horizontal line k and a point A on k. Construct line j through A and perpendicular to k.

2. Draw a horizontal line p and a point B not on p. Construct line q through B so that $q \perp p$.

3. Do exercises 1 and 2 with lines k and p drawn vertically.

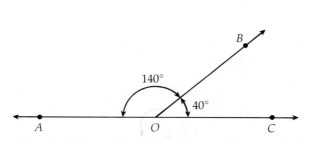

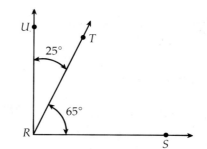

Two angles are **supplementary** if the sum of their measures is 180°. ∠AOB is supplementary to ∠BOC.

Two angles are **complementary** if the sum of their measures is 90°. ∠URT is complementary to ∠TRS.

When two straight lines intersect, two pairs of **vertical angles** are formed.

∠1 and ∠3 are vertical angles.
∠2 and ∠4 are vertical angles.

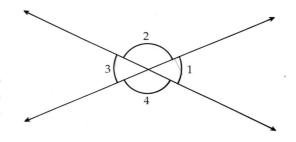

If $m\angle 1 = 50°$, then $m\angle 2 = 130°$. Why?
If $m\angle 2 = 130°$, then $m\angle 3 = 50°$. Why?
If $m\angle 3 = 50°$, then $m\angle 4 = 130°$. Why?
    $m\angle 1 = m\angle 3$ and $m\angle 2 = m\angle 4$

The angles in each pair of vertical angles have the same measure.

Give the number of degrees for x in each figure.

1.

2.

3.

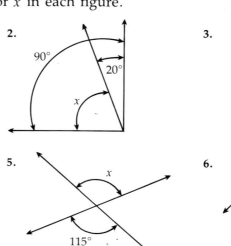

4.

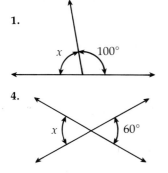

5.

6.

7. $m\angle A = 123°$
What is the measure of an angle which is supplementary to ∠A?

8. $m\angle B = 19°$
What is the measure of an angle which is complementary to ∠B?

Each of 8 strangers in a room shakes hands with each of the others once. How many handshakes are there?

Angles and parallel lines

Try these constructions. Test to see if lines are parallel by measuring the perpendicular distance between them at two or three places. The distances should all be equal.

Construct a line parallel to a given line by constructing perpendicular lines.

Step 1

P
•

l ⟷   given line

Step 2

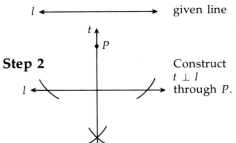

Construct
$t \perp l$
through P.

Step 3

Construct
$m \perp t$
through P.

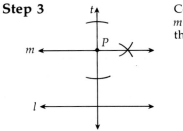

Line m is parallel to line l.

$$m \parallel l$$

Make two copies of line l and point A. Use each of the methods above to construct a line through A and parallel to l.

Construct a line parallel to a given line by copying an angle.

Step 1

P
•

s ⟷   given line

Step 2

Draw any line through P that intersects s.

Step 3

Copy $\angle 1$ on ray PA to produce line r.

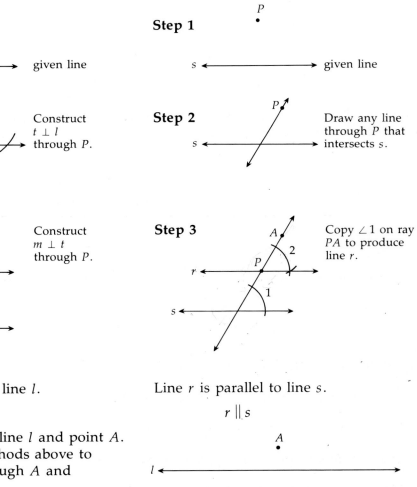

Line r is parallel to line s.

$$r \parallel s$$

A
•

l ⟷

Copy each line and point. Construct a line through the point parallel to the given line.

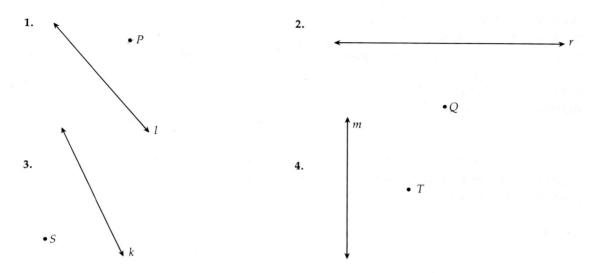

1. • *P*   *l*

2. *r*   • *Q*   *m*

3. • *S*   *k*

4. • *T*

When parallel lines are cut by a transversal, certain pairs of congruent or supplementary angles are formed.

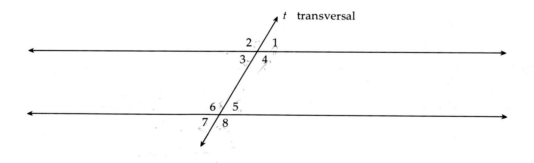

t transversal

Use your protractor, if needed, to complete the following:

5. List three angles that are congruent to ∠1.

6. List three angles that are congruent to ∠2.

7. List four angles that are supplementary to ∠4.

8. List four angles that are supplementary to ∠3.

✪ Regular polygons

All of the sides of a **regular polygon** have the same length and all of the vertex angles have the same measure.

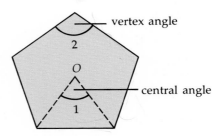

Regular pentagon

∠2 is a **vertex angle** of the regular pentagon. Point O is the center of the pentagon. ∠1 is a **central angle** of the pentagon.

The measure of the central angle of a regular polygon is

$\dfrac{360°}{n}$, where n is the number of sides of the polygon.

$$m(\angle 1) = \frac{360°}{5} = 72°$$

The vertex angle of a regular polygon is the supplement of the central angle.

$$m(\angle 2) + m(\angle 1) = 180°$$
$$m(\angle 2) = 180° - m(\angle 1)$$
$$= 180° - 72°$$
$$= 108°$$

1. How many sides does a regular octagon have?

2. Find the measure of the central angle, ∠1.

3. Find the measure of the vertex angle, ∠2.

4. Find the total number of degrees in all 8 vertex angles of a regular octagon.

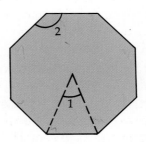

Regular octagon

Compute the measure of a central angle and a vertex angle
of each regular polygon below.

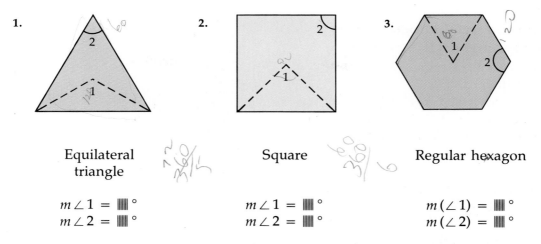

1.	**2.**	**3.**
Equilateral triangle	Square	Regular hexagon
$m \angle 1 =$ ▓ °	$m \angle 1 =$ ▓ °	$m (\angle 1) =$ ▓ °
$m \angle 2 =$ ▓ °	$m \angle 2 =$ ▓ °	$m (\angle 2) =$ ▓ °

An n-gon is a polygon with n sides.

Compute the measure of a central angle and a vertex angle
of each regular n-gon.

4. 9-gon   **5.** 10-gon   **6.** 12-gon   **7.** 15-gon

8. 18-gon   **9.** 20-gon   **10.** 24-gon   **11.** 36-gon

12. Find the total number of degrees in the vertex angles
of each n-gon in exercises 1–11.

☆ **13.** A regular heptagon has 7 sides.
Find the measure of a central
angle and vertex angle of a regular
heptagon. Using a protractor and
ruler, draw a regular heptagon with
each side 2 cm long.

☆ **14.** When the mathematician K. F. Gauss (1777–1855) was
17 years old he discovered that a regular 17-gon
could be constructed with a ruler and compass.
Find the measure of a central angle of a regular
17-gon to the nearest tenth of a degree.
Find the measure of each vertex angle
to the nearest tenth of a degree.

⊛ Angles and circles

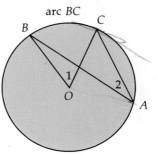

O is the **center** of the circle.
∠1 is a **central angle**.

A is on the circle.
∠2 is an **inscribed angle**.

∠1 and ∠2 intercept the same **arc** on the circle.

Measure the central angle and the inscribed angle in each circle below. Copy and complete the table.

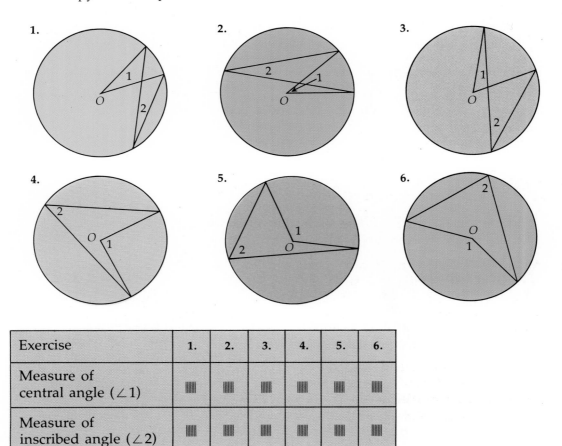

1.

2.

3.

4.

5.

6.

Exercise	1.	2.	3.	4.	5.	6.
Measure of central angle (∠1)	▓	▓	▓	▓	▓	▓
Measure of inscribed angle (∠2)	▓	▓	▓	▓	▓	▓

7. The measure of an inscribed angle is __?__ the measure of a central angle which intercepts the same arc.

Give the degree measure of the central or inscribed angle without measuring.

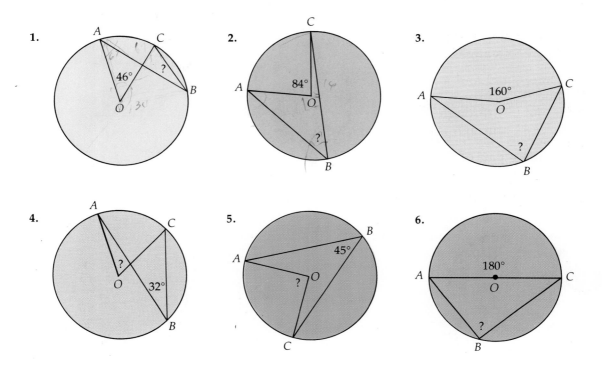

1. 46° ?

2. 84° ?

3. 160° ?

4. ? 32°

5. 45° ?

6. 180° ?

7. If the measure of an inscribed angle is 53°, what is the measure of a central angle that intercepts the same arc?

8. Angle *AOC*, formed by two rays from *O* in opposite directions, is a straight angle. $m(\angle AOC) = 180°$. $\angle 1$ intercepts the same semicircle arc as $\angle AOC$. What is $m(\angle 1)$?

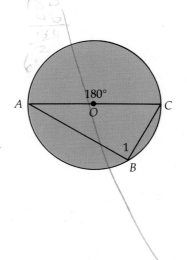

180°

9. Draw a circle and draw 4 different angles inscribed in a semicircular arc as in exercise 8. What is the measure of each of these angles?

Answers for Self-check **4.** congruent angles: $\angle 1$ and $\angle 4$, $\angle 2$ and $\angle 3$; supplementary angles: $\angle 1$ and $\angle 2$, $\angle 2$ and $\angle 4$, $\angle 3$ and $\angle 4$, $\angle 1$ and $\angle 3$; vertical angles: $\angle 1$ and $\angle 4$, $\angle 2$ and $\angle 3$ **5.** $m(\angle 1) = 72°$; $m(\angle 2) = 108°$ **6.** $m(\angle 3) = 30°$

Self-check

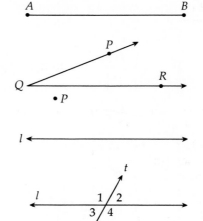

1. Copy segment AB. Then bisect it.

2. Copy this angle. Then bisect it.

3. Draw line l and a point P not on line l. Construct:
   a. $m \perp l$, through P.
   b. $k \parallel l$, through P.

4. Name a pair of congruent angles, a pair of supplementary angles, and a pair of vertical angles.

☆ 5. Without measuring, give the measures of $\angle 1$ and $\angle 2$ in this regular pentagon.

☆ 6. Without measuring, give the measure of inscribed $\angle 3$ in this circle.

Answers for Self-check—page 65

Test

1. Draw a segment. Then bisect it.

2. Draw an angle. Then bisect it.

3. Draw a line j and a point Q not on the line.
   Construct: a. $r \parallel j$, through Q.
   b. $s \perp j$, through Q.

4. Name a pair of vertical angles, a pair of supplementary angles, and a pair of congruent angles.

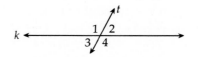

☆ 5. Without measuring, give the measures of $\angle 1$ and $\angle 2$ in this regular hexagon.

☆ 6. Without measuring, give the measure of inscribed $\angle 3$ in this circle.

Math lab

Ruler-Compass Designs

Many interesting designs can be made with a ruler and compass.

1. Designs based on squares and octagons

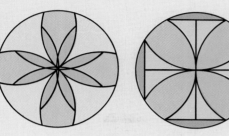

2. Designs based on equilateral triangles and hexagons

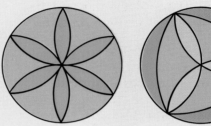

3. Designs based on pentagons*

4. Mixed designs

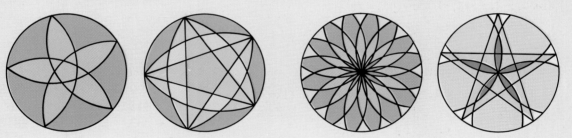

Use the ideas above to create
some designs of your own!

*A compass opening of 33 mm will divide a circle with a radius of
28 mm into approximately 5 equal parts.

Unit 7 review

Write the standard numeral.

1. four hundred eighty-three

2. two hundred six million

3. 7.5×10^8

4. 4.38×10^6

Give the correct sign, $<$ or $>$, for each ⬤.

5. 3.9 ⬤ 4.2

6. 6.82 ⬤ 6.79

7. 0.261 ⬤ 0.257

8. 3.804 ⬤ 3.798

Round to the nearest hundred.

9. 76 829

10. 324 261

Round to the nearest thousand.

11. 76 829

12. 324 261

Round to the nearest tenth.

13. 5.284

14. 36.078

Round to the nearest hundredth.

15. 5.284

16. 36.078

Add.

17.	97 + 65	18.	483 + 129	19.	6287 + 4376	20.	729 846 + 283	21.	4628 1765 + 9842

22.	7.8 + 6.5	23.	9.36 + 8.74	24.	36.84 + 17.27	25.	0.732 0.840 + 0.695	26.	476.3 287.4 + 396.0

Subtract.

27.	42 − 19	28.	764 − 392	29.	6052 − 1378	30.	7301 − 4625	31.	26 431 − 9 283

32.	7.5 − 3.8	33.	5.03 − 1.67	34.	32.36 − 14.43	35.	2.076 − 0.395	36.	43.281 − 17.653

Multiplication
Division
Problem Solving—Using Your Skills
Measurement Concepts

Multiplication

Review the basic principles for multiplication by studying the examples.

Commutative principle (multiplication)

For any whole numbers a and b,
$$a \cdot b = b \cdot a$$

Examples: $5 \cdot 7 = 7 \cdot 5$

$x \cdot 6 = 6 \cdot x = 6x$

Associative principle (multiplication)

For any whole numbers a, b, and c,
$$(a \cdot b) \cdot c = a \cdot (b \cdot c)$$

Examples: $(3 \cdot 2) \cdot 5 = 3 \cdot (2 \cdot 5)$

$7 \cdot (4x) = (7 \cdot 4)x = 28x$

One principle

For any whole number a,
$$a \cdot 1 = a$$

Examples: $8 \cdot 1 = 8$

$x \cdot 1 = 1 \cdot x = x$

Distributive principle

For any whole numbers a, b, and c,
$$a \cdot (b + c) = (a \cdot b) + (a \cdot c)$$

Examples: $3 \cdot (2 + 5) = (3 \cdot 2) + (3 \cdot 5)$

$4x + 3x = (4 + 3) \cdot x = 7x$

True or *false*

If the statement is true, give the name of the principle used. Do not compute.

1. $23 \cdot 46 = 46 \cdot 23$

2. $879 \cdot 1 = 879$

3. $18 \cdot 0 = 18$

4. $9 \cdot (20 + 7) = (9 \cdot 20) + (9 \cdot 7)$

5. $23 + (9 \cdot 6) = (23 + 9) \cdot (23 + 6)$

6. $(12 \cdot 5) \cdot 2 = 12 \cdot (5 \cdot 2)$

7. $6 \cdot (9 + 4) = (6 \cdot 9) + 4$

Find the products.

1. $4 \cdot 10$ 2. $7 \cdot 10$ 3. $8 \cdot 100$ 4. $9 \cdot 1000$ 5. $17 \cdot 10$

6. $9 \cdot 100$ 7. $23 \cdot 10$ 8. $14 \cdot 1000$ 9. $6 \cdot 100$ 10. $25 \cdot 10$

11. $28 \cdot 1000$ 12. $34 \cdot 10$ 13. $64 \cdot 100$ 14. $10 \cdot 100$ 15. $100 \cdot 100$

Other special products can be found mentally by using the basic principles for multiplication.

Examples: $3 \cdot 40 = (3 \cdot 4) \cdot 10 = 12 \cdot 10 = 120$
$8 \cdot 3000 = (8 \cdot 3) \cdot 1000 = 24 \cdot 1000 = 24\ 000$

Find the products.

16. $4 \cdot 20$ 17. $7 \cdot 80$ 18. $9 \cdot 60$ 19. $8 \cdot 30$ 20. $9 \cdot 70$

21. $20 \cdot 30$ 22. $60 \cdot 60$ 23. $80 \cdot 40$ 24. $50 \cdot 50$ 25. $90 \cdot 60$

Other examples: $70 \cdot 60 = (7 \cdot 6) \cdot (10 \cdot 10) = 42 \cdot 100 = 4200$
$50 \cdot 40 = (5 \cdot 4) \cdot (10 \cdot 10) = 20 \cdot 100 = 2000$

26. $7 \cdot 4000$ 27. $6 \cdot 2000$ 28. $9 \cdot 3000$ 29. $8 \cdot 7000$ 30. $3 \cdot 9000$

31. $8 \cdot 80$ 32. $6 \cdot 800$ 33. $5 \cdot 400$ 34. $3 \cdot 8000$ 35. $4 \cdot 400$

Simplify each expression.
Examples: $2x + 3x = 5x$; $5(3y) = 15y$

36. $(4x) \cdot 9$ 37. $(12 - 7)x$ 38. $4x + 2x$ 39. $t \cdot 1$ 40. $6 \cdot (4s)$

41. $7q + 2q$ 42. $m(7 + 5)$ 43. $(6r) \cdot 3$ 44. $3x + x$ 45. $(7 + 3)n$

Multiplying whole numbers

Sound travels through air at a speed
of about 1195 km/h (kilometers per hour).
Some earth satellites travel
23 times that fast. How fast do
these satellites travel?

Finding the answer

Multiply by the ones' digit	Multiply by the tens' digit	Add the products

$$\begin{array}{r} 1195 \\ \times \quad 23 \\ \hline 3585 \end{array}$$

$$\begin{array}{r} 1195 \\ \times \quad 23 \\ \hline 3585 \\ 2390 \\ \hline \end{array}$$

$$\begin{array}{r} 1195 \\ \times \quad 23 \\ \hline 3585 \\ 2390 \\ \hline 27485 \end{array}$$

The satellites travel about 27 485 km/h.

Other examples

$$\begin{array}{r} 386 \\ \times \quad 7 \\ \hline 2702 \end{array}$$

$$\begin{array}{r} 5283 \\ \times \quad 46 \\ \hline 31\,698 \\ 211\,32 \\ \hline 243\,018 \end{array}$$

$$\begin{array}{r} 374 \\ \times 592 \\ \hline 748 \\ 33\,66 \\ 187\,0 \\ \hline 221\,408 \end{array}$$

Find the products.

1. $\begin{array}{r} 54 \\ \times \ 8 \\ \hline \end{array}$
2. $\begin{array}{r} 376 \\ \times \ 4 \\ \hline \end{array}$
3. $\begin{array}{r} 4578 \\ \times \ 6 \\ \hline \end{array}$
4. $\begin{array}{r} 274 \\ \times \ 93 \\ \hline \end{array}$
5. $\begin{array}{r} 659 \\ \times \ 75 \\ \hline \end{array}$

6. $\begin{array}{r} 8371 \\ \times \ 82 \\ \hline \end{array}$
7. $\begin{array}{r} 654 \\ \times 726 \\ \hline \end{array}$
8. $\begin{array}{r} 782 \\ \times 347 \\ \hline \end{array}$
9. $\begin{array}{r} 2634 \\ \times 829 \\ \hline \end{array}$
10. $\begin{array}{r} 5729 \\ \times 603 \\ \hline \end{array}$

Find the products.

1.	39 × 3	**2.**	46 × 8	**3.**	275 × 7

4.	7326 × 6	**5.**	74 × 29	**6.**	83 × 54

7. 723 × 62   **8.** 608 × 37   **9.** 375 × 48

10. 2635 × 26   **11.** 7806 × 92   **12.** 472 × 24

13. 981 × 257   **14.** 307 × 683   **15.** 562 × 427

16. 740 × 956   **17.** 1375 × 807   **18.** 2486 × 342

19. 1750 × 651   **20.** 6053 × 108   **21.** 7562 × 640

22. 49×68 **23.** 175×23 **24.** 98×87 **25.** 46×224 **26.** 92×50

27. 77×163 **28.** 382×5803 **29.** 468×1094 **30.** 37×379 **31.** 744×9376

32. Some rocket planes can fly at a rate of about 5 times the speed of sound. How fast is this?

33. The earth travels in its orbit at a rate of about 90 times the speed of sound. How fast is this?

Light travels at about $2.998 \cdot 10^5$ km/s. How many kilometers per hour does light travel? How many kilometers does light travel in a day?

Decimal multiplication

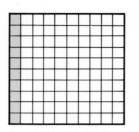

1 **tenth** is shaded pink.   1 **tenth** of 1 **tenth** is shaded red.

1 **tenth** of 1 **tenth** is 1 **hundredth**.

$$0.1 \times 0.1 = 0.01$$

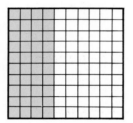

4 **tenths** is shaded pink.   3 **tenths** of 4 **tenths** is shaded red.

3 **tenths** of 4 **tenths** is 12 **hundredths**.

$$0.3 \times 0.4 = 0.12$$

Complete each sentence. Then give the product.

1. 2 tenths of 4 tenths is ____?____ .
    $0.2 \times 0.4 = $ ▥

2. 6 tenths of 1 tenth is ____?____ .
    $0.6 \times 0.1 = $ ▥

3. 7 tenths of 5 tenths is ____?____ .
    $0.7 \times 0.5 = $ ▥

4. 1 tenth of 8 tenths is ____?____ .
    $0.1 \times 0.8 = $ ▥

5. 9 tenths of 4 tenths is ____?____ .
    $0.9 \times 0.4 = $ ▥

6. 8 tenths of 3 tenths is ____?____ .
    $0.8 \times 0.3 = $ ▥

7. 5 tenths of 5 tenths is ____?____ .
    $0.5 \times 0.5 = $ ▥

8. 3 tenths of 7 tenths is ____?____ .
    $0.3 \times 0.7 = $ ▥

The number of decimal places in a numeral is important when multiplying decimals.

Decimal	Kind of decimal	Examples		
whole numbers	0-place	25	643	8920
tenths	1-place	0.3	5.2	236.7
hundredths	2-place	0.07	0.22	57.84
thousandths	3-place	0.003	1.249	67.075
ten-thousandths	4-place	0.0004	0.7865	2.4093

Study each example. Then give the missing numbers.

1. $0.3 \times 0.02 = 0.006$
   A 1-place decimal times a 2-place decimal gives a ▥-place decimal.

2. $4 \times 0.3 = 1.2$
   A 0-place decimal times a 1-place decimal gives a ▥-place decimal.

3. $0.04 \times 0.07 = 0.0028$
   A 2-place decimal times a 2-place decimal gives a ▥-place decimal.

4. $0.8 \times 0.006 = 0.0048$
   A 1-place decimal times a 3-place decimal gives a ▥-place decimal.

Find the products.

5. 0.7×0.6

6. 3×0.5

7. 8×0.02

8. 0.1×0.01

9. 0.1×0.001

10. 0.01×0.01

11. 0.4×0.03

12. 0.05×0.5

13. 0.003×7

14. 0.09×0.02

15. 0.2×0.9

16. 0.04×4

17. 0.9×0.9

18. 6×0.6

19. 0.03×0.07

20. 8×0.1

21. 9×0.01

22. $7 \times .0001$

23. $(0.1 \times 0.2) \times 0.3$

24. $(6 \times 0.2) \times 0.1$

25. $(0.3 \times 0.2) \times 4$

Multiplying decimals

The painters can figure out how much
paint they need if they can find
the area of the wall. The
wall is 3.65 m by 2.75 m.
What is the area of the wall
in square meters?

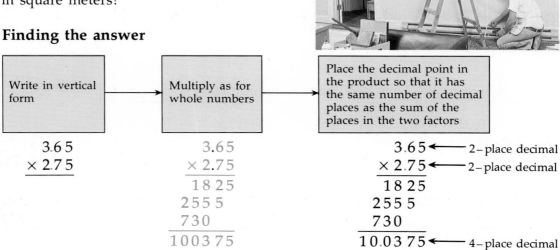

Finding the answer

Write in vertical form	Multiply as for whole numbers	Place the decimal point in the product so that it has the same number of decimal places as the sum of the places in the two factors

$$
\begin{array}{r}
3.65 \\
\times\ 2.75 \\
\hline
\end{array}
$$

$$
\begin{array}{r}
3.65 \\
\times\ 2.75 \\
\hline
1825 \\
2555 \\
730 \\
\hline
100375
\end{array}
$$

$$
\begin{array}{r}
3.65 \longleftarrow 2\text{-place decimal} \\
\times\ 2.75 \longleftarrow 2\text{-place decimal} \\
\hline
1825 \\
2555 \\
730 \\
\hline
10.0375 \longleftarrow 4\text{-place decimal}
\end{array}
$$

The area of the wall is about 10 m².

Other examples

$$
\begin{array}{r}
32.67 \\
\times\ \ \ \ 45 \\
\hline
16335 \\
13068 \\
\hline
1470.15
\end{array}
\qquad
\begin{array}{r}
3.86 \\
\times\ \ 0.7 \\
\hline
2.702
\end{array}
\qquad
\begin{array}{r}
2.85 \\
\times\ 0.63 \\
\hline
855 \\
1710 \\
\hline
1.7955
\end{array}
\qquad
\begin{array}{r}
0.34 \\
\times\ 0.27 \\
\hline
238 \\
68 \\
\hline
0.0918
\end{array}
$$

Find the products.

1. $\begin{array}{r} 3.76 \\ \times\ \ \ \ 4 \\ \hline \end{array}$
2. $\begin{array}{r} 3.76 \\ \times\ \ 0.4 \\ \hline \end{array}$
3. $\begin{array}{r} 37.6 \\ \times\ \ 0.4 \\ \hline \end{array}$
4. $\begin{array}{r} 376 \\ \times\ 0.04 \\ \hline \end{array}$
5. $\begin{array}{r} 3.76 \\ \times\ 0.04 \\ \hline \end{array}$

6. $\begin{array}{r} 2.59 \\ \times\ \ 3.4 \\ \hline \end{array}$
7. $\begin{array}{r} 6.82 \\ \times\ 0.57 \\ \hline \end{array}$
8. $\begin{array}{r} 46.3 \\ \times\ \ 2.8 \\ \hline \end{array}$
9. $\begin{array}{r} 79.8 \\ \times\ 0.16 \\ \hline \end{array}$
10. $\begin{array}{r} 5.23 \\ \times\ \ 4.1 \\ \hline \end{array}$

Multiply.

1. $\begin{array}{r} 7.6 \\ \times\ 0.4 \\ \hline \end{array}$	**2.** $\begin{array}{r} 8.23 \\ \times\quad 3 \\ \hline \end{array}$	**3.** $\begin{array}{r} 6.9 \\ \times\ 0.6 \\ \hline \end{array}$	**4.** $\begin{array}{r} 543 \\ \times\ 0.08 \\ \hline \end{array}$	**5.** $\begin{array}{r} 27.6 \\ \times\ 0.05 \\ \hline \end{array}$
6. $\begin{array}{r} 4.6 \\ \times\ 2.7 \\ \hline \end{array}$	**7.** $\begin{array}{r} 0.32 \\ \times\ 0.83 \\ \hline \end{array}$	**8.** $\begin{array}{r} 56.4 \\ \times\ 92 \\ \hline \end{array}$	**9.** $\begin{array}{r} 7.83 \\ \times\ 5.6 \\ \hline \end{array}$	**10.** $\begin{array}{r} 0.92 \\ \times\ 0.74 \\ \hline \end{array}$
11. $\begin{array}{r} 0.86 \\ \times\ 3.2 \\ \hline \end{array}$	**12.** $\begin{array}{r} 517 \\ \times\ 0.48 \\ \hline \end{array}$	**13.** $\begin{array}{r} 8.33 \\ \times\ 5.7 \\ \hline \end{array}$	**14.** $\begin{array}{r} 0.64 \\ \times\ 7.6 \\ \hline \end{array}$	**15.** $\begin{array}{r} 3.8 \\ \times\ 0.28 \\ \hline \end{array}$
16. $\begin{array}{r} 2.66 \\ \times\ 1.32 \\ \hline \end{array}$	**17.** $\begin{array}{r} 1.73 \\ \times\ 30.4 \\ \hline \end{array}$	**18.** $\begin{array}{r} 0.624 \\ \times\ 6.21 \\ \hline \end{array}$	**19.** $\begin{array}{r} 7.65 \\ \times\ 0.314 \\ \hline \end{array}$	**20.** $\begin{array}{r} 8.54 \\ \times\ 70.2 \\ \hline \end{array}$
21. $\begin{array}{r} 0.764 \\ \times\ 0.619 \\ \hline \end{array}$	**22.** $\begin{array}{r} 3.98 \\ \times\ 9.81 \\ \hline \end{array}$	**23.** $\begin{array}{r} 5.26 \\ \times\ 24.3 \\ \hline \end{array}$	**24.** $\begin{array}{r} 7.81 \\ \times\ 0.675 \\ \hline \end{array}$	**25.** $\begin{array}{r} 0.675 \\ \times\ 8.29 \\ \hline \end{array}$
26. $\begin{array}{r} 129.6 \\ \times\ 0.065 \\ \hline \end{array}$	**27.** $\begin{array}{r} 38\ 192 \\ \times\ 0.09 \\ \hline \end{array}$	**28.** $\begin{array}{r} 0.774 \\ \times\ 23.4 \\ \hline \end{array}$	**29.** $\begin{array}{r} 8.29 \\ \times\ 38.5 \\ \hline \end{array}$	**30.** $\begin{array}{r} 37\ 429 \\ \times\ 0.125 \\ \hline \end{array}$

31. A room to be carpeted is 4.27 m long and 3.10 m wide. What is the area of the floor of this room?

☆ **32.** Estimate the length and width of your classroom. What is the area of the floor? Check your results by measuring.

Calculator problems.

☆ Find the products.

33. 8.14×6.092

34. 0.7142×0.849

35. $0.29 \times 12.4 \times 6.29$

36. $33.4 \times 19.3 \times 17.6$

37. $0.07 \times 0.11 \times 0.13$

38. $0.7 \times 1.1 \times 1.3$

39. $0.999 \times 0.99 \times 0.9$

40. $7.38 \times 3.14 \times 9.7$

More practice, page 383, Set A

Using multiplication to solve equations

A cook prepared some soup. The soup was then divided equally into 8 bowls, each holding 200 mL. How many milliliters of soup did the cook prepare?

Let m = number of milliliters of soup in the pot

Equation: $\dfrac{m}{8} = 200$

Solving the equation

Equation	$\dfrac{m}{8} = 200$

Multiply each side of the equation by the same number

$8 \cdot \dfrac{m}{8} = 8 \cdot 200$

To undo dividing by 8, we multiply by 8. Multiplying both sides by 8 maintains the equality.

Simplify to find the solution

$m = 1600$ Check: $\dfrac{1600}{8} = 200$

The cook prepared 1600 mL of soup.

Other examples

$$\dfrac{x}{10} = 80 \qquad\qquad \dfrac{a}{4} = 5.7 \qquad\qquad \dfrac{z}{0.7} = 9.2$$

$$10 \cdot \dfrac{x}{10} = 10 \cdot 80 \qquad 4 \cdot \dfrac{a}{4} = 4 \cdot 5.7 \qquad 0.7 \cdot \dfrac{z}{0.7} = 0.7 \cdot 9.2$$

$$x = 800 \qquad\qquad a = 22.8 \qquad\qquad z = 6.44$$

Solve these equations. Show each step.

1. $\dfrac{n}{6} = 5$ 2. $\dfrac{x}{4} = 8$ 3. $\dfrac{c}{8} = 11$ 4. $\dfrac{d}{9} = 40$ 5. $\dfrac{r}{7} = 3$ 6. $\dfrac{s}{4} = 25$

7. $\dfrac{y}{8} = 3$ 8. $\dfrac{t}{6} = 9$ 9. $\dfrac{n}{3} = 1.2$ 10. $\dfrac{x}{5} = 8.4$ 11. $\dfrac{c}{0.2} = 5.0$ 12. $\dfrac{p}{0.3} = 0.3$

Solve these equations. Show each step.

1. $\dfrac{n}{3} = 10$ 2. $\dfrac{x}{8} = 20$ 3. $\dfrac{y}{9} = 20$

4. $\dfrac{c}{7} = 30$ 5. $\dfrac{d}{4} = 40$ 6. $\dfrac{t}{12} = 4$

7. $\dfrac{r}{6} = 9$ 8. $\dfrac{p}{9} = 3$ 9. $\dfrac{a}{5} = 30$

10. $\dfrac{b}{7} = 5$ 11. $\dfrac{d}{2} = 25$ 12. $\dfrac{x}{4} = 20$

13. $\dfrac{x}{3.2} = 5.1$

14. $\dfrac{a}{8.72} = 0.25$

15. $\dfrac{y}{0.25} = 62.8$ 16. $\dfrac{b}{2.95} = 10.3$

17. $\dfrac{s}{4.8} = 146$ 18. $\dfrac{t}{6.73} = 12.85$

19. $\dfrac{c}{4.5} = 9.81$ 20. $\dfrac{r}{5.46} = 3.89$

21. $\dfrac{u}{0.33} + 75 = 103$ 22. $\dfrac{w}{0.037} = 3000$

Calculate the two products in each box and write them on your paper. Do you see anything unusual about the two numbers?

10 989 × 1	10 989 × 2	10 989 × 3	10 989 × 4
10 989 × 9	10 989 × 8	10 989 × 7	10 989 × 6

Try this using 109 989 instead of 10 989. Does it work?
Try this using 1 099 989 instead of 10 989. Does it work?

Can you describe a pattern?

Answers for Self-check 1. 30 2. 80 3. 2100 4. 2400 5. 8000 6. 152 7. 434 8. 472 9. 1482
10. 29 466 11. 2666 12. 1305 13. 13 050 14. 294 354 15. 4 201 098 16. 0.42 17. 0.0156
18. 3.56 19. 229.62 20. 13.7934 21. $r = 24$ 22. $x = 91$ 23. $n = 152$ 24. $t = 6.48$
25. $k = 10.00$ 26. $b = 27.170$

Self-check

Find the products.

1. 3×10
2. 4×20
3. 7×300
4. 6×400
5. 8×1000

6. $\begin{array}{r} 38 \\ \times\ 4 \\ \hline \end{array}$
7. $\begin{array}{r} 62 \\ \times\ 7 \\ \hline \end{array}$
8. $\begin{array}{r} 59 \\ \times\ 8 \\ \hline \end{array}$
9. $\begin{array}{r} 247 \\ \times\ 6 \\ \hline \end{array}$
10. $\begin{array}{r} 3274 \\ \times\ 9 \\ \hline \end{array}$

11. $\begin{array}{r} 62 \\ \times 43 \\ \hline \end{array}$
12. $\begin{array}{r} 87 \\ \times 15 \\ \hline \end{array}$
13. $\begin{array}{r} 225 \\ \times\ 58 \\ \hline \end{array}$
14. $\begin{array}{r} 621 \\ \times 474 \\ \hline \end{array}$
15. $\begin{array}{r} 7206 \\ \times\ 583 \\ \hline \end{array}$

16. $\begin{array}{r} 0.7 \\ \times 0.6 \\ \hline \end{array}$
17. $\begin{array}{r} 0.26 \\ \times 0.06 \\ \hline \end{array}$
18. $\begin{array}{r} 8.9 \\ \times 0.4 \\ \hline \end{array}$
19. $\begin{array}{r} 26.7 \\ \times\ 8.6 \\ \hline \end{array}$
20. $\begin{array}{r} 5.82 \\ \times 2.37 \\ \hline \end{array}$

Solve the equations.

21. $\dfrac{r}{3} = 8$
22. $\dfrac{x}{7} = 13$
23. $\dfrac{n}{8} = 19$

24. $\dfrac{t}{1.2} = 5.4$
25. $\dfrac{k}{0.8} = 12.5$
26. $\dfrac{b}{0.95} = 28.6$

Answers for Self-check—page 79

Test

Find the products.

1. 8×10
2. 3×30
3. 8×200
4. 7×1000
5. 40×20

6. $\begin{array}{r} 26 \\ \times\ 3 \\ \hline \end{array}$
7. $\begin{array}{r} 87 \\ \times\ 9 \\ \hline \end{array}$
8. $\begin{array}{r} 19 \\ \times\ 7 \\ \hline \end{array}$
9. $\begin{array}{r} 537 \\ \times\ 8 \\ \hline \end{array}$
10. $\begin{array}{r} 4473 \\ \times\ 6 \\ \hline \end{array}$

11. $\begin{array}{r} 73 \\ \times 27 \\ \hline \end{array}$
12. $\begin{array}{r} 96 \\ \times 54 \\ \hline \end{array}$
13. $\begin{array}{r} 179 \\ \times\ 37 \\ \hline \end{array}$
14. $\begin{array}{r} 608 \\ \times 388 \\ \hline \end{array}$
15. $\begin{array}{r} 2571 \\ \times\ 362 \\ \hline \end{array}$

16. $\begin{array}{r} 0.9 \\ \times 0.3 \\ \hline \end{array}$
17. $\begin{array}{r} 3.8 \\ \times 0.4 \\ \hline \end{array}$
18. $\begin{array}{r} 0.43 \\ \times\ 0.9 \\ \hline \end{array}$
19. $\begin{array}{r} 47.3 \\ \times\ 2.8 \\ \hline \end{array}$
20. $\begin{array}{r} 3.48 \\ \times 0.672 \\ \hline \end{array}$

Solve the equations.

21. $\dfrac{x}{4} = 9$
22. $\dfrac{n}{6} = 14$
23. $\dfrac{t}{7} = 28$

24. $\dfrac{r}{5} = 3.8$
25. $\dfrac{s}{2.1} = 6.3$
26. $\dfrac{c}{0.75} = 24.8$

Multiplication Magic

With a little practice you can learn to write the **answer only** for
2- and 3-digit multiplication problems. Study the examples to discover
the method.

Find 56 × 34.

Step 1

$$\begin{array}{r} 34 \\ \times\,56 \\ \hline 4 \end{array}$$

Think:
6 × 4 = 24

Write 4.

Remember 2.

Step 2

$$\begin{array}{r} 34 \\ \times\,56 \\ \hline 04 \end{array}$$

Think:
6 × 3 = 18
5 × 4 = 20
$$\begin{array}{r} +\,2 \\ \hline 40 \end{array}$$

Write 0.
Remember 4

Step 3

$$\begin{array}{r} 34 \\ \times\,56 \\ \hline 1904 \end{array}$$

Think:
5 × 3 = 15
$$\begin{array}{r} +\,4 \\ \hline 19 \end{array}$$

Write 19.

Now try these.

1.	2.	3.	4.	5.	6.
36	52	35	72	56	83
× 24	× 46	× 27	× 34	× 72	× 24

Find 326 × 452.

Step 1

$$\begin{array}{r} 452 \\ \times\,326 \\ \hline 2 \end{array}$$

6 × 2 = 12

Step 2

$$\begin{array}{r} 452 \\ \times\,326 \\ \hline 52 \end{array}$$

6 × 5 = 30
2 × 2 = 4
$$\begin{array}{r} +\,1 \\ \hline 35 \end{array}$$

Step 3

$$\begin{array}{r} 452 \\ \times\,326 \\ \hline 352 \end{array}$$

6 × 4 = 24
3 × 2 = 6
2 × 5 = 10
$$\begin{array}{r} +\,3 \\ \hline 43 \end{array}$$

Step 4

$$\begin{array}{r} 452 \\ \times\,326 \\ \hline 7352 \end{array}$$

2 × 4 = 8
3 × 5 = 15
$$\begin{array}{r} +\,4 \\ \hline 27 \end{array}$$

Step 5

$$\begin{array}{r} 452 \\ \times\,326 \\ \hline 147\,352 \end{array}$$

3 × 4 = 12
$$\begin{array}{r} +\,2 \\ \hline 14 \end{array}$$

Now try these.

7.	8.	9.	10.	11.	12.
273	253	724	372	538	463
× 324	× 346	× 263	× 426	× 232	× 352

Division

Division and multiplication are related operations.

$$24 \div 4 = 6 \qquad \text{because} \qquad 6 \times 4 = 24$$
$$32 \div 8 = 4 \qquad \text{because} \qquad 4 \times 8 = 32$$
$$54 \div 9 = 6 \qquad \text{because} \qquad 6 \times 9 = 54$$

The two examples below show why we do not divide by 0.

$$48 \div 0 = ? \qquad ? \times 0 = 48$$

There is **no** number times 0 that equals 48. There is **no** number for the quotient.

$$0 \div 0 = ? \qquad ? \times 0 = 0$$

Every number times 0 equals 0. There is **no single** number for the quotient.

Find the quotients.

1. $18 \div 2$	2. $15 \div 3$	3. $24 \div 6$	4. $20 \div 5$
5. $12 \div 6$	6. $36 \div 4$	7. $40 \div 8$	8. $42 \div 7$
9. $27 \div 9$	10. $48 \div 8$	11. $56 \div 7$	12. $81 \div 9$
13. $21 \div 3$	14. $24 \div 8$	15. $54 \div 6$	16. $10 \div 5$
17. $28 \div 4$	18. $63 \div 9$	19. $16 \div 8$	20. $49 \div 7$
21. $35 \div 7$	22. $32 \div 8$	23. $45 \div 9$	24. $56 \div 8$
25. $12 \div 12$	26. $0 \div 9$	27. $7 \div 1$	28. $72 \div 8$
29. $14 \div 7$	30. $16 \div 2$	31. $54 \div 9$	32. $64 \div 8$

Basic multiplication facts and special products can help you
find special quotients.

$$28 \div 7 = 4 \qquad \text{because} \qquad 4 \times 7 = 28$$
$$280 \div 7 = 40 \qquad \text{because} \qquad 40 \times 7 = 280$$
$$2800 \div 7 = 400 \qquad \text{because} \qquad 400 \times 7 = 2800$$
$$2800 \div 70 = 40 \qquad \text{because} \qquad 40 \times 70 = 2800$$

Complete each table.

	Divide by 2	
1.	4	
2.	40	
3.	400	
4.	4000	
5.	40 000	

	Divide by 8	
6.	24	
7.	240	
8.	2400	
9.	24 000	
10.	240 000	

	Divide by 7	
11.	35	
12.	350	
13.	3500	
14.	35 000	
15.	350 000	

	Divide by 30	
16.	60	
17.	120	
18.	150	
19.	240	
20.	270	

	Divide by 40	
21.	120	
22.	160	
23.	200	
24.	400	
25.	800	

	Divide by 60	
26.	60	
27.	600	
28.	6000	
29.	60 000	
30.	600 000	

Find the quotients.

31. $450 \div 9$

32. $630 \div 70$

33. $5000 \div 50$

34. $1200 \div 20$

35. $1800 \div 300$

36. $490 \div 70$

37. $6000 \div 2000$

38. $560 \div 80$

39. $5400 \div 9$

40. $500 \div 100$

41. $1500 \div 3$

42. $1500 \div 30$

43. $1000 \div 100$

44. $2000 \div 500$

45. $1200 \div 60$

46. $720 \div 90$

47. $4200 \div 700$

48. $8100 \div 90$

Dividing whole numbers

During one day, a San Francisco cable car made 36 trips from one end of its line to the other. A total of 1481 passengers rode on the cable car that day. About how many persons rode on each trip of the cable car?

Finding the answer

Estimate the tens	Multiply and subtract	Estimate the ones	Multiply and subtract

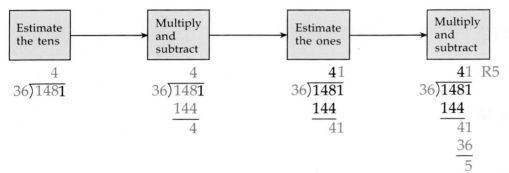

$$
\begin{array}{r}
4 \\
36\overline{)1481}
\end{array}
\qquad
\begin{array}{r}
4 \\
36\overline{)1481} \\
144 \\
\hline
4
\end{array}
\qquad
\begin{array}{r}
41 \\
36\overline{)1481} \\
144 \\
\hline
41
\end{array}
\qquad
\begin{array}{r}
41 \text{ R5} \\
36\overline{)1481} \\
144 \\
\hline
41 \\
36 \\
\hline
5
\end{array}
$$

About 41 persons rode on each trip.

Other examples

$$
\begin{array}{r}
306 \text{ R25} \\
48\overline{)14\,713} \\
14\,4 \\
\hline
313 \\
288 \\
\hline
25
\end{array}
\qquad
\begin{array}{r}
470 \text{ R8} \\
62\overline{)29\,148} \\
24\,8 \\
\hline
4\,34 \\
4\,34 \\
\hline
8
\end{array}
\qquad
\begin{array}{r}
73 \text{ R132} \\
294\overline{)21\,594} \\
20\,58 \\
\hline
1\,014 \\
882 \\
\hline
132
\end{array}
$$

Find the quotients and remainders.

1. $29\overline{)1263}$

2. $61\overline{)4575}$

3. $38\overline{)7842}$

4. $73\overline{)25\,603}$

5. $227\overline{)6232}$

6. $481\overline{)27\,171}$

7. $628\overline{)44\,386}$

8. $782\overline{)25\,080}$

Find the quotients and remainders.

1. $57\overline{)3669}$
2. $21\overline{)1940}$
3. $48\overline{)3649}$
4. $94\overline{)7144}$

5. $35\overline{)823}$
6. $64\overline{)1957}$
7. $77\overline{)6468}$
8. $81\overline{)5732}$

9. $27\overline{)8815}$
10. $46\overline{)22\,263}$
11. $32\overline{)4704}$
12. $17\overline{)11\,604}$

13. $75\overline{)23\,245}$
14. $40\overline{)30\,429}$
15. $23\overline{)9384}$
16. $65\overline{)24\,114}$

17. $317\overline{)9003}$
18. $806\overline{)36\,732}$
19. $732\overline{)47\,580}$
20. $284\overline{)20\,651}$

21. $914\overline{)12\,759}$
22. $637\overline{)51\,522}$
23. $452\overline{)41\,592}$
24. $378\overline{)18\,754}$

25. $827\overline{)26\,842}$
26. $575\overline{)38\,906}$
27. $162\overline{)20\,000}$
28. $953\overline{)48\,711}$

29. $408\overline{)38\,062}$
30. $810\overline{)43\,821}$
31. $777\overline{)62\,913}$
32. $386\overline{)15\,125}$

33. $129\overline{)42\,684}$
34. $279\overline{)58\,413}$
35. $371\overline{)84\,900}$
36. $457\overline{)95\,589}$

37. During one day, 27 cable cars carried 36 819 people. About how many people did each car carry?

38. The cable for the Hyde Street cable car route costs about $8000. It must be replaced about every 125 days. How much does the cable cost per day?

Find the missing digits.

```
        ▓ 6              ▓ 6
▓ 7 )▓ ▓ 0 ▓      ▓ 8 )2 6 ▓ ▓
    1 8 5              ▓ ▓ 0
    ▓ ▓ ▓              ▓ ▓ ▓
    2 2 2              ▓ ▓ ▓
      2 8                  0
```

Dividing a decimal by a whole number

An installer of telephones needs to cut a 14.6 m telephone cord into 4 equal pieces. How long should each piece be?

Finding the answer

Divide the ones	Place the decimal point Divide the tenths	Annex a zero Divide the hundredths

$$
\begin{array}{r}
3 \\
4\overline{)14.6} \\
12 \\
\hline
2
\end{array}
\qquad
\begin{array}{r}
3.6 \\
4\overline{)14.6} \\
12 \\
\hline
2\,6 \\
2\,4 \\
\hline
2
\end{array}
\qquad
\begin{array}{r}
3.65 \\
4\overline{)14.60} \\
12 \\
\hline
2\,6 \\
2\,4 \\
\hline
20 \\
20 \\
\hline
0
\end{array}
$$

Each of the 4 pieces should be 3.65 m long.

Other examples

$$
\begin{array}{r}
3.42 \\
28\overline{)95.76} \\
84 \\
\hline
11\,7 \\
11\,2 \\
\hline
56 \\
56 \\
\hline
0
\end{array}
\qquad
\begin{array}{r}
0.032 \\
25\overline{)0.800} \\
75 \\
\hline
50 \\
50 \\
\hline
0
\end{array}
\qquad
\begin{array}{r}
3.45 \\
16\overline{)55.20} \\
48 \\
\hline
7\,2 \\
6\,4 \\
\hline
80 \\
80 \\
\hline
0
\end{array}
$$

Find the quotients. Continue to annex zeros and divide until the remainder is zero.

1. $4\overline{)15}$
2. $7\overline{)43.96}$
3. $8\overline{)43}$
4. $54\overline{)1873.8}$

5. $16\overline{)7}$
6. $16\overline{)1.2}$
7. $286\overline{)134.42}$
8. $32\overline{)148.8}$

Find the quotients.

1. $4\overline{)31}$
2. $4\overline{)5}$
3. $6\overline{)28.2}$
4. $8\overline{)15}$
5. $9\overline{)4.41}$

6. $7\overline{)436.8}$
7. $5\overline{)378}$
8. $8\overline{)0.3}$
9. $12\overline{)18}$
10. $75\overline{)4.5}$

11. $28\overline{)101.36}$
12. $16\overline{)14}$
13. $19\overline{)148.77}$
14. $64\overline{)40}$
15. $26\overline{)7.28}$

16. $25\overline{)16}$
17. $80\overline{)0.8}$
18. $37\overline{)28.86}$
19. $125\overline{)50}$
20. $32\overline{)4.8}$

21. $26\overline{)36.4}$
22. $50\overline{)1.7}$
23. $128\overline{)96}$
24. $96\overline{)885.12}$
25. $52\overline{)209.56}$

26. $59\overline{)48.97}$
27. $92\overline{)588.8}$
28. $27\overline{)399.6}$
29. $215\overline{)89.225}$
30. $371\overline{)36.729}$

31. $742\overline{)5.194}$
32. $80\overline{)88}$
33. $600\overline{)584.4}$
34. $99\overline{)2.673}$
35. $85\overline{)268.345}$

36. A telephone bill for the month of May was $25.74. About how much was this a week? A day?

☆ 37. Find the amount of your family's phone bill for a recent month. About how much was it per day?

Suppose you are offered a job that will take 10 hours. You will be paid 10 cents the first hour, 20 cents the second hour, 40 cents the third hour and so on, doubling your pay each hour. How much would you make?

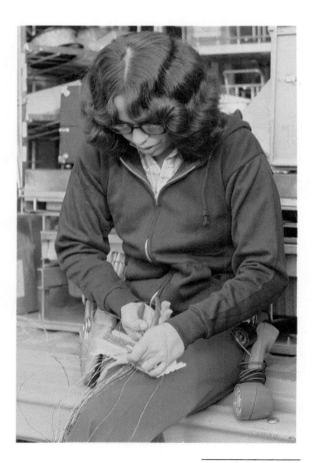

Dividing a decimal by a decimal

In many school books, each sheet of paper is about 0.008 cm thick. Together, the pages of a certain school book measure 1.8 cm thick. About how many sheets of paper are in the book? (Each sheet is 2 pages, front and back.)

Finding the answer

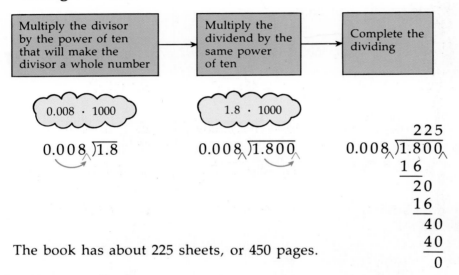

Multiply the divisor by the power of ten that will make the divisor a whole number	→	Multiply the dividend by the same power of ten	→	Complete the dividing

0.008 · 1000

$0.008\overline{)1.8}$

1.8 · 1000

$0.008\overline{)1.800}$

```
           225
0.008)1.800
      1 6
        20
        16
         40
         40
          0
```

The book has about 225 sheets, or 450 pages.

Other examples

```
        2.7
4.3)11.6 1
    8 6
    3 01
    3 01
       0
```

```
          0.366
1.2)0.4 400
      3 6
        80
        72
         80
         72
```

The quotient rounded to the nearest hundredth is 0.37.

Find the quotients to the nearest hundredth.

1. $7.4\overline{)31.4}$ 2. $0.23\overline{)3.62}$ 3. $0.8\overline{)17.4}$ 4. $0.006\overline{)3.4}$

5. $6.8\overline{)0.8}$ 6. $4.71\overline{)5.762}$ 7. $0.146\overline{)3.1}$ 8. $1.5\overline{)39.4}$

Find the quotients to the nearest tenth.

1. $0.03\overline{)0.47}$
2. $0.7\overline{)5.82}$
3. $0.12\overline{)6.73}$
4. $3.6\overline{)4.7}$

5. $0.006\overline{)7.6}$
6. $0.37\overline{)24}$
7. $4.26\overline{)3.81}$
8. $0.0032\overline{)2.54}$

9. $5.8\overline{)30.8}$
10. $2.14\overline{)63.05}$
11. $1.5\overline{)54.8}$
12. $1.42\overline{)63.21}$

13. $7.42\overline{)12.87}$
14. $16.8\overline{)59.1}$
15. $0.76\overline{)1.883}$
16. $0.0049\overline{)0.1388}$

Find the quotients to the nearest hundredth.

17. $6.1\overline{)52.6}$
18. $3.7\overline{)3.94}$
19. $9.2\overline{)57.8}$
20. $4.8\overline{)2.5}$

21. $0.36\overline{)65}$
22. $0.72\overline{)7.8}$
23. $0.48\overline{)1.33}$
24. $0.72\overline{)5}$

25. $0.009\overline{)0.07}$
26. $0.012\overline{)0.86}$
27. $0.036\overline{)0.009}$
28. $0.021\overline{)0.6}$

29. $4.76\overline{)53.2}$
30. $0.381\overline{)6.4}$
31. $42.8\overline{)3.17}$
32. $3.4\overline{)12.5}$

33. $9.02\overline{)38.44}$
34. $0.507\overline{)3}$
35. $69.5\overline{)100}$
36. $12.7\overline{)349.33}$

37. Some workbook sheets have a thickness of about 0.009 cm. About how many sheets would fit in a book 0.5 cm thick?

☆ 38. Measure the thickness of one of your books (not counting the covers). Divide by the number of sheets (half the number of pages) to find the thickness of each sheet.

A dollar bill has a thickness of about 0.012 cm. How much money would it take for a stack of dollar bills to be as high as the 443-meter Sears Tower in Chicago?

More practice, page 383, Set B

Using division to solve equations

A landscape architect's plan for landscaping a small park called for 6 evergreen trees, at a total cost of $240. If each tree is the same price what is the cost of each tree?

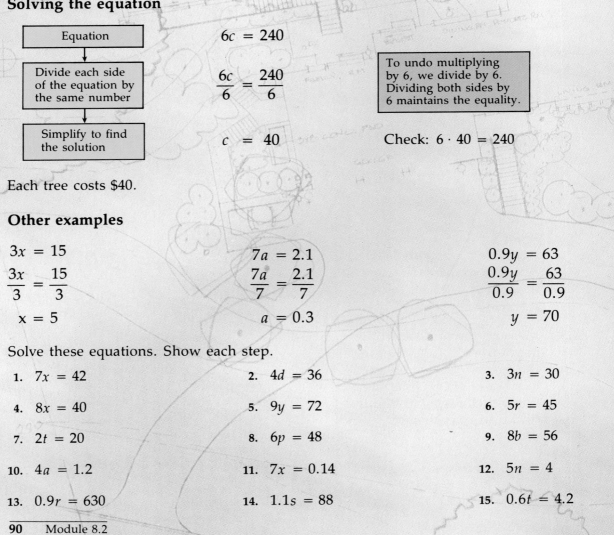

Let c = the cost of each tree

Equation: $6c = 240$

Solving the equation

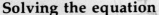

| Equation | $6c = 240$ |

| Divide each side of the equation by the same number | $\dfrac{6c}{6} = \dfrac{240}{6}$ |

To undo multiplying by 6, we divide by 6. Dividing both sides by 6 maintains the equality.

| Simplify to find the solution | $c = 40$ |

Check: $6 \cdot 40 = 240$

Each tree costs $40.

Other examples

$3x = 15$
$\dfrac{3x}{3} = \dfrac{15}{3}$
$x = 5$

$7a = 2.1$
$\dfrac{7a}{7} = \dfrac{2.1}{7}$
$a = 0.3$

$0.9y = 63$
$\dfrac{0.9y}{0.9} = \dfrac{63}{0.9}$
$y = 70$

Solve these equations. Show each step.

1. $7x = 42$

2. $4d = 36$

3. $3n = 30$

4. $8x = 40$

5. $9y = 72$

6. $5r = 45$

7. $2t = 20$

8. $6p = 48$

9. $8b = 56$

10. $4a = 1.2$

11. $7x = 0.14$

12. $5n = 4$

13. $0.9r = 630$

14. $1.1s = 88$

15. $0.6t = 4.2$

Solve these equations. Show each step.

1. $7x = 560$
2. $24n = 240$
3. $70d = 420$
4. $50a = 250$
5. $60r = 120$
6. $12t = 108$
7. $10x = 100$
8. $30y = 210$
9. $80b = 400$
10. $90p = 2700$
11. $20t = 1600$
12. $50s = 3500$

Solve these equations. Show each step.

13. $0.6r = 0.3$
14. $3.1s = 7.44$
15. $5.2x = 2.34$
16. $0.36n = 0.1512$
17. $4.8y = 35.04$
18. $6.5z = 53.95$
19. $0.18x = 8.136$
20. $7.25n = 58$
21. $0.054z = 1.5336$
22. $125t = 8$
23. $3.14b = 50.24$
24. $0.064n = 1.0$

Calculator problems

Use your calculator to solve these equations.

25. $96x = 7488$
26. $\dfrac{p}{467} = 28$
27. $x + 96\ 784 = 123\ 476$

28. $127x = 16\ 129$
29. $r - 19\ 768 = 4876$
30. $\dfrac{n}{799} = 899$

31. $d + 99\ 999 = 888\ 888$
32. $142\ 857x = 428\ 571$
33. $b - 12\ 345 = 87\ 655$

Start with any number.
Double it. Add 1. Add
the number you started
with. Then add 38. Divide
by 3. Subtract the
number you started with.
What is the result?
Try this with some other
numbers.

Answers for Self-check 1. 9 2. 5 3. 9 4. 6 5. 20 6. 40 7. 3 000 8. 4 9. 87 10. 56 R10
11. 14.3 12. 0.83 13. 0.36 14. 40.00 15. 13.04 16. 3.33 17. $x = 8$ 18. $n = 25$ 19. $y = 0.2$
20. $z = 18$

Self-check

Find the quotients.

1. $72 \div 8$
2. $45 \div 9$
3. $54 \div 6$
4. $48 \div 8$

5. $80 \div 4$
6. $200 \div 5$
7. $9000 \div 3$
8. $360 \div 90$

Find the quotients and remainders.

9. $9\overline{)783}$
10. $39\overline{)2194}$
11. $39\overline{)557.7}$
12. $25\overline{)20.75}$

Find the quotient to the nearest hundredth.

13. $7.2\overline{)2.6208}$
14. $0.8\overline{)32}$
15. $0.56\overline{)7.3}$
16. $5.38\overline{)17.9}$

Solve these equations.

17. $9x = 72$
18. $6n = 150$
19. $8y = 1.6$
20. $0.4z = 7.2$

Answers for Self-check—page 91

Test

Find the quotients.

1. $18 \div 3$
2. $40 \div 5$
3. $27 \div 9$
4. $72 \div 9$

5. $60 \div 2$
6. $400 \div 8$
7. $6000 \div 6$
8. $240 \div 40$

Find the quotients and remainders.

9. $52\overline{)3900}$
10. $19\overline{)475}$
11. $28\overline{)907.2}$
12. $42\overline{)2.646}$

Round each quotient to the nearest hundredth.

13. $5.3\overline{)3.5616}$
14. $0.7\overline{)35.42}$
15. $0.39\overline{)4.62}$
16. $5.26\overline{)8.6}$

Solve these equations.

17. $5t = 60$
18. $5r = 250$
19. $7z = 1.4$
20. $2.3n = 6.9$

Math lab

The **greatest common factor (GCF)** of two numbers is the
largest number that is a common factor of both numbers.

Sometimes the GCF is called the **greatest common divisor**.

The greatest common factor of 18 and 24 is 6 because 6
is the largest number that will divide both 18 and 24 exactly.

To find the GCF of two large numbers you can use a method
called the Euclidean Algorithm. The flow chart below shows
the steps.

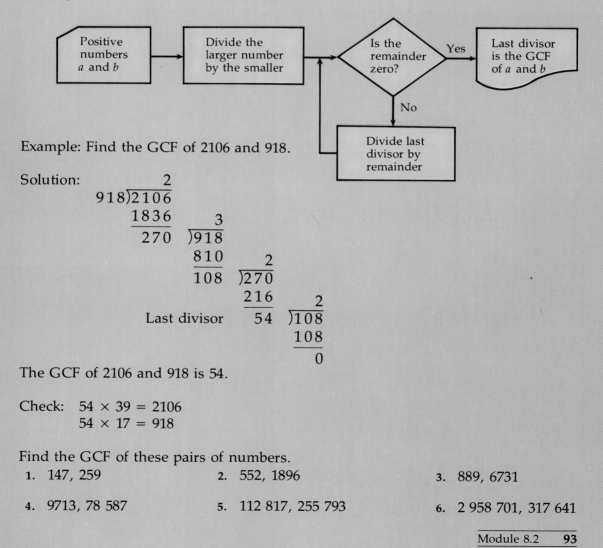

Example: Find the GCF of 2106 and 918.

Solution:

$$
\begin{array}{r} 2 \\ 918\overline{)2106} \\ 1836 \\ \hline 270 \end{array}
$$

$$
\begin{array}{r} 3 \\ 270\overline{)918} \\ 810 \\ \hline 108 \end{array}
$$

$$
\begin{array}{r} 2 \\ 108\overline{)270} \\ 216 \\ \hline 54 \end{array}
$$

Last divisor

$$
\begin{array}{r} 2 \\ 54\overline{)108} \\ 108 \\ \hline 0 \end{array}
$$

The GCF of 2106 and 918 is 54.

Check: $54 \times 39 = 2106$
$54 \times 17 = 918$

Find the GCF of these pairs of numbers.

1. 147, 259
2. 552, 1896
3. 889, 6731
4. 9713, 78 587
5. 112 817, 255 793
6. 2 958 701, 317 641

Problem Solving
Using Your Skills

Park rangers manage the many state and national parks in America. They try to conserve the natural beauty of the parks. They control the number of visitors and campers who use the parks. They organize trips, talks, and outings for the visitors. Although most of their work is outdoors, the park rangers also order supplies and prepare reports.

Some problems are more easily solved by writing an equation.

An important step in writing an equation is to decide what is unknown in the problem. Then *choose a variable to represent this unknown number*.

Example: The total number of bison and moose in Yellowstone Park is about 2150. About 1000 of these are moose. About how many bison are in the park?

The number of bison is unknown and the question asks us to find that number. Therefore we choose a variable to represent the number of bison.

Let x = number of bison.

In each problem below, tell which is the correct choice for the variable.

<table>
<tr><td>

Problem-solving guidelines using equations

1. Read the problem carefully.
2. Choose a variable to represent the unknown number.
3. Write an equation.
4. Solve the equation.
5. Check your answer in the original words of the problem.

</td></tr>
</table>

1. In the summer there are about 500 black bears at Yellowstone. This is about twice the number of grizzly bears. How many grizzly bears are there?

   A   Let n = number of black bears
   B   Let n = number of grizzly bears

2. In the summer, for every mule deer at Yellowstone there are about 30 elk. There are 21 000 elk. How many mule deer are there?

   A   Let y = number of mule deer
   B   Let y = number of elk

3. There are about 10 000 hot springs in Yellowstone Park. This is about 50 times the number of geysers in the park. About how many geysers are in the park?

   A   Let z = number of hot springs
   B   Let z = number of geysers

Writing expressions

The examples below show how expressions with one variable can be written when a word phrase is given.

Choice of variable	Phrase	Expression
Let x = an unknown number	6 more than the number	$x + 6$
Let t = an unknown number	12 less than the number	$t - 12$
Let r = an unknown number	10 times the number	$10r$
Let y = an unknown number	the number divided by 3	$\dfrac{y}{3}$

Give the letter for the expression that matches each phrase.

Choice of variable	Phrase	Expression
	1. 2 more than a number	**A** $n - 2$
	2. 2 less than a number	**B** $\dfrac{n}{2}$
Let n = a number	3. 2 times a number	**C** $n + 2$
	4. a number divided by 2	**D** $2n$
	5. a number increased by 3	**E** $3a$
	6. a number decreased by 3	**F** $a + 3$
Let a = a number	7. the product of 3 and a number	**G** $\dfrac{a}{3}$
	8. a number divided by 3	**H** $a - 3$
	9. 4 decreased by a number	**I** $\dfrac{4}{r}$
	10. 4 divided by a number	**J** $4 + r$
Let r = a number	11. 4 increased by a number	**K** $r + 4$
	12. the sum of a number and 4	**L** $4 - r$
	13. 5 less than twice a number	**M** $5 + 2s$
	14. 5 more than a number divided by 2	**N** $5 - 2s$
Let s = a number	15. 2 times a number subtracted from 5	**O** $2s - 5$
	16. 5 increased by 2 times a number	**P** $\dfrac{s}{2} + 5$

Write an expression for each phrase.

1. 12 more than r
2. 3 less than t
3. twice as many as r
4. p divided by 6

Use n for the number in exercises 5 through 26.

5. 4 more than a number
6. a number increased by 11
7. the product of 7 and a number
8. a number decreased by 9
9. 10 less than a number
10. a number divided by 6
11. the sum of a number and 8
12. the difference of a number and 8
13. 15 increased by a number
14. a number subtracted from 20
15. 9 times a number
16. 12 divided by a number
17. the double of a number
18. a number n more than 25
19. a number multiplied by 6
20. a number n less than 100
21. 4 less than twice a number
22. 12 more than 8 times a number
23. the difference of 3 times a number and 4
24. 6 less than one half of a number
25. 5 times a number subtracted from 100
26. 100 less than a number divided by 1000

Think!

Arlene had 6 apples in a bag.
She gave each of 6 persons one
apple and left one in the bag.
How did she do this?
Coded Answer: Let A = 1, B = 2,
C = 3, . . ., Z = 26
Answer: 19857122520851211920165181915 14
2085217239208208512119201161612591 4920

Writing and solving equations

Some treasure hunters, diving near sunken Spanish galleons off the coast of Florida, found a number of gold coins. When a diver found 12 more coins, they had 45 in all. How many coins had they found at first?

Let n = number of coins at first

$$n + 12 = 45$$
$$n + 12 - 12 = 45 - 12$$
$$n = 33$$

They had found 33 coins at first.

Write an equation for each sentence. Solve the equation.

1. 5 more than a number is 32.

2. A number increased by 17 is 85.

3. A number times 8 is 72.

4. A number divided by 9 is 6.

5. The product of 7 and a number is 63.

6. A number decreased by 57 is 39.

7. 3 times a number is 216.

8. 7 less than a number is 11.

9. The sum of a number and 18 is 48.

10. A number divided by 6 is 5.

11. 16 less than a number is 66.

12. 39 more than a number is 54.

Write and solve an equation for each problem.

1. A certain Spanish fleet had 28 ships. 8 ships sank in a storm. How many ships did not sink?

2. One Spanish galleon had 180 cannons. It had 3 times as many cannons as muskets. How many muskets did it have?

3. After 3 divers were added to the diving crew, there were 12 divers in all. How many were in the crew at first?

4. The crew found 10 gold coins on Monday. By the end of the week they had found a total of 36 coins. How many coins were found after Monday?

5. There were 12 divers searching for gold bars. If the number of gold bars were divided equally among the divers, each diver would get 8 bars. How many gold bars were there?

6. The divers found a ship's anchor. Then 2 m below the anchor they found a gold cup. The cup was found at a depth of 23 m. At what depth was the anchor found?

7. A diving crew found 6 times as many coins on Tuesday as they did on Monday. On Tuesday they found 78 coins. How many coins did they find on Monday?

8. The Spanish treasure ship Atocha was discovered in 1971. This was 349 years after it had sunk during a storm. In what year did the Atocha sink?

What facts are needed?

In some of these problems, more information is given than you need. In other problems, not enough information is given to solve the problem. Solve the problems that have enough information. Tell what additional facts are needed before the other problems can be solved.

1. There are 4 classes of science students going on a field trip. Altogether, 135 students are going to ride on 3 buses. If the same number of students ride on each bus, how many will that be?

2. There were 387 students and 95 parents at the basketball game. Only 189 students stayed for the party after the game. How many students did not stay for the party?

3. Tickets for the class play were priced at $1.00 for adults and $0.50 for students. In all, $209.50 was collected from ticket sales. How many tickets were sold?

4. There are 675 students in Wilson Junior High School. Each student has a homeroom class. What is the average number of students in each homeroom class?

5. The score at half time was: Wilson 28, Jordan 27. Wilson scored 34 points in the second half. Who won the game?

6. During the first week of school, the attendance for Wilson Junior High School was: Mon. 647, Tues. 658, Wed. 652, Thurs. 649, and Fri. 637. There are 675 students enrolled at Wilson. What was the average daily attendance for the first week?

Solve the problems that have enough facts given. Tell what facts are needed for those problems that do not have enough facts.

Enrollment and Attendance Statistics for Jefferson School					
Second floor homeroom class enrollment		Ms. Wood's science class enrollment		School attendance	
Room 217	34	First period	26	Monday	473
Room 219	29	Second period	25	Tuesday	462
Room 221	35	Third period	29	Wednesday	459
Room 223	31	Fourth period	28	Thursday	460
Room 225	26	Fifth period	27	Friday	481

1. How many students are enrolled in the five homeroom classes on the second floor?

2. What is the average number of students enrolled in the five second-floor homerooms?

3. How many students attend Jefferson school?

4. Twenty-three students from homeroom 217 take Ms. Wood's second-period science class. How many students from room 217 do not take Ms. Wood's second period science class?

5. What is Ms. Wood's average class size for her five classes?

6. How many students were absent from school on Tuesday and Thursday combined?

7. How many more were absent from school on Wednesday than on Monday?

8. One day Ms. Wood had only 102 students in all five of her classes. No one was absent first period. How many were absent in the other four periods combined?

9. Rooms 219 and 221 put on a school play. In all, 24 students had parts. How many in Room 219 had a part in the play?

10. All of the students in homeroom 225 take third-period science. How many third-period science students are not in homeroom 225?

Estimation and problem solving

The distance formula
$$rate \cdot time = distance$$
is written as
$$rt = d.$$

How long does it take for an airplane to travel 3237 km at the rate of 498 km/h?

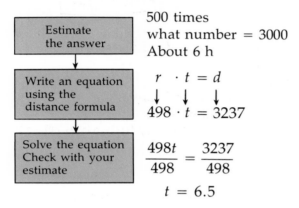

Estimate the answer	500 times what number = 3000 About 6 h
Write an equation using the distance formula	$r \cdot t = d$ $\downarrow \quad \downarrow \quad \downarrow$ $498 \cdot t = 3237$
Solve the equation Check with your estimate	$\dfrac{498t}{498} = \dfrac{3237}{498}$ $t = 6.5$

It takes 6.5 hours for the plane to make the trip. Checking this solution with the estimate shows that the answer is reasonable.

Choose the best estimate. Then write and solve an equation. Does your solution seem reasonable?

1. Traveling at an average rate of 83 km/h, an auto trip from Chicago to Denver takes 19 h. What is the distance?

   A 4 km   B 1600 km   C 800 km

2. A jet is traveling at a rate of 1021 km/h. How long will it take it to make a 4084 km trip to Hawaii?

   A 4 h   B 40 h   C 400 h

3. A racing motorcycle went 1683 km in 9 h. What was the average rate of speed of the motorcycle?

   A 200 km/h   B 16 km/h   C 160 km/h

4. If a satellite is traveling 9 km/s, how long will it take it to orbit the earth? The circumference of its path is 40 500 km.

   A 4000 s   B 400 s   C 40 000 s

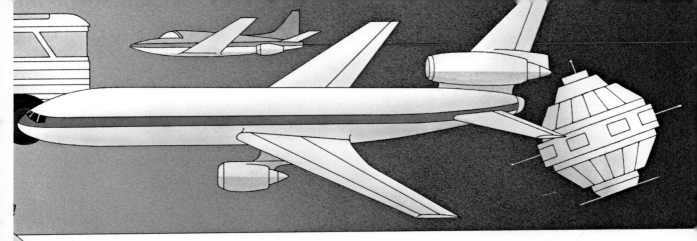

Estimate the answer to each problem. Then write and solve an equation. Compare your estimate with the solution.

1. A bus driver drove 546 km from noon to 6 o'clock in the evening. What was the average rate of speed for the trip?

2. An auto trip of 4788 km, from Vancouver to Montreal, took 57 h of driving time. What was the average rate of speed?

3. A recent water speed record was 459 km/h. If you could travel at this rate, how long would it take you to travel the 5967 km from New York City to Southampton, England?

4. Sound travels 332 m/s. How long does it take the sound of thunder to travel 6308 m?

5. A runner ran 1500 m at the rate of 6 m/s. How many seconds did it take? How many minutes and seconds?

☆ 6. Light travels 299 792.5 km/s. About how many minutes and seconds does it take for light to travel the 149 597 870 km from the sun to the earth?

A certain auto with a diesel engine costs $2400 more than the standard gasoline model.

Assume the following fuel and maintenance costs:

Diesel: 1.5¢/km
Standard model: 4.5¢/km

About how far would you have to drive the car in order for the diesel to be the most economical buy?

A	25 000 km
B	45 000 km
C	65 000 km
D	85 000 km
E	105 000 km

Guess first. Then calculate by trying the numbers of kilometers given.

Equations with two operations

Renata had 5 dollars. She worked 4 hours. She then had 13 dollars. How much did she earn each hour?

Let x = amount earned each hour
$\quad 4x$ = amount earned in 4 hours
Equation: $4x + 5 = 13$

Solving the equation

| Equation | $4x + 5 = 13$ |

| Subtract the same number from both sides of the equation | $4x + 5 - 5 = 13 - 5$ |

To undo multiplying by 4 and adding 5, we subtract 5 and divide by 4. Subtracting from, and dividing both sides of the equation maintains the equality.

| Divide each side of the equation by the same number | $\dfrac{4x}{4} = \dfrac{8}{4}$ |

| Simplify to find the solution | $x = 2$ |

Check: $4 \cdot 2 + 5 = 8 + 5$
$\qquad\qquad\quad = 13$

Renata earned $2 each hour.

Other examples

$$8b - 1 = 23$$
$$8b - 1 + 1 = 23 + 1$$
$$\frac{8b}{8} = \frac{24}{8}$$
$$b = 3$$

$$24 = 5x + 4$$
$$24 - 4 = 5x + 4 - 4$$
$$\frac{20}{5} = \frac{5x}{5}$$
$$4 = x, \text{ or } x = 4$$

$$16 = 3n - 2$$
$$16 + 2 = 3n - 2 + 2$$
$$\frac{18}{3} = \frac{3n}{3}$$
$$6 = n, \text{ or } n = 6$$

Solve these equations.

1. $3n + 2 = 8$

2. $4b + 3 = 23$

3. $2a + 5 = 17$

4. $5r + 1 = 16$

5. $3s + 6 = 18$

6. $4x - 1 = 11$

7. $5d - 4 = 6$

8. $6c - 4 = 20$

9. $8s - 6 = 10$

Solve these equations. Show each step.

1. $4c + 2 = 22$
2. $3n + 8 = 20$
3. $5p + 3 = 28$

4. $6d + 3 = 45$
5. $2x + 9 = 27$
6. $7r + 2 = 30$

7. $12s + 6 = 30$
8. $8t + 10 = 50$
9. $9a + 4 = 49$

10. $4b + 17 = 25$
11. $5n + 8 = 38$
12. $6r + 6 = 24$

13. $8p + 5 = 85$
14. $6x + 3 = 51$
15. $5n + 15 = 60$

16. $7d + 8 = 29$
17. $12r + 6 = 42$
18. $3s + 4 = 28$

19. $40x + 10 = 130$
20. $7p + 5 = 75$
21. $8c + 52 = 100$

22. $15 = 4r + 7$
23. $28 = 3t + 10$
24. $32 = 5n + 12$

25. $60 = 8d + 4$
26. $64 = 20s + 4$
27. $70 = 9p + 7$

28. $50 = 12n + 2$
29. $48 = 9q + 12$
30. $32 = 7t + 11$

☆ 31. Choose the equation which describes the problem and solve it to answer the question.

Brian worked 9 hours. After he spent 3 dollars of his earnings he had 15 dollars left. How much did he earn each hour?

Let y = amount earned each hour

A $3 + 9y = 15$

B $15 - 3 = 9y$

C $9y - 3 = 15$

D $3y - 9 = 15$

Study this pattern.

$15 \cdot 15 = (10 \cdot 20) + (5 \cdot 5)$
$25 \cdot 25 = (20 \cdot 30) + (5 \cdot 5)$
$35 \cdot 35 = (30 \cdot 40) + (5 \cdot 5)$

Use the idea of the pattern to do these without writing or using a calculator.

$45 \cdot 45 = ||||$ $55 \cdot 55 = ||||$
$65 \cdot 65 = ||||$ $75 \cdot 75 = ||||$
$85 \cdot 85 = ||||$ $95 \cdot 95 = ||||$

Check your answers on a calculator.

✪ Equations for two-step problems

A new gear cutting machine can make 20 more than 3 times the number of gears an old gear cutting machine could make in one day. The new machine makes 170 gears in a day. How many gears did the older machine make in a day?

Let b = the number of gears the old machine made in a day

$$3b + 20 = 170$$
$$3b = 150$$
$$b = 50$$

Check:
$$(3 \cdot 50) + 20 = 170$$

The old machine made 50 gears in one day.

Write and solve an equation for each problem.

1. One week an employee worked a total of 45 h. This employee worked 5 h of overtime plus 5 regular shifts. How long was each regular shift?

2. A new machine was able to make 7 more than twice the number of parts an old machine could make in an hour. The new machine made 53 parts in an hour. How many parts did the old machine make in an hour?

3. One section of the factory had a total of 274 workers who worked in 3 shifts. There were an equal number of workers in the first two shifts, and 80 workers in the third shift. How many workers were in the first two shifts?

4. A machine operator worked 40 hours at her regular hourly rate of pay. She also earned $63.00 in overtime pay. Her total pay was $423.00. What was her hourly rate of pay?

5. An inspector checked 701 parts. There were 17 parts that were faulty. The other parts were packed in 19 boxes with the same number in each box. How many parts were in each box?

6. One week a company received 123 orders. This was 12 more than 3 times the number of orders received the week before. How many orders did it get the first week?

7. A gear machine operator had to use the formula

$$2S_1 + p = D.$$

If $p = 4$, and $D = 4.5$, find the number for S.

8. There were 238 people working in Building A. This number was 13 more than 3 times the number of people working in Building B. How many people were working in Building B?

9. An employee took 3 vacation periods of equal length plus 7 days of sick leave. Altogether the employee was not at work 22 days. How long was each vacation period?

10. Another employee had 8 days remaining of his total 20 days of vacation. He had already taken 2 equal vacation periods. How long was each vacation period?

11. An experienced machine operator produced 18 less than twice as many items as an inexperienced operator. The inexperienced operator produced 32 items. How many items did the experienced operator produce?

12. A group of 43 employees was hired to make a new machine. This group was 7 less than twice the number of employees hired for the old machine. How many had been hired for the old machine?

Answers for Self-check 1. $n + 3$ 2. $2n$ 3. $\frac{n}{4}$ 4. $5n$ 5. $4n = 20$, $n = 5$ 6. $2n = 12$, $n = 6$
7. $5n + 3 = 8$, $n = 3$ 8. $\frac{n}{5} = 8$, $n = 40$ 9. $n + 27 = 98$, $n = 71$ 10. $2n - 11 = 53$, $n = 32$

Self-check

Write an expression for each phrase.

1. 3 more than a number

2. twice a number

3. a number divided by 4

4. the product of a number and 5

Write and solve an equation for each statement.

5. 4 times a number is 20.

6. Twice a number is 12.

7. Five times a number increased by 3 is 18.

8. A number divided by 5 is 8.

Write and solve an equation for each problem.

9. A small factory increased the number of its employees by 27. The new total of workers is 98. How many workers were there before the increase?

☆10. Jason worked 53 hours one week. This was 11 hours less than twice the number of hours Jason worked the week before. How many hours did Jason work the week before?

Answers for Self-check—page 107

Test

Write an expression for each phrase.

1. 4 less than a number

2. 3 more than 5 times a number

3. the product of a number and 6

4. twice a number

Write and solve an equation for each statement.

5. A number increased by 8 is 15.

6. 6 more than twice a number is 16.

7. A number divided by 4 is 3.

8. 3 times a number is 21.

Write and solve an equation for each problem.

9. A train traveled at an average speed of 90 km/h for 48 h. How far did it travel?

☆10. Mila worked a total of 39 hours one week. This was 5 regular shifts plus 4 hours of overtime work. How many hours long was each regular shift?

Math lab

A Soap Film Experiment

The Belgian physicist, Joseph Plateau (1801–1833), found a way to show the shape of the smallest surface area that would span the outline of a space figure. Plateau dipped wire models of space figures into a heavy soap solution. The soap film formed a surface of minimum area which connected the boundaries of the space figure.

The pictures below show some soap film surfaces for a cube and a tetrahedron.

Try making wire models of some space figures. Tie thread to a model and dip it in liquid soap to which a few drops of glycerin have been added. Watch to see the beautiful surfaces the soap film will form when the model is lifted from the soap solution.

Measurement Concepts

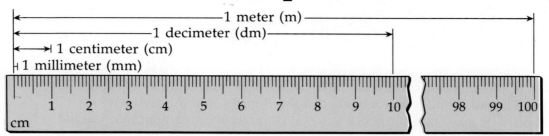

1 meter (m)
1 decimeter (dm)
1 centimeter (cm)
1 millimeter (mm)

| 1 | 2 | 3 | 4 | 5 | 6 | 7 | 8 | 9 | 10 | 98 | 99 | 100 |

cm

The **meter** is the basic unit of length in the metric system.
The ruler above shows how smaller units are related to the meter.

thickness of a dime	radius of a nickel	eye distance	length of a baseball bat
about 1 mm	about 1 cm	about 1 dm	about 1 m

Estimate each of the following lengths.
Then measure to find the actual length.
Find the difference between your estimate and the actual length.

1. width of your little
    fingernail in millimeters

2. length of this page
    in centimeters

3. width of your desk or
    table in centimeters

4. length of your pencil
    or pen in centimeters

5. distance from your
    elbow to your fingertips
    in decimeters

6. distance from your
    desk to the floor in
    decimeters

7. height of a door
    in meters

8. length of a chalkboard
    in meters

9. classroom length
    in meters

10. classroom width in
    meters

Metric prefix	Symbol	Meaning	Measure	Symbol	Relation to the meter
kilo	k	1000	kilometer	km	1000 m
hecto	h	100	hectometer	hm	100 m
deka	da	10	dekameter	dam	10 m
deci	d	0.1	decimeter	dm	0.1 m
centi	c	0.01	centimeter	cm	0.01 m
milli	m	0.001	millimeter	mm	0.001 m

The hectometer, dekameter, and decimeter are not often used in practical measurement.

Complete each statement using **km**, **m**, **cm**, or **mm**.

1. The length of a pencil is 19 ___?___ .

2. The thickness of a pencil lead is 2 ___?___ .

3. The length of a picnic table is 2 ___?___ .

4. The distance from Chicago to St. Louis is 460 ___?___ .

5. The length of a baseball bat is 94 ___?___ .

6. An airplane might fly at an altitude of 8 ___?___ .

7. A very tall person might be about 2 ___?___ tall.

8. A certain book is 3 ___?___ thick.

9. The length of a walking step might be 70 ___?___ .

10. The diameter of a quarter is 23 ___?___ .

Complete the following.

11. 1 m = ▦ dm

12. 1 m = ▦ cm

13. 1 m = ▦ mm

14. 1 km = ▦ m

15. 1 km = ▦ dam

16. 1 km = ▦ hm

17. 1 cm = ▦ mm

18. 1 dm = ▦ cm

19. 1 cm = ▦ m

20. 1 cm = ▦ dm

21. 1 mm = ▦ cm

22. 1 mm = ▦ dm

Changing metric units

Kathy's height is 157 cm.
What is her height in decimeters,
meters, and millimeters?

The metric units are related to each
other by factors of 10, 100, and
1000. The table shows how the units
can be changed by multiplying and
dividing by these factors.

m	dm	cm	mm
1	5	7.		⟷ 157 cm
1	5.	7		⟷ 15.7 dm = 157 ÷ 10
1.	5	7		⟷ 1.57 m = 157 ÷ 100
1	5	7	0.	⟷ 1570 mm = 157 · 10

Give the measures shown by each line of the tables.

	m	dm	cm	mm
	1	3	8	4.	1384 mm
1.	1	3	8	4	▥
2.	1	3.	8	4	▥
3.	1.	3	8	4	▥

	m	dm	cm	mm
	6.	4	2	8	6.428 m
4.	6	4.	2	8	▥
5.	6	4	2.	8	▥
6.	6	4	2	8.	▥

Give the missing numbers.

7. 7.42 m = ▥ cm

8. 92.7 cm = ▥ mm

9. 4.5 cm = ▥ mm

10. 687 mm = ▥ cm

11. 26.8 cm = ▥ m

12. 6.8 cm = ▥ m

13. 3.2 m = ▥ cm

14. 5.8 cm = ▥ mm

15. 237 cm = ▥ m

16. 17.4 cm = ▥ mm

17. 21.72 m = ▥ cm

18. 0.98 m = ▥ cm

Think about the charts to help you give the missing numbers.

1.

km	hm	dam	m	dm	cm	mm
7.	6	5	8	9		

7.6589 km = ▥ m

2.

km	hm	dam	m	dm	cm	mm
4	3	7	6.	8		

4376.8 m = ▥ km

3.

km	hm	dam	m	dm	cm	mm
			9.	6	7	1

9.671 m = ▥ cm

4.

km	hm	dam	m	dm	cm	mm
		6	3	8	4.	2

6384.2 cm = ▥ m

Complete the following.

5. 437 cm = ▥ m

6. 4.6892 km = ▥ m

7. 32.46 m = ▥ cm

8. 386 mm = ▥ cm

9. 3785.46 m = ▥ km

10. 46.3 cm = ▥ mm

11. 1649 cm = ▥ m

12. 4.88 m = ▥ mm

Give the missing symbol.

13. 2.37 m = 237 ____?____

14. 9250 m = 9.250 ____?____

15. 345 mm = 34.5 ____?____

16. 847 cm = 8.47 ____?____

17. 15 km = 1500 ____?____

18. 5209 mm = 5.209 ____?____

19. 2894 mm = 2.894 ____?____

20. 1.06 m = 1060 ____?____

A small automobile gets 12 km/L using regular gasoline. Regular costs 16.9¢ per liter. It can get 13.2 km/L using premium gasoline. Premium costs 18.4¢ per liter.

If the car is driven 16 000 km in one year, which type gas would cost less? How much would be saved?

Area

The area of a region is the number of square units it takes to cover the region. The table gives some metric units of area.

Units of Area	
square kilometer (km²)	1 000 000 m²
square hectometer (hm²) or hectare (ha)	10 000 m²
square dekameter (dam²)	100 m²
square meter (m²)	1 m²
square decimeter (dm²)	0.01 m²
square centimeter (cm²)	0.0001 m²
square millimeter (mm²)	0.000001 m²

The **square kilometer** (km²) is used for measuring large areas such as the areas of cities, counties, and states.

The **hectare** (ha) is used for measuring smaller regions. The area of a city park 100 m by 100 m is 1 hectare.

For measuring still smaller areas, the **square meter** (m²) and the **square centimeter** (cm²) are used. The area of the top of a card table is about 1 m². The area of the fingerhole of a telephone dial is about 1 cm².

Complete the area for each of the following using **cm²**, **m²**, **ha**, or **km²**.

1. a classroom floor: 35 ___?___

2. land area of a state: 109 405 ___?___

3. a small photo: 80 ___?___

4. a picnic table top: 2 ___?___

5. a football field: about 0.5 ___?___

6. a post card: 120 ___?___

7. a basketball court: about 400 ___?___

The area of a rectangle is found by multiplying the length times the width.

$A = lw$

What is the area in hectares of a 400 m by 600 m rectangular shopping center?

$A = lw$
$= 400 \cdot 600$
$= 240\ 000\ m^2$

$240\ 000 \div 10\ 000 = 24$

The area is 24 hectares.

Solve these problems.

1. A lot for a house is 40 m long and 25 m wide. What is the area of the lot in square meters?

2. A tennis court is 23.8 m long and 11 m wide. What is the area of the court in square meters?

3. A field is 200 m wide and 500 m long. What is the area of the field in hectares?

4. A square field is 396 m on each side. What is the area of the field in hectares?

5. A soccer field is 102 m long and 65 m wide. What is the area of the field in hectares?

6. A city block has an area of 1.2 hectares. What is the area of the block in square meters?

☆ 7. A large airport is 10 km long and 5 km wide. What is the area of the airport in square meters? In hectares?

 A gardener made a fence around a square garden. When he finished there were 10 fence posts on each side. Each post was 5 m from the next post in line. What was the area of the garden? How many posts were used?

Volume and capacity

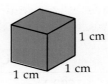

1 cubic centimeter
1 cm³

The volume of a space is the number of cubic units it takes to fill the space.

Metric Units of Volume			
cubic meter (m³)	1 m³		
cubic kilometer (km³)	1 000 000 000 m³	cubic decimeter (dm³)	0.001 m³
cubic hectometer (hm³)	1 000 000 m³	cubic centimeter (cm³)	0.000001 m³
cubic dekameter (dam³)	1000 m³	cubic millimeter (m³)	0.000000001 m³

The most commonly used units of volume are the cubic meter, cubic centimeter, and the cubic decimeter.

a marble
about 2 cm³

common red brick
about 1 dm³

refrigerator packing case
about 1 m³

The volume of a box is found by multiplying the length times the width times the height.

$$V = lwh$$

Find the volume of each.

1.

3 m
9 m
4 m

refrigerator truck

2.

0.80 m
1.8 m
0.95 m

freezer

3.

3.5 m
12 m
4.2 m

box car

4.

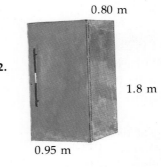

9 cm
31 cm
14 cm

shoe box

The volume of a liquid is often given as a number of liters or milliliters, called capacity units, rather than in cubic units.

Metric Units of Capacity			
kiloliter (kL)	1000 L	deciliter (dL) 0.1 L	
hectoliter (hL)	100 L	centiliter (cL) 0.01 L	
dekaliter (daL)	10 L	milliliter (mL) 0.001 L	
liter (L)	1 L		

There is a simple relationship between cubic units of volume and units of capacity.

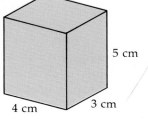

$1 \text{ cm}^3 = 1 \text{ mL}$
$1 \text{ dm}^3 = 1 \text{ L}$
$1 \text{ m}^3 = 1 \text{ kL}$

Example:

$V = 4 \cdot 3 \cdot 5 = 60 \text{ cm}^3$
$V = 60 \text{ mL}$

5 cm
4 cm
3 cm

Most measures of capacity are given in liters or milliliters.

1000 mL = 1 L

Find the volumes in cubic centimeters.
Find the capacity in milliliters and liters.

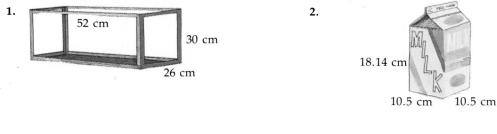

1. 52 cm, 30 cm, 26 cm

2. 18.14 cm, 10.5 cm, 10.5 cm

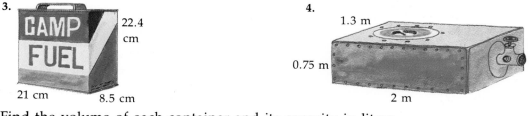

3. CAMP FUEL, 22.4 cm, 21 cm, 8.5 cm

4. 1.3 m, 0.75 m, 2 m

Find the volume of each container and its capacity in liters.

5. $l = 4$ cm, $w = 2.5$ cm, $h = 1.8$ cm

6. $l = 12$ m, $w = 8$ m, $h = 3.5$ m

7. $l = 2$ m, $w = 1.4$ m, $h = 0.9$ m

8. $l = 6$ cm, $w = 4$ cm, $h = 2.8$ cm

9. $l = 3$ dm, $w = 1.8$ dm, $h = 2$ dm

10. $l = 25$ cm, $w = 18$ cm, $h = 7$ cm

Mass

Metric Units of Mass			
metric ton (t) (megagram)	1000 kg	gram (g)	1 g
kilogram (kg)	1000 g	decigram (dg)	0.1 g
hectogram (hg)	100 g	centigram (cg)	0.01 g
dekagram (dag)	10 g	milligram (mg)	0.001 g

The kilogram, gram, and milligram are the most common metric units of mass. The milligram is used to measure very small masses such as the amount of vitamins or minerals in a serving of food. For measuring very large masses, the metric ton is used.

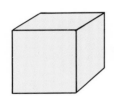

1 L of water—
1 kg

large paper clip—
about 1 g

1 mL of water—
1 g

an encyclopedia volume—
about 1 kg

Give the masses of the following. Use **mg**, **g**, **kg**, or **t**.

1. a sack of apples: 3 __?__

2. an adult person: 75 __?__

3. a pencil: 12 __?__

4. an egg: 50 __?__

5. a truckload of peaches: 2 __?__

6. a vitamin pill: 450 __?__

7. a liter of soda: 1 __?__

8. a golf ball: 42 __?__

9. a raisin: 600 __?__

10. a new-born baby: 4 __?__

11. an apple: 275 __?__

12. a bowling ball: 6 __?__

13. a straight pin: 120 __?__

14. a school bus: 5 __?__

15. a postage stamp: 20 __?__

16. a can of soup: 305 __?__

Give the missing numbers.

1. 7.384 kg = ▮▮▮ mg   2. 5694 g = ▮▮▮ kg

3. 8 kg = ▮▮▮ g   4. 7989 g = ▮▮▮ kg

5. 0.645 kg = ▮▮▮ g   6. 75 g = ▮▮▮ kg

7. 0.001 kg = ▮▮▮ g   8. 5498 g = ▮▮▮ kg

9. 5.768 g = ▮▮▮ mg   10. 0.794 g = ▮▮▮ mg

11. 7432 mg = ▮▮▮ g   12. 0.575 g = ▮▮▮ mg

13. 18 g = ▮▮▮ mg   14. 45 g = ▮▮▮ mg

Give the missing metric unit.

15. 8 kg = 800 __?__   16. 6.52 kg = 6520 __?__   17. 1.428 kg = 1428 __?__

18. 2600 g = 2.6 __?__   19. 4774 g = 4.774 __?__   20. 500 g = 0.5 __?__

21. 3 g = 3000 __?__   22. 1540 mg = 1.540 __?__   23. 6.835 g = 6835 __?__

Give the approximate mass of each amount of water.

24. 5 L   25. 250 mL   26. 3.5 L   27. 427 mL   28. 0.796 L   29. 56.5 mL

☆ 30. When a rock was placed in a container full of water, it displaced 235 mL of the water. The mass of the rock was 5.63 times as much as the mass of the same amount of water. What was the volume (cm³) and mass (g) of the rock?

Choose a number and multiply it by itself. Now multiply 5 less than the number by 5 more than the number.

Is the first product

A greater than the second,
B less than the second, or
C equal to the second?

Try at least five examples. What is your conclusion?

Temperature

The metric unit of temperature is the kelvin (K). The kelvin is used largely in scientific work. For ordinary use, the Celsius temperature scale is used. The intervals on the two scales are the same. However, the kelvin units are 273.15 more than the corresponding Celsius units.

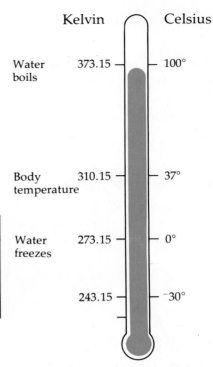

Miscellaneous Temperatures	
6000°C	surface of sun
3000°C	iron melts
1063°C	gold melts
327.5°C	lead melts
⁻37.87°C	mercury freezes
⁻273.15°C	absolute zero

Oven Temperatures	
230°–245°C	very hot
205°–220°C	hot
175°–190°C	moderate
150°–165°C	warm
120°–135°C	low

Choose the most appropriate temperature.

1. hot summer day
   A 30°C   B 15°C   C 50°C

2. iced beverage
   A 5°C   B ⁻10°C   C 19°C

3. oven for baking pizza
   A 100°C   B 220°C   C 675°C

4. ice cream
   A 15°C   B 5°C   C ⁻3°C

5. inside a refrigerator
   A 5°C   B ⁻10°C   C 20°C

6. inside a freezer
   A 6°C   B ⁻4°C   C ⁻100°C

7. soft candy while it is cooking
   A 130°C   B 101°C   C 240°C

8. fever
   A 36.5°C   B 98.9°C   C 38.5°C

9. blast furnace in a steel mill
   A 250°C   B 3500°C   C 8000°C

10. absolute zero
    A ⁻50°C   B ⁻37.87°C   C ⁻273.15°C

11. The lowest recorded temperature in the world is ⁻88°C (in Antarctica). By how many degrees Celsius does it differ from the highest recorded temperature of 56.7°C (in Libya)?

12. Copper melts at a temperature 100.5°C more than 3 times the melting point of lead. What is the melting point of copper?

Time

Time can be measured with great precision. Scientists have devised atomic clocks which are accurate to a few seconds in 100 000 years.

The **second** is the basic unit of time in the metric system.

Some Units of Time
1 hour (h) = 60 minutes (min)
1 minute = 60 seconds (s)
1 millisecond (ms) = 0.001 s
1 nanosecond (ns) = 0.000000001 s

The millisecond and nanosecond are very small units of time and are used in scientific work. A very fast runner can run about 1 cm in 1 millisecond. Light travels about 30 cm in 1 nanosecond.

Complete.

1. 1 h = |||| s

2. 4 min = |||| s

3. 1000 ms = |||| s

4. 1 h 23 min = |||| min

5. 5 min 19 s = |||| s

6. 1 h 15 min 45 s = |||| s

7. 255 min = 4 h |||| min

8. 187 min = |||| h 7 min

9. 375 min = 6 h |||| min

Solve the problems.

10. Cooking time for a beef roast is 12 min for each 1 kg of beef. For how many hours and minutes should an 11 kg roast be cooked?

11. A 9.5 kg turkey is to be roasted 33 minutes per kilogram. For how many hours and minutes should the turkey be cooked?

12. A 4.8 kg leg of lamb is to be roasted 65 minutes per kilogram. How long will it take the lamb to cook?

13. A 1.8 kg chicken is to be roasted 1 h 30 min per kilogram. How long will it take to roast the chicken?

✪ Precision and significant digits

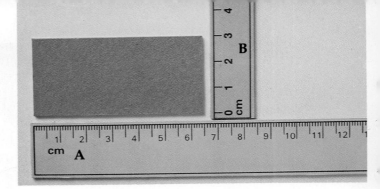

Two different rulers
are used to measure
the length and width
of a rectangle.

Ruler A measures to the nearest
tenth of a centimeter (0.1 cm).
The **greatest possible error** using
ruler A is one half of a tenth
of a centimeter, or 0.05 cm.

Ruler B measures to the nearest
whole centimeter. The **greatest
possible error** using ruler B is
one half of a centimeter or 0.5 cm.

6.4 cm is a more **precise** measure than 3 cm because the
greatest possible error is smaller.

When adding or subtracting measures, use this rule of rounding:

> Add or subtract the given measures. Then round
> the answer to the same precision as the least
> precise measure.

Example: Find the perimeter of a rectangle
with length 6.4 cm and
width 3 cm.

Perimeter = 6.4 + 3 + 6.4 + 3
= 18.8 cm

The least precise measure, 3 cm, was measured to the
nearest centimeter. Round 18.8 cm to the nearest
centimeter. Perimeter = 19 cm

Tell which measure is more precise.

1. 6.4 cm or 1.53 cm

2. 8.15 cm or 7.2 cm

3. 4 km or 6.15 km

Give the greatest possible error of each measure.

4. 12 cm   5. 2.7 cm   6. 8 mm   7. 1.83 km   8. 0.9 cm

Find the perimeter. Round the answer according to the rule above.

9. [rectangle] 1.946 cm
12.7 cm

10. [triangle] 8.77 cm   8.77 cm   16 cm

Problems involving multiplication or division of measurements require an understanding of **significant digits**.

The significant digits of a measure are those digits which are considered to be correct.

Examples:

Distance between Boston, Massachusetts, and Montreal, Quebec:

536 km
3 significant digits

Earth's circumference:

40 074.06 km
7 significant digits

Moon's diameter:

3500 km
2 significant digits

Thickness of a paper:

0.009 cm
1 significant digit

When multiplying or dividing measures, use this rule of rounding:

> Multiply or divide the given measures. Then round the answer to the same number of significant digits as the measure with the least number of significant digits.

Example:

Find the area of a rectangle that has width 3.4 cm and length 1.623 cm.

$A = lw$
$= 3.4 \cdot 1.623$
$= 5.5182 \text{ cm}^2$ $A = 5.5 \text{ cm}^2$ (rounded to 2 significant digits)

Give the number of significant digits of each measure.

1. 240 000 km   **2.** 12.4 cm   **3.** 8.137 km   **4.** 6 km   **5.** 0.07 cm

Find the area of each rectangle.
Round the answers according to the rule above.

6.  0.775 cm

4.1 cm

7. 11.5 mm

20.4 mm

Answers for Self-check **1.** 1.48 m **2.** 8.965 km **3.** 3.695 m **4.** 586 cm **5.** 7456 mL
6. 5.280 L **7.** 864 g **8.** 0.249 kg **9.** 5 h 12 min **10. B** **11. A** **12.** 396 m²
13. 28 800 cm³, 28.8 L **14.** 3 h 51 min ☆ **15. A:** 3; **B:** 4; 7.42 is more precise.

Self-check

Give the missing numbers.

1. 148 cm = ▥ m

2. 8965 m = ▥ km

3. 369.5 cm = ▥ m

4. 5.86 m = ▥ cm

5. 7.456 L = ▥ mL

6. 5280 mL = ▥ L

7. 0.864 kg = ▥ g

8. 249 g = ▥ kg

9. 312 min = ▥ h ▥ min

10. The area of a basketball court is about
    A 400 cm² **B** 400 m² **C** 400 km²

11. The temperature on a hot day might be
    A 31°C **B** 45°C **C** 98°C

12. A rectangular field has a length of 22 m and a width of 18 m. What is the area of the field?

13. An aquarium is 40 cm long, 24 cm wide, and 30 cm high. What is its volume? What is its capacity in liters?

14. A 7 kg turkey is to be roasted 33 minutes per kilogram. For how many hours and minutes should it be cooked?

☆ 15. Give the number of significant digits of each. Tell which measure is more precise.
    A 7.42 cm **B** 123.6 cm

Answers for Self-check—page 123

Test

Give the missing numbers.

1. 0.376 km = ▥ m

2. 463 cm = ▥ m

3. 42 cm = ▥ mm

4. 5.67 m = ▥ cm

5. 6842 mL = ▥ L

6. 5.1 L = ▥ mL

7. 5.679 kg = ▥ g

8. 869 g = ▥ kg

9. 250 min = ▥ h ▥ min

10. The area of a kitchen floor might be
    A 15 km² **B** 15 m² **C** 15 cm²

11. Normal body temperature is
    A 36°C **B** 37°C **C** 38°C

12. How many square meters of carpet are needed to cover a floor that is 9 m by 12 m?

13. A storage box is 3 m long, 1.5 m wide, and 2 m high. What is the volume?

14. A 2 kg roasting chicken should be cooked 1 h 30 min for each kilogram. How long should it be cooked?

☆ 15. Give the number of significant digits of each. Tell which measure is more precise.
    A 794.3 cm **B** 8.25 cm

Math lab

A Paperfolded Cube

By following the instructions, you can fold a square sheet of paper into a cube.

Fold a square sheet
of paper three times
as shown.

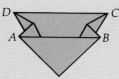

Make a
triangular
shape.

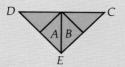

Fold points *A* and *B*
down to *E*.

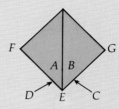

Fold points *D* and *C*
down to *E*, behind
A and *B*.

Fold the top corners
inward at *F* and *G*
to the center line.

Fold the other two
corners backward
to the center line
on the back.

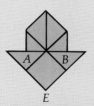

Fold back loose
corners *A* and *B*.
Do the same for the
loose corners in the back.

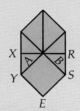

Fold points *A* and *B*
to the center. Repeat
for the points in
the back.

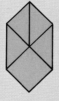

Tuck △*AXY* and
△*BRS* into the
pockets under
A and *B*. Repeat
for the triangles
in the back.

Blow in the hole
at point *O* to
inflate the cube.

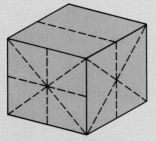

Crease the edges
to complete the cube.

Unit 8 review

Multiply.

1.	68 × 42	**2.**	237 × 65	**3.**	4893 × 8	**4.**	741 × 376	**5.**	929 × 474
6.	3.8 × 0.7	**7.**	0.48 × 96	**8.**	6.72 × 3.9	**9.**	0.084 × 3.16	**10.**	8.37 × 6.92

Find the quotients and remainders.

11. $57\overline{)4674}$ **12.** $34\overline{)5695}$ **13.** $93\overline{)19\ 276}$ **14.** $316\overline{)29\ 000}$

Find the exact quotients. Annex zeros as necessary.

15. $8\overline{)12.4}$ **16.** $3.1\overline{)16.74}$ **17.** $0.09\overline{)1.386}$ **18.** $1.28\overline{)1.6}$

Find each quotient to the nearest hundredth.

19. $9\overline{)23}$ **20.** $2.7\overline{)8.45}$ **21.** $0.77\overline{)0.418}$ **22.** $34.8\overline{)9.44}$

Solve the equations.

23. $\dfrac{u}{42} = 54$ **24.** $\dfrac{c}{2.5} = 0.08$ **25.** $\dfrac{k}{3.94} = 14.78$

26. $\dfrac{d}{0.25} = 8.72$ **27.** $\dfrac{e}{6.8} = 1.235$ **28.** $\dfrac{f}{52} = 0.0041$

29. $83t = 5312$ **30.** $474v = 74\ 418$ **31.** $258s = 176\ 214$

32. $4.4g = 28.028$ **33.** $72.9m = 364.5$ **34.** $0.38n = 2.1052$

35. $7c = 21$ **36.** $3n + 5 = 14$ **37.** $5k - 4 = 21$

Use n to write an expression for each phrase.

38. a number decreased by 5

39. 6 more than a number

40. 4 less than one half of a number

41. 28 divided by a number

42. a number multiplied by 9

43. 2 less than twice a number

Write and solve an equation for each problem.

44. When 4 is subtracted from 7 times a number the result is 59. What is the number?

45. A number is multiplied by 9. Then 17 is added to the product. The sum is 73. What is the number?

Fractional Numbers
Computing with Fractions
Ratio and Proportion
Congruent and Similar Triangles

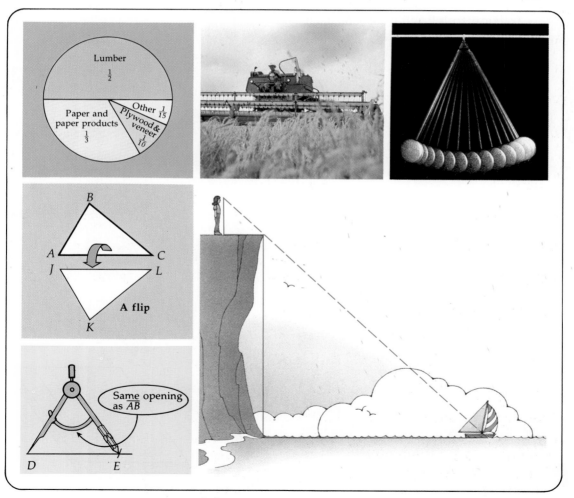

Fractional Numbers

Students shared tables to show their collections at the Collectors' Fair.

1 table is shared by 2 students.

1 table is divided into 2 equal parts.

Each student is using $\frac{1}{2}$ of a table.

Give a fraction to tell what part of each table top is covered by the colored paper.

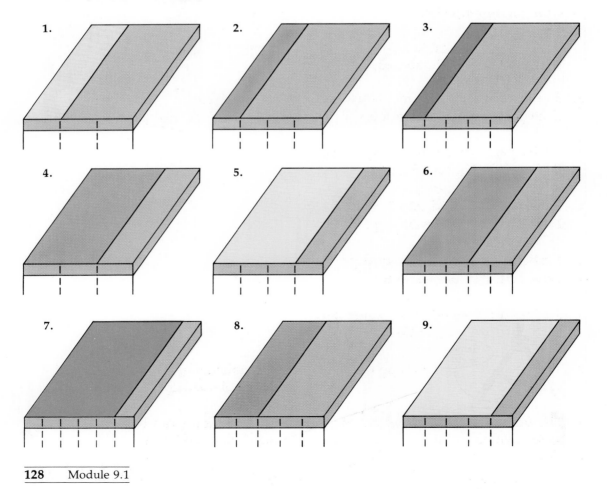

1.

2.

3.

4.

5.

6.

7.

8.

9.

Some students shared more than one table.

3 tables are shared by 4 students.

3 tables are divided into 4 equal parts.

Each student is using $\frac{1}{4}$ of 3 tables or $\frac{3}{4}$ of a table.

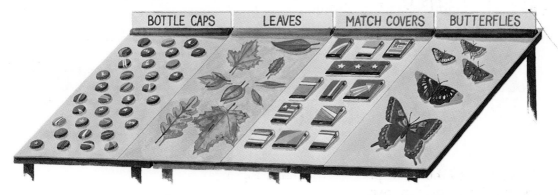

Give the missing numbers.

1. 2 tables are divided into 3 equal parts.
   Each part is ▥ of a table top.

2. 3 tables are divided into 5 equal parts.
   Each part is ▥ of a table top.

3. 2 tables are divided into 4 equal parts.
   Each part is ▥ of a table top.

4. 4 tables are divided into 5 equal parts.
   Each part is ▥ of a table top.

5. 1 table is divided into 3 equal parts.
   Each part is ▥ of a table top.

6. 3 tables are divided into 6 equal parts.
   Each part is ▥ of a table top.

7. The fraction $\frac{3}{5}$ can be thought of
   as 3 divided by ▥ .

8. The fraction $\frac{5}{8}$ can be thought of
   as ▥ divided by 8.

9. The fraction $\frac{3}{10}$ can be thought of
   as ▥ divided by 10.

10. The fraction $\frac{2}{3}$ can be thought of
    as ▥ divided by ▥ .

Writing decimals for fractions

A 3 m board is cut into 8 pieces of equal length. Each piece is $\frac{3}{8}$ m long. What is the decimal for this length?

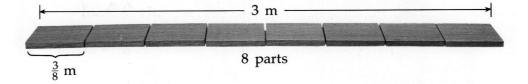

3 m

$\frac{3}{8}$ m

8 parts

Finding the answer

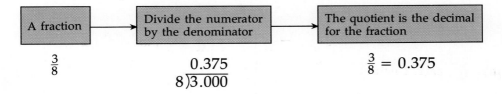

| A fraction | Divide the numerator by the denominator | The quotient is the decimal for the fraction |

$\frac{3}{8}$

$$\begin{array}{r} 0.375 \\ 8\overline{)3.000} \end{array}$$

$\frac{3}{8} = 0.375$

Each piece has a length of 0.375 m.

Other examples

$\frac{7}{5}$ $\longrightarrow$ $\begin{array}{r} 1.4 \\ 5\overline{)7.0} \end{array}$ $\longrightarrow$ $\frac{7}{5} = 1.4$

$\frac{3}{4}$ $\longrightarrow$ $\begin{array}{r} 0.75 \\ 4\overline{)3.00} \end{array}$ $\longrightarrow$ $\frac{3}{4} = 0.75$

Write a decimal for each fraction.

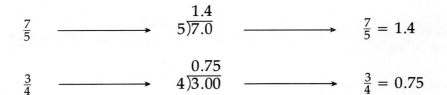

1. $\frac{1}{4}$	**2.** $\frac{7}{8}$	**3.** $\frac{7}{20}$	**4.** $\frac{1}{2}$	**5.** $\frac{5}{16}$	**6.** $\frac{7}{4}$
7. $\frac{2}{5}$	**8.** $\frac{63}{50}$	**9.** $\frac{3}{2}$	**10.** $\frac{11}{8}$	**11.** $\frac{7}{10}$	**12.** $\frac{5}{8}$
13. $\frac{17}{50}$	**14.** $\frac{3}{16}$	**15.** $\frac{5}{4}$	**16.** $\frac{1}{8}$	**17.** $\frac{19}{20}$	**18.** $\frac{1}{16}$
19. $\frac{5}{2}$	**20.** $\frac{4}{5}$	**21.** $\frac{3}{10}$	**22.** $\frac{7}{16}$	**23.** $\frac{9}{4}$	**24.** $\frac{9}{8}$

Every fractional number can be written as a **repeating decimal**. These decimals have one digit or a group of digits that repeat over and over without end. When the repeating digit in a decimal is zero, the decimal is a **terminating** decimal.

Find a decimal for $\frac{7}{11}$.

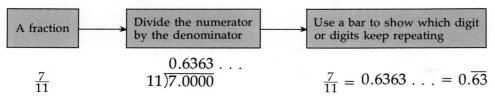

| A fraction | Divide the numerator by the denominator | Use a bar to show which digit or digits keep repeating |

$$\frac{7}{11} \qquad \begin{array}{r} 0.6363\ldots \\ 11\overline{)7.0000} \end{array} \qquad \frac{7}{11} = 0.6363\ldots = 0.\overline{63}$$

Other examples

$$\frac{13}{6} \longrightarrow \begin{array}{r} 2.166\ldots \\ 6\overline{)13.000} \end{array} \longrightarrow \frac{13}{6} = 2.1\overline{6}$$

$$\frac{15}{12} \longrightarrow \begin{array}{r} 1.250\ldots \\ 12\overline{)15.000} \end{array} \longrightarrow \frac{15}{12} = 1.25$$

Write a decimal for each fraction.

1. $\frac{2}{3}$ 2. $\frac{5}{6}$ 3. $\frac{3}{11}$ 4. $\frac{6}{24}$ 5. $\frac{11}{6}$ 6. $\frac{25}{99}$

7. $\frac{27}{22}$ 8. $\frac{13}{16}$ 9. $\frac{47}{99}$ 10. $\frac{4}{33}$ 11. $\frac{7}{9}$ 12. $\frac{15}{12}$

You can also write mixed decimals for fractions. The remainder is written as a fraction.
Examples:

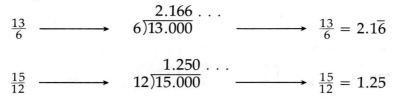

$$\frac{1}{3} = \longrightarrow \begin{array}{r} 0.33 \\ 3\overline{)1.00} \\ \underline{9} \\ 10 \\ \underline{9} \\ 1 \end{array} \longrightarrow \frac{1}{3} = 0.33\frac{1}{3} \qquad \frac{13}{8} \longrightarrow \begin{array}{r} 1.62 \\ 8\overline{)13.00} \\ \underline{8} \\ 5\,0 \\ \underline{4\,8} \\ 20 \\ \underline{16} \\ 4 \end{array} \longrightarrow \frac{13}{8} = 1.62\frac{1}{2}$$

Write mixed decimals in hundredths for each fraction.

13. $\frac{5}{6}$ 14. $\frac{3}{8}$ 15. $\frac{5}{3}$ 16. $\frac{5}{7}$ 17. $\frac{11}{9}$ 18. $\frac{41}{8}$

19. $\frac{26}{9}$ 20. $\frac{15}{8}$ 21. $\frac{7}{6}$ 22. $\frac{10}{3}$ 23. $\frac{12}{9}$ 24. $\frac{14}{6}$

More practice, page 384, Set A

Equivalent fractions and lowest terms

Are the fractions $\frac{9}{24}$ and $\frac{15}{40}$ equivalent?

Different fractions that are equal to the same decimal are equivalent to each other.

Finding the answer

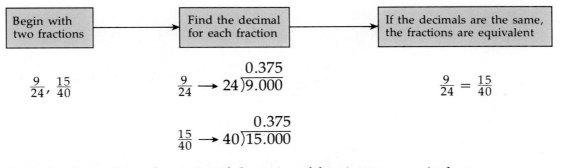

Find the decimals to determine if the pairs of fractions are equivalent.

1. $\frac{6}{8}, \frac{15}{20}$ 2. $\frac{15}{24}, \frac{20}{32}$ 3. $\frac{6}{9}, \frac{10}{15}$ 4. $\frac{8}{10}, \frac{12}{16}$ 5. $\frac{5}{40}, \frac{6}{48}$

6. $\frac{15}{18}, \frac{20}{24}$ 7. $\frac{12}{20}, \frac{21}{36}$ 8. $\frac{6}{22}, \frac{18}{66}$ 9. $\frac{15}{27}, \frac{35}{63}$ 10. $\frac{6}{35}, \frac{8}{48}$

Are the fractions $\frac{9}{12}$ and $\frac{15}{20}$ equivalent?

Different fractions that have equal cross products are equivalent to each other.

Finding the answer

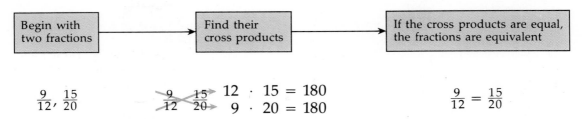

Find the cross products to determine if the pairs of fractions are equivalent.

11. $\frac{4}{32}, \frac{5}{40}$ 12. $\frac{10}{15}, \frac{25}{40}$ 13. $\frac{10}{15}, \frac{12}{18}$ 14. $\frac{12}{15}, \frac{16}{20}$ 15. $\frac{12}{16}, \frac{15}{20}$

16. $\frac{4}{25}, \frac{6}{36}$ 17. $\frac{25}{45}, \frac{30}{54}$ 18. $\frac{9}{15}, \frac{18}{30}$ 19. $\frac{12}{44}, \frac{16}{55}$ 20. $\frac{15}{18}, \frac{25}{30}$

Of all the fractions that are equal to the same decimal, there is one "simplest" fraction for that decimal. This fraction is the **lowest-terms fraction** for that decimal.

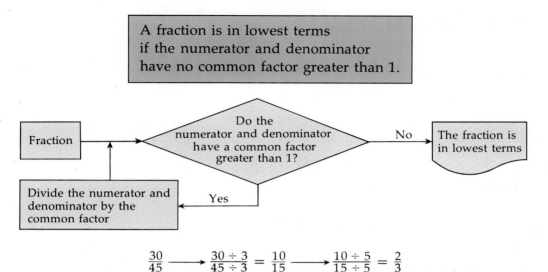

A fraction is in lowest terms
if the numerator and denominator
have no common factor greater than 1.

$$\frac{30}{45} \longrightarrow \frac{30 \div 3}{45 \div 3} = \frac{10}{15} \longrightarrow \frac{10 \div 5}{15 \div 5} = \frac{2}{3}$$

Using the greatest common factor first can save some steps.

$$\frac{30}{45} \longrightarrow \frac{30 \div 15}{45 \div 15} = \frac{2}{3}$$

The lowest-terms fraction for $\frac{30}{45}$ is $\frac{2}{3}$.

Find the lowest-terms fraction for each.

1. $\frac{24}{32}$

2. $\frac{16}{24}$

3. $\frac{12}{32}$

4. $\frac{15}{20}$

5. $\frac{32}{40}$

6. $\frac{12}{18}$

7. $\frac{24}{30}$

8. $\frac{6}{9}$

9. $\frac{40}{48}$

10. $\frac{45}{60}$

11. $\frac{30}{36}$

12. $\frac{36}{96}$

13. $\frac{10}{15}$

14. $\frac{6}{8}$

15. $\frac{12}{15}$

16. $\frac{20}{30}$

17. $\frac{27}{72}$

18. $\frac{18}{24}$

19. $\frac{75}{90}$

20. $\frac{18}{48}$

21. $\frac{45}{54}$

22. $\frac{36}{45}$

23. $\frac{76}{100}$

24. $\frac{48}{120}$

Which pairs of fractions are equivalent? Use both the decimal method and the cross-product method.

1. $\frac{1185}{1659}$, $\frac{2265}{3171}$

2. $\frac{952}{1632}$, $\frac{1519}{2604}$

3. $\frac{1812}{2331}$, $\frac{2233}{2871}$

4. $\frac{1248}{768}$, $\frac{2223}{1368}$

Writing fractions for decimals

Each terminating decimal can be expressed as a lowest-terms fraction.

Give the lowest-terms fraction for 0.625.

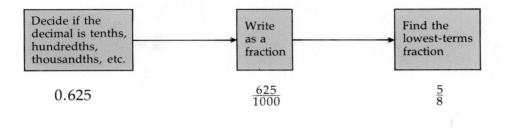

Decide if the decimal is tenths, hundredths, thousandths, etc.	Write as a fraction	Find the lowest-terms fraction
0.625	$\frac{625}{1000}$	$\frac{5}{8}$

Other examples

$0.25 \longrightarrow \frac{25}{100} \longrightarrow \frac{1}{4}$

$0.6 \longrightarrow \frac{6}{10} \longrightarrow \frac{3}{5}$

$0.4375 \longrightarrow \frac{4375}{10\ 000} \longrightarrow \frac{7}{16}$

$0.17 \longrightarrow \frac{17}{100} \longrightarrow \frac{17}{100}$

Give the lowest-terms fraction for each decimal.

1. 0.35
2. 0.875
3. 0.12
4. 0.2
5. 0.55

6. 0.7
7. 0.125
8. 0.24
9. 0.5
10. 0.1875

11. 0.02
12. 0.6
13. 0.08
14. 0.375
15. 0.14

16. 0.3
17. 0.75
18. 0.5625
19. 0.8125
20. 0.4

21. 0.16
22. 0.65
23. 0.8
24. 0.15
25. 0.4025

26. 0.50
27. 0.46
28. 0.115
29. 0.025
30. 0.66

31. 0.004
32. 0.175
33. 0.64
34. 0.23
35. 0.96

36. 0.0935
37. 0.408
38. 0.0625
39. 0.0125
40. 0.6875

Each repeating decimal can also be expressed as a lowest-terms fraction.
The flow chart shows how to find the lowest-terms fraction for a repeating
decimal in which all the digits in the decimal repeat.

Give the lowest-terms fraction for $0.\overline{135}$

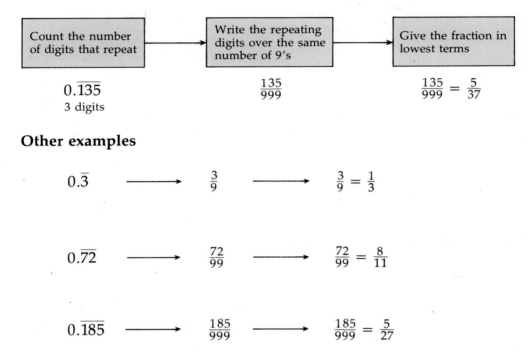

| Count the number of digits that repeat | Write the repeating digits over the same number of 9's | Give the fraction in lowest terms |

$$0.\overline{135}$$
3 digits

$$\frac{135}{999}$$

$$\frac{135}{999} = \frac{5}{37}$$

Other examples

$0.\overline{3}$ $\longrightarrow$ $\frac{3}{9}$ $\longrightarrow$ $\frac{3}{9} = \frac{1}{3}$

$0.\overline{72}$ $\longrightarrow$ $\frac{72}{99}$ $\longrightarrow$ $\frac{72}{99} = \frac{8}{11}$

$0.\overline{185}$ $\longrightarrow$ $\frac{185}{999}$ $\longrightarrow$ $\frac{185}{999} = \frac{5}{27}$

Give the lowest-terms fraction for each decimal.

1. $0.\overline{6}$ 2. $0.\overline{45}$ 3. $0.\overline{4}$

4. $0.\overline{12}$ 5. $0.\overline{30}$ 6. $0.\overline{90}$

7. $0.\overline{54}$ 8. $0.\overline{1}$ 9. $0.\overline{18}$

10. $0.\overline{5}$ 11. $0.\overline{27}$ 12. $0.\overline{24}$

13. $0.\overline{63}$ 14. $0.\overline{054}$ 15. $0.\overline{7}$

16. $0.\overline{09}$ ☆ 17. $0.\overline{481}$ ☆ 18. $0.\overline{0594}$

☆ 19. $0.\overline{962}$ ☆ 20. $0.\overline{8613}$ ☆ 21. $0.\overline{405}$

☆ 22. $0.\overline{428571}$ ☆ 23. $0.\overline{3213}$ ☆ 24. $0.\overline{1001}$

Find the lowest-terms fraction
for each of these fractions.

Hint: First find the decimal.

1. $\frac{47\,374}{71\,061}$ 2. $\frac{127\,932}{287\,847}$

3. $\frac{174\,500}{479\,875}$ 4. $\frac{544\,502}{2\,343\,726}$

More practice, page 384, Set B

Improper fractions and mixed numerals

The numerator of an **improper fraction** is greater than or equal to the denominator of the fraction.

$\frac{7}{2}$, $\frac{8}{3}$, and $\frac{6}{6}$ are improper fractions.

Mixed numerals are sums of whole numbers and fractions.

$2\frac{1}{2}$, $7\frac{2}{3}$, and $10\frac{3}{8}$ are mixed numerals.

What is the mixed numeral for $\frac{34}{6}$?

Finding the answer

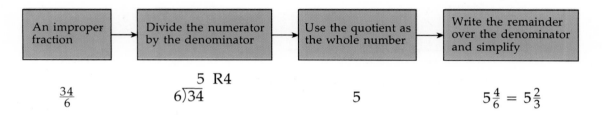

| An improper fraction | Divide the numerator by the denominator | Use the quotient as the whole number | Write the remainder over the denominator and simplify |

$$\frac{34}{6} \qquad 6\overline{)34}^{\,5\ R4} \qquad 5 \qquad 5\frac{4}{6} = 5\frac{2}{3}$$

The mixed numeral for $\frac{34}{6}$ is $5\frac{2}{3}$.

Other examples

$$\frac{37}{5} \longrightarrow 5\overline{)37}^{\,7\ R2} \longrightarrow 7\frac{2}{5} \qquad\qquad \frac{98}{4} \longrightarrow 4\overline{)98}^{\,24\ R2} \longrightarrow 24\frac{2}{4} = 24\frac{1}{2}$$

Write the mixed numeral or whole number for each improper fraction.

1. $\frac{25}{3}$ 2. $\frac{51}{4}$ 3. $\frac{37}{6}$ 4. $\frac{7}{1}$ 5. $\frac{42}{5}$ 6. $\frac{26}{3}$

7. $\frac{34}{4}$ 8. $\frac{18}{2}$ 9. $\frac{46}{8}$ 10. $\frac{59}{2}$ 11. $\frac{24}{3}$ 12. $\frac{77}{5}$

13. $\frac{38}{8}$ 14. $\frac{46}{7}$ 15. $\frac{27}{1}$ 16. $\frac{35}{3}$ 17. $\frac{66}{4}$ 18. $\frac{46}{8}$

19. $\frac{27}{2}$ 20. $\frac{59}{6}$ 21. $\frac{37}{3}$ 22. $\frac{92}{4}$ 23. $\frac{61}{2}$ 24. $\frac{28}{5}$

What improper fraction names
point *A* on the number line?

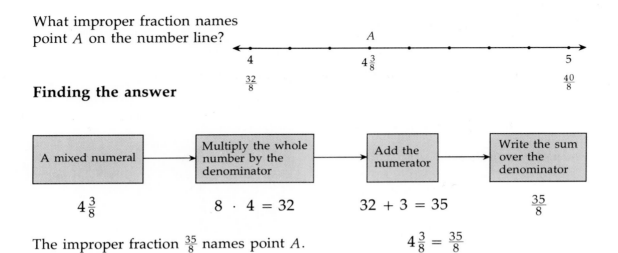

Finding the answer

| A mixed numeral | → | Multiply the whole number by the denominator | → | Add the numerator | → | Write the sum over the denominator |

$$4\frac{3}{8} \qquad\qquad 8 \cdot 4 = 32 \qquad\qquad 32 + 3 = 35 \qquad\qquad \frac{35}{8}$$

The improper fraction $\frac{35}{8}$ names point *A*. $\qquad\qquad 4\frac{3}{8} = \frac{35}{8}$

Other examples

$$3\frac{2}{5} = \frac{17}{5} \qquad\qquad 6\frac{7}{8} = \frac{55}{8} \qquad\qquad 8\frac{2}{3} = \frac{26}{3}$$

Write an improper fraction for each mixed numeral.

1. $5\frac{3}{8}$
2. $9\frac{3}{4}$
3. $1\frac{5}{8}$
4. $8\frac{2}{5}$
5. $2\frac{3}{4}$

6. $1\frac{5}{6}$
7. $7\frac{3}{5}$
8. $3\frac{1}{6}$
9. $5\frac{3}{4}$
10. $7\frac{5}{6}$

11. $2\frac{7}{10}$
12. $6\frac{1}{10}$
13. $9\frac{4}{5}$
14. $6\frac{1}{4}$
15. $1\frac{1}{8}$

16. $2\frac{1}{5}$
17. $5\frac{7}{8}$
18. $3\frac{1}{4}$
19. $6\frac{1}{8}$
20. $4\frac{1}{2}$

21. $7\frac{2}{3}$
22. $9\frac{2}{7}$
23. $4\frac{3}{5}$
24. $8\frac{9}{10}$
25. $3\frac{2}{3}$

Calculator problems

Find the mixed numeral for
each improper fraction.

26. $\frac{33\,912}{15\,072}$
27. $\frac{17\,436}{13\,077}$

28. $\frac{27\,858}{18\,572}$
29. $\frac{37\,401}{21\,372}$

30. $\frac{30\,371}{24\,849}$
31. $\frac{11\,760}{8624}$

Draw a figure like the one below.
Now trace over the entire figure by
drawing a path that does not cross
itself or retrace itself.

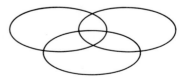

Fractional number inequality

One tennis team, the Hornets, won $\frac{5}{8}$ of their games. Another tennis team, the Cougars, won $\frac{3}{4}$ of their games. Which team had a better record of wins?

To compare fractions with simple denominators, compare their equivalent fractions using common denominators.

$$\frac{5}{8} \quad \bullet \quad \frac{3}{4}$$

$$\frac{5}{8} < \frac{6}{8} \quad \text{so} \quad \frac{5}{8} < \frac{3}{4}$$

The Cougars had a better record of wins.

To compare some fractional numbers, it is easier to compare their decimals.

Compare $\frac{22}{25}$ and $\frac{28}{30}$.

$$\frac{22}{25} = 0.88 \qquad \frac{28}{30} = 0.9\overline{3} \qquad 0.88 < 0.9\overline{3}$$

$$\text{so } \frac{22}{25} < \frac{28}{30}$$

Other examples

Compare $\frac{5}{6}$ and $\frac{7}{12}$

$$\frac{10}{12} > \frac{7}{12}$$

$$\text{so } \frac{5}{6} > \frac{7}{12}$$

Compare $\frac{8}{11}$ and $\frac{11}{15}$

$$\frac{8}{11} = 0.\overline{72} \qquad \frac{11}{15} = 0.7\overline{3}$$

$$0.\overline{72} < 0.7\overline{3}$$

$$\text{so } \frac{8}{11} < \frac{11}{15}$$

Compare these fractions.

1. $\frac{1}{2}$ and $\frac{5}{8}$ 2. $\frac{3}{4}$ and $\frac{7}{8}$ 3. $\frac{1}{4}$ and $\frac{1}{3}$ 4. $\frac{5}{6}$ and $\frac{7}{12}$

Use decimals to compare these fractions.

5. $\frac{13}{16}$ and $\frac{7}{9}$ 6. $\frac{4}{7}$ and $\frac{8}{13}$ 7. $\frac{8}{11}$ and $\frac{11}{15}$ 8. $\frac{6}{7}$ and $\frac{17}{20}$

Compare these fractions.

9. $\frac{1}{4}$ and $\frac{2}{5}$ 10. $\frac{1}{2}$ and $\frac{7}{12}$ 11. $\frac{2}{7}$ and $\frac{1}{3}$ 12. $\frac{2}{3}$ and $\frac{3}{5}$

13. $\frac{5}{6}$ and $\frac{3}{4}$ 14. $\frac{4}{7}$ and $\frac{5}{8}$ 15. $\frac{3}{4}$ and $\frac{2}{3}$ 16. $\frac{1}{6}$ and $\frac{1}{8}$

17. $\frac{3}{5}$ and $\frac{6}{10}$ 18. $\frac{2}{9}$ and $\frac{1}{4}$ 19. $\frac{4}{5}$ and $\frac{5}{6}$ 20. $\frac{5}{8}$ and $\frac{1}{2}$

21. $\frac{5}{8}$ and $\frac{3}{4}$ 22. $\frac{1}{7}$ and $\frac{1}{6}$ 23. $\frac{9}{10}$ and $\frac{7}{8}$ 24. $\frac{5}{7}$ and $\frac{4}{5}$

Calculator problems

Compare the fractions.

25. $\frac{27}{43}$ and $\frac{26}{42}$ 26. $\frac{38}{75}$ and $\frac{38}{74}$ 27. $\frac{52}{86}$ and $\frac{52}{85}$ 28. $\frac{43}{76}$ and $\frac{44}{67}$

29. $\frac{65}{27}$ and $\frac{76}{33}$ 30. $\frac{42}{88}$ and $\frac{69}{94}$ 31. $\frac{37}{42}$ and $\frac{49}{57}$ 32. $\frac{68}{17}$ and $\frac{73}{21}$

The rates for Want Ads in a newspaper are
92¢ per line per day for 4 to 8 days,
68¢ per line per day for 9 to 11 days, and
50¢ per line per day for 12 to 26 days.
How much would it cost to run a 3-line ad for

1. 8 days?   2. 9 days?
3. 11 days?   4. 12 days?
5. 14 days?

Which number of days costs least?

Answers for Self-check   1. 0.7   2. 0.375   3. 0.$\overline{6}$ 4. 0.1$\overline{6}$ 5. 0.$\overline{3}$ 6. yes   7. no   8. yes
9. $\frac{7}{8}$ 10. $\frac{5}{6}$ 11. $\frac{1}{4}$ 12. $\frac{3}{8}$ 13. 0.62$\frac{1}{2}$ 14. 1.33$\frac{1}{3}$ 15. 1.33$\frac{1}{3}$ 16. 1.87$\frac{1}{2}$ 17. $\frac{17}{3}$ 18. $\frac{31}{8}$ 19. $\frac{19}{4}$
20. $\frac{42}{5}$ 21. <   22. >   23. >   24. >

Self-check

Write a decimal or repeating decimal for each fraction.

1. $\frac{7}{10}$ **2.** $\frac{3}{8}$ **3.** $\frac{2}{3}$ **4.** $\frac{1}{6}$ **5.** $\frac{2}{6}$

Tell whether or not the two fractions are equivalent.

Find the lowest-terms fraction for each decimal or fraction.

6. $\frac{15}{20}, \frac{21}{28}$ **7.** $\frac{16}{24}, \frac{6}{10}$ **8.** $\frac{15}{40}, \frac{6}{16}$ **9.** $\frac{42}{48}$ **10.** $\frac{45}{54}$

11. 0.25   **12.** 0.375

Write a mixed decimal for each fraction.

Write the improper fraction for each mixed numeral.

13. $\frac{5}{8}$ **14.** $\frac{4}{3}$ **17.** $5\frac{2}{3}$ **18.** $3\frac{7}{8}$

15. $\frac{12}{9}$ **16.** $\frac{15}{8}$ **19.** $4\frac{3}{4}$ **20.** $8\frac{2}{5}$

Give the correct symbol, < or >, for each ●.

21. $\frac{2}{3}$ ● $\frac{3}{4}$ **22.** $\frac{7}{8}$ ● $\frac{6}{7}$ **23.** $\frac{5}{6}$ ● $\frac{4}{5}$ **24.** $\frac{1}{2}$ ● $\frac{4}{9}$

Answers for Self-check—page 139

Test

Write a decimal or repeating decimal for each fraction.

1. $\frac{3}{4}$ **2.** $\frac{1}{5}$ **3.** $\frac{5}{6}$ **4.** $\frac{3}{11}$ **5.** $\frac{5}{9}$

Tell whether or not the two fractions are equivalent.

Find the lowest-terms fraction for each decimal or fraction.

6. $\frac{12}{16}, \frac{9}{12}$ **7.** $\frac{8}{12}, \frac{14}{21}$ **8.** $\frac{18}{48}, \frac{16}{40}$ **9.** $\frac{12}{32}$ **10.** $\frac{42}{54}$

11. 0.625   **12.** 0.75

Write a mixed decimal for each fraction.

Write the improper fraction for each mixed numeral.

13. $\frac{13}{8}$ **14.** $\frac{2}{3}$ **17.** $6\frac{3}{4}$ **18.** $9\frac{3}{10}$

15. $\frac{3}{8}$ **16.** $\frac{11}{9}$ **19.** $7\frac{2}{3}$ **20.** $4\frac{3}{8}$

Give the correct symbol, < or >, for each ●.

21. $\frac{5}{8}$ ● $\frac{2}{3}$ **22.** $\frac{4}{5}$ ● $\frac{3}{4}$ **23.** $\frac{9}{10}$ ● $\frac{8}{9}$ **24.** $\frac{7}{12}$ ● $\frac{1}{2}$

Math lab

Geoboard Fractions

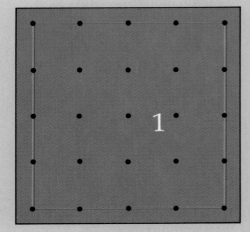

Example:

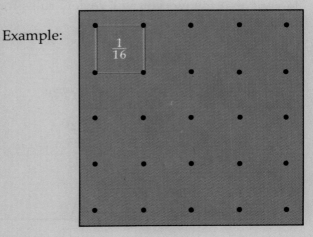

Using the large square
as the unit, each small
square is $\frac{1}{16}$ unit.
Show the fractions $\frac{1}{32}, \frac{1}{16}, \frac{1}{8}, \frac{1}{4}, \frac{1}{2}$
on dot paper or a geoboard.

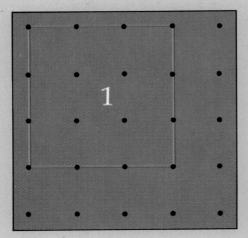

Using this square
as the unit, each small
square is $\frac{1}{9}$ of a unit.
Show the fractions $\frac{1}{18}, \frac{1}{9}, \frac{1}{3}, \frac{1}{2}, \frac{1}{6}$.

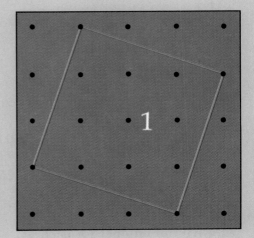

Using this square
as the unit, each small
square is $\frac{1}{10}$ of a unit.
Show the fractions $\frac{1}{20}, \frac{1}{10}, \frac{1}{5}, \frac{1}{2}, \frac{1}{4}$.

Computing with Fractions

This lesson will help you understand computing with fractions. In the lessons that follow, you will review rules for more rapid computing with fractions.

Addition

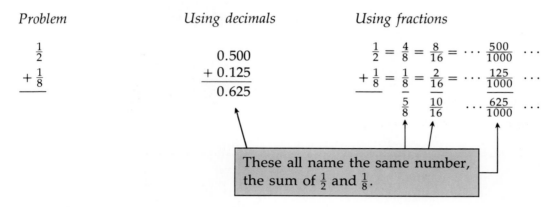

Problem	Using decimals	Using fractions
$\frac{1}{2}$	0.500	$\frac{1}{2} = \frac{4}{8} = \frac{8}{16} = \cdots \frac{500}{1000} \cdots$
$+\frac{1}{8}$	$+0.125$	$+\frac{1}{8} = \frac{1}{8} = \frac{2}{16} = \cdots \frac{125}{1000} \cdots$
	0.625	$\frac{5}{8} \quad \frac{10}{16} \quad \cdots \frac{625}{1000} \cdots$

These all name the same number, the sum of $\frac{1}{2}$ and $\frac{1}{8}$.

1. Give the number for each ▐.

$\frac{1}{2}$	0.50	$\frac{1}{2} = \frac{2}{4} = \frac{4}{8} = \cdots \frac{50}{100} \cdots$
$+\frac{1}{4}$	$+0.25$	$+\frac{1}{4} = \frac{1}{4} = \frac{2}{8} = \cdots \frac{25}{100} \cdots$
	▐	▐ ▐ ▐

Subtraction

Problem	Using decimals	Using fractions
$\frac{1}{2}$	0.500	$\frac{1}{2} = \frac{4}{8} = \frac{8}{16} = \cdots \frac{500}{1000} \cdots$
$-\frac{3}{8}$	-0.375	$-\frac{3}{8} = \frac{3}{8} = \frac{6}{16} = \cdots \frac{375}{1000} \cdots$
	0.125	$\frac{1}{8} \quad \frac{2}{16} \quad \cdots \frac{125}{1000}$

2. Give the number for each ▐.

$\frac{3}{4}$	0.750	$\frac{3}{4} = \frac{6}{8} = \frac{12}{16} = \cdots \frac{750}{1000} \cdots$
$-\frac{1}{8}$	-0.125	$-\frac{1}{8} = \frac{1}{8} = \frac{2}{16} = \cdots \frac{125}{1000} \cdots$
	▐	▐ ▐ ▐

Multiplication

Problem   *Using decimals*   *Using fractions*

$\frac{3}{4} \cdot \frac{2}{5}$

$$\begin{array}{r} 0.75 \\ \times\ \ 0.4 \\ \hline 0.300 \end{array}$$

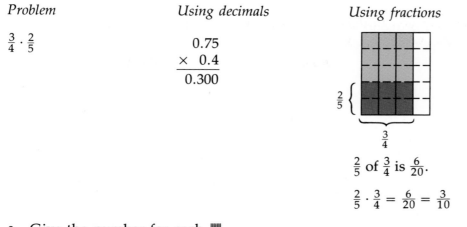

$\frac{2}{5}$ of $\frac{3}{4}$ is $\frac{6}{20}$.

$$\frac{2}{5} \cdot \frac{3}{4} = \frac{6}{20} = \frac{3}{10}$$

3. Give the number for each ▥.

$\frac{3}{4} \cdot \frac{1}{2}$

$$\begin{array}{r} 0.75 \\ \times\ \ 0.5 \\ \hline \text{▥} \end{array}$$

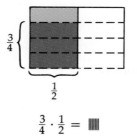

$$\frac{3}{4} \cdot \frac{1}{2} = \text{▥}$$

Division

Problem   *Using decimals*   *Using fractions*

$\frac{3}{4} \div \frac{1}{2}$

$$0.5\overline{)0.7\ 5}\ ^{1.5}$$

$\frac{3}{4} \div \frac{1}{2} = \left(\frac{3}{4} \cdot \frac{2}{1}\right) \div \left(\frac{1}{2} \cdot \frac{2}{1}\right)$

$\qquad = \left(\frac{3}{4} \cdot \frac{2}{1}\right) \div 1$

$\qquad = \frac{6}{4}$

$\qquad = 1\frac{1}{2}$

4. Give the number for each ▥.

$\frac{1}{2} \div \frac{5}{8}$

$$0.625\overline{)0.500\ 0}\ ^{0.8}$$

$\frac{1}{2} \div \frac{5}{8} = \left(\frac{1}{2} \cdot \frac{8}{5}\right) \div \left(\frac{5}{8} \cdot \frac{8}{5}\right)$

$\qquad = \left(\frac{1}{2} \cdot \frac{8}{5}\right) \div 1$

$\qquad = \text{▥}$

Addition of fractional numbers

What fractional part of wood is used for lumber and paper combined?

Uses of Wood in the United States

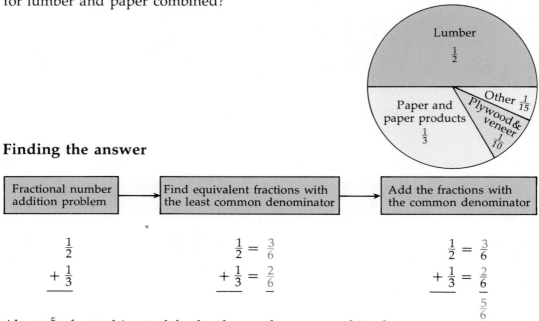

Finding the answer

Fractional number addition problem	→	Find equivalent fractions with the least common denominator	→	Add the fractions with the common denominator

$$\begin{array}{r} \frac{1}{2} \\ +\frac{1}{3} \\ \hline \end{array}$$

$$\begin{array}{r} \frac{1}{2} = \frac{3}{6} \\ +\frac{1}{3} = \frac{2}{6} \\ \hline \end{array}$$

$$\begin{array}{r} \frac{1}{2} = \frac{3}{6} \\ +\frac{1}{3} = \frac{2}{6} \\ \hline \frac{5}{6} \end{array}$$

About $\frac{5}{6}$ of wood is used for lumber and paper combined.

Other examples

$$\begin{array}{r} \frac{3}{8} = \frac{3}{8} \\ +\frac{1}{4} = \frac{2}{8} \\ \hline \frac{5}{8} \end{array}$$

$$\begin{array}{r} \frac{3}{4} = \frac{9}{12} \\ +\frac{2}{3} = \frac{8}{12} \\ \hline \frac{17}{12} = 1\frac{5}{12} \end{array}$$

$$\begin{array}{r} \frac{4}{5} = \frac{16}{20} \\ +\frac{1}{4} = \frac{5}{20} \\ \hline \frac{21}{20} = 1\frac{1}{20} \end{array}$$

Find the sums.

1. $\frac{1}{2}$
    $+\frac{3}{8}$

2. $\frac{2}{3}$
    $+\frac{1}{4}$

3. $\frac{1}{6}$
    $+\frac{3}{4}$

4. $\frac{1}{4}$
    $+\frac{3}{8}$

5. $\frac{3}{5}$
    $+\frac{1}{6}$

6. $\frac{1}{4}$
    $+\frac{7}{10}$

7. $\frac{7}{8}$
    $+\frac{1}{6}$

8. $\frac{1}{2}$
    $+\frac{3}{5}$

9. $\frac{5}{12}$
    $+\frac{3}{8}$

10. $\frac{3}{8}$
    $+\frac{2}{3}$

11. $\frac{5}{6}$
    $+\frac{1}{4}$

12. $\frac{3}{4}$
    $+\frac{5}{8}$

These examples show how to add using mixed numerals.

$$7\frac{1}{4} = 7\frac{3}{12}$$
$$+8\frac{5}{6} = 8\frac{10}{12}$$
$$15\frac{13}{12} = 16\frac{1}{12}$$

$$2\frac{1}{2} = 2\frac{6}{12}$$
$$1\frac{2}{3} = 1\frac{8}{12}$$
$$+3\frac{1}{4} = 3\frac{3}{12}$$
$$6\frac{17}{12} = 7\frac{5}{12}$$

Find the sums.

1. $8\frac{1}{2}$ $+7\frac{1}{8}$

2. $5\frac{1}{4}$ $+6\frac{1}{3}$

3. $9\frac{5}{6}$ $+6\frac{1}{2}$

4. $3\frac{3}{4}$ $+4\frac{1}{3}$

5. $7\frac{1}{4}$ $+3\frac{1}{3}$

6. $2\frac{1}{8}$ $+4\frac{3}{4}$

7. $36\frac{1}{2}$ $+75\frac{5}{6}$

8. $83\frac{1}{8}$ $+79\frac{1}{6}$

9. $56\frac{7}{8}$ $+27\frac{1}{2}$

10. $38\frac{1}{4}$ $+17\frac{5}{6}$

11. $59\frac{3}{8}$ $+67\frac{7}{8}$

12. $83\frac{1}{4}$ $+92\frac{1}{2}$

13. $\frac{1}{2}$ $\frac{1}{4}$ $+\frac{1}{8}$

14. $\frac{3}{8}$ $\frac{1}{4}$ $+\frac{1}{2}$

15. $\frac{1}{6}$ $\frac{1}{4}$ $+\frac{1}{2}$

16. $\frac{1}{5}$ $\frac{1}{2}$ $+\frac{3}{4}$

17. $\frac{5}{6}$ $\frac{1}{3}$ $+\frac{1}{2}$

18. $\frac{3}{8}$ $\frac{5}{6}$ $+\frac{3}{4}$

19. $7\frac{1}{2}$ $6\frac{1}{4}$ $+5\frac{1}{2}$

20. $3\frac{1}{8}$ $8\frac{1}{2}$ $+2\frac{1}{4}$

21. $4\frac{1}{3}$ $3\frac{1}{6}$ $+6\frac{1}{4}$

22. $27\frac{1}{2}$ $56\frac{3}{4}$ $+39\frac{2}{3}$

23. $47\frac{5}{6}$ $28\frac{3}{8}$ $+36\frac{3}{4}$

24. $52\frac{7}{8}$ $38\frac{1}{2}$ $+75\frac{2}{3}$

25. What fractional part of wood is used for paper products, plywood, and veneer combined?

26. What fractional part of wood is used for lumber, paper products, plywood, and veneer combined?

Find the repeating decimal for each of these fractions:

$$\frac{1}{7}, \frac{2}{7}, \frac{3}{7}, \frac{4}{7}, \frac{5}{7}, \frac{6}{7}$$

What do these repeating decimals have in common?

More practice, page 385, Set A

Subtraction of fractional numbers

Lincoln School band is scheduled to practice $3\frac{1}{2}$ hours a week. By Wednesday it has practiced $1\frac{3}{4}$ hours. How many more hours of practice are needed?

Finding the answer

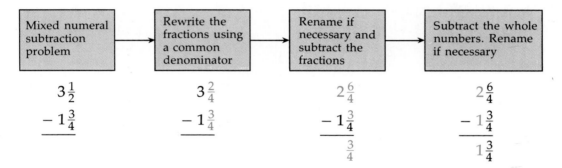

Mixed numeral subtraction problem	Rewrite the fractions using a common denominator	Rename if necessary and subtract the fractions	Subtract the whole numbers. Rename if necessary

$$3\frac{1}{2}$$
$$-1\frac{3}{4}$$

$$3\frac{2}{4}$$
$$-1\frac{3}{4}$$

$$2\frac{6}{4}$$
$$-1\frac{3}{4}$$
$$\frac{3}{4}$$

$$2\frac{6}{4}$$
$$-1\frac{3}{4}$$
$$1\frac{3}{4}$$

The band needs to practice $1\frac{3}{4}$ hours more.

Other examples

$$\frac{2}{3} = \frac{4}{6}$$
$$-\frac{1}{6} = \frac{1}{6}$$
$$\frac{3}{6} = \frac{1}{2}$$

$$6 = 5\frac{6}{6}$$
$$-1\frac{1}{6} = 1\frac{1}{6}$$
$$4\frac{5}{6}$$

$$7\frac{1}{8} = 7\frac{1}{8} = 6\frac{9}{8}$$
$$-2\frac{3}{4} = 2\frac{6}{8} = 2\frac{6}{8}$$
$$4\frac{3}{8}$$

Find the differences.

1. $\frac{7}{8}$
$-\frac{1}{2}$

2. $\frac{5}{6}$
$-\frac{1}{4}$

3. $\frac{1}{2}$
$-\frac{1}{3}$

4. $\frac{2}{3}$
$-\frac{1}{4}$

5. $\frac{3}{4}$
$-\frac{1}{6}$

6. $\frac{4}{5}$
$-\frac{1}{2}$

7. $9\frac{1}{2}$
$-2\frac{1}{4}$

8. $6\frac{1}{4}$
$-1\frac{1}{2}$

9. $8\frac{3}{8}$
$-3\frac{5}{6}$

10. $7\frac{3}{4}$
$-4\frac{7}{8}$

11. 5
$-2\frac{7}{8}$

12. $9\frac{1}{4}$
$-7\frac{2}{3}$

Find the differences.

1. $\frac{2}{3}$ $-\frac{1}{2}$
2. $\frac{1}{2}$ $-\frac{3}{10}$
3. $\frac{2}{3}$ $-\frac{1}{4}$

4. $\frac{3}{8}$ $-\frac{1}{3}$
5. $\frac{2}{5}$ $-\frac{1}{3}$
6. $\frac{1}{4}$ $-\frac{1}{5}$

7. $\frac{3}{4}$ $-\frac{3}{8}$
8. $\frac{3}{8}$ $-\frac{1}{4}$
9. $\frac{7}{10}$ $-\frac{1}{6}$

10. $\frac{2}{3}$ $-\frac{1}{6}$
11. $\frac{2}{5}$ $-\frac{1}{10}$
12. $\frac{1}{2}$ $-\frac{2}{5}$

13. $9\frac{7}{8}$ $-3\frac{1}{3}$
14. $8\frac{3}{10}$ $-4\frac{1}{3}$
15. $4\frac{1}{6}$ $-1\frac{3}{8}$
16. $6\frac{2}{3}$ $-2\frac{3}{4}$
17. $7\frac{5}{6}$ $-2\frac{1}{8}$
18. $5\frac{3}{10}$ $-3\frac{1}{2}$

19. $75\frac{1}{2}$ $-28\frac{3}{4}$
20. $69\frac{3}{8}$ $-32\frac{3}{4}$
21. $43\frac{3}{5}$ $-18\frac{5}{8}$
22. $71\frac{1}{2}$ $-64\frac{9}{10}$
23. $30\frac{1}{4}$ $-14\frac{2}{3}$
24. $52\frac{7}{10}$ $-13\frac{1}{2}$

25. $65\frac{1}{2}$ $-11\frac{1}{8}$
26. $37\frac{1}{8}$ $-21\frac{1}{6}$
27. $62\frac{7}{10}$ $-18\frac{3}{4}$
28. $90\frac{1}{10}$ $-74\frac{1}{8}$
29. $31\frac{1}{8}$ $-27\frac{3}{5}$
30. $76\frac{1}{2}$ $-58\frac{5}{6}$

31. The band concert was supposed to last 3 hours. How much time was left after $1\frac{3}{4}$ hours?

32. The director wanted the marching band to practice 8 hours during the week before the season opened. By Wednesday they had practiced only $3\frac{1}{4}$ hours. How many more hours of practice were needed?

Choose a 3-digit number.
  Example: 691
Use it twice to make a 6-digit number.
  691 691
1. Divide by 7.
2. Divide by the original number.
3. Divide by 13.
Try these steps with several 3-digit numbers. What do you conclude?

More practice, page 385, Set B

Multiplication of fractional numbers

About $\frac{3}{5}$ of all coal mined in the United States is used to produce electrical energy. About $\frac{5}{8}$ of this amount of coal produces electricity for commercial and industrial users. What fraction of the coal is used to produce electricity for commercial and industrial users?

Finding the answer

Fractional number multiplication problem	Multiply the numerators	Multiply the denominators Rename if necessary

$$\frac{5}{8} \cdot \frac{3}{5}$$

$$\frac{5}{8} \cdot \frac{3}{5} = \frac{15}{}$$

$$\frac{5}{8} \cdot \frac{3}{5} = \frac{15}{40} = \frac{3}{8}$$

About $\frac{3}{8}$ of the coal is used to produce electricity for commercial and industrial users.

Other examples

$$\frac{7}{8} \cdot \frac{4}{5} = \frac{28}{40} = \frac{7}{10} \qquad \frac{3}{4} \cdot \frac{5}{6} = \frac{15}{24} = \frac{5}{8} \qquad \frac{4}{3} \cdot \frac{3}{5} = \frac{12}{15} = \frac{4}{5}$$

Short cut: Divide numerators and denominators by the same number before multiplying.

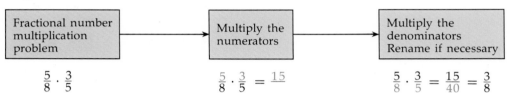

$$\frac{7}{\overset{8}{\underset{2}{\cancel{8}}}} \cdot \frac{\overset{1}{\cancel{4}}}{5} = \frac{7}{10} \qquad \frac{\overset{1}{\cancel{3}}}{4} \cdot \frac{5}{\underset{2}{\cancel{6}}} = \frac{5}{8} \qquad \frac{4}{\underset{1}{\cancel{3}}} \cdot \frac{\overset{1}{\cancel{3}}}{5} = \frac{4}{5}$$

Find the products.

1. $\frac{2}{3} \cdot \frac{1}{2} = e$

2. $\frac{1}{4} \cdot \frac{2}{3} = b$

3. $\frac{5}{6} \cdot \frac{3}{5} = h$

4. $\frac{4}{5} \cdot \frac{1}{2} = d$

5. $\frac{5}{8} \cdot \frac{2}{3} = i$

6. $\frac{1}{6} \cdot \frac{3}{4} = m$

7. $\frac{2}{3} \cdot \frac{3}{4} = a$

8. $\frac{3}{8} \cdot \frac{2}{3} = g$

9. $\frac{7}{10} \cdot \frac{5}{6} = c$

10. $\frac{2}{3} \cdot \frac{3}{10} = j$

11. $\frac{1}{2} \cdot \frac{1}{3} = f$

12. $\frac{4}{5} \cdot \frac{7}{10} = k$

The example below shows how to multiply using mixed numerals.

$$2\frac{2}{5} \cdot 3\frac{1}{4}$$

$$\frac{\overset{3}{\cancel{12}}}{5} \cdot \frac{13}{\cancel{4}_{1}} = \frac{39}{5} = 7\frac{4}{5}$$

Find the products.

1. $\frac{2}{3} \cdot \frac{3}{10} = g$ 2. $\frac{3}{4} \cdot \frac{1}{2} = b$

3. $\frac{3}{4} \cdot \frac{7}{12} = m$ 4. $\frac{4}{5} \cdot \frac{1}{8} = k$

5. $\frac{7}{8} \cdot \frac{2}{3} = r$ 6. $\frac{5}{6} \cdot \frac{1}{10} = e$ 7. $\frac{1}{4} \cdot \frac{1}{5} = s$ 8. $\frac{5}{8} \cdot \frac{9}{10} = t$

9. $1\frac{2}{3} \cdot 2\frac{1}{2} = i$ 10. $3\frac{1}{4} \cdot 1\frac{2}{5} = o$ 11. $3\frac{1}{4} \cdot 1\frac{1}{2} = a$ 12. $2\frac{2}{3} \cdot 2\frac{1}{2} = h$

13. $1\frac{1}{4} \cdot 4\frac{1}{2} = d$ 14. $2\frac{1}{8} \cdot 1\frac{3}{4} = p$ 15. $\frac{7}{8} \cdot 2\frac{1}{2} = n$ 16. $3\frac{1}{4} \cdot \frac{1}{2} = m$

17. $1\frac{1}{3} \cdot \frac{3}{4} = q$ 18. $\frac{2}{3} \cdot 1\frac{1}{2} = f$ 19. $2\frac{1}{2} \cdot \frac{2}{5} = j$ 20. $\frac{4}{5} \cdot 1\frac{1}{4} = c$

When the product of two numbers is 1, they are **reciprocals** of each other. The reciprocal of $\frac{2}{3}$ is $\frac{3}{2}$ because $\frac{2}{3} \cdot \frac{3}{2} = 1$.

Find the reciprocal of each number.

21. $\frac{3}{4}$ 22. $\frac{2}{5}$ 23. $\frac{7}{2}$ 24. $2\frac{2}{3}$ 25. $1\frac{1}{4}$ 26. $3\frac{1}{2}$ 27. $4\frac{2}{5}$

What number is 16 times as large as its reciprocal?

Hint: $n \cdot \frac{1}{n} = 1$

More practice, page 386, Set A

Division of fractional numbers

A full pitcher can fill 6 glasses. Each glass is $\frac{1}{6}$ of a pitcher. How many glasses of lemonade are in $\frac{3}{4}$ of a pitcher?

Finding the answer

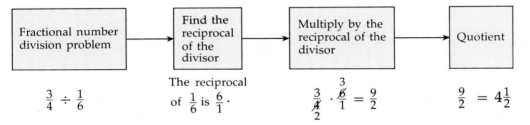

Fractional number division problem	Find the reciprocal of the divisor	Multiply by the reciprocal of the divisor	Quotient

$$\frac{3}{4} \div \frac{1}{6} \qquad \text{The reciprocal of } \frac{1}{6} \text{ is } \frac{6}{1}. \qquad \frac{3}{\underset{2}{4}} \cdot \frac{\overset{3}{6}}{1} = \frac{9}{2} \qquad \frac{9}{2} = 4\frac{1}{2}$$

There are $4\frac{1}{2}$ glasses of lemonade in $\frac{3}{4}$ of a pitcher.

Other examples

$$\frac{2}{3} \div \frac{3}{4} = \frac{2}{3} \cdot \frac{4}{3} \qquad\qquad \frac{3}{4} \div \frac{5}{6} = \frac{3}{\underset{2}{4}} \cdot \frac{\overset{3}{6}}{5} \qquad\qquad \frac{4}{5} \div \frac{1}{3} = \frac{4}{5} \cdot \frac{3}{1}$$

$$= \frac{8}{9} \qquad\qquad\qquad\qquad = \frac{9}{10} \qquad\qquad\qquad\qquad = \frac{12}{5} = 2\frac{2}{5}$$

Find the quotients.

1. $\frac{2}{5} \div \frac{1}{10} = e$
2. $\frac{3}{10} \div \frac{4}{5} = o$
3. $\frac{2}{3} \div \frac{5}{8} = i$
4. $\frac{3}{5} \div \frac{3}{4} = c$

5. $\frac{5}{6} \div \frac{3}{4} = k$
6. $\frac{2}{3} \div \frac{5}{6} = f$
7. $\frac{3}{4} \div \frac{3}{4} = a$
8. $\frac{1}{4} \div \frac{5}{8} = p$

9. $\frac{4}{5} \div \frac{2}{5} = b$
10. $\frac{1}{2} \div \frac{1}{10} = m$
11. $\frac{3}{8} \div \frac{3}{4} = g$
12. $\frac{1}{3} \div \frac{2}{3} = m$

13. $\frac{1}{8} \div \frac{1}{6} = j$
14. $\frac{7}{10} \div \frac{3}{4} = d$
15. $\frac{3}{10} \div \frac{7}{10} = n$
16. $\frac{2}{3} \div \frac{1}{2} = h$

17. $\frac{3}{4} \div \frac{1}{4} = s$
18. $\frac{7}{12} \div \frac{5}{8} = t$
19. $\frac{5}{6} \div \frac{1}{12} = q$
20. $\frac{9}{10} \div \frac{1}{5} = r$

The examples below show how to divide using mixed numerals.

$$2\frac{1}{4} \div 2\frac{2}{5}$$

$$\frac{9}{4} \div \frac{12}{5} = \frac{\cancel{9}^{3}}{4} \cdot \frac{5}{\cancel{12}_{4}}$$

$$= \frac{15}{16}$$

$$5\frac{5}{8} \div 3\frac{3}{4}$$

$$\frac{45}{8} \div \frac{15}{4} = \frac{\cancel{45}^{3}}{\cancel{8}_{2}} \cdot \frac{\cancel{4}^{1}}{\cancel{15}_{1}}$$

$$= \frac{3}{2} = 1\frac{1}{2}$$

Find the quotients.

1. $4\frac{1}{2} \div 2\frac{3}{4} = c$ 2. $1\frac{5}{8} \div \frac{5}{6} = n$ 3. $3\frac{1}{2} \div 1\frac{1}{4} = i$ 4. $2\frac{1}{2} \div 1\frac{1}{4} = s$

5. $2\frac{1}{8} \div 1\frac{1}{3} = m$ 6. $2\frac{1}{4} \div 1\frac{3}{4} = h$ 7. $5\frac{1}{2} \div 2 = a$ 8. $2 \div \frac{7}{8} = d$

9. $2 \div 1\frac{1}{4} = g$ 10. $4\frac{5}{8} \div 1\frac{1}{2} = r$ 11. $1\frac{3}{8} \div 4\frac{1}{4} = k$ 12. $6\frac{1}{2} \div 2\frac{2}{3} = o$

13. $3\frac{1}{4} \div 1\frac{3}{4} = q$ 14. $\frac{2}{3} \div 2\frac{1}{2} = b$ 15. $4\frac{1}{3} \div 1\frac{2}{3} = p$ 16. $3\frac{1}{4} \div 1\frac{2}{3} = n$

17. $5 \div 2\frac{1}{2} = f$ 18. $3\frac{5}{8} \div 2\frac{5}{6} = t$ 19. $1\frac{7}{8} \div \frac{5}{12} = j$ 20. $1\frac{2}{3} \div 2\frac{3}{4} = e$

21. If 1 pitcher of iced tea fills 8 glasses, how many glasses of tea are in $\frac{5}{6}$ of a pitcher?

22. How many glasses of orange juice are in $\frac{1}{2}$ of a pitcher, if each glass is $\frac{1}{6}$ of the pitcher?

23. How many glasses of grape juice are in $\frac{2}{3}$ of a pitcher, if each glass is $\frac{1}{8}$ of the pitcher?

24. How many people will 60 cups of fruit punch serve if each person drinks $2\frac{1}{2}$ cups?

☆ 25. A recipe for lemonade calls for the juice from 1 lemon for every $2\frac{1}{2}$ cups of water. The juice from 1 lemon is about $\frac{1}{4}$ cup. How many cups of lemonade can be made from the juice of 9 lemons?

A professional golfer can hit a golf ball about 260 m. How many such hits would it take to hit a golf ball across the United States? (Use a distance of 4800 km.)

More practice, page 386, Set B

Fraction problems—paint mixtures

The primary colors are red, blue, and yellow. Other colors can be made by mixing different amounts of these colors together. White can be used to give lighter shades of color.

1. To make a light green paint, $1\frac{1}{3}$ cans of blue paint, $1\frac{3}{4}$ cans of yellow paint, and $3\frac{1}{2}$ cans of white paint were mixed together. How many cans of the light green paint did this make?

2. How much more white paint than yellow and blue combined were used to make the light green paint?

3. A light red mixture of paint was made by mixing $1\frac{2}{3}$ cans of red paint with white paint. How much white paint was used if the resulting mixture filled $4\frac{1}{2}$ cans?

4. To make a shade of orange, $\frac{1}{3}$ can of red paint was mixed with $1\frac{1}{2}$ cans of yellow paint. How many cans of orange paint were made?

5. How much red paint would be needed to make 5 times the amount of orange paint in problem 4? How much yellow paint would be needed? How much orange paint would there be?

6. How much paint is needed for painting a room with 3 coats of paint if each coat requires $2\frac{2}{3}$ cans of paint?

7. To make a purple paint, it takes $\frac{1}{2}$ can of red paint, $\frac{1}{4}$ can of blue paint, and $\frac{1}{3}$ can of white paint. How many cans of purple paint does this make?

8. A light pink paint can be made by mixing $\frac{1}{3}$ can of red paint to $8\frac{1}{4}$ times as much white paint. How many cans of white paint should be used?

9. How many cans of white paint should be mixed with $1\frac{1}{3}$ cans of red paint to give the same light pink paint as in problem 8?

10. It took $2\frac{2}{3}$ cans of paint to paint a wooden patio deck. How many times could the deck be painted with 8 cans of paint?

11. To paint the exterior of a house, a painter mixed $\frac{1}{8}$ can of blue paint, $\frac{2}{3}$ can of yellow paint, and $5\frac{1}{2}$ cans of white paint. The painter estimated that 4 times that amount of paint would be needed. How much of each color would be needed? How many cans of the mixture would that make?

☆ 12. A shade of green paint was made from $\frac{1}{6}$ can of blue, $\frac{3}{4}$ cans of yellow, and $\frac{1}{3}$ can of white paint. How much paint was in this mixture? How much of each color paint would it take to make $6\frac{1}{4}$ cans of the mixture?

☆ 13. A mixture of $5\frac{3}{4}$ cans of orange paint was made from red, yellow, and white paint. There was $\frac{1}{2}$ can of red in the mixture. Twice as much yellow was used as white. How much white paint was used in the mixture?

Fraction problems—small airplanes

1. A small airplane uses 16 liters of gasoline an hour while flying. How many liters of gasoline would be used for a $\frac{3}{4}$ hour flight?

2. A small airplane uses 24 liters of gasoline per hour. How many liters of gasoline will be used for a flight that takes 1 hour and 20 minutes?

3. A small airplane uses 18 liters of gasoline per hour. How much gasoline would be used for a flight that takes $2\frac{1}{2}$ hours?

4. A small airplane has a capacity of 75 liters of gasoline. What is the greatest length of time the airplane could fly if it uses gasoline at the rate of 30 liters an hour?

5. A trip in a small plane is estimated to last $2\frac{3}{4}$ hours. If the plane uses 20 liters of gasoline per hour, how many liters of gasoline will be used for the trip?

6. The fuel tank of a small plane holds 64 liters. The plane uses 16 liters of fuel an hour. After $1\frac{1}{2}$ hours of flying, how many liters of gasoline would be left in the tank?

7. A flying instructor gave four lessons in one day. The first lesson was $1\frac{1}{4}$ hours long, the second lesson was 45 minutes long and the last two lessons were each 30 minutes long. What was the total amount of time the instructor used for lessons that day?

8. The smallest plane ever flown was 300 cm long and had a wingspan that was 82 cm less than the length of the plane. What was its wingspan?

9. A pilot estimated that a trip to another city would take 1 hour and 15 minutes. The return time was estimated to be 1 hour and 30 minutes. If the airplane used 22 liters of gasoline per hour, how many liters would be used for the complete trip?

10. On a flight of $3\frac{1}{2}$ hours, a pilot found that the airplane had used 84 liters of gasoline. How many liters per hour were used?

☆11. On December 17, 1903, Orville Wright became the first person to successfully fly an engine-propelled airplane. The airplane flew for 12 seconds at a ground speed of 11 km/h. How far did it fly?

Answers for Self-check 1. $1\frac{5}{24}$ 2. $1\frac{5}{12}$ 3. $14\frac{1}{40}$ 4. $1\frac{7}{12}$ 5. $14\frac{17}{24}$ 6. $\frac{3}{8}$ 7. $\frac{1}{2}$ 8. $4\frac{3}{8}$ 9. $3\frac{9}{20}$
10. $34\frac{13}{24}$ 11. $x = \frac{1}{3}$ 12. $m = 8\frac{1}{3}$ 13. $n = 1\frac{1}{6}$ 14. $g = 2\frac{2}{9}$ 15. $1\frac{7}{12}$ 16. 32 L

Self-check

Find the sums.

1. $\frac{3}{8}$
$+\frac{5}{6}$

2. $\frac{2}{3}$
$+\frac{3}{4}$

3. $7\frac{1}{8}$
$+6\frac{9}{10}$

4. $\frac{1}{3}$
$\frac{1}{2}$
$+\frac{3}{4}$

5. $3\frac{1}{8}$
$4\frac{1}{3}$
$+7\frac{1}{4}$

Find the differences.

6. $\frac{7}{8}$
$-\frac{1}{2}$

7. $\frac{5}{6}$
$-\frac{1}{3}$

8. $6\frac{1}{2}$
$-2\frac{1}{8}$

9. $6\frac{1}{5}$
$-2\frac{3}{4}$

10. $52\frac{3}{8}$
$-17\frac{5}{6}$

Find the products and quotients.

11. $\frac{1}{2} \cdot \frac{2}{3} = x$

12. $2\frac{1}{2} \cdot 3\frac{1}{3} = m$

13. $\frac{7}{8} \div \frac{3}{4} = n$

14. $2\frac{1}{2} \div 1\frac{1}{8} = g$

15. If $3\frac{1}{3}$ cans of white paint are mixed with $1\frac{3}{4}$ cans of red paint, how many more cans of white are used?

16. A $2\frac{1}{2}$ hour flight used 80 liters of gasoline. How many liters of gasoline per hour did the plane use?

Answers for Self-check—page 155

Test

Find the sums.

1. $\frac{5}{6}$
$+\frac{3}{4}$

2. $\frac{3}{5}$
$+\frac{2}{3}$

3. $14\frac{3}{4}$
$+19\frac{1}{3}$

4. $\frac{1}{4}$
$\frac{2}{3}$
$+\frac{3}{8}$

5. $6\frac{1}{2}$
$5\frac{2}{3}$
$+2\frac{1}{4}$

Find the differences.

6. $\frac{5}{8}$
$-\frac{1}{4}$

7. $\frac{7}{10}$
$-\frac{1}{2}$

8. $7\frac{3}{4}$
$-2\frac{1}{2}$

9. $7\frac{1}{4}$
$-4\frac{3}{5}$

10. $71\frac{2}{5}$
$-28\frac{3}{4}$

Find the products and quotients.

11. $\frac{4}{5} \cdot \frac{7}{8} = b$

12. $3\frac{1}{4} \cdot 6\frac{1}{2} = j$

13. $\frac{5}{6} \div \frac{2}{3} = n$

14. $2\frac{1}{8} \div 1\frac{2}{3} = h$

15. If $3\frac{2}{3}$ cans of blue paint are mixed with $4\frac{1}{2}$ cans of yellow paint, how many cans of green paint are made?

16. A small plane uses 28 liters of gasoline per hour. How many liters would it use for a $1\frac{3}{4}$ hour flight?

Math lab

The Brussels Sprouts Game

A British mathematician, J. H. Conway, invented this game for two players.

Rules:

1. Mark two or more large plus signs on a piece of paper.

2. A move consists of connecting two free ends of the plus signs with a curve and marking a crossbar along a point of the curve.

3. No end of a plus sign may be used twice and no curve can cross itself or any other previously drawn curve.

4. Players take turns connecting the plus signs or crossbars.

5. The game ends when it is not possible to draw another connecting curve. The player making the last move is the winner.

A sample game starting with two plus signs is shown below.

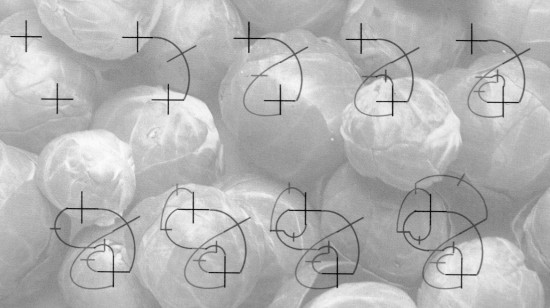

Can you decide who will win a game, the first player or the second player?

Ratio and Proportion

The **ratio** of lemonade to ginger ale in the lemon punch is 9 to 4. The ratio 9 to 4 is written as 9:4 or $\frac{9}{4}$.

1. Write the ratio of ginger ale to crushed strawberries.

2. In the Hawaiian punch, what is the ratio of pineapple juice to orange juice?

3. Write the ratio of orange juice to lemon-lime soda.

4. Write the ratio of juice to soda.

5. In the grape punch, what is the ratio of grape juice to grapefruit juice?

6. Write the ratio of grape juice to grape soda.

7. Write the ratio of juice to soda.

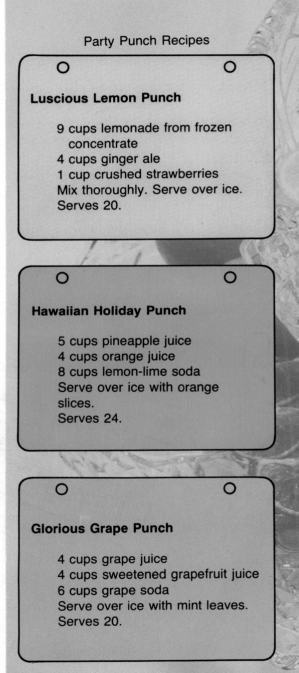

Party Punch Recipes

Luscious Lemon Punch

9 cups lemonade from frozen concentrate
4 cups ginger ale
1 cup crushed strawberries
Mix thoroughly. Serve over ice.
Serves 20.

Hawaiian Holiday Punch

5 cups pineapple juice
4 cups orange juice
8 cups lemon-lime soda
Serve over ice with orange slices.
Serves 24.

Glorious Grape Punch

4 cups grape juice
4 cups sweetened grapefruit juice
6 cups grape soda
Serve over ice with mint leaves.
Serves 20.

The same ratios of juices to soda could be used to make larger amounts of punch.

	For 20 people	For 40 people	For 60 people
lemonade ⟶	$\dfrac{9}{4}$	$\dfrac{18}{8}$	$\dfrac{27}{12}$ ...
ginger ale ⟶			

All of these ratios would give the same mixture. They are **equal ratios**.

$$\frac{9}{4} = \frac{18}{8} = \frac{27}{12} = \frac{36}{16} = \cdots$$

Two ratios are equal if, and only if, the cross products are equal.

$$4 \cdot 27 \quad 9 \cdot 12$$
$$108 \qquad 108$$

A statement that two ratios are equal is called a **proportion**.

We write: $\frac{9}{4} = \frac{27}{12}$ We read: 9 is to 4 as 27 is to 12.

Give 4 equal ratios for each of the following.
Luscious Lemon Punch

1. $\dfrac{\text{ginger ale}}{\text{crushed strawberries}}$

2. $\dfrac{\text{ginger ale}}{\text{lemonade}}$

3. $\dfrac{\text{lemonade}}{\text{crushed strawberries}}$

Hawaiian Holiday Punch

4. $\dfrac{\text{pineapple juice}}{\text{orange juice}}$

5. $\dfrac{\text{orange juice}}{\text{pineapple juice}}$

6. $\dfrac{\text{orange juice}}{\text{lemon-lime soda}}$

Glorious Grape Punch

7. $\dfrac{\text{grape juice}}{\text{grapefruit juice}}$

8. $\dfrac{\text{grape juice}}{\text{grape soda}}$

9. $\dfrac{\text{grape soda}}{\text{grapefruit juice}}$

Find the cross products. Write a proportion for the ratios that are equal.

10. $\dfrac{2}{3}, \dfrac{12}{15}$

11. $\dfrac{12}{16}, \dfrac{21}{28}$

12. $\dfrac{12}{30}, \dfrac{15}{40}$

13. $\dfrac{10}{16}, \dfrac{25}{40}$

14. $\dfrac{7}{21}, \dfrac{3}{9}$

15. $\dfrac{45}{54}, \dfrac{35}{40}$

16. $\dfrac{17}{34}, \dfrac{14}{28}$

17. $\dfrac{12}{16}, \dfrac{24}{32}$

Solving proportions

A pendulum 56 cm long will make about 2 complete swings every 3 seconds. At that rate, how many complete swings will the pendulum make in 1 minute, or 60 seconds? (In 1 complete swing the pendulum moves from A to B and back to A.)

56 cm

A   B

Finding the answer

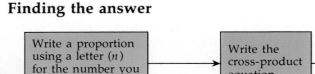

Write a proportion using a letter (n) for the number you want to find	Write the cross-product equation	Solve the equation

swings $\longrightarrow$ $\dfrac{2}{3} = \dfrac{n}{60}$ $\longleftarrow$ seconds

$3n = 120$

$n = 40$

The pendulum will make 40 complete swings in 1 minute.

Other examples

$\dfrac{2}{3} = \dfrac{24}{n}$

$2n = 72$

$n = 36$

$\dfrac{6}{8} = \dfrac{n}{60}$

$8n = 360$

$n = 45$

$\dfrac{2}{5} = \dfrac{n}{72}$

$5n = 144$

$n = 28\frac{4}{5}$ or 28.8

Solve each proportion.

1. $\dfrac{6}{10} = \dfrac{9}{n}$

2. $\dfrac{2}{5} = \dfrac{n}{70}$

3. $\dfrac{2}{3} = \dfrac{n}{39}$

4. $\dfrac{9}{15} = \dfrac{24}{n}$

5. $\dfrac{9}{12} = \dfrac{n}{68}$

6. $\dfrac{6}{8} = \dfrac{63}{n}$

7. $\dfrac{4}{5} = \dfrac{n}{27}$

8. $\dfrac{3}{8} = \dfrac{n}{72}$

9. $\dfrac{4}{10} = \dfrac{14}{n}$

10. $\dfrac{7}{8} = \dfrac{n}{60}$

11. $\dfrac{5}{6} = \dfrac{n}{72}$

12. $\dfrac{3}{5} = \dfrac{n}{95}$

The **period** for a pendulum is the time for 1 complete swing.

The period may be found by solving a proportion. Let n = the period.

swings $\longrightarrow$ $\dfrac{2}{3} = \dfrac{1}{n}$ $\longleftarrow$ swings
seconds $\longrightarrow$ $\phantom{\dfrac{2}{3}}$ $\longleftarrow$ seconds

$$2n = 3$$
$$n = 1.5$$

The period is 1.5 seconds.

Write and solve a proportion for each problem.

1. A certain pendulum completes 5 swings every 4 seconds. How many swings does it complete in a minute? What is its period?

2. If a pendulum completes 2 swings in 5 seconds, what is its period? How many swings does it complete in a minute? In an hour? In a day?

Find the period to the nearest hundredth of a second for each of the following.

3. $\dfrac{3 \text{ swings}}{4 \text{ seconds}}$

4. $\dfrac{6 \text{ swings}}{5 \text{ seconds}}$

5. $\dfrac{6 \text{ swings}}{2 \text{ seconds}}$

6. $\dfrac{7 \text{ swings}}{6 \text{ seconds}}$

7. $\dfrac{8 \text{ swings}}{5 \text{ seconds}}$

8. $\dfrac{4 \text{ swings}}{5 \text{ seconds}}$

☆ 9. A pendulum of 24.8 cm has a period of 1 second. A pendulum 4 times as long has a period of 2 seconds. A pendulum 9 times as long has a period of 3 seconds; 16 times as long, 4 seconds; and so on. Give the lengths of pendulums with periods of 2, 3, 4, and 5 seconds.

☆ 10. Make a pendulum. Count the swings your pendulum makes for different numbers of seconds. Check to see if the ratios of swings to seconds are all equal to each other.

More practice, page 387, Set A

Unit pricing

Which market has the lowest price for grapefruit?

Safebuy Markets	Value Markets
white fancy grapefruit	white fancy grapefruit
6 for 99¢	4 for 59¢

To compare the prices, find the cost for one grapefruit at each store.

Let x = cost of one grapefruit at Safebuy Market

Total cost $\longrightarrow$ $\dfrac{99¢}{6} = \dfrac{x}{1}$
Number $\longrightarrow$

$$x = \frac{99¢}{6} = 16.5¢$$

Let y = cost of one grapefruit at Value Market

Total cost $\longrightarrow$ $\dfrac{59¢}{4} = \dfrac{y}{1}$
Number $\longrightarrow$

$$y = \frac{59¢}{4} = 14.75¢$$

The grapefruit costs less at Value Markets.

The cost of one item or unit is called the unit price.

Some stores show unit prices of items they sell.

$$\text{Unit price} = \frac{\text{total cost of units}}{\text{number of units}}$$

Find the unit price.

1. 3 for 69¢

2. 12 for 84¢

3. 8 for 96¢

4. 10 for $1.29

5. 12 for $4.68

6. 24 for $23.28

7. 5 for 98¢

8. 16 for $3.92

9. 6 for 57¢

Find the unit price for each. Then tell which is lower in price.

1. Fresh strawberries:
   4 baskets for $1.00
      or
   3 baskets for 69¢

2. Avocados:
   3 for 99¢
      or
   2 for 69¢

3. Detergent:
   1.4 kg for $1.19
      or
   4.2 kg for $3.59

4. Cheese slices:
   16 slices for $1.37
      or
   12 slices for $1.09

5. Pet food:
   4.5 kg for $1.79
      or
   2.2 kg for 99¢

6. Fresh lemons:
   6 for 49¢
      or
   2 for 15¢

7. Cantaloupes:
   3 for 81¢
      or
   2 for 49¢

8. Canned cat food:
   5 cans for $1.00
      or
   3 cans for 57¢

9. Fresh apples:
   3 kg for $1.29
      or
   4 kg for $1.88

10. Sausage:
    0.45 kg for $1.39
       or
    0.34 kg for $1.19

A roll of cellophane tape 2.03 m long costs 49¢.
Another roll of tape which has the same width
is 1.14 m long and costs 37¢. Find the unit
price of each kind of tape. Which costs less
per unit?

Career problems using proportions

In a sample of 25 fish a naturalist found that 3 of the fish were undersized. About how many undersized fish would be found in a sample of 200 fish?

Write and solve a proportion to find the answer.

Let x be the number of undersized fish in a sample of 200.

$$\frac{\text{number of undersized fish} \longrightarrow}{\text{number in sample} \longrightarrow} \frac{3}{25} = \frac{x}{200}$$

$$25x = 600$$

$$x = 24$$

There would be about 24 undersized fish in a sample of 200.

Write and solve a proportion for each problem.

1. Carpenter:
    A carpenter found that there are about 15 cm of scrap wood for each of 2 boards needed in a project. How many centimeters of scrap wood are there if 26 boards are used for the project?

2. Shipping clerk:
    For every 2 mixers ordered, there were 3 toasters ordered. If orders were filled for 42 mixers, how many were filled for toasters?

3. Photographer:

   Some photographers found that they actually used only about 3 of every 8 pictures they took. About how many would they use out of 120 shots?

4. Restaurant manager:

   At a certain restaurant about 5 of every 12 people order dessert. Out of 180 people, how many desserts would be ordered?

5. Pollster:

   It was found that 56 of every 100 people favored the bond issue. There were 1250 people surveyed. How many of the 1250 favored the bond issue?

6. Plumber:

   The ratio of the length of pipe cut off to the length remaining is 5 to 8. If 115 cm of pipe is cut off, how much remains?

7. Musician:

   The band leader pays a drummer $50 for each 4-hour job. One month the drummer worked 68 hours. How much did the drummer make?

8. Quality-control supervisor:
   A quality-control supervisor found that 2 parts of every 135 machines were defective. How many new parts are needed to repair 675 machines?

☆ 9. Farmer:

   The ratio of land planted in soybeans to land planted in rice is 2 to 5. If 294 hectares are planted, how much land is in soybeans and how much land is in rice?

Scale drawings and ratios

N

W ✦ E

S

The scale for a scale drawing gives the ratio of the dimensions of the drawing to the dimensions of the actual object.

6.1 cm

Yellowstone
National Park

WYOMING

4.6 cm   4.6 cm

What is the north-south distance across Wyoming?

Let x = north-south distance in km.

$$\begin{array}{c} \text{cm} \longrightarrow \\ \text{km} \longrightarrow \end{array} \dfrac{1}{95} = \dfrac{4.6}{x}$$

$x = 4.6 \cdot 95$

$x = 437$ km

6.2 cm

Scale: 1 cm = 95 km

The north-south distance
is about 437 km.

Write and solve a proportion for each problem.

1. Find the distance from east to west along the southern border of Wyoming.

2. Find the east-west distance along the northern border of Wyoming.

3. The north-south distance across Yellowstone National Park in Wyoming is about 100 km. How many centimeters is this distance on the map?

4. The east-west distance across Yellowstone Park along its southern border is about 85 km. How many centimeters is this distance on the map?

A **draftsman** makes **mechanical drawings** to scale. The drawing below shows a house plan. Plans such as this one, with much more detail, are used to build the house.

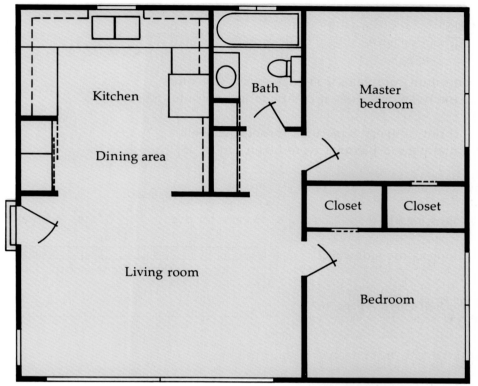

Scale 1 cm = 1.2 m

Measure to the nearest tenth of a centimeter.

1. Find the outside length of the house.

2. Find the outside width of the house.

3. Find the length of the living room.

4. Find the width of the living room.

5. Find the dimensions of the smaller bedroom (include the closet).

6. Give the dimensions of the kitchen and dining area.

☆ 7. What is the area of the kitchen and dining area?

Answers for Self-check 1. $n = 20$ 2. $n = 20$ 3. $n = 14$ 4. $n = 45$ 5. 140 6. 18 7. 12.5¢
8. $29\frac{2}{3}$¢ or $29.\overline{6}$¢ 9. 16.5¢ 10. 28 m

Self-check

Solve each proportion.

1. $\dfrac{3}{4} = \dfrac{15}{n}$ 2. $\dfrac{5}{8} = \dfrac{n}{32}$ 3. $\dfrac{6}{9} = \dfrac{n}{21}$ 4. $\dfrac{6}{10} = \dfrac{27}{n}$

5. A pendulum completes 7 swings every 3 seconds.
   How many swings does it complete in a minute (60 seconds)?

6. Only 3 out of every 8 pictures turned out well.
   How many good pictures were taken out of 48?

Find the unit price.

7. 8 oranges for $1.00   8. 3 cans for 89¢   9. 6 limes for 99¢

8 cm

10. How long is the sidewalk?

Scale: 2 cm = 7 m

Answers for Self-check—page 167

Test

Solve the proportions.

1. $\dfrac{2}{3} = \dfrac{n}{21}$ 2. $\dfrac{3}{8} = \dfrac{24}{n}$ 3. $\dfrac{9}{12} = \dfrac{30}{n}$ 4. $\dfrac{4}{10} = \dfrac{n}{35}$

5. A pendulum completes 5 swings every 4 seconds.
   How many swings does it complete in a minute (60 seconds)?

6. An average of 3 bicycles were manufactured every 20 minutes.
   How many were manufactured each hour?

Find the unit price.

7. 3 kg for $2.07   8. 5 cans for $1.00   9. 1.8ℓ for 90¢

9 cm

10. How long is the board?

Scale: 3 cm = 2 m

Math lab

Heights of Bounces

When a hard rubber ball was dropped 100 cm onto a hard surface, it bounced 0.90 of the height from which it was dropped.

A golf ball bounced 0.67 of its original height.

A tennis ball bounced 0.63 of its original height.

Assuming these numbers are true for each bounce, complete the table, rounding the results to the nearest centimeter.

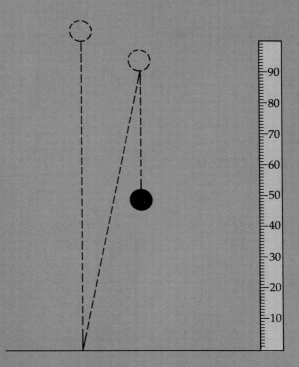

	100 cm Drop			300 cm Drop		
	First bounce	Second bounce	Third bounce	First bounce	Second bounce	Third bounce
Hard rubber ball	90 cm	81 cm	73 cm	270 cm	243 cm	▓▓
Golf ball	67 cm	45 cm	▓▓	201 cm	135 cm	▓▓
Tennis ball	63 cm	▓▓	▓▓	189 cm	▓▓	▓▓

Drop several different kinds of balls from the same height. Note the heights to which they bounce. Record your results in a table.

Kind of ball	Original height	First bounce	Second bounce
Basketball	▓▓	▓▓	▓▓
Baseball	▓▓	▓▓	▓▓
Soccerball	▓▓	▓▓	▓▓
?	▓▓	▓▓	▓▓
?	▓▓	▓▓	▓▓

Congruent and Similar Triangles

In each picture below the motion or combination of motions given will make △ABC fit exactly on the other triangle.

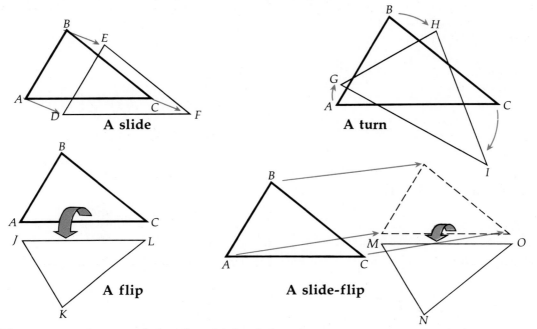

A slide

A turn

A flip

A slide-flip

Use tracing paper and decide which of the above motions are needed to make a tracing of △ABC fit exactly on △DEF.

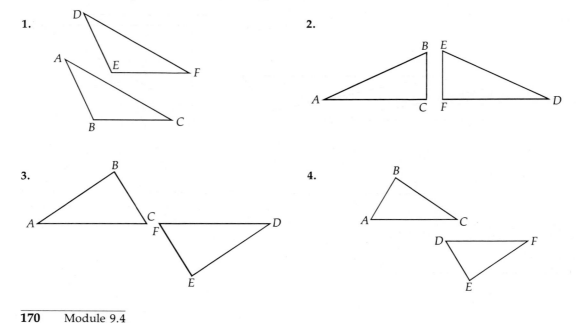

1.

2.

3.

4.

Two triangles are **congruent** if they can be made to fit exactly on each other by a slide, turn, flip, or slide-flip. The same number of slash marks shows matching sides. The same number of arcs on angles shows matching angles. Whenever two triangles are congruent,

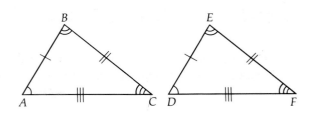

A matching sides of the triangles are congruent and

$$\overline{AB} \cong \overline{DE}$$
$$\overline{AC} \cong \overline{DF}$$
$$\overline{BC} \cong \overline{EF}$$

$$\angle A \cong \angle D$$
$$\angle B \cong \angle E$$
$$\angle C \cong \angle F$$

B matching angles of the triangles are congruent.

We write: $\triangle ABC \cong \triangle DEF$.

List the pairs of congruent matching sides and angles for each pair of congruent triangles. Use $\cong$ to show congruence.

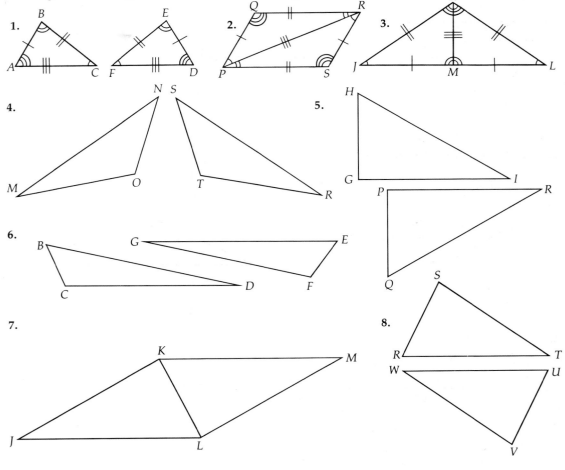

⊗ Side-side-side (SSS) congruence

The construction below shows how to construct a pair of congruent triangles by constructing three congruent sides.

Step 1

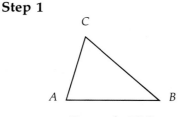

Draw △ABC.

Step 2

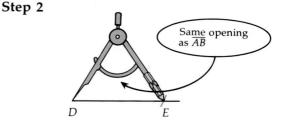

Same opening as $\overline{AB}$

Step 3

Same opening as $\overline{AC}$

Step 4

Same opening as $\overline{BC}$

Step 5

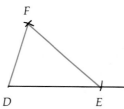

The three sides of △DEF are congruent to the three sides of △ABC. The matching angles will also be congruent.
△DEF ≅ △ABC

This suggests the **side-side-side (SSS) theorem**.

> If the three sides of one triangle are congruent to the three matching sides of another triangle, then the two triangles are congruent.

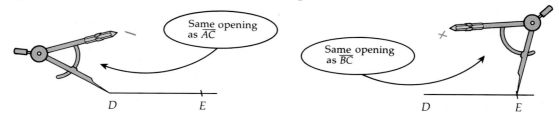

1. Use the above method to construct △XYZ ≅ △PQR.

2. List the congruent sides and angles.

Write a statement of congruence for the pairs of triangles that are congruent.

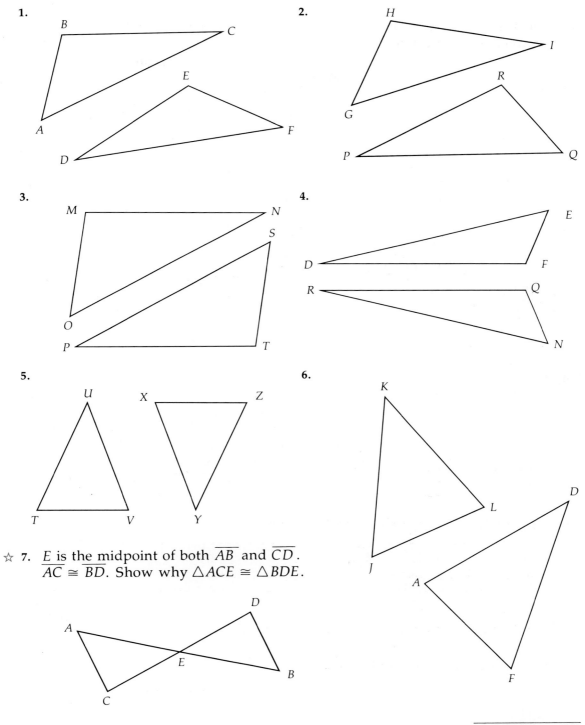

1.

2.

3.

4.

5.

6.

☆ 7. E is the midpoint of both $\overline{AB}$ and $\overline{CD}$.
$\overline{AC} \cong \overline{BD}$. Show why $\triangle ACE \cong \triangle BDE$.

✪ Side-angle-side (SAS) congruence

The construction below shows how to construct a pair
of congruent triangles by making two sides and the
included angle of each triangle congruent.

Step 1

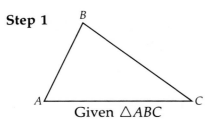

Given △ABC

Step 2

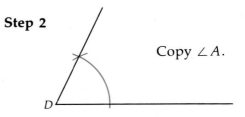

Copy ∠A.

Step 3

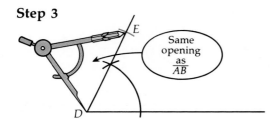

Same opening as $\overline{AB}$

Step 4

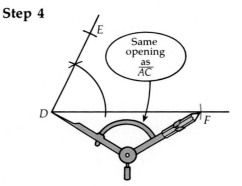

Same opening as $\overline{AC}$

Step 5

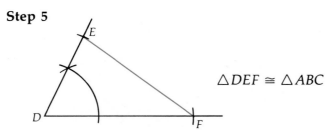

△DEF ≅ △ABC

This suggests the **side-angle-side (SAS) theorem**.

> If two sides and the included angle of one triangle are
> congruent to two matching sides and the included angle
> of another triangle, the two triangles are congruent.

1. Use the above method to construct △XYZ ≅ △JKL.

2. List the congruent sides and angles.

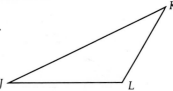

Write a statement of congruence for the pairs of triangles that are congruent.

1.

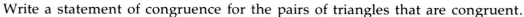

2.

3.

4.

5.

☆ **6.**

$$\overline{AB} \cong \overline{DE}$$
$$\overline{AC} \cong \overline{DF}$$
$$\angle B \cong \angle E$$

Here two sides and an angle
of each triangle are congruent.
Does the SAS Theorem show that
the two triangles are congruent?

✪ Angle-side-angle (ASA) congruence

The construction below shows how to construct a pair of congruent triangles by making two angles and a common side congruent.

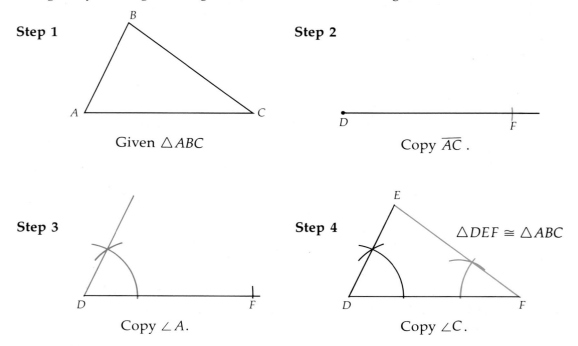

Step 1

Given △ABC

Step 2

Copy $\overline{AC}$.

Step 3

Copy ∠A.

Step 4

Copy ∠C.

△DEF ≅ △ABC

This suggests the **angle-side-angle (ASA) theorem**.

> If two angles and their common side of one triangle are congruent to two matching angles and common side of a second triangle, the two triangles are congruent.

1. Use the above method to construct △XYZ ≅ △MNO.

2. List the congruent sides and angles.

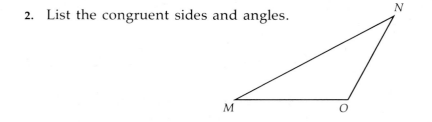

Write a statement of congruence for the pairs of triangles that are congruent.

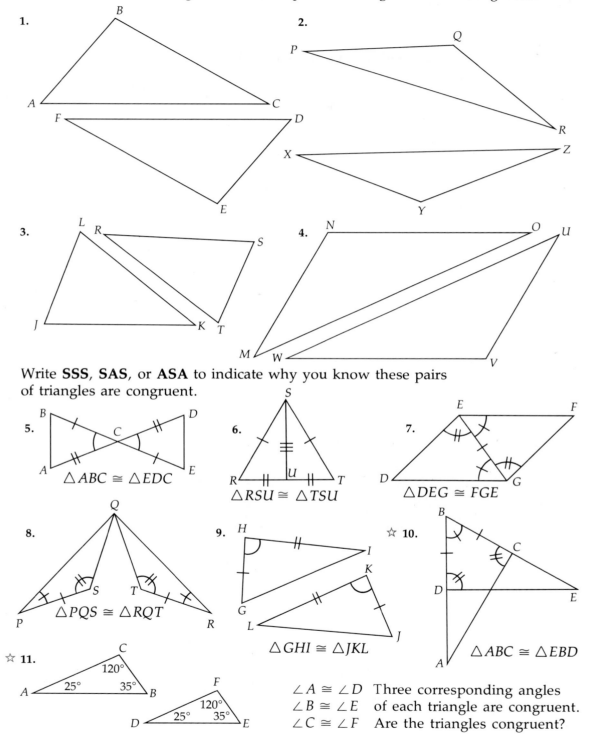

1.

2.

3.

4.

Write **SSS**, **SAS**, or **ASA** to indicate why you know these pairs
of triangles are congruent.

5.
△ABC ≅ △EDC

6.
△RSU ≅ △TSU

7.
△DEG ≅ FGE

8.
△PQS ≅ △RQT

9.
△GHI ≅ △JKL

☆ **10.**
△ABC ≅ △EBD

☆ **11.**

∠A ≅ ∠D   Three corresponding angles
∠B ≅ ∠E   of each triangle are congruent.
∠C ≅ ∠F   Are the triangles congruent?

Similar triangles

$\triangle ABC$ has the same shape but not the same size as $\triangle DEF$.

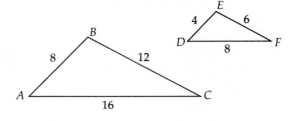

The matching angles are congruent. $\angle A \cong \angle D$, $\angle B \cong \angle E$, and $\angle C \cong \angle F$

The ratios of lengths of corresponding sides are equal. $\frac{4}{8} = \frac{6}{12} = \frac{8}{16}$

Two triangles are **similar** whenever

A matching angles are congruent or

B the ratios of lengths of corresponding sides are equal.

$\triangle DEF$ is similar to $\triangle ABC$. We write: $\triangle DEF \sim \triangle ABC$.

Write a statement of similarity to show which pairs of triangles are similar. Write the ratios of the lengths of the corresponding sides.

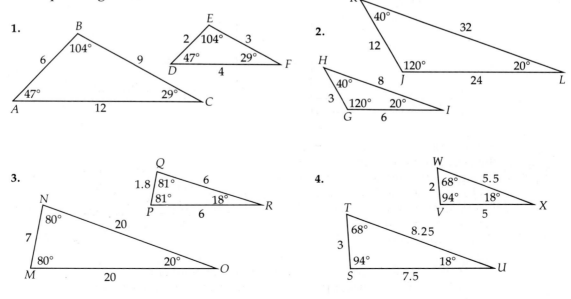

Each pair of triangles below are similar.
Find the missing side length or angle measure.

Example: Since the ratios of matching sides are equal when triangles are similar,

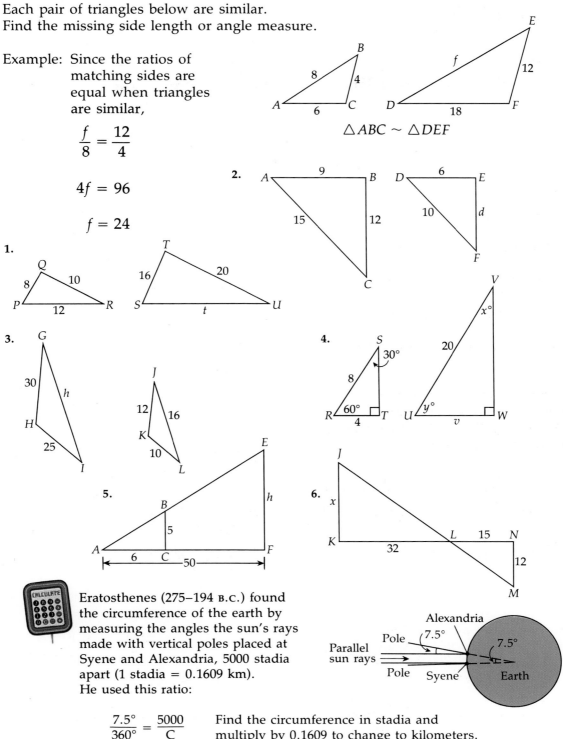

$$\frac{f}{8} = \frac{12}{4}$$

$$4f = 96$$

$$f = 24$$

$\triangle ABC \sim \triangle DEF$

1.

2.

3.

4.

5.

6.

Eratosthenes (275–194 B.C.) found the circumference of the earth by measuring the angles the sun's rays made with vertical poles placed at Syene and Alexandria, 5000 stadia apart (1 stadia = 0.1609 km). He used this ratio:

$$\frac{7.5°}{360°} = \frac{5000}{C}$$

Find the circumference in stadia and multiply by 0.1609 to change to kilometers.

Similar right triangles

A water tower casts a shadow
of 35 m at the same time that
a person 1.75 m tall casts a shadow
of 2 m. The diagram shows how
two similar triangles are formed.
What is the height (h) of the tower?

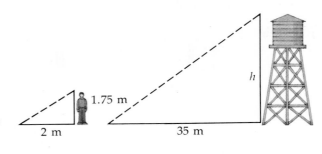

1.75 m

h

2 m   35 m

Finding the answer

The triangles are similar. We write a proportion
using the lengths of the corresponding sides.

$$\frac{h}{1.75} = \frac{35}{2}$$

$$2h = 1.75 \cdot 35$$

$$2h = 61.25$$

$$h = 30.625$$

The height of the tower is about 31 m.

Use similar triangles to find these heights.

1. A Ferris wheel casts a shadow of 23 m
    at the same time that a 3 m basketball
    goal casts a shadow of 4.5 m. What is
    the height of the Ferris wheel to the
    nearest meter?

2. A person 1.9 m tall looks into a mirror
    lying on the ground and sees the top of a
    tree. The mirror is 2.4 m from the person
    and 20.0 m from the tree. What is the
    height of the tree to the nearest meter?

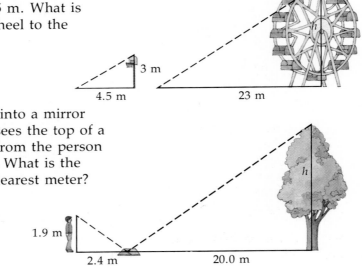

3 m

4.5 m   23 m

1.9 m

2.4 m   20.0 m

Find corresponding sides of similar triangles. Write and solve a proportion to answer each question.

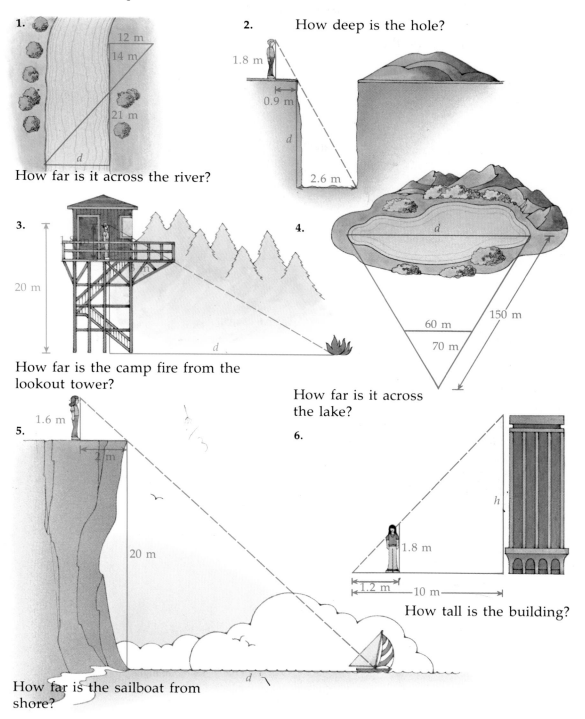

1.

12 m

14 m

21 m

d

How far is it across the river?

2. How deep is the hole?

1.8 m

0.9 m

d

2.6 m

3.

20 m

d

How far is the camp fire from the lookout tower?

4.

d

60 m

70 m

150 m

How far is it across the lake?

5.

1.6 m

2 m

20 m

d

How far is the sailboat from shore?

6.

h

1.8 m

1.2 m

10 m

How tall is the building?

✪ The tangent ratio

In right triangle *ABC*, ∠*C* is a right angle. Side *a* is the side opposite ∠*A* and side *b* is the side adjacent to∠ *A*.

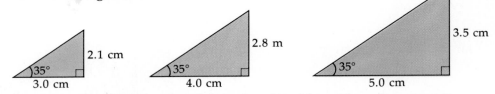

The following three triangles are similar triangles. Each has an acute angle of 35°.

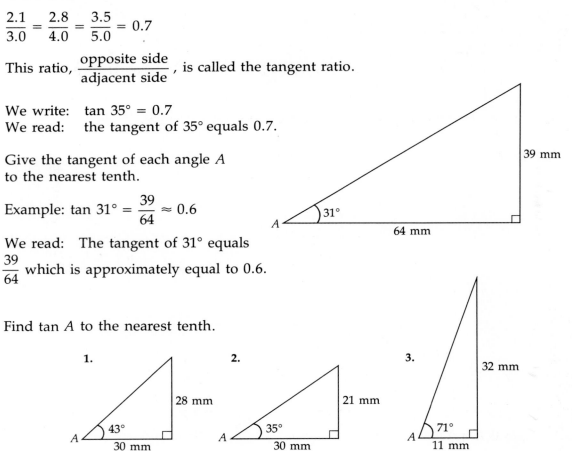

In each of these triangles the ratio of the opposite side to the adjacent side is the same.

$$\frac{2.1}{3.0} = \frac{2.8}{4.0} = \frac{3.5}{5.0} = 0.7$$

This ratio, $\dfrac{\text{opposite side}}{\text{adjacent side}}$, is called the tangent ratio.

We write: tan 35° = 0.7
We read: the tangent of 35° equals 0.7.

Give the tangent of each angle *A* to the nearest tenth.

Example: $\tan 31° = \dfrac{39}{64} \approx 0.6$

We read: The tangent of 31° equals $\dfrac{39}{64}$ which is approximately equal to 0.6

Find tan *A* to the nearest tenth.

1.   28 mm   43°   30 mm

2.   21 mm   35°   30 mm

3.   32 mm   71°   11 mm

Find length *a* to the nearest tenth of a centimeter for each triangle.

Example:

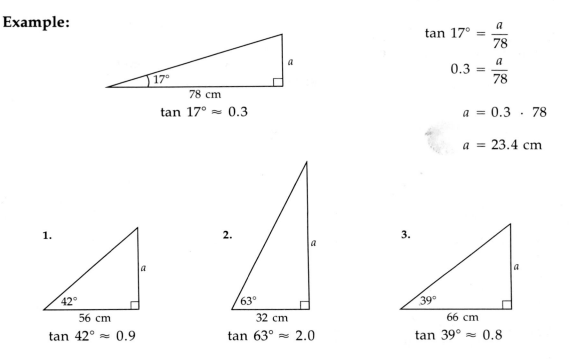

$$\tan 17° = \frac{a}{78}$$

$$0.3 = \frac{a}{78}$$

$$a = 0.3 \cdot 78$$

$$a = 23.4 \text{ cm}$$

tan 17° ≈ 0.3

1.

42°

56 cm

a

tan 42° ≈ 0.9

2.

63°

32 cm

a

tan 63° ≈ 2.0

3.

39°

66 cm

a

tan 39° ≈ 0.8

Find length *b* to the nearest tenth of a meter for each triangle.

Example:

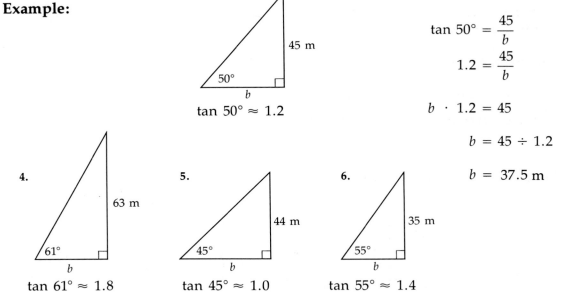

45 m

50°

b

tan 50° ≈ 1.2

$$\tan 50° = \frac{45}{b}$$

$$1.2 = \frac{45}{b}$$

$$b \cdot 1.2 = 45$$

$$b = 45 \div 1.2$$

$$b = 37.5 \text{ m}$$

4.

63 m

61°

b

tan 61° ≈ 1.8

5.

44 m

45°

b

tan 45° ≈ 1.0

6.

35 m

55°

b

tan 55° ≈ 1.4

✪ Solving problems using the tangent ratio

The table gives the tangent ratios rounded to the nearest thousandth.

Angle	Tan
0°	0.000
1°	0.017
2°	0.035
3°	0.052
4°	0.070
5°	0.087
6°	0.105
7°	0.123
8°	0.141
9°	0.158
10°	0.176
11°	0.194
12°	0.213
13°	0.231
14°	0.249
15°	0.268
16°	0.287
17°	0.306
18°	0.325
19°	0.344
20°	0.364
21°	0.384
22°	0.404
23°	0.424
24°	0.445
25°	0.466
26°	0.488
27°	0.510
28°	0.532
29°	0.554
30°	0.577

Angle	Tan
31°	0.601
32°	0.625
33°	0.649
34°	0.675
35°	0.700
36°	0.727
37°	0.754
38°	0.781
39°	0.810
40°	0.839
41°	0.869
42°	0.900
43°	0.933
44°	0.966
45°	1.000
46°	1.036
47°	1.072
48°	1.111
49°	1.150
50°	1.192
51°	1.235
52°	1.280
53°	1.327
54°	1.376
55°	1.428
56°	1.483
57°	1.540
58°	1.600
59°	1.664
60°	1.732

Angle	Tan
61°	1.804
62°	1.881
63°	1.963
64°	2.050
65°	2.145
66°	2.246
67°	2.356
68°	2.475
69°	2.605
70°	2.748
71°	2.904
72°	3.078
73°	3.271
74°	3.487
75°	3.732
76°	4.011
77°	4.332
78°	4.705
79°	5.145
80°	5.671
81°	6.314
82°	7.115
83°	8.144
84°	9.514
85°	11.430
86°	14.301
87°	19.081
88°	28.636
89°	57.290
90°	———

Use the table to find each tangent ratio.

1. $\tan 28°$ 2. $\tan 56°$ 3. $\tan 45°$ 4. $\tan 15°$

5. $\tan 75°$ 6. $\tan 32°$ 7. $\tan 60°$ 8. $\tan 89°$

Use the table to find the degree measure for angle A.

9. $\tan A \approx 1.327$ 10. $\tan A \approx 8.144$ 11. $\tan A \approx 2.356$ 12. $\tan A \approx 19.081$

13. $\tan A \approx 0.488$ 14. $\tan A \approx 0.839$ 15. $\tan A \approx 0.087$ 16. $\tan A \approx 1.150$

Use the tangent ratio from the table to find the height of each object to the nearest hundredth.

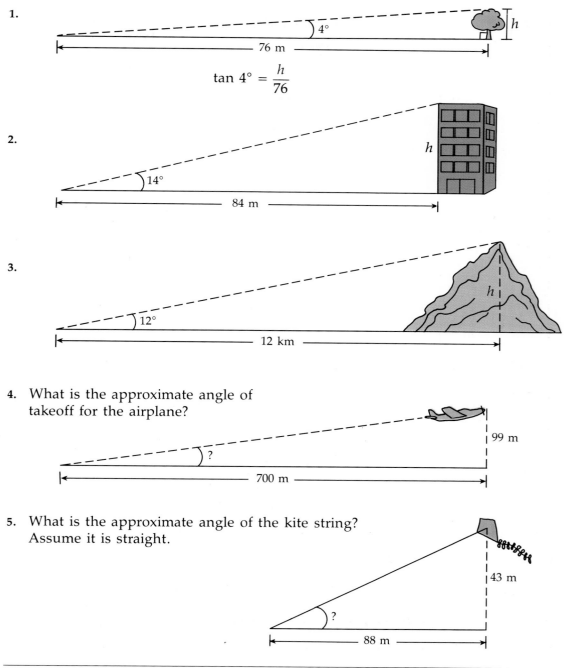

1.

$4°$

76 m

$$\tan 4° = \frac{h}{76}$$

2.

$14°$

84 m

3.

$12°$

12 km

4. What is the approximate angle of takeoff for the airplane?

99 m

?

700 m

5. What is the approximate angle of the kite string? Assume it is straight.

43 m

?

88 m

Answers for Self-check   3. ASA   4. SAS   5. 56 m

Self-check

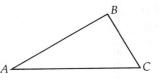

☆ 1. Use the SSS, ASA, and SAS methods to construct three triangles congruent to △ABC.

2. Construct a triangle similar to △ABC, with sides twice as long.

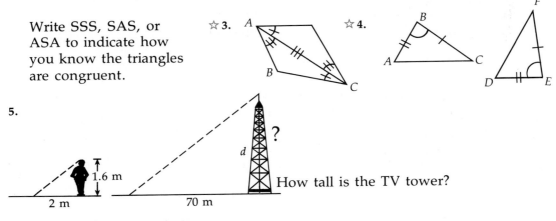

Write SSS, SAS, or ASA to indicate how you know the triangles are congruent.

☆ 3.

☆ 4.

5.

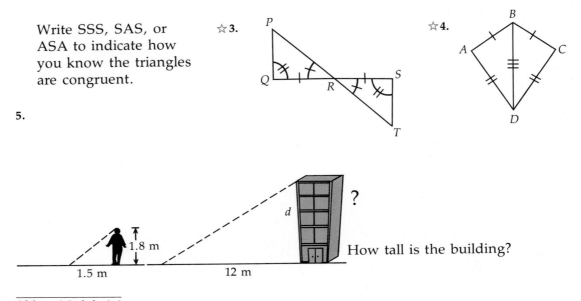

How tall is the TV tower?

Answers for Self-check—page 185

Test

☆ 1. Use the SSS, ASA, and SAS methods to construct three triangles congruent to △PQR.

2. Construct a triangle similar to △PQR, with sides 3 times as long.

Write SSS, SAS, or ASA to indicate how you know the triangles are congruent.

☆ 3.

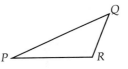

☆ 4.

5.

How tall is the building?

Mirror Measurements

Use this method to find the height of a pole, building, tower, or other object near your school. Estimate the height first.

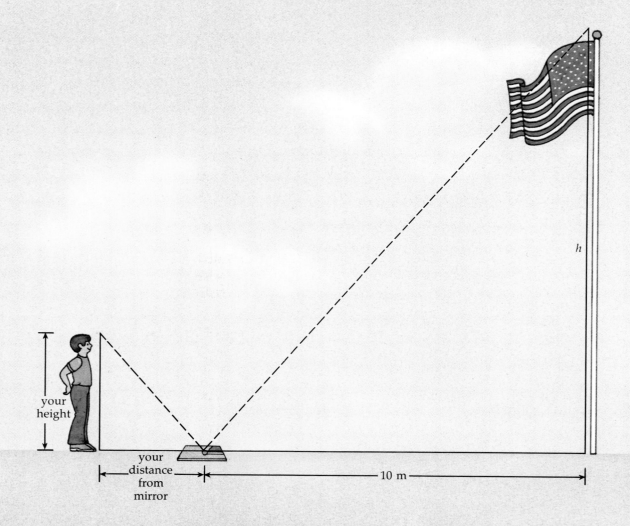

Place a mirror a convenient distance, such as 10 m, from the base of the object. Look in the mirror and move so that you can see the top of the object in the center of the mirror. Measure your height and your distance from the center of the mirror. Solve a proportion to find the height of the object.

Unit 9 Review

Write a decimal for each fraction.

1. $\frac{3}{5}$ 2. $\frac{9}{10}$ 3. $\frac{1}{8}$ 4. $\frac{27}{100}$ 5. $\frac{11}{50}$

Find the lowest-terms fraction for each fraction.

6. $\frac{10}{15}$ 7. $\frac{27}{36}$ 8. $\frac{28}{32}$ 9. $\frac{24}{48}$ 10. $\frac{3}{18}$

Write a mixed numeral for each fraction.

11. $\frac{8}{3}$ 12. $\frac{19}{5}$ 13. $\frac{33}{4}$ 14. $\frac{17}{2}$ 15. $\frac{67}{8}$

Write an improper fraction for each mixed numeral.

16. $3\frac{1}{2}$ 17. $6\frac{1}{4}$ 18. $2\frac{2}{3}$ 19. $4\frac{3}{8}$ 20. $10\frac{2}{3}$

Give the correct symbol, $>$ or $<$, for each ●.

21. $\frac{1}{2}$ ● $\frac{2}{3}$ 22. $\frac{4}{5}$ ● $\frac{3}{4}$ 23. $\frac{1}{6}$ ● $\frac{1}{10}$ 24. $\frac{2}{5}$ ● $\frac{5}{8}$

Add or subtract.

25. $\begin{array}{r} \frac{7}{8} \\ + \frac{1}{4} \\ \hline \end{array}$ 26. $\begin{array}{r} \frac{9}{10} \\ - \frac{1}{2} \\ \hline \end{array}$ 27. $\begin{array}{r} 25\frac{3}{4} \\ + 37\frac{1}{2} \\ \hline \end{array}$ 28. $\begin{array}{r} 36\frac{1}{3} \\ - 18\frac{2}{3} \\ \hline \end{array}$ 29. $\begin{array}{r} 75\frac{5}{8} \\ + 19\frac{3}{4} \\ \hline \end{array}$

Multiply or divide.

30. $\frac{2}{3} \cdot \frac{4}{5}$ 31. $2\frac{1}{2} \cdot \frac{1}{5}$ 32. $3\frac{1}{4} \cdot 5\frac{1}{2}$ 33. $\frac{7}{8} \div \frac{1}{2}$ 34. $4\frac{1}{3} \div 1\frac{1}{2}$

Solve each proportion.

35. $\frac{3}{5} = \frac{n}{20}$ 36. $\frac{2}{3} = \frac{10}{n}$ 37. $\frac{5}{6} = \frac{n}{24}$ 38. $\frac{16}{20} = \frac{4}{n}$

39. On a map a distance of 2 cm represented 50 km. How many kilometers would 5 cm represent?

40. Find the unit price of an orange if 12 oranges cost 99¢.

Percent Concepts
Types of Percent Problems
Problem Solving—Using Your Skills
Measurement Formulas

Percent Concepts

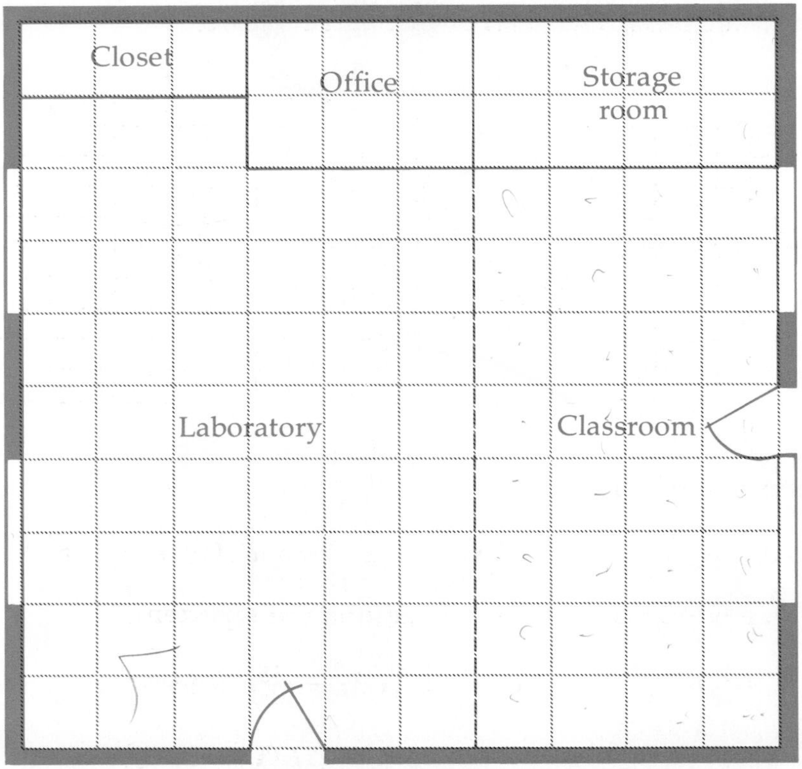

Floor Plan of Science Area

The floor plan shows that the storage room covers $\frac{8}{100}$ of the science area.

$\frac{8}{100}$ means **8 per hundred** or **8 percent**.

We write: 8%

The storage room covers 8% of the science area.

Write a percent that tells what part of the science area is covered by each section.

1. the office
2. the closet
3. the classroom
4. the laboratory
5. the storage room, office, and closet together
6. the classroom and laboratory together
7. the classroom, office, and closet
8. the laboratory and storage room

Percent is a special ratio that compares a number to 100.
12% means **12 out of 100** or $\frac{12}{100}$.

Give the percent for the shaded part of each large square.

1.   **2.**   **3.**

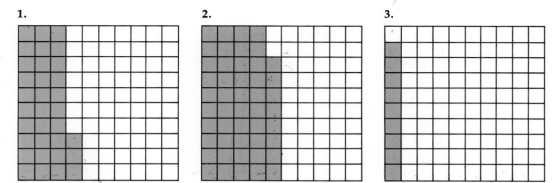

Write each ratio as a percent.

4. 7 out of 100   **5.** 19 out of 100   **6.** 26 out of 100   **7.** 98 out of 100

A number can be written as a fraction, a decimal, or a percent.

$\frac{23}{100} = 0.23 = 23\%$ $0.85 = \frac{85}{100} = 85\%$

$67\% = \frac{67}{100} = 0.67$ $\frac{100}{100} = 1.00 = 100\%$

Copy and complete the table.

	Fraction	Decimal	Percent
8.	$\frac{37}{100}$	▥	▥
9.	$\frac{59}{100}$	▥	▥
10.	▥	▥	82%
11.	▥	0.16	▥
12.	$\frac{1}{100}$	▥	▥
13.	▥	0.93	▥
14.	$\frac{79}{100}$	▥	▥
15.	▥	▥	11%
16.	▥	0.09	▥

Percents and decimals

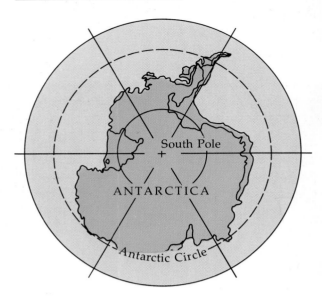

Antarctica has 9.3% of the land area of the world.

What is 9.3% written as a decimal?

$$9.3\% = \frac{9.3}{100} = 0.093$$

You can use a shortcut to write a decimal for a percent.

$$9.3\% = 0.093 \longleftarrow$$

> Move the decimal point two places to the left and drop the percent symbol

Other examples

$16\% = 0.16$	$12.5\% = 0.125$	$135\% = 1.35$

Write each percent as a decimal.

1. 8%	**2.** 25%	**3.** 66%	**4.** 17%	**5.** 83%
6. 6.8%	**7.** 3.1%	**8.** 185%	**9.** 67.4%	**10.** 81.1%
11. 4.2%	**12.** 213%	**13.** 1.5%	**14.** 16.6%	**15.** 15.8%
16. 87.5%	**17.** 99.9%	**18.** 150%	**19.** 2.7%	**20.** 325%

The ice and snow of Antarctica contain about 0.715 of the total fresh water in the world. What percent is 0.715?

$$0.715 = \frac{715}{1000} = \frac{715 \div 10}{1000 \div 10} = \frac{71.5}{100} = 71.5\%$$

You can use a shortcut to find the percent for a decimal.

$0.715 = 71.5\%$ ← Move the decimal point two places to the right and write the percent symbol

Other examples

$0.23 = 23\%$ $\qquad$ $1.25 = 125\%$

$0.087 = 8.7\%$ $\qquad$ $2.3 = 2.30 = 230\%$

Write each decimal as a percent.

1. 0.16	**2.** 0.07	**3.** 0.38	**4.** 0.67	**5.** 0.83
6. 0.625	**7.** 0.187	**8.** 0.095	**9.** 0.018	**10.** 0.776
11. 1.38	**12.** 2.6	**13.** 1.09	**14.** 3.75	**15.** 2.45
16. 0.166	**17.** 0.053	**18.** 0.081	**19.** 0.386	**20.** 1.3

More practice, page 387, Set B

Fractions and percents

The conical candle can be made with only $\frac{1}{3}$ as much wax as is needed for the cylindrical candle. The wax needed for the conical candle is what percent of the wax needed for the cylindrical candle?

Finding the answer

A fraction or ratio		Find a decimal or mixed decimal in hundredths		Write the percent for the decimal

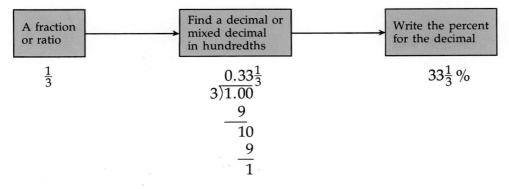

$$\frac{1}{3}$$

$$3\overline{)1.00}^{\ \ 0.33\frac{1}{3}}$$
$$\underline{9}$$
$$10$$
$$\underline{9}$$
$$1$$

$$33\frac{1}{3}\%$$

The percent for $\frac{1}{3}$ is $33\frac{1}{3}\%$. $\frac{1}{3} = 33\frac{1}{3}\%$

Other examples

$$\frac{5}{8} \longrightarrow 8\overline{)5.00}^{\ \ 0.62\frac{1}{2}}$$
$$\underline{4\ 8}$$
$$20$$
$$\underline{16}$$
$$4$$

$$\frac{5}{8} = 62\frac{1}{2}\%$$

$$\frac{2}{5} \longrightarrow 5\overline{)2.00}^{\ \ 0.40}$$
$$\underline{2\ 0}$$
$$0$$

$$\frac{2}{5} = 40\%$$

Find the percent for each fraction.

1. $\frac{1}{2}$ 2. $\frac{1}{4}$ 3. $\frac{3}{10}$ 4. $\frac{2}{5}$ 5. $\frac{7}{10}$

6. $\frac{2}{3}$ 7. $\frac{1}{6}$ 8. $\frac{1}{8}$ 9. $\frac{7}{12}$ 10. $\frac{4}{11}$

11. $\frac{5}{16}$ 12. $\frac{1}{10}$ 13. $\frac{13}{20}$ 14. $\frac{11}{15}$ 15. $\frac{1}{7}$

16. $\frac{5}{6}$ 17. $\frac{47}{50}$ 18. $\frac{17}{25}$ 19. $\frac{19}{24}$ 20. $\frac{13}{18}$

Find a percent for each fraction to the **nearest tenth** of a percent.

Example:

$$\frac{5}{7} \longrightarrow 7\overline{)5.0000} \longrightarrow 0.7142 = 71.42\%$$

$$\begin{array}{r} 0.7142 \\ 7\overline{)5.0000} \\ \underline{4\ 9} \\ 10 \\ \underline{7} \\ 30 \\ \underline{28} \\ 20 \\ \underline{14} \\ 6 \end{array}$$

71.42% rounded to the nearest tenth of a percent is 71.4%.

1. $\frac{2}{3}$　　2. $\frac{7}{12}$　　3. $\frac{8}{15}$　　4. $\frac{11}{16}$　　5. $\frac{14}{27}$

6. $\frac{3}{8}$　　7. $\frac{19}{30}$　　8. $\frac{31}{40}$　　9. $\frac{3}{7}$　　10. $\frac{5}{6}$

11. $\frac{13}{24}$　　12. $\frac{11}{12}$　　13. $\frac{7}{8}$　　14. $\frac{1}{15}$　　15. $\frac{5}{9}$

16. $\frac{7}{9}$　　17. $\frac{10}{13}$　　18. $\frac{9}{16}$　　19. $\frac{4}{11}$　　20. $\frac{6}{21}$

21. $\frac{13}{17}$　　22. $\frac{5}{29}$　　23. $\frac{17}{60}$　　24. $\frac{7}{32}$　　25. $\frac{5}{12}$

26. The candle will just fit inside the box. The candle fills about $\frac{11}{14}$ of the space in the box. What percent of the space to the nearest tenth of a percent does the candle fill?

27. The 12-cm candle takes only $\frac{27}{64}$ the amount of wax that the 16-cm candle takes. Write $\frac{27}{64}$ as a percent.

A candle in the shape of a ball is packed in a cubical box. The candle just touches all six sides of the box. Estimate the percent of the space inside the box which the candle occupies.

The candle occupies $\frac{\pi}{6}$ of the space in the box. Use 3.14159 for π and find the percent to the nearest tenth of a percent.

More practice, page 388, Set A

Writing percents as fractions

A wildlife scientist banded a number of birds. During a year's time $6\frac{1}{4}\%$ of the banded birds were reported. What fractional part of the banded birds were reported?

Finding the answer

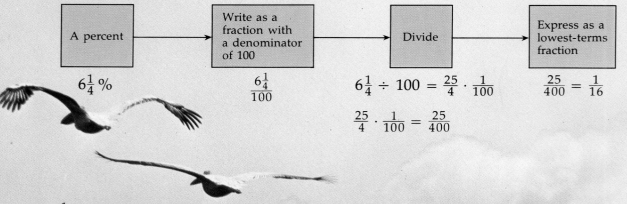

A percent	Write as a fraction with a denominator of 100	Divide	Express as a lowest-terms fraction
$6\frac{1}{4}\%$	$\dfrac{6\frac{1}{4}}{100}$	$6\frac{1}{4} \div 100 = \dfrac{25}{4} \cdot \dfrac{1}{100}$	$\dfrac{25}{400} = \dfrac{1}{16}$

$$\frac{25}{4} \cdot \frac{1}{100} = \frac{25}{400}$$

$\frac{1}{16}$ of the banded birds were reported.

Other examples

$$1\frac{1}{2}\% = \frac{1\frac{1}{2}}{100} = \frac{3}{2} \div 100 = \frac{3}{200}$$

$$87\frac{1}{2}\% = \frac{\frac{175}{2}}{100} = \frac{175}{2} \div 100 = \frac{175}{200} = \frac{7}{8}$$

Find the lowest-terms fraction for each percent.

1. $12\frac{1}{2}\%$
2. $4\frac{1}{2}\%$
3. $33\frac{1}{3}\%$
4. $37\frac{1}{2}\%$

5. $66\frac{2}{3}\%$
6. $14\frac{2}{7}\%$
7. $16\frac{2}{3}\%$
8. $2\frac{1}{2}\%$

9. $3\frac{3}{4}\%$
10. $3\frac{1}{3}\%$
11. $87\frac{1}{2}\%$
12. $83\frac{1}{3}\%$

13. $62\frac{1}{2}\%$
14. $6\frac{2}{3}\%$
15. $1\frac{3}{5}\%$
16. $7\frac{3}{4}\%$

17. $8\frac{1}{3}\%$
18. $5\frac{5}{6}\%$
19. $\frac{1}{2}\%$
20. $43\frac{3}{4}\%$

Write each percent as a lowest-terms fraction.

Examples:

$15\% = \frac{15}{100} = \frac{3}{20}$

$4.5\% = \frac{4.5}{100} = \frac{45}{1000} = \frac{9}{200}$

$3.25\% = \frac{3.25}{100} = \frac{325}{10\ 000} = \frac{13}{400}$

1. 20%   2. 25%   3. 60%   4. 50%   5. 80%

6. 44%   7. 75%   8. 95%   9. 8.5%   10. 1.5%

11. 6.4%   12. 2.5%   13. 4.25%   14. 2.8%   15. 7.25%

16. 8.3%   17. 37.5%   18. 0.5%   19. 0.25%   20. 0.1%

21. 8.4%   22. 96%   23. 7.5%   24. 1.25%   25. 0.05%

26. A starling egg was 40 mm long. A redwing blackbird egg was 87.5% as long. Express this percent as a lowest-terms fraction.

27. The mass of a hummingbird egg was only 12.5% of the mass of a mockingbird egg. Express this percent as a lowest-terms fraction.

Suppose you and a friend divide a pile of pennies like this:

Your friend takes 1 penny.
You take 2 pennies.
Your friend takes 3 pennies.
You take 4 pennies.

Each time, each person takes one more than the other person. When all the pennies have been taken you have 10 pennies more than your friend.

How much money does each of you have?

How many pennies were in the pile?

More practice, page 388, Set B

Larger percents

When 100 mL of water at 20°C are heated
to 100°C, the water expands to 102 mL.

Express the ratio

$$\frac{\text{volume at } 100°\text{C}}{\text{volume at } 20°\text{C}}$$

as a percent.

100 mL
at 20°C

102 mL
at 100°C

Finding the answer

volume at 100°C $\longrightarrow$
volume at 20°C $\longrightarrow$ $\dfrac{102 \text{ mL}}{100 \text{ mL}} = 102\%$

The volume of water at 100°C is 102% of the
volume at 20°C.

Other examples

$1.15 = \frac{115}{100} = 115\%$ $\qquad \frac{5}{4} = \frac{5 \cdot 25}{4 \cdot 25} = \frac{125}{100} = 125\%$

$\frac{8}{5} = \frac{8 \cdot 20}{5 \cdot 20} = \frac{160}{100} = 160\%$ $\qquad 1 = \frac{100}{100} = 100\% \qquad 6 = \frac{6}{1} = \frac{600}{100} = 600\%$

Write as a percent.

1. $\frac{112}{100}$ 2. $\frac{250}{100}$ 3. $\frac{101}{100}$ 4. $\frac{175}{100}$ 5. $\frac{300}{100}$

6. $\frac{3}{2}$ 7. $\frac{11}{10}$ 8. $\frac{7}{4}$ 9. $\frac{6}{5}$ 10. $\frac{5}{2}$

11. $\frac{9}{4}$ 12. $\frac{13}{10}$ 13. $\frac{12}{5}$ 14. $\frac{27}{25}$ 15. $\frac{33}{20}$

16. 2   17. 7.25   18. 4.33   19. 10   20. 3

21. 5   22. 1.3   23. 1.04   24. 12   25. 1.36

26. $\frac{9}{2}$ 27. $\frac{17}{10}$ 28. $\frac{71}{50}$ 29. $\frac{11}{4}$ 30. $\frac{21}{14}$

Write 135% as a decimal.

$$135\% = \frac{135}{100} = 1.35$$

Write 1000% as a decimal.

$$1000\% = \frac{1000}{100} = 10.00$$

Write each percent as a decimal.

1. 125%	**2.** 138%	**3.** 108%	**4.** 200%	**5.** 150%
6. 101%	**7.** 500%	**8.** 250%	**9.** 177%	**10.** 193%
11. 2000%	**12.** 750%	**13.** 119%	**14.** 104%	**15.** 225%
16. 400%	**17.** 166%	**18.** 283%	**19.** 1200%	**20.** 103%

Write each percent as a lowest-terms fraction.

Example: $150\% = \frac{150}{100} = \frac{15}{10} = \frac{3}{2}$

21. 180%	**22.** 250%	**23.** 125%	**24.** 300%	**25.** 110%
26. 220%	**27.** 160%	**28.** 120%	**29.** 240%	**30.** 750%

31. When 1000 mL of mercury at 0°C are heated to 100°C, the mercury expands to 1018 mL. Express the ratio

$$\frac{\text{volume at } 100°C}{\text{volume at } 0°C}$$

as a percent.

Here are two ways to express 99 as a sum of four squares:

$$99 = 9^2 + 4^2 + 1^2 + 1^2$$
$$99 = 8^2 + 5^2 + 3^2 + 1^2$$

Find four ways of expressing 63 as the sum of four squares.

Answers for Self-check 1. 24%   2. 30%   3. 93%   4. 25%   5. 8%   6. 62.3%   7. 20%
8. 70%   9. 12.5% or $12\frac{1}{2}$%   10. $83\frac{1}{3}$%   11. $\frac{23}{100}$ 12. $\frac{12}{25}$ 13. $\frac{1}{3}$ 14. $\frac{1}{16}$ 15. $\frac{7}{5}$ or $1\frac{2}{5}$ 16. $\frac{1}{4}$
17. $\frac{1}{200}$ 18. $\frac{4}{5}$ 19. $\frac{19}{20}$ 20. $\frac{3}{4}$ 21. 250%   22. 112%   23. 250%   24. 745%   25. 400%

Self-check

Write as a percent.

1. 24 out of 100
2. $\frac{30}{100}$
3. $\frac{93}{100}$
4. 0.25
5. 0.08
6. 0.623
7. $\frac{1}{5}$
8. $\frac{7}{10}$
9. $\frac{1}{8}$
10. $\frac{5}{6}$

Write each percent as a lowest-terms fraction.

11. 23%
12. 48%
13. $33\frac{1}{3}\%$
14. $6\frac{1}{4}\%$
15. 140%
16. 25%
17. 0.5%
18. 80%
19. 95%
20. 75%

Write each as a percent.

21. $\frac{250}{100}$
22. $\frac{28}{25}$
23. $\frac{5}{2}$
24. 7.45
25. 4

Answers for Self-check—page 199

Test

Write as a percent.

1. 33 out of 100
2. $\frac{75}{100}$
3. $\frac{22}{100}$
4. 0.42
5. 0.02
6. 0.915
7. $\frac{2}{5}$
8. $\frac{9}{10}$
9. $\frac{3}{8}$
10. $\frac{1}{6}$

Write each percent as a lowest-terms fraction.

11. 41%
12. 13%
13. $66\frac{2}{3}\%$
14. $5\frac{1}{2}\%$
15. 120%
16. 75%
17. 0.4%
18. 60%
19. 35%
20. 20%

Write each as a percent.

21. $\frac{350}{100}$
22. $\frac{23}{20}$
23. $\frac{7}{4}$
24. 8
25. 6.05

Math lab

Making a Percent Calculator

You can make a **percent calculator** from a flat rubber band.

Stretch the rubber band over a centimeter ruler. Use a felt pen to mark points on the band from 0 to 10 cm, one centimeter apart.

Stretched rubber band

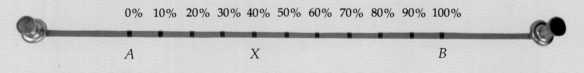

When the rubber band is not stretched, the marks will be close together and evenly spaced.

Unstretched rubber band

Here is one way to use the percent calculator:

What percent of the distance from A to B is point X?

Stretch the rubber band so that the two end marks fall on A and B.

0% 10% 20% 30% 40% 50% 60% 70% 80% 90% 100%

A   X   B

Each space between the marks is 10% of the distance from A to B.
Point X is 40% of the distance from A to B.

What percent of the distance from A to B is point X on each segment below?

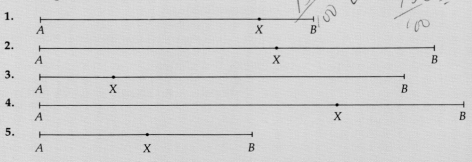

1.
A   X   B

2.
A   X   B

3.
A   X   B

4.
A   X   B

5.
A   X   B

Types of Percent Problems

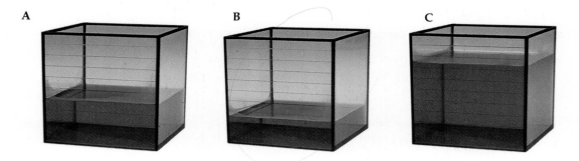

A   B   C

Which of the liter measures is 25% full?

Each box can hold 1500 cm³. One of the boxes contains 900 cm³ of liquid. Which picture shows this?

A   B   C

30% full   50% full   60% full

250 mL of liquid filled 10% of the large container.

How many milliliters will this container hold?

A 2500 mL   B 25 mL   C 25 000 mL

1. A 120 mL container is 50% full. How many milliliters are in the container?

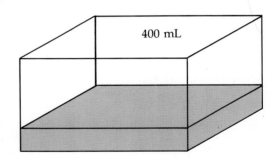

2. A 200 mL container is 75% full. How many milliliters are in the container?

3. A 400 mL container has 100 mL of liquid in it. What fractional part of the container is filled?

4. What percent of the 400 mL container is filled?

   A 50%   **B** 75%   **C** 25%

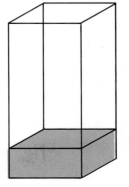

5. There are 100 mL of liquid in the container. It is 20% full. Give the amount of liquid that will be in the container when it is:

   A 40% full
   B 60% full
   C 80% full
   D 100% full

Finding a percent of a number

A new musical group performed
before an audience of 500 people.
18% of the audience purchased
records of the performance.
How many people purchased records?

Finding the answer

Let x = number of people who purchased records

18% of $500 = x$

$0.18 \cdot 500 = x$

$90 = x$

90 people purchased records.

Other examples

Find 32% of 45.

32% of $45 = x$

$0.32 \cdot 45 = x$

$14.4 = x$

Find 6.5% of 750.

6.5% of $750 = x$

$0.065 \cdot 750 = x$

$48.75 = x$

Find 15% of 12.95.

15% of $12.95 = x$

$0.15 \cdot 12.95 = x$

$1.9425 = x$

Find the percent of each number.

1. 20% of 600

2. 33% of 1000

3. 3% of 250

4. 67% of 400

5. 12% of 125

6. 2% of 155

7. 2.5% of 200

8. 8.2% of 500

9. 7% of 82.5

Find the percent of each number.

1. 15% of 500
2. 8% of 65
3. 75% of 96
4. 5% of 2700

5. 25% of 56
6. 14% of 350
7. 33% of 200
8. 50% of 362

9. 2% of 150
10. 9% of 15.88
11. 24% of 78.4
12. 1% of 843.5

13. 95% of 66.8
14. 150% of 400
15. 3.5% of 610
16. 8.4% of 286

Solve each equation.

17. $20\% \cdot 75 = x$
18. $65\% \cdot 340 = x$
19. $72\% \cdot 520 = x$

20. $5\% \cdot 12.4 = x$
21. $10\% \cdot 897 = x$
22. $7\% \cdot 265 = x$

23. $2\% \cdot 750 = x$
24. $25\% \cdot 76 = x$
25. $1.5\% \cdot 850 = x$

26. $6.1\% \cdot 3000 = x$
27. $11\% \cdot 489.50 = x$
28. $13\% \cdot 84.60 = x$

29. A total of 100 000 records of a new song were released. In the first week 42% of them were sold. How many records were sold in the first week?

30. Out of 15 songs a performer had recorded, 20% sold a million copies. How many songs sold a million copies?

Think! A photocopying machine can make reduced-size copies of pictures. The machine can reduce a picture to $83\frac{1}{3}\%$, 75%, or $66\frac{2}{3}\%$ of its original size. How would you use the machine to make a copy that is 50% of the size of the original picture?

More practice, page 389, Set A

Finding what percent one number is of another

An airline company owns 360 jet airplanes. 54 of the planes are jumbo jets. What percent of the 360 planes are the 54 jumbo jets?

Problem: What percent of 360 is 54?

Equation: $n \cdot 360 = 54$

$$n = \frac{54}{360}$$

$$n = 0.15$$

$$n = 15\%$$

$$
\begin{array}{r}
0.15 \\
360\overline{)54.00} \\
36\ 0 \\
\hline
18\ 00 \\
18\ 00 \\
\hline
0
\end{array}
$$

15% of the planes are jumbo jets.

Other Examples

What percent of 25 is 15?

Equation: $n \cdot 25 = 15$

$$n = \frac{15}{25}$$

$$n = 0.60$$

$$n = 60\%$$

$$
\begin{array}{r}
0.60 \\
25\overline{)15.00} \\
15\ 0 \\
\hline
00
\end{array}
$$

What percent of 87 is 29?

Equation: $n \cdot 87 = 29$

$$n = \frac{29}{87}$$

$$n = 0.33\tfrac{1}{3}$$

$$n = 33\tfrac{1}{3}\%$$

$$
\begin{array}{r}
0.33\tfrac{1}{3} \\
87\overline{)29.00} \\
26\ 1 \\
\hline
2\ 90 \\
2\ 61 \\
\hline
29
\end{array}
$$

1. What percent of 75 is 15?
3. What percent of 54 is 9?
5. What percent of 80 is 45?
7. What percent of 10 is 9?
9. What percent of 25 is 4?
11. What percent of 350 is 329?

2. What percent of 30 is 21?
4. What percent of 250 is 20?
6. What percent of 325 is 65?
8. What percent of 40 is 1?
10. What percent of 65 is 13?
12. What percent of 30 is 18?

Compute.

1. What percent of 72 is 18?
2. What percent of 96 is 32?
3. What percent of 130 is 26?
4. What percent of 100 is 7?
5. What percent of 90 is 72?
6. What percent of 40 is 13?
7. What percent of 200 is 14?
8. What percent of 125 is 65?
9. What percent of 65 is 39?
10. What percent of 18 is 2.7?

11. Out of 360 planes, 18 are cargo planes. What percent of the planes are cargo planes?

12. 36 out of 360 airplanes are DC-10's. What percent of the planes are DC-10's?

13. 60 out of 360 airplanes are 737-jet planes. What percent of the planes are 737-jets? Round the answer to the nearest whole percent.

14. 85 out of 360 airplanes are DC-8's. What percent of the planes are DC-8's? Round the answer to the nearest whole percent.

The air temperature outside an airplane drops about 1°C for every 150 m rise in altitude. If the ground temperature is 15°C, what is the outside temperature of a plane flying at an altitude of 9000 m?

More practice, page 389, Set B

Another type of percent problem

A bookstore sold 27 mystery books in one day. This was 18% of all the books sold that day. How many books were sold during the day?

Problem: 18% of some number is 27.

Equation: $18\% \cdot n = 27$

$$0.18n = 27$$

$$n = \frac{27}{0.18}$$

$$n = 150$$

There were 150 books sold during the day.

Other examples

15% of a number is 24.
What is the number?
Let n = the number.
$15\% \cdot n = 24$
$0.15n = 24$
$n = \frac{24}{0.15}$
$n = 160$

32% of a number is 20.8.
What is the number?
Let n = the number.
$32\% \cdot n = 20.8$
$0.32n = 20.8$
$n = \frac{20.8}{0.32}$
$n = 65$

Solve.

1. 5% of a number is 12.
   What is the number?

2. 56% of a number is 28.
   What is the number?

3. 30% of a number is 4.5.
   What is the number?

4. 35% of a number is 14.7.
   What is the number?

Solve each equation.

1. $20\% \cdot n = 18$

2. $6\% \cdot n = 15$

3. $50\% \cdot n = 29$

4. $42\% \cdot n = 63$

5. $10\% \cdot n = 17$

6. $75\% \cdot n = 24$

7. $6\% \cdot n = 5.1$

8. $18\% \cdot n = 42.3$

9. $1\% \cdot n = 2.95$

Write and solve an equation for each.

10. 30% of a number is 15. What is the number?

11. 25% of a number is 10. What is the number?

12. 26% of a number is 13. What is the number?

13. 4% of a number is 20. What is the number?

14. 55% of a number is 22. What is the number?

15. 7% of a number is 84. What is the number?

16. 9% of a number is 6.30. What is the number?

17. 19% of a number is 5.70. What is the number?

18. 38% of a number is 45.60. What is the number?

19. 64% of a number is 46.08 What is the number?

20. 6% of a number is 1.2. What is the number?

21. 75% of a number is 120. What is the number?

22. In a day, 18 books about crafts were sold. This was 10% of all the books sold that day. How many books were sold that day?

23. In one day, 12% of all the books sold were about sports. If 30 sports books were sold, how many books of all kinds were sold?

 This multiplication problem is written in Chinese numerals.

Write the problem in ordinary numerals.

	二	五	九
	二	五	九
	二	三	三	二
一	二	九	五
五	一	八	
六	七	十	八	一

Answers for Self-check 1. 70 2. 5.95 3. 520.80 4. 25% 5. 30% 6. 75% 7. 34%
8. $n = 700$ 9. $n = 60$ 10. $n = 75$ 11. $0.20n = 3$, $n = 15$ 12. $0.75n = 18$, $n = 24$
13. $0.03n = 8.7$, $n = 290$ 14. $0.12n = 15$, $n = 125$

More practice, page 390

Self-check

Find the percent of each number.

1. 20% of 350

2. 7% of 85

3. 84% of 620

Compute.

4. What percent of 96 is 24?

5. What percent of 70 is 21?

6. What percent of 36 is 27?

7. What percent of 150 is 51?

Solve each equation.

8. $0.08n = 56$

9. $0.25n = 15$

10. $0.66n = 49.5$

Write and solve an equation for each.

11. 20% of a number is 3. What is the number?

12. 75% of a number is 18. What is the number?

13. 3% of a number is 8.7. What is the number?

14. 12% of a number is 15. What is the number?

Answers for Self-check—page 209

Test

Find the percent of each number.

1. 60% of 55

2. 8% of 180

3. 72% of 265

Compute.

4. What percent of 50 is 30?

5. What percent of 75 is 60?

6. What percent of 120 is 42?

7. What percent of 38 is 19?

Solve each equation.

8. $0.06n = 54$

9. $0.45n = 9$

10. $0.16n = 6.4$

Write and solve an equation for each.

11. 40% of a number is 18. What is the number?

12. 22% of a number is 7.7. What is the number?

13. 95% of a number is 285. What is the number?

14. 2% of a number is 5.4. What is the number?

Heptamond Patterns

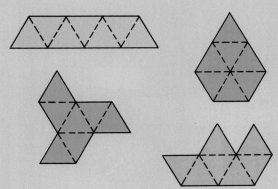

A heptamond is a region formed
by 7 equilateral triangles joined
edge to edge. There are exactly
24 different heptamonds. Some
of them are shown.

How many of the other heptamonds can you construct?

The 24 heptamonds can be placed together
to form parallelograms and other more
complex shapes.

Some interesting heptamond patterns are
shown below.

Construct some patterns of your own
using the 24 heptamonds.

Problem Solving
Using Your Skills

Environmental scientists study the earth's land, water, and air.
They are much concerned with conservation of natural resources
and with the problem of pollution.

A **hydrologist** is an environmental scientist whose special field
of interest is **water**. A hydrologist studies the properties,
circulation, and distribution of water.

A hydrologist might prepare a table of information like the one below.

Estimated Daily Use of Water in the U.S. (Billions of liters)						
Year	Irrigation	Water utilities	Rural use	Industrial use	Electric utilities	Total
1940	311	49	22	132	88	602
1950	453	68	33	172	174	900
1960	644	105	44	275	374	1442
1970	577	127	32	251	458	1443
1980 (projected)	659	156	36	334	732	1917

Source: *Statistical Abstract of the United States, 1975*

Example:

In 1970 about 22% of all the water used for irrigation came from wells. The estimated daily use for irrigation was 577 billion liters. About how many liters per day came from wells?

Let x = number of billions of liters per day from wells

$$22\% \cdot 577 = x$$
$$0.22 \cdot 577 = x$$
$$126.94 = x$$

About 127 billion liters of water used for irrigation per day came from wells.

1. The state of California uses about 35 billion liters of water a day. About 80% of this is used for irrigation of crops. How much water is used per day for irrigation?

2. In 1940 about 602 billion liters of water were used daily in the U.S. In 1980 it is estimated that about 1917 billion liters of water a day will be used. How many times as much water will be used in 1980 as in 1940? Round the answer to the nearest tenth.

3. During a water shortage a household that had been using 1200 L a day reduced its use 25%. How many liters a day did the household use during the shortage?

4. The table shows the daily use of water in the U.S. for a recent year.

Irrigation	609 billion L
Water utilities	139 billion L
Rural use	34 billion L
Industrial use	284 billion L
Electric utilities	568 billion L

What is the total daily use of water?

Percent and estimation

A pair of running shoes costs $19.90.
The sales tax is 6% of the cost.
Estimate the sales tax on the shoes.

Think: $19.90 is about $20.00.
        6% sales tax rate means 6¢ tax on each dollar.

        $6 \cdot 20 = 120$

        The sales tax is about 120¢ or $1.20.

Choose the best estimate.

1. 4% of $9.88
    A 30¢   **B** 35¢   **C** 40¢

2. 8.06% of $893
    A 72¢   **B** $7.20   **C** $72.00

3. $6\frac{1}{4}$% of $189
    A $12.00   **B** $1.20   **C** $120.00

4. 25% of $99.95
    A $2.50   **B** $25.00   **C** $0.25

5. 15% of $29.50
    A $3.50   **B** $4.00   **C** $4.50

6. $7\frac{3}{4}$% of $479
    A $30   **B** $40   **C** $50

Estimate each amount.

7. 52% of $78

8. $7\frac{3}{4}$% of $219

9. 5.1% of $621

10. $6\frac{2}{3}$% of $522

11. $1\frac{3}{4}$% of $475

12. 8.2% of $109

13. 9.8% of $39.50

14. 5.9% of $386

15. 7.14% of $193

16. $33\frac{1}{3}$% of $612

17. 3.9% of $59.95

18. 15% of $81.14

In making estimates of percents, it is often useful to know the percent equivalents for some simple fractional numbers.

$\frac{1}{4} = 25\%$	$\frac{1}{2} = 50\%$	$\frac{3}{4} = 75\%$	
$\frac{1}{5} = 20\%$	$\frac{2}{5} = 40\%$	$\frac{3}{5} = 60\%$	$\frac{4}{5} = 80\%$
$\frac{1}{6} = 16\frac{2}{3}\%$	$\frac{1}{3} = 33\frac{1}{3}\%$	$\frac{2}{3} = 66\frac{2}{3}\%$	$\frac{5}{6} = 83\frac{1}{3}\%$
$\frac{1}{8} = 12\frac{1}{2}\%$	$\frac{3}{8} = 37\frac{1}{2}\%$	$\frac{5}{8} = 62\frac{1}{2}\%$	$\frac{7}{8} = 87\frac{1}{2}\%$

6 out of 29 students in one room are wearing glasses. About what percent are wearing glasses?

Think: $\frac{6}{29}$ of the students wear glasses.

29 is about 30.

$$\frac{6}{30} = \frac{1}{5} = 20\%$$

About 20% of the students are wearing glasses.

Choose the best estimate of percent for each ratio.

1. $\frac{19}{40}$

    A 30%   **B** 40%   **C** 50%

2. $\frac{8}{24}$

    A 12%   **B** 30%   **C** 40%

3. $\frac{10.7}{42.3}$

    A 20%   **B** 25%   **C** 30%

4. $\frac{31}{92}$

    A 25%   **B** $33\frac{1}{3}\%$ **C** 50%

Estimate the percent for each ratio.

5. $\frac{9.3}{35.7}$ 6. $\frac{212}{311}$ 7. $\frac{66}{125}$ 8. $\frac{29}{79}$ 9. $\frac{11}{52}$

10. $\frac{92}{121}$ 11. $\frac{4.2}{5.3}$ 12. $\frac{748}{859}$ 13. $\frac{3.8}{15.9}$ 14. $\frac{79}{419}$

15. There are 58 students in the school band. There are 309 students in the school. Estimate the percent of students who are in the band.

☆ 16. A bicycle costs $93.77. The sales tax rate is 6% of the cost. Estimate the sales tax and give the estimated total cost of the bicycle (tax included).

Change ADD to SUM by changing one letter at a time. Each letter change must make a new 3-letter word.

    ADD
    AID
    . . .
    . . .
    . . .
    SUM

Nutritionists

Nutritionists study the composition of foods. They often work in laboratories weighing, filtering, drying, and analyzing foods to determine their nutritional values.

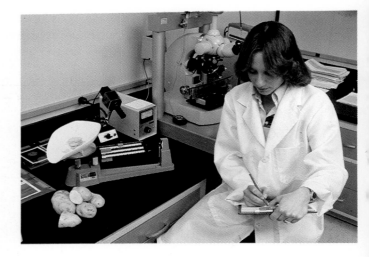

To determine the amount of water in potatoes, a nutritionist carefully measured 50 g of thinly sliced fresh potatoes. The potatoes were then dried to remove the water in them. After drying, the potatoes had a mass of 11 g.

The amount of water in the fresh potatoes was

$$50 \text{ g} - 11 \text{ g} = 39 \text{ g}$$

$$\frac{\text{mass of water}}{\text{mass of fresh potatoes}} = \frac{39}{50} = \frac{78}{100} = 78\%$$

The fresh potatoes contained 78% water.

Find the amount and percent of water in each of the following foods.

1. Fresh tomatoes
   Original mass: 50 g
   Dried mass: 3 g
   Amount of water: ▦
   Percent of water: ▦

2. Bananas
   Original mass: 50 g
   Dried mass: 14 g
   Amount of water: ▦
   Percent of water: ▦

3. Watermelon
   Original mass: 100 g
   Dried mass: 18 g
   Amount of water: ▦
   Percent of water: ▦

Copy and complete the table.

	Kind of food	Original mass	Dried mass	Amount of water	Percent water
1.	Carrots	50 g	7 g	▨	▨
2.	Apples	50 g	8 g	▨	▨
3.	Cucumbers	50 g	2 g	▨	▨
4.	Celery	100 g	6 g	▨	▨
5.	Bread	100 g	64 g	▨	▨
6.	Spinach	100 g	7 g	▨	▨
7.	Sweet potatoes	25 g	8 g	▨	▨
8.	Yellow onion	25 g	3 g	▨	▨
9.	Honey	10 g	8 g	▨	▨
10.	Milk	100 g	13 g	▨	▨
11.	Cheese	20 g	8 g	▨	▨
12.	Round Steak	50 g	13 g	▨	▨

13. When 100 g of water from Great Salt Lake, Utah, is evaporated, the salt and other remaining minerals have a mass of 22 g. What percent of the water from the lake is pure water?

14. If 1000 g of sea water is evaporated, the remaining mass will be about 3.5 g. What percent of sea water is pure water?

A faucet is dripping 1 drop of water each second. Ten drops of water make 1 milliliter. How much water drips in 24 hours? How much water is wasted by the leaky faucet in a year?

Discounts

A digital watch was regularly priced
at $60.00. During a sale it was sold
at "30% off" the regular price.

What was the sale price?

The percent "off" the regular price is the **discount rate**.
The amount "taken off" the regular price is the **discount**.

Sale price = Regular price − discount

Regular price	$60.00		Regular Price	$60.00
Discount rate	× 0.30		Discount	− 18.00
Discount	$18.00		Sale Price	$42.00

The sale price of the watch was $42.00.

Find the discount and sale price for each.

1. Regular price: $35.00
   Discount rate: 10%

2. Regular price: $16.00
   Discount rate: 25%

3. Regular price: $84.00
   Discount rate: 50%

4. Regular price: $12.00
   Discount rate: 40%

5. Regular price: $18.75
   Discount rate: 20%

6. Regular price: $6.95
   Discount rate: 15%

7. Regular price: $37.50
   Discount rate: $33\frac{1}{3}$%

8. Regular price: $72.00
   Discount rate: 12.5%

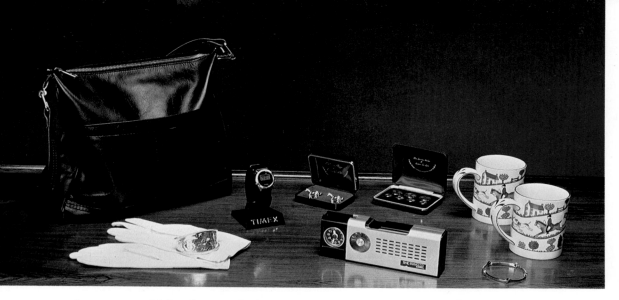

1. A ten-speed bicycle regularly priced at $84.95 was on sale at 25% off. Find the sale price.

2. A piece of costume jewelry regularly priced at $6.00 was on sale at 30% off. What was the sale price?

3. A candle-making kit was on sale with a discount rate of 20%. The regular price of the kit was $12.95. What was the sale price?

4. The regular price of a guitar was $149.95. During a sale it was reduced 15%. What was the sale price?

5. A leather shoulder bag was regularly priced at $25.00. What was the sale price of the bag during a 10% off sale?

6. A tether ball set was regularly priced at $15.88. During a sale the price was reduced by 18%. What was the sale price?

7. A croquet set was on sale at 50% off. If the regular price was $29.98, what was the sale price?

8. The regular price of a pair of binoculars was $124.50. The price was reduced by 12%. What was the reduced price?

☆ 9. An article regularly priced at $80.00 was on sale at 25% off. Later the sale price was reduced by 25%. What was the new sale price?

 A furniture store put a $100 chair on sale at 20% off. Each week the sale price was reduced by 20%. The chair finally sold for $40.96. How many times was the price reduced?

More practice, page 391, Set A

Interest

A family borrowed $3000 to remodel their kitchen. The loan was for 2 years. The interest rate was 12% per year. What was the interest for the 2 years?

Interest is found by applying the formula
$$I = Prt$$
where I means **interest**, P means **principal**, r means **rate**, and t means **time**.

Here $P = \$3000$
$r = 12\%$ per year
$t = 2$ years
$I = \$3000 \cdot 0.12 \cdot 2$
$= \$720.00$

The interest for 2 years was $720.

Other examples

Find the interest, I.
$P = \$500$
$r = 6\%$ per year
$t = 3$ years
$I = \$500 \cdot 0.06 \cdot 3$
$= \$90.00$

Find the interest, I.
$P = \$2400$
$r = 8\%$ per year
$t = \frac{1}{2}$ year
$I = \$2400 \cdot 0.08 \cdot \frac{1}{2}$
$= \$96.00$

Find the interest.

1. $P = \$700$
$r = 5\%$ per year
$t = 4$ yr

2. $P = \$250$
$r = 9\%$ per year
$t = 5$ yr

3. $P = \$500$
$r = 4\%$ per year
$t = 1$ yr

4. $P = \$1000$
$r = 7\%$ per year
$t = 15$ yr

5. $P = \$620$
$r = 11\%$ per year
$t = 3$ yr

6. $P = \$125$
$r = 5\%$ per year
$t = 2$ yr

When money is borrowed the amount to be repaid is
the **principal** P, plus the **interest** I. This is called the **amount**, A.
$$A = P + I$$

Example:

Find the amount on $1500 when the interest rate is 6% per year for 3 years.

$I = Prt$	$A = P + I$
$I = \$1500 \cdot 0.06 \cdot 3$	$A = \$1500 + \$270$
$I = \$270$	$A = \$1770$

Find the interest and the amount in each exercise.

	Principal	Rate per year	Time	Interest	Amount
1.	$1000	5%	6 yr		
2.	$2400	7%	3 yr		
3.	$250	18%	1 yr		
4.	$6800	9%	4 yr		
5.	$20 000	10%	12 yr		
6.	$600	12%	$\frac{1}{2}$ yr		
7.	$2000	6.5%	2 yr		
8.	$360	15%	$\frac{1}{4}$ yr		
9.	$980	$5\frac{1}{4}$%	1 yr		
10.	$40 000	7%	29 yr		
11.	$16 000	9.5%	$6\frac{1}{2}$ yr		
12.	$12 000	$5\frac{3}{4}$%	5 yr		

 A bank pays 6% yearly interest on money left in savings for a year. If you put $100 in a savings account, at the end of the year you would have $100 plus $6 interest or $106. At the end of the second year you would have the interest on $106 or $6.36 and a total amount of $112.36.

How many years would it take you to have at least $200 in savings?

Year	Principal	Rate	Interest	Amount
1	$100.00	6%	$6.00	$106.00
2	$106.00	6%	$6.36	$112.36
3	$112.36	6%	$6.74	
4				

More practice, page 391, Set B

Using a credit card

Many people make purchases on credit. For example, a bank credit card may be used at the time of purchase. The bank pays the store where the buyer makes a purchase. Each month the bank sends the buyer a bill for the total. The bank charges an interest rate of $1\frac{1}{2}\%$ per month on the unpaid balance on amounts under $1000.

Example:

A buyer has purchases totaling $219.20.
The buyer made a payment of $50.00.
What is the interest charge and the
new balance?

$$
\begin{array}{rr}
\text{Purchases} \rightarrow & \$219.20 \\
\text{Payment} \rightarrow & -\ 50.00 \\
\text{Unpaid balance} \rightarrow & 169.20 \\
\text{Monthly interest rate: } 1\frac{1}{2}\% = 0.015 \rightarrow & \times\ 0.015 \\
\hline
& 84600 \\
& 16920 \\
\hline
\text{Interest} \rightarrow & \$2.53800
\end{array}
$$

$\$169.20 \leftarrow$ Unpaid balance
$+\ \ 2.54 \leftarrow$ Interest
$\$171.74 \leftarrow$ New balance

Interest rounded to nearest cent $\rightarrow \$2.54$

The interest charge on the unpaid balance for one month is $2.54.
The new balance is $171.74.

Find the unpaid balance, the interest, and the new balance.
Use $1\frac{1}{2}\%$ per month as the interest rate.

1. Purchases: $315.50
   Payment: $100.00

2. Purchases: $89.95
   Payment: $10.00

3. Purchases: $186.66
   Payment: $75.00

4. Purchases: $220.10
   Payment: $120.10

5. Purchases: $116.75
   Payment: $40.00

6. Purchases: $642.96
   Payment: $325.00

Copy and complete the table below. Use a monthly interest rate of $1\frac{1}{2}\%$.

	Purchases	Payment	Unpaid balance	Interest	New balance
1.	$160.50	$ 60.50			
2.	$336.80	$175.00			
3.	$ 88.45	$ 10.00			
4.	$261.73	$100.00			
5.	$501.92	$200.00			
6.	$109.66	$ 25.00			
7.	$ 38.44	$ 10.00			
8.	$451.76	$ 22.59			
9.	$184.22	$ 40.00			
10.	$803.69	$500.00			
11.	$201.38	$ 65.00			
12.	$360.91	$ 80.00			
13.	$ 63.65	$ 10.00			
14.	$714.09	$ 50.00			
15.	$464.13	$175.00			

☆ 16. A person made a payment of $75.00 on a credit card bill of $180.00. Find the interest at a rate of $1\frac{1}{2}\%$ per month on the unpaid balance. If items totaling $48 are purchased during the next month, what will the new balance be?

☆ 17. A person made purchases totaling $195.25 using a credit card. The person paid $50.00 per month on the unpaid balance and made no new purchases. What was the amount of the last payment if the interest rate is $1\frac{1}{2}\%$ per month?

Answers for Self-check 1. B 2. A 3. B 4. $54.40 5. $220.00 6. $47.08
7. $137.40 unpaid balance; $2.06 interest; $139.46 new balance

Self-check

Choose the best estimate.

1. 6.25% of $812
   A $4.80
   B $48.00
   C $480.00

2. 29% of $59.95
   A $18.00
   B $24.00
   C $28.00

3. 8.1% of $19.33
   A $0.16
   B $1.60
   C $16.00

4. An article regularly priced at $64.00 was on sale at 15% off. What was the sale price?

Find the interest.

5. $P = \$1100$
   $r = 5\%$
   $t = 4\,\text{yr}$

6. $P = \$856.00$
   $r = 11\%$
   $t = \frac{1}{2}\,\text{yr}$

7. Mr. Franks made purchases totaling $217.40 with his credit card. He made a payment of $80.00. What is the unpaid balance, the interest, and the new balance?
   Use $1\frac{1}{2}\%$ per month as the interest rate.

Answers for Self-check—page 223

Test

Choose the best estimate.

1. 3.2% of $88.50
   A $27.00
   B $2.70
   C $0.27

2. 52% of 886
   A 450
   B 400
   C 500

3. 18% of $24.00
   A $2.00
   B $3.00
   C $4.00

4. A parka regularly sold for $56.00. During an end-of-season sale it was marked down 20%. What was the sale price?

Find the interest.

5. $P = \$900$
   $r = 8\%$
   $t = 2\,\text{yr}$

6. $P = \$750$
   $r = 10\%$
   $t = 1\,\text{yr}$

7. Cindy Aoki made purchases totaling $372.46 with her credit card. She made a payment of $100. Find the unpaid balance, the interest, and the new balance.
   Use $1\frac{1}{2}\%$ monthly as the interest rate.

Math lab

Measuring Speeds

Study this example to help you measure some speeds in kilometers per hour.

A very fast runner ran 100 m in 12 s.

What is this speed in kilometers per hour?

Step 1   Write a ratio.

$$\frac{100 \text{ m}}{12 \text{ s}}$$

Step 2   Write the ratio as a decimal.

8.33 m/s

Step 3   Change to kilometers per hour by multiplying by 3.6.

$8.33 \cdot 3.6 = 29.988$ or 30 km/h

A   Measure off a distance of 100 m.

B   Use a stopwatch to find the amount of time it takes to travel 100 m.

C   Find some of the following speeds in kilometers per hour.

Normal walking

Running

Fast bicycle

Cars passing the school

Measurement Formulas

The distance around a circle is called
the **circumference** of the circle.

Circumference: $C = 201$ cm   Diameter: $d = 64$ cm

$$\frac{C}{d} = \frac{201}{64} \approx 3.14$$

$C = 69$ cm

$d = 22$ cm

$$\frac{C}{d} = \frac{69}{22} \approx 3.14$$

The quotient $\dfrac{C}{d}$ is the same for **all** circles.

It is symbolized by the Greek letter π.
The decimal value of π has been computed to
thousands of decimal places. The decimal
for π does not repeat and does not end.
π computed to ten decimal places is 3.1415926538.

Since $\dfrac{C}{d} = \pi$, the formula for the circumference

of a circle is $C = \pi d$.
The diameter d is 2 times the radius r of a
circle. Therefore the circumference formula
can also be written as $C = \pi \cdot (2r)$ or $C = 2\pi r$.

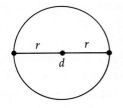

Measure the circumferences and diameters of some circular objects
with a tape measure. Find an approximate value of π by dividing
the circumference by the diameter for each object.

Use the formula $C = \pi d$ or $C = 2\pi r$ to find the circumference of each circle.
Use 3.14 for π.

Example: $C = 2\pi r$
$C \approx 2 \cdot 3.14 \cdot 1.5$
$C \approx 9.42$ cm

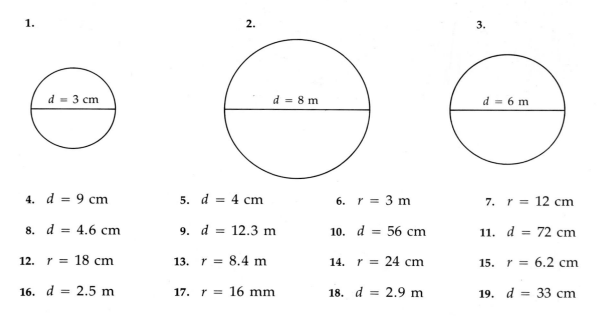

$r = 1.5$ cm

The circumference is about 9.4 cm.

1.

$d = 3$ cm

2.

$d = 8$ m

3.

$d = 6$ m

4. $d = 9$ cm

5. $d = 4$ cm

6. $r = 3$ m

7. $r = 12$ cm

8. $d = 4.6$ cm

9. $d = 12.3$ m

10. $d = 56$ cm

11. $d = 72$ cm

12. $r = 18$ cm

13. $r = 8.4$ m

14. $r = 24$ cm

15. $r = 6.2$ cm

16. $d = 2.5$ m

17. $r = 16$ mm

18. $d = 2.9$ m

19. $d = 33$ cm

Solve the problems.

20. A small bicycle wheel has a diameter of 61 cm. How far does the bicycle travel as the wheel turns once?

21. A gear on a bicycle has a diameter of 19 cm. What is the circumference of the gear?

22. A small gear on a bicycle has a diameter of 8 cm. A larger gear has a diameter of twice that. Is the circumference of the larger gear twice that of the smaller gear?

☆ **23.** A circular track has a radius of 12 m. A bicycle wheel has a diameter of 66 cm. About how many times must you ride the bicycle around the track to go 1 km? About how many times will the wheel of the bike turn as you go 1 km?

Areas of rectangles and parallelograms

The area A of a rectangle with base b
and height h is the base times the height.
$$A = bh$$
The drawings below show why the formula
for the area of a parallelogram is the
same as for the area of a rectangle.

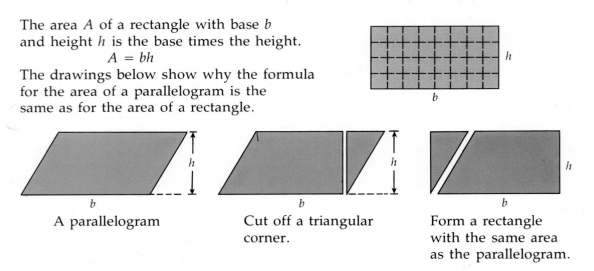

| A parallelogram | Cut off a triangular corner. | Form a rectangle with the same area as the parallelogram. |

The formula for the area of a parallelogram is $A = bh$.

Find the area of each rectangle.

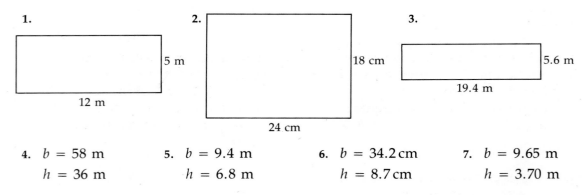

1. 5 m, 12 m
2. 18 cm, 24 cm
3. 5.6 m, 19.4 m

4. $b = 58$ m
   $h = 36$ m

5. $b = 9.4$ m
   $h = 6.8$ m

6. $b = 34.2$ cm
   $h = 8.7$ cm

7. $b = 9.65$ m
   $h = 3.70$ m

Find the area of each parallelogram.

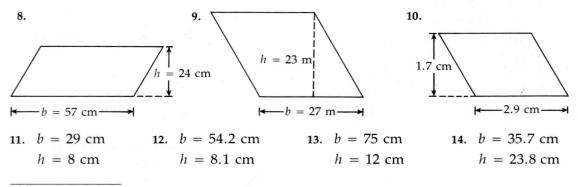

8. $b = 57$ cm, $h = 24$ cm
9. $h = 23$ m, $b = 27$ m
10. 1.7 cm, 2.9 cm

11. $b = 29$ cm
    $h = 8$ cm

12. $b = 54.2$ cm
    $h = 8.1$ cm

13. $b = 75$ cm
    $h = 12$ cm

14. $b = 35.7$ cm
    $h = 23.8$ cm

Find the area of each rectangular
room. Use these dimensions, where
l = length and w = width.

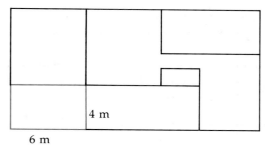

1. $l = 6$ m
   $w = 4$ m

2. $l = 5.0$ m
   $w = 6.2$ m

3. $l = 8.1$ m
   $w = 3.6$ m

4. $l = 6.0$ m
   $w = 6.3$ m

5. $l = 9$ m
   $w = 4$ m

6. $l = 12.0$ m
   $w = 6.3$ m

Find the area of each parallelogram. Use these dimensions.

7. $b = 35$ m
   $h = 26$ m

8. $b = 29$ m
   $h = 24$ m

9. $b = 42$ m
   $h = 25$ m

10. $b = 35.7$ m
    $h = 26.3$ m

11. $b = 39$ m
    $h = 18$ m

12. $b = 40.7$ m
    $h = 29.2$ m

13. $b = 45$ m
    $h = 28$ m

14. $b = 38$ m
    $h = 14$ m

Solve these problems.

15. A bedroom has dimensions of
    4.6 m by 3.7 m. How much will
    it cost to carpet the floor if
    carpet costs $12.95 per square
    meter?

16. A rectangular house 22.8 m
    by 11.5 m is to be built on
    a lot 36.5 m by 33.5 m.
    How many square meters of the
    lot will not be covered by the
    house?

☆ 17. A hexagonal house
    with these dimensions
    was built on a 36 m
    by 36 m lot. How
    many square meters
    of the lot will not
    be covered by the
    house?

Suppose you want to build a
rectangular dog pen that has an
area of 48 m². The lengths and
widths are to be whole numbers.

1. Give the dimensions of
   different pens you could
   make.

2. Which pen would require the
   most fence? The least fence?

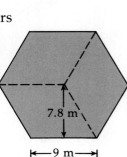

7.8 m

9 m

Areas of triangles and trapezoids

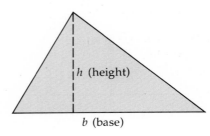

Start with
a triangle.

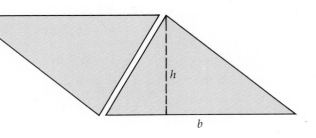

Put a congruent triangle
with it to make a
parallelogram.

Find the area of the triangle by finding
half the area of the parallelogram.

The formula for finding the area of a
triangle is:

$A = \frac{1}{2} bh$

Use the formula to find the areas of these triangles.

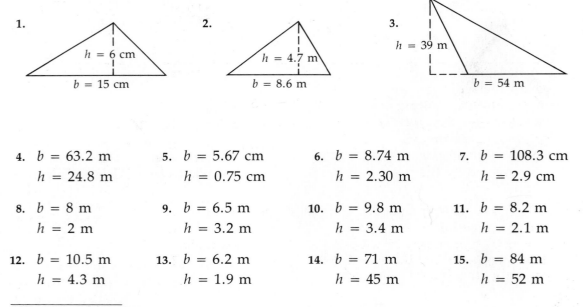

1. $h = 6$ cm $b = 15$ cm

2. $h = 4.7$ m $b = 8.6$ m

3. $h = 39$ m $b = 54$ m

4. $b = 63.2$ m
   $h = 24.8$ m

5. $b = 5.67$ cm
   $h = 0.75$ cm

6. $b = 8.74$ m
   $h = 2.30$ m

7. $b = 108.3$ cm
   $h = 2.9$ cm

8. $b = 8$ m
   $h = 2$ m

9. $b = 6.5$ m
   $h = 3.2$ m

10. $b = 9.8$ m
    $h = 3.4$ m

11. $b = 8.2$ m
    $h = 2.1$ m

12. $b = 10.5$ m
    $h = 4.3$ m

13. $b = 6.2$ m
    $h = 1.9$ m

14. $b = 71$ m
    $h = 45$ m

15. $b = 84$ m
    $h = 52$ m

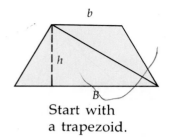

Start with
a trapezoid.

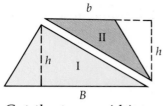

Cut the trapezoid into
two triangles and find
their areas.

$$\text{Area } (\triangle \text{I}) = \tfrac{1}{2} Bh$$

$$\text{Area } (\triangle \text{II}) = \tfrac{1}{2} bh$$

Find the area of the trapezoid by adding the
areas of the triangles.

$$A = \tfrac{1}{2} Bh + \tfrac{1}{2} bh = \tfrac{1}{2} h (B + b)$$

The formula for finding the area of a
trapezoid is:

$$A = \tfrac{1}{2} h (B + b)$$

Use the formula to find the areas of these trapezoids.

1.
8 cm
7 cm
15 cm

2.
6 m
14 m
24 m

3.
4.8 cm
4.5 cm
9.6 cm

4.
6.4 m
8.2 m
10.5 m

5. $b = 3.86$ m
$B = 5.97$ m
$h = 8.64$ m

6. $b = 24$ cm
$B = 48$ cm
$h = 64$ cm

7. $b = 9.6$ m
$B = 4.2$ m
$h = 3.8$ m

8. $b = 12$ m
$B = 16$ m
$h = 8$ m

9. Which has the larger area:
a triangle with $b = 8$ m and
$h = 6$ m, or a trapezoid with
$B = 8$ m, $b = 6$ m, and $h = 4$ m?
How much larger?

10. What is the
area of this
triangular
corner lot?

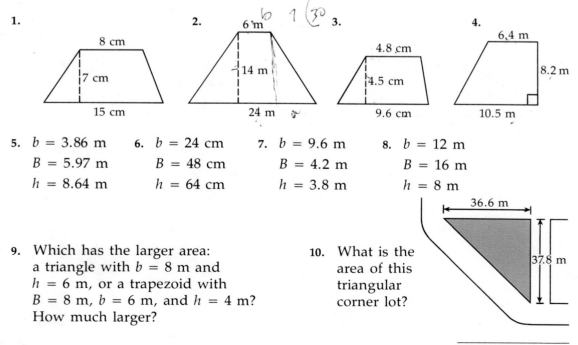

36.6 m

37.8 m

Area of a circle

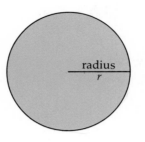
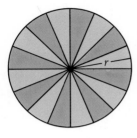

half the circumference

r

πr

| Start with a circle with radius r. | Divide the circle into "triangles." | Put the "triangles" together to form a "parallelogram." Find its area to find the area of the circle. |

$$A = \pi r \cdot r = \pi r^2$$

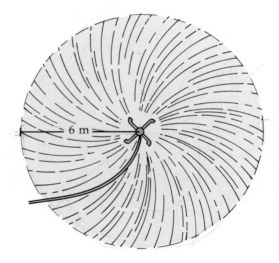

6 m

A rotating lawn sprinkler sprays water in a circle 6 m from the sprinkler. What is the area of the lawn watered?

$$A = \pi r^2$$
$$\approx 3.14 \, (6^2)$$
$$\approx 3.14 \cdot 6 \cdot 6$$
$$\approx 113.04$$

The area watered is about 100 m².

Find the areas of circles with the following dimensions.

1. $r = 4$ cm   2. $r = 12$ m   3. $r = 3.6$ m   4. $r = 5.9$ cm

5. $d = 10$ cm   6. $d = 32$ m   7. $d = 24$ m   8. $d = 64.8$ cm

9. $r = 15$ cm   10. $r = 100$ m   11. $r = 0.75$ m   12. $d = 56.4$ cm

1. Find the areas of the table top and the throw rug. The diameter of the rug is 2 times the diameter of the table. How many times the area of the table is the area of the rug?

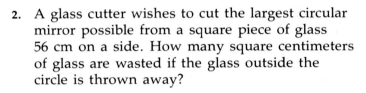

0.8 m

1.6 m

2. A glass cutter wishes to cut the largest circular mirror possible from a square piece of glass 56 cm on a side. How many square centimeters of glass are wasted if the glass outside the circle is thrown away?

56 cm

56 cm

3. A landscape architect designed a cement sidewalk around a circular fountain flower garden. The diameter of the fountain flower garden is 12 m and the sidewalk is 1 m wide. What is the area of the sidewalk?

12 m — 1 m

4. A rectangular patio is to be made using 48 circular cement slabs with decorative rock in between. The patio is 3 m by 4 m. Each slab has a diameter of 0.5 m. How many square meters of the patio will be covered by the cement slabs? How many square meters will be covered by the decorative rock?

3 m

4 m

5. A decorative window has the shape shown here. The top is a semicircle. What is the area of the glass in the window?

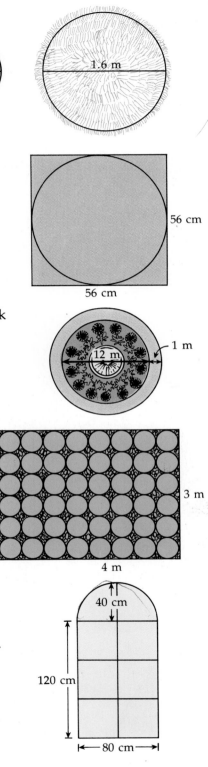

40 cm

120 cm

|← 80 cm →|

Surface area

The **surface area** of a space figure is the **sum** of the areas of all its polygonal faces or curved surfaces. To find surface area, it often helps to think about how the space figure would look unfolded.

Find these surface areas.

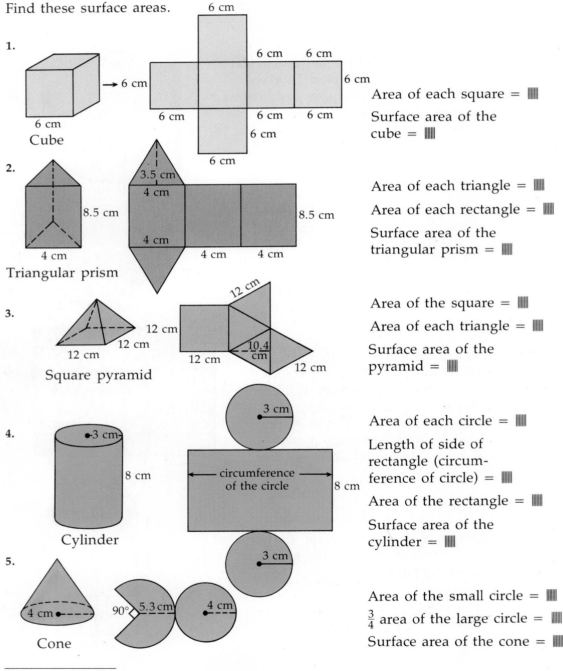

1. Cube

Area of each square = ▥

Surface area of the cube = ▥

2. Triangular prism

Area of each triangle = ▥

Area of each rectangle = ▥

Surface area of the triangular prism = ▥

3. Square pyramid

Area of the square = ▥

Area of each triangle = ▥

Surface area of the pyramid = ▥

4. Cylinder

Area of each circle = ▥

Length of side of rectangle (circumference of circle) = ▥

Area of the rectangle = ▥

Surface area of the cylinder = ▥

5. Cone

Area of the small circle = ▥

$\frac{3}{4}$ area of the large circle = ▥

Surface area of the cone = ▥

Find the surface areas. Give answers to the nearest tenth.

1.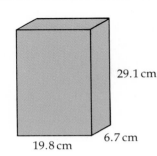
29.1 cm
19.8 cm
6.7 cm

2.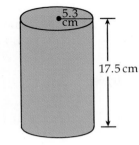
5.3 cm
17.5 cm

3.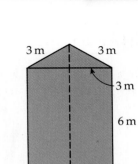
3 m   3 m
3 m
6 m
2.6 m

4. The Great Pyramid at El Gizeh in Egypt was built more than 4500 years ago.

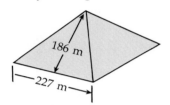
186 m
227 m

What is the surface area of this square pyramid, not including the floor?

5. A certain airplane hangar is half a cylinder.

80 m
40 m

What is the surface area of this hangar, not including the floor?

6. If 1 L of paint covers 5 m², how many liters of paint are needed to paint the sides and door of this garage?

1.5 m
3 m
9 m
7 m

(The garage has one 0.8 m by 1.25 m window on each of three sides.)

7. The surface area of any cone (not counting a circular "lid" for the cone) is:

$$S = \pi rs$$

How many square centimeters of paper were used to make this cone?

r = 4 cm
Grape Ice
s = 11 cm

This truncated icosahedron has 12 pentagonal faces and 20 hexagonal faces. Find the surface area using these dimensions.

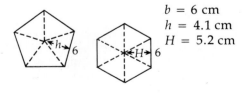

h → 6
H → 6

b = 6 cm
h = 4.1 cm
H = 5.2 cm

Volumes of prisms

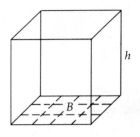 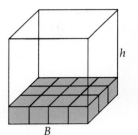 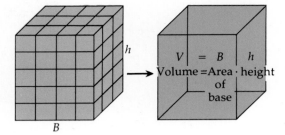

| Start with a rectangular prism with base area B and height h. | Put one layer of B cubes in the prism. | Fill the prism with h layers of cubes with B cubes in each layer, or Bh cubes. | Formula for finding the volume of a prism $$V = Bh$$ |

The formula above can also be used to find the volume of any prism. Find these volumes.

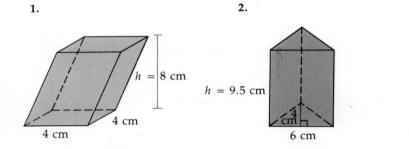

1. $h = 8$ cm, 4 cm, 4 cm

2. $h = 9.5$ cm, 4 cm, 6 cm

3. $h = 17.4$ cm, $B = 24$ cm^2

Find the volumes of boxes with these dimensions.

4. $l = 15$ cm
$w = 6$ cm
$h = 26$ cm

5. $l = 12$ cm
$w = 7$ cm
$h = 30$ cm

6. $l = 19$ cm
$w = 8$ cm
$h = 29$ cm

7. $l = 4$ m
$w = 2$ m
$h = 4$ m

8. $l = 8.5$ m
$w = 4.5$ m
$h = 10.5$ m

9. $l = 24$ cm
$w = 12$ cm
$h = 15$ cm

10. $l = 8.2$ cm
$w = 4.9$ cm
$h = 10$ cm

11. $l = 6.8$ m
$w = 3.2$ m
$h = 4.0$ m

12. Box **A** has $l = 20$ cm, $w = 12$ cm, and $h = 7$ cm.
Box **B** has $l = 12$ cm, $w = 12$ cm, and $h = 12$ cm.
Which box has the greater volume? How much greater?

⊛ Volume of pyramids

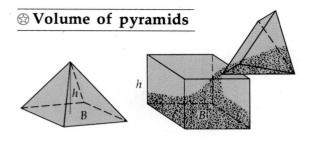

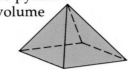

The volume of the pyramid is **one third** the volume of the prism.

Start with a square pyramid with base area B and height h.

Pour three pyramids full of sand to fill a rectangular prism with the same base area B and height h.

Formula for finding the volume of a pyramid

$$V = \frac{1}{3} Bh$$

The formula above can be used to find the volume of any pyramid. Find these volumes.

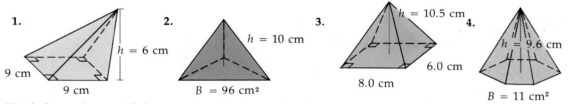

1. 9 cm, 9 cm, $h = 6$ cm

2. $h = 10$ cm, $B = 96$ cm²

3. $h = 10.5$ cm, 6.0 cm, 8.0 cm

4. $h = 9.6$ cm, $B = 11$ cm²

Find the volume of these square pyramids where B = area of base, h = height, and s = length of a side of the base.

5. $B = 2025$ m²
    $h = 85$ m

6. $B = 1225$ m²
    $h = 65$ m

7. $B = 4225$ m²
    $h = 73$ m

8. $B = 576$ m²
    $h = 41$ m

9. $s = 24$ m
    $h = 37$ m

10. $s = 59$ m
    $h = 26.2$ m

11. $s = 12$ m
    $h = 18.4$ m

12. $s = 16$ m
    $h = 22$ m

13. The pyramidal container of popcorn costs the same as the box. Which is the best buy? How many more cubic centimeters of popcorn do you get?

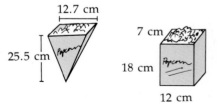

☆ 14. A company sold a small box of raisins for 20¢. They doubled each dimension to make a larger box. If the raisins are sold according to the volume of the box, what should be the price of the larger box?

Think — What is the length of a side of a cube that has as many cubic centimeters of volume as it has square centimeters of surface area?

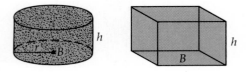

⊛ Volumes of cylinders and cones

A circular cylinder which has the same base area B and height h as a rectangular prism is filled with sand.

The sand in the cylinder will exactly fill the prism. The volume of the cylinder and the prism are the same.

The volume V of the rectangular prism: $V = Bh$
The volume V of the circular cylinder: $V = Bh$

The area of the base B of a cylinder with radius r is $B = \pi r^2$. Therefore the formula for the volume of a circular cylinder is

$$V = Bh \text{ or } V = \pi r^2 h$$

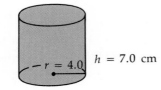

$h = 7.0$ cm
$r = 4.0$

$V = \pi \cdot 4^2 \cdot 7$
$V = 112\pi$
$V \approx 112 \cdot 3.14 = 351.68$
$V \approx 350$ cm^3

Find the volume of each circular cylinder.

1.

12 cm
8 cm

2.

4.0 cm
6.5 cm

3.

10.3 cm
2.0 cm

4.

$h = 6$ cm
3 cm

5. $r = 5$ cm
$h = 16$ cm

6. $r = 1.5$ m
$h = 2.0$ m

7. $r = 6$ cm
$h = 30$ cm

8. $r = 2.0$ m
$h = 4.5$ m

9.

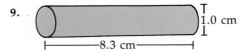

1.0 cm

8.3 cm

A new piece of chalk is 8.3 cm long and 1.0 cm in diameter. What is the total volume of 12 pieces of chalk?

10. Find the volume of each can of juice. Which costs less per cubic centimeter?

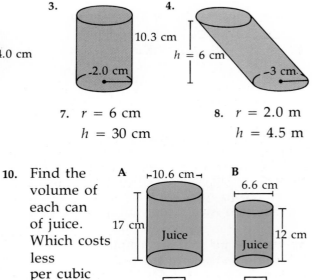

A ⊢10.6 cm⊣

17 cm

Juice

95¢

B

6.6 cm

12 cm

Juice

24¢

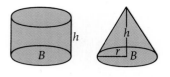

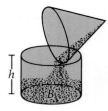

A circular cylinder and a cone have the same base area B and the same height h.

Three cones of sand will exactly fill the cylinder.

The volume of the cone is one third the volume of the cylinder.

Volume of the cylinder: $V = Bh$

Volume of the cone: $V = \frac{1}{3} Bh$

If r is the radius of the base, then $B = \pi r^2$.

Volume of the cone: $V = \frac{1}{3} \pi r^2 h$

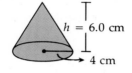

$V = \frac{1}{3} \cdot \pi \cdot 4^2 \cdot 6$

$V = 32\pi \approx 32 \cdot 3.14$

$V \approx 100.48$ cm³

$V \approx 100$ cm³

Find the volume of each cone.

1.
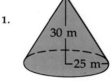
30 m
25 m

2.
4.5 cm
6 cm

3.
8.6 cm
3.4 cm

4.
24 mm
17 mm

5. $r = 1.4$ m
    $h = 2.2$ m

6. $r = 2$ m
    $h = 2$ m

7. $r = 2.7$ cm
    $h = 3.1$ cm

8. $r = 10$ cm
    $h = 8$ cm

9. Which drinking cup will hold more liquid? How much more?

A ⊢8 cm⊣
8 cm

B ⊢10 cm⊣
10 cm

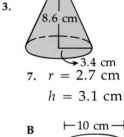

The formula for the volume of a sphere is $V = \frac{4}{3} \pi r^3$.

Using a scale 1 cm = 100 km, the earth can be represented by a sphere with radius 64.0 cm and the moon by a sphere with radius 17.3 cm. How many "moons" would it take to make a volume equal to that of the "earth"?

"Earth"

"Moon"

17.3 cm

$r = 64.0$ cm

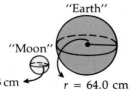

Answers for Self-check   1. $128.78 \approx 130$ m²   2. $37.68 \approx 38$ cm 3. $113.04 \approx 110$ cm²
4. $116.25 \approx 116$ cm²   5. $208 \approx 200$ m²   6. $107.90 \approx 110$ m²
7. $544 \approx 500$ cm²   8. $768 \approx 800$ cm³   ☆ 9. $412.8 \approx 410$ cm²   ☆ 10. $456 \approx 460$ cm³
☆ 11. $226.08 \approx 230$ m²   ☆ 12. $254.34 \approx 250$ m³   ☆ 13. $235.5 \approx 200$ cm³

Self-check

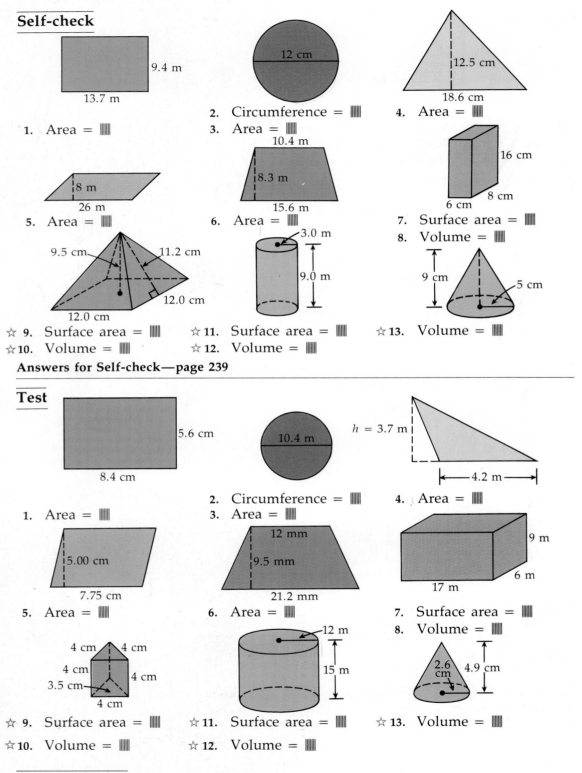

1. Area = ▥

2. Circumference = ▥
3. Area = ▥

4. Area = ▥

5. Area = ▥

6. Area = ▥

7. Surface area = ▥
8. Volume = ▥

☆ **9.** Surface area = ▥
☆ **10.** Volume = ▥

☆ **11.** Surface area = ▥
☆ **12.** Volume = ▥

☆ **13.** Volume = ▥

Answers for Self-check—page 239

Test

1. Area = ▥

2. Circumference = ▥
3. Area = ▥

4. Area = ▥

5. Area = ▥

6. Area = ▥

7. Surface area = ▥
8. Volume = ▥

☆ **9.** Surface area = ▥
☆ **10.** Volume = ▥

☆ **11.** Surface area = ▥
☆ **12.** Volume = ▥

☆ **13.** Volume = ▥

Math lab

Measuring Record Grooves

Have you ever noticed how close the grooves
of a phonograph record are to each other?
Here is a way to compute the average distance
between the grooves.

1. Find the number of revolutions per minute
   (rpm) for the record.

2. Find the playing time t of the record.
   This is usually printed on the record.

3. Measure the distance d across the
   playing surface of the record.

4. Use the formula below to find the average
   distance G between the grooves.

$$G = \frac{d}{\text{rpm} \cdot t}$$

Example: rpm $= 45$
$t = 2{:}18 = 2\frac{18}{60} = 2.3$ minutes
$d = 29$ mm

$$G = \frac{29}{45 \cdot 2.3} = 0.280 \text{ mm}$$

Find the average distance between
the grooves on some of your
records. Use records of different
sizes and rpm's.

Find a way to compute the total
length of the spiral groove
on one side of a record.

Unit 10 review

Write each as a percent.

1. 0.75 2. 0.01 3. 0.33 4. 0.84 5. 0.05

6. $\frac{1}{5}$ 7. $\frac{1}{4}$ 8. $\frac{5}{6}$ 9. $\frac{2}{3}$ 10. $\frac{3}{8}$

11. $\frac{27}{20}$ 12. $\frac{150}{100}$ 13. $\frac{6}{2}$ 14. 3.00 15. 2.05

Write each percent as a lowest-terms fraction.

16. 25% 17. $12\frac{1}{2}$% 18. $66\frac{2}{3}$% 19. 20% 20. 80%

Find the percent of each number.

21. 36% of 480 22. 25% of 200 23. 12% of 415

24. 65% of 80 25. 55% of 20 26. 33% of 25

27. 48% of 212 28. 75% of 400 29. 6% of 30

Compute.

30. What percent of 80 is 20? 31. What percent of 110 is 35?

32. What percent of 56 is 18? 33. What percent of 250 is 25?

34. What percent of 438 is 120? 35. What percent of 16 is 4?

Write and solve an equation for each.

36. 8% of a number is 12.
    What is the number?

37. 35% of a number if 189.
    What is the number?

38. 12% of a number is 84.
    What is the number?

39. 76% of a number is 228.
    What is the number?

40. Find $1\frac{1}{2}$% of $325.44
    to the nearest cent.

41. Find 8% of $1242.75
    to the nearest cent.

Adding and Subtracting Positive and Negative Numbers
Other Operations with Positive and Negative Numbers
Equations
Coordinate Geometry
Symmetry and Transformations

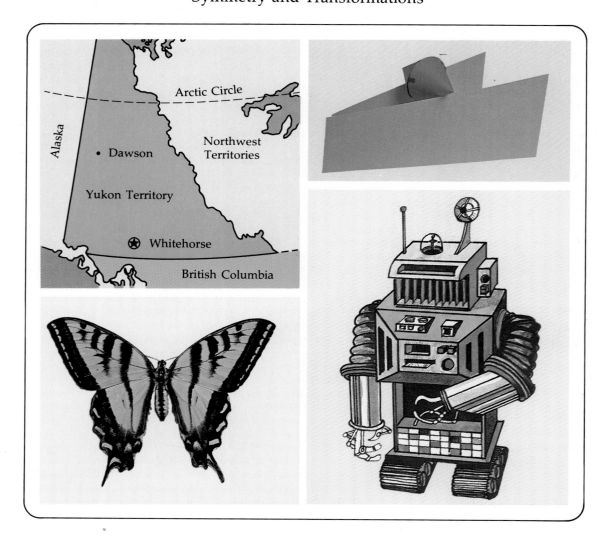

Adding and Subtracting Positive and Negative Numbers

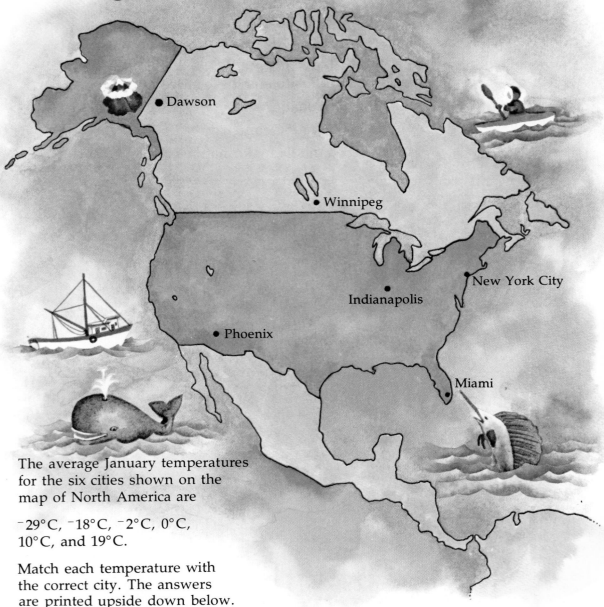

The average January temperatures for the six cities shown on the map of North America are

⁻29°C, ⁻18°C, ⁻2°C, 0°C, 10°C, and 19°C.

Match each temperature with the correct city. The answers are printed upside down below.

Answers: Miami, Florida, 19°C; Phoenix, Arizona, 10°C; New York City, 0°C; Indianapolis, Indiana, ⁻2°C; Winnipeg, Manitoba, ⁻18°C; Dawson, Yukon, ⁻29°C

Points on the number line can be named by positive numbers, negative numbers, or zero.

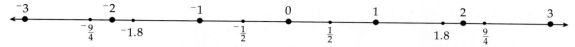

Each positive fractional number has an **opposite** that is a negative fractional number. The opposite of $\frac{1}{2}$ is negative $\frac{1}{2}$. We write: $^-\frac{1}{2}$.

$^-\frac{1}{2}$ is the opposite of $\frac{1}{2}$.

The opposite of 3 is negative 3. We write: $^-3$.

$^-3$ is the opposite of 3.

1 and $^-1$ are opposites.
1.8 and $^-1.8$ are opposites.

$\frac{9}{4}$ and $^-\frac{9}{4}$ are opposites.

The basic relation between pairs of numbers that are opposites is given by the **opposites principle**.

> ### The Opposites Principle
> The sum of each number and its opposite is zero.

Examples: $6 + {}^-6 = 0$ $^-3 + 3 = 0$ $\frac{1}{2} + {}^-\frac{1}{2} = 0$

The positive fractional numbers, the negative fractional numbers, and 0 are called the set of **rational numbers**. The positive whole numbers, the negative whole numbers, and 0 are called the set of **integers**.

The set of integers: $\{\ldots {}^-4, {}^-3, {}^-2, {}^-1, 0, 1, 2, 3, 4, \ldots\}$

Give the opposite of each number.

1. 7   2. $^-2$ 3. 13   4. $^-4$ 5. 10   6. 14   7. $^-9$ 8. $^-1$

9. 20   10. $^-3.1$ 11. $^-\frac{3}{8}$ 12. $^-100$ 13. 4.2   14. $\frac{2}{3}$ 15. $^-6.9$ 16. $^-\frac{1}{4}$

Give the number for n in each equation.

17. $6 + {}^-6 = n$ 18. $^-11 + 11 = n$ 19. $n + {}^-5 = 0$

20. $7 + n = 0$ 21. $\frac{1}{3} + {}^-\frac{1}{3} = n$ 22. $3.2 + {}^-3.2 = n$

Comparing integers

The coldest temperature ever recorded in North Dakota was ⁻51°C. The coldest recorded temperature in Maine was ⁻44°C. Which state recorded the lower temperature?

⁻51°C is "below" ⁻44°C on the thermometer. North Dakota had the lower temperature.

We say: ⁻51 is less than ⁻44,
        or ⁻44 is greater than ⁻51.

We write: ⁻51 < ⁻44 or ⁻44 > ⁻51

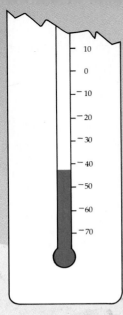

The number line can help you compare two integers.

  ⁻7 < ⁻2 because ⁻7 is to the left of ⁻2.
  ⁻3 > ⁻5 because ⁻3 is to the right of ⁻5.
   1 > ⁻8 because 1 is to the right of ⁻8.
  ⁻6 < 0 because ⁻6 is to the left of 0.

Tell which integer is the smaller.

1. 9, ⁻3   2. ⁻1, ⁻2   3. ⁻10, ⁻16   4. 0, 7

5. ⁻2, ⁻84   6. 38, 83   7. ⁻2, 0   8. ⁻1, 1

Tell which integer is the greater.

9. ⁻9, ⁻6   10. ⁻23, ⁻33   11. 2, ⁻2   12. ⁻10, ⁻9

13. ⁻39, ⁻31   14. 0, 7   15. ⁻1, ⁻8   16. ⁻99, ⁻999

Copy and give the correct symbol, > or <, for each ●.

1. ⁻6 ● ⁻4
2. ⁻1 ● 3
3. 11 ● 9
4. ⁻3 ● ⁻5
5. ⁻8 ● ⁻12
6. ⁻10 ● ⁻4
7. 0 ● 5
8. 0 ● ⁻6
9. ⁻30 ● ⁻20
10. ⁻7 ● ⁻8
11. 1 ● ⁻1
12. 53 ● 54
13. ⁻53 ● ⁻54
14. ⁻5 ● 2
15. ⁻19 ● ⁻17
16. ⁻13 ● ⁻18

Repeated inequalities can be used to compare three or more numbers.

⁻6 < ⁻4 < 2 means ⁻6 is less than ⁻4 *and* ⁻4 is less than 2.
We say: ⁻4 is between ⁻6 and 2.

7 > ⁻3 > ⁻5 means 7 is greater than ⁻3 *and* ⁻3 is greater than ⁻5.
We say: ⁻3 is between ⁻5 and 7.

Write repeated inequalities to compare each group of numbers.

17. ⁻1, 4, ⁻7
18. 6, ⁻3, 9
19. ⁻11, ⁻10, ⁻20
20. 0, ⁻1, 1
21. 5, ⁻14, ⁻8
22. ⁻4, ⁻11, ⁻2
23. ⁻5, ⁻7, ⁻9
24. 15, ⁻15, 0
25. ⁻3, ⁻9, ⁻20
26. 31, ⁻67, 76
27. ⁻10, ⁻15, ⁻8
28. ⁻6, 6, ⁻3

29. The low temperature on one winter day was ⁻14°C in Duluth, ⁻6°C in Minneapolis, and ⁻10°C in Northfield. Which city had the coldest temperature?

☆ 30. The lowest temperature recorded on earth is ⁻88.3°C. The highest recorded temperature on earth is 58.0°C. How many degrees would the temperature have to rise to go from the coldest to the hottest temperature?

Upside-Down Calculator Crossword Puzzle

Copy the puzzle. Calculate each answer and turn the calculator upside down to find the word to put in the puzzle.

Across
1. Famous book (18 765 + 19 053)
4. Little islands (19 × 2829)
5. A military action (45 × 807)

Down
1. Happiness (96 423 − 41 245)
2. Water found in a ship (1669 × 22)
3. Girl's name (177^2 + 244)

Adding integers

The number line can be used to add integers.

Adding a positive integer

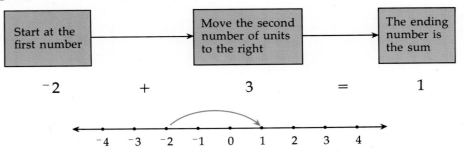

Start at the first number → Move the second number of units to the right → The ending number is the sum

$$^-2 \quad + \quad 3 \quad = \quad 1$$

Adding a negative integer

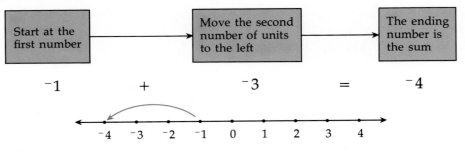

Start at the first number → Move the second number of units to the left → The ending number is the sum

$$^-1 \quad + \quad ^-3 \quad = \quad ^-4$$

Other examples

$$^-3 + 2 = ^-1 \qquad 2 + ^-4 = ^-2 \qquad 4 + ^-3 = 1$$

Find the sums. Use the number line to help you.

-10 -9 -8 -7 -6 -5 -4 -3 -2 -1 0 1 2 3 4 5 6 7 8 9 10

1. $5 + ^-1$ 2. $4 + ^-3$ 3. $^-2 + 6$ 4. $2 + ^-5$

5. $1 + ^-4$ 6. $9 + ^-5$ 7. $^-4 + ^-3$ 8. $^-1 + ^-5$

9. $3 + 7$ 10. $8 + ^-8$ 11. $7 + ^-10$ 12. $^-9 + 6$

13. $^-3 + ^-4$ 14. $10 + ^-1$ 15. $6 + ^-9$ 16. $4 + ^-8$

17. $7 + ^-9$ 18. $^-5 + ^-5$ 19. $9 + ^-11$ 20. $2 + ^-12$

21. $^-5 + 5$ 22. $^-1 + ^-9$ 23. $^-5 + 10$ 24. $^-4 + ^-6$

Find the sums.

1. $2 + {}^-7$ —5
2. $^-3 + {}^-5$
3. $6 + {}^-5$
4. $7 + {}^-7$

5. $^-1 + {}^-3$ —4
6. $4 + {}^-8$
7. $^-6 + {}^-3$
8. $7 + {}^-11$

9. $^-8 + 12$ 4
10. $^-3 + {}^-1$
11. $8 + {}^-6$
12. $^-10 + 8$

13. $^-2 + {}^-2$ —4
14. $9 + {}^-13$
15. $^-10 + 1$
16. $^-4 + {}^-5$

17. $0 + {}^-8$ —8
18. $^-6 + 7$
19. $3 + 5$
20. $^-7 + 3$

21. $5 + {}^-12$ —7
22. $^-4 + {}^-4$
23. $^-6 + 13$
24. $9 + {}^-4$

25. $3 + {}^-9$ —6
26. $8 + {}^-14$
27. $7 + {}^-2$
28. $^-3 + {}^-5$

29. $^-6 + {}^-1$ —7
30. $10 + {}^-10$
31. $^-2 + 1$
32. $^-7 + 8$

Give the missing integer. Check your answer.

Example: $6 + n = 5$ Check: $6 + {}^-1 = 5$
$n = {}^-1$

33. $8 + n = 2$
34. $^-2 + n = {}^-5$
35. $^-1 + n = 6$
36. $3 + n = {}^-1$

37. $4 + n = 0$
38. $^-5 + n = {}^-2$
39. $7 + n = {}^-3$
40. $^-8 + n = {}^-4$

41. $5 + n = 2$
42. $^-3 + n = 3$
43. $^-6 + n = {}^-10$
44. $12 + n = 5$

45. $0 + n = {}^-7$
46. $13 + n = 0$
47. $9 + n = 17$
48. $14 + n = 6$

49. $^-10 + n = {}^-20$
50. $^-7 + n = {}^-7$
51. $^-11 + n = 4$
52. $^-9 + n = 18$

Choose two numbers a and b.
Find $a - b$.

Use the same two numbers.
Find $b - a$.

What do you notice about
the two answers? Try this
with other pairs of numbers.

⊛ Basic principles for addition

The same basic principles hold for negative numbers as for positive numbers. Using the basic principles for addition, you can prove that the sums of integers you find by using the number line are correct.

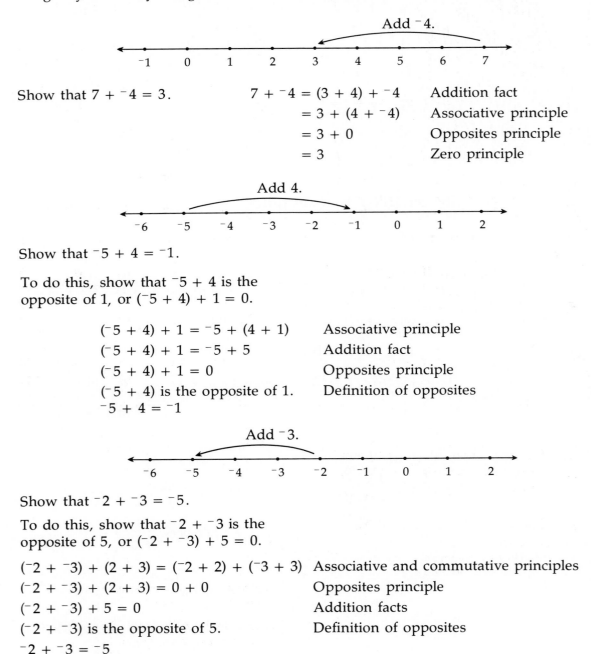

Show that 7 + ⁻4 = 3.

7 + ⁻4 = (3 + 4) + ⁻4	Addition fact
= 3 + (4 + ⁻4)	Associative principle
= 3 + 0	Opposites principle
= 3	Zero principle

Add 4.

Show that ⁻5 + 4 = ⁻1.

To do this, show that ⁻5 + 4 is the opposite of 1, or (⁻5 + 4) + 1 = 0.

(⁻5 + 4) + 1 = ⁻5 + (4 + 1)	Associative principle
(⁻5 + 4) + 1 = ⁻5 + 5	Addition fact
(⁻5 + 4) + 1 = 0	Opposites principle
(⁻5 + 4) is the opposite of 1.	Definition of opposites
⁻5 + 4 = ⁻1	

Add ⁻3.

Show that ⁻2 + ⁻3 = ⁻5.

To do this, show that ⁻2 + ⁻3 is the opposite of 5, or (⁻2 + ⁻3) + 5 = 0.

(⁻2 + ⁻3) + (2 + 3) = (⁻2 + 2) + (⁻3 + 3)	Associative and commutative principles
(⁻2 + ⁻3) + (2 + 3) = 0 + 0	Opposites principle
(⁻2 + ⁻3) + 5 = 0	Addition facts
(⁻2 + ⁻3) is the opposite of 5.	Definition of opposites
⁻2 + ⁻3 = ⁻5	

Find the sums.

1. $3 + {}^-2$
2. ${}^-9 + 5$
3. ${}^-4 + {}^-7$
4. $6 + {}^-9$

5. $12 + {}^-8$
6. ${}^-3 + 6$
7. ${}^-12 + 10$
8. $5 + {}^-8$

9. $10 + {}^-12$
10. ${}^-13 + 9$
11. ${}^-2 + {}^-6$
12. ${}^-4 + {}^-9$

13. $\begin{array}{r} {}^-6 \\ + {}^-8 \\ \hline \end{array}$
14. $\begin{array}{r} 11 \\ + {}^-11 \\ \hline \end{array}$
15. $\begin{array}{r} {}^-12 \\ + \quad 3 \\ \hline \end{array}$
16. $\begin{array}{r} 5 \\ + {}^-14 \\ \hline \end{array}$
17. $\begin{array}{r} 7 \\ + {}^-6 \\ \hline \end{array}$
18. $\begin{array}{r} 15 \\ + {}^-8 \\ \hline \end{array}$

19. $\begin{array}{r} 9 \\ + {}^-8 \\ \hline \end{array}$
20. $\begin{array}{r} {}^-17 \\ + \quad 12 \\ \hline \end{array}$
21. $\begin{array}{r} 13 \\ + {}^-15 \\ \hline \end{array}$
22. $\begin{array}{r} {}^-6 \\ + {}^-13 \\ \hline \end{array}$
23. $\begin{array}{r} 10 \\ + {}^-5 \\ \hline \end{array}$
24. $\begin{array}{r} {}^-10 \\ + \quad 5 \\ \hline \end{array}$

25. $3 + {}^-8 + {}^-2$
26. ${}^-1 + 4 + {}^-6$
27. $9 + {}^-2 + {}^-6$

28. $9 + {}^-7 + 4$
29. ${}^-3 + {}^-5 + {}^-4$
30. ${}^-12 + 6 + 5$

31. ${}^-2 + {}^-3 + 7 + 1$
32. $4 + {}^-5 + {}^-7 + 6$
33. ${}^-5 + {}^-6 + {}^-1 + {}^-2$

34. $\begin{array}{r} {}^-2 \\ 7 \\ {}^-5 \\ + \quad 6 \\ \hline \end{array}$
35. $\begin{array}{r} 10 \\ {}^-4 \\ {}^-7 \\ + {}^-3 \\ \hline \end{array}$
36. $\begin{array}{r} {}^-9 \\ {}^-7 \\ 10 \\ + \quad 8 \\ \hline \end{array}$
37. $\begin{array}{r} {}^-4 \\ {}^-8 \\ 9 \\ + {}^-3 \\ \hline \end{array}$
38. $\begin{array}{r} 12 \\ {}^-3 \\ {}^-9 \\ + {}^-5 \\ \hline \end{array}$
39. $\begin{array}{r} 6 \\ {}^-8 \\ {}^-7 \\ + \quad 4 \\ \hline \end{array}$

40. $\begin{array}{r} 12 \\ {}^-9 \\ + {}^-8 \\ \hline \end{array}$
41. $\begin{array}{r} {}^-20 \\ {}^-11 \\ + \quad 16 \\ \hline \end{array}$
42. $\begin{array}{r} {}^-8 \\ {}^-13 \\ + {}^-9 \\ \hline \end{array}$
43. $\begin{array}{r} 16 \\ 18 \\ + {}^-10 \\ \hline \end{array}$
44. $\begin{array}{r} {}^-25 \\ {}^-12 \\ + {}^-17 \\ \hline \end{array}$
45. $\begin{array}{r} {}^-83 \\ 42 \\ + \quad 37 \\ \hline \end{array}$

46. If all the addends in a problem are positive numbers, is the sum positive or negative?

47. If all the addends in a problem are negative, is the sum positive or negative?

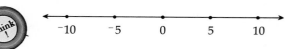

Choose pairs of integers from 10 to ${}^-10$ which have a sum of 5.

Write as many different addition equations as you can using the pairs.

More practice, page 392, Set A

Subtracting integers

You can check a subtraction equation by using the related addition equation.

$$6 - 2 = 4 \text{ because } 4 + 2 = 6$$
$$8 - 3 = 5 \text{ because } 5 + 3 = 8$$
$$7 - {}^-2 = 9 \text{ because } 9 + {}^-2 = 7$$
$${}^-1 - 4 = {}^-5 \text{ because } {}^-5 + 4 = {}^-1$$
$${}^-2 - {}^-3 = 1 \text{ because } 1 + {}^-3 = {}^-2$$
$$5 - 7 = {}^-2 \text{ because } {}^-2 + 7 = 5$$

Give an addition equation for each subtraction equation.

1. $5 - {}^-2 = 7$ *7+⁻2=5*
2. ${}^-4 - 3 = {}^-7$ *⁻7+3=⁻4*
3. $8 - {}^-6 = 14$

4. ${}^-3 - {}^-2 = {}^-1$ *⁻1+⁻2=⁻3*
5. $8 - 10 = {}^-2$ *⁻2+10=8*
6. $0 - {}^-3 = 3$

7. ${}^-4 - 6 = {}^-10$ *⁻10+6=⁻4*
8. ${}^-7 - 5 = {}^-12$ *⁻12+5=⁻7*
9. $4 - {}^-4 = 8$

0+⁻2=⁻2

10. ${}^-2 - {}^-2 = 0$
11. ${}^-9 - 4 = {}^-13$ *⁻13+4=⁻9*
12. ${}^-13 - {}^-5 = {}^-8$

13. ${}^-10 - {}^-6 = {}^-4$ *⁻4+⁻6=⁻10*
14. ${}^-1 - 8 = {}^-9$ *⁻9+8=⁻1*
15. $3 - {}^-8 = 11$

Find the number for n.

What number
plus 4 equals 1?
↓
16. $1 - 4 = n$

What number
plus 2 equals ⁻5?
↓
17. ${}^-5 - 2 = n$

What number
plus ⁻3 equals 7?
↓
18. $7 - {}^-3 = n$

What number
plus 3 equals ⁻1?
↓
19. ${}^-1 - 3 = n$

What number
plus ⁻11 equals 7?
↓
20. $7 - {}^-11 = n$

What number
plus ⁻4 equals ⁻6?
↓
21. ${}^-6 - {}^-4 = n$

Find the number for n.

1. $2 - 4 = n$ 2. $^-3 - 2 = n$ 3. $6 - {}^-3 = n$ 4. $^-8 - 5 = n$

5. $0 - 6 = n$ 6. $^-5 - 1 = n$ 7. $7 - 10 = n$ 8. $4 - {}^-8 = n$

9. $^-1 - {}^-2 = n$ 10. $^-7 - {}^-6 = n$ 11. $^-3 - 5 = n$ 12. $10 - 9 = n$

13. $0 - {}^-9 = n$ 14. $1 - {}^-10 = n$ 15. $4 - {}^-9 = n$ 16. $^-8 - {}^-2 = n$

17. $7 - {}^-7 = n$ 18. $^-3 - 0 = n$ 19. $^-5 - {}^-5 = n$ 20. $10 - {}^-5 = n$

21. $13 - 20 = n$ 22. $^-13 - {}^-9 = n$ 23. $14 - 18 = n$ 24. $^-9 - {}^-8 = n$

25. $^-7 - 8 = n$ 26. $6 - {}^-8 = n$ 27. $^-16 - {}^-9 = n$ 28. $^-15 - {}^-3 = n$

29. $^-1 - {}^-6 = n$ 30. $^-10 - {}^-14 = n$ 31. $11 - {}^-3 = n$ 32. $^-6 - 8 = n$

Find the differences.

33. $\begin{array}{r} ^-8 \\ -\ 2 \\ \hline \end{array}$ 34. $\begin{array}{r} ^-9 \\ -\ ^-5 \\ \hline \end{array}$ 35. $\begin{array}{r} 6 \\ -\ ^-5 \\ \hline \end{array}$ 36. $\begin{array}{r} ^-12 \\ -\ ^-6 \\ \hline \end{array}$ 37. $\begin{array}{r} 15 \\ -\ 20 \\ \hline \end{array}$ 38. $\begin{array}{r} 12 \\ -\ ^-9 \\ \hline \end{array}$

39. $\begin{array}{r} ^-11 \\ -\ ^-7 \\ \hline \end{array}$ 40. $\begin{array}{r} 6 \\ -\ ^-8 \\ \hline \end{array}$ 41. $\begin{array}{r} 0 \\ -\ ^-5 \\ \hline \end{array}$ 42. $\begin{array}{r} ^-7 \\ -\ 9 \\ \hline \end{array}$ 43. $\begin{array}{r} 10 \\ -\ 16 \\ \hline \end{array}$ 44. $\begin{array}{r} ^-4 \\ -\ ^-8 \\ \hline \end{array}$

45. $6 - {}^-7$ 46. $^-9 - {}^-8$ 47. $8 - 12$ 48. $9 - {}^-9$

49. $0 - 8$ 50. $4 - {}^-11$ 51. $^-20 - {}^-10$ 52. $7 - {}^-4$

53. $16 - 9$ 54. $^-5 - 3$ 55. $^-7 - 0$ 56. $^-1 - {}^-1$

57. $^-2 - 8$ 58. $12 - {}^-5$ 59. $^-6 - {}^-5$ 60. $^-17 - {}^-19$

61. $100 - {}^-9$ 62. $^-84 - 16$ 63. $^-27 - {}^-68$ 64. $65 - 94$

Give the integer for n.

☆ 65. $3 - n = 9$

☆ 66. $^-6 - n = {}^-2$

☆ 67. $^-5 - n = 5$

☆ 68. $1 - n = {}^-10$

The sum of two numbers is zero.

The difference of the same two numbers is 8.

What are the two numbers?

Relating subtraction and addition of integers

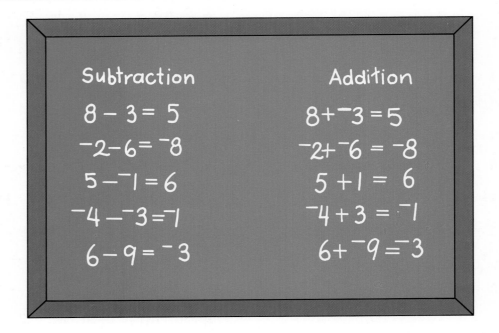

Subtraction
$8 - 3 = 5$
$^-2 - 6 = ^-8$
$5 - ^-1 = 6$
$^-4 - ^-3 = ^-1$
$6 - 9 = ^-3$

Addition
$8 + ^-3 = 5$
$^-2 + ^-6 = ^-8$
$5 + 1 = 6$
$^-4 + 3 = ^-1$
$6 + ^-9 = ^-3$

The addition and subtraction equations on the chalkboard show that you get the same answer when you subtract a number as when you add its opposite.

$$3 - ^-2 = 3 + 2 = 5$$
opposites

$$^-4 - 7 = ^-4 + ^-7 = ^-11$$
opposites

Write each subtraction problem as an addition problem. Then find the answer.

1. $6 - 2$ 2. $^-1 - 3$ 3. $5 - ^-7$ 4. $^-1 - ^-4$

5. $3 - 10$ 6. $12 - 7$ 7. $^-5 - ^-2$ 8. $^-2 - ^-8$

9. $9 - ^-4$ 10. $^-4 - 4$ 11. $^-15 - ^-9$ 12. $4 - 11$

13. $0 - ^-5$ 14. $^-3 - ^-3$ 15. $12 - 7$ 16. $6 - ^-6$

17. $4 - ^-1$ 18. $20 - ^-10$ 19. $8 - 14$ 20. $^-12 - 9$

Find the differences.

1. $4 - {}^-3$
2. $10 - {}^-8$
3. $1 - 5$
4. ${}^-6 - {}^-5$

5. ${}^-7 - 4$
6. ${}^-11 - {}^-12$
7. ${}^-9 - {}^-7$
8. $3 - 11$

9. ${}^-1 - {}^-2$
10. $0 - 6$
11. $25 - {}^-10$
12. $14 - 6$

13. ${}^-13 - {}^-14$
14. $7 - {}^-5$
15. ${}^-9 - 1$
16. $8 - {}^-7$

17. ${}^-4 - 4$
18. ${}^-15 - {}^-6$
19. $3 - 12$
20. $11 - {}^-9$

21. ${}^-9 - {}^-7$
22. ${}^-6 - 9$
23. ${}^-19 - 0$
24. ${}^-99 - 1$

25. ${}^-14 - 2$
26. ${}^-7 - {}^-5$
27. $0 - {}^-3$
28. $1 - 13$

29. $18 - {}^-9$
30. ${}^-6 - 6$
31. ${}^-16 - {}^-9$
32. ${}^-8 - {}^-14$

33. $23 - 33$
34. $1 - {}^-1$
35. ${}^-5 - {}^-12$
36. $16 - {}^-8$

37. ${}^-3 - 0$
38. ${}^-11 - 7$
39. $5 - {}^-6$
40. $12 - 18$

41. ${}^-4 - 9$
42. $15 - {}^-5$
43. $6 - 13$
44. ${}^-17 - {}^-10$

Find the number for n.

45. $(3 - 8) + {}^-4 = n$
46. ${}^-4 + (6 - 9) = n$

47. $({}^-1 - {}^-2) - {}^-3 = n$
48. $(11 - {}^-4) - 15 = n$

49. $10 + ({}^-2 - {}^-7) = n$
50. $(7 + {}^-9) - {}^-6 = n$

51. $(9 - 15) - {}^-4 = n$
52. $(1 - 2) - 3 = n$

53. $(9 - 8) - 7 = n$
54. $({}^-2 - {}^-3) - {}^-4 = n$

☆ 55. Is subtraction a commutative operation?

Does $a - b = b - a$, for all numbers a and b?

☆ 56. Is subtraction an associative operation?

Does $(a - b) - c = a - (b - c)$ for all numbers a, b, and c?

Make an **antimagic** square.

(Think)

Place the digits from 1 through 9 in the nine squares so that each row, column, and diagonal has a different sum.

More practice, page 392, Set B

✪ Adding and subtracting rational numbers

Facts about Yukon Territory
Area: 536 324 km²
Population: 21 800
Capital: Whitehorse
Coldest temperature: ⁻62.8°C
Highest temperature: 35.0°C
Highest mountain: Mt. Logan

What is the difference between the highest and the lowest temperatures for Yukon Territory?

$$35.0 - {}^-62.8 = 35.0 + 62.8$$
$$= 97.8$$

The difference is 97.8°C.

Other examples

$$\begin{array}{r} {}^-17.4 \\ + \;\; {}^-8.5 \\ \hline {}^-25.9 \end{array}$$

$$^-6.4 + 2.1 = {}^-4.3 \qquad 12.5 - 20.0 = {}^-7.5$$

Find the sums.

1. $5.4 + {}^-3.2$ 2. $^-1.7 + {}^-2.5$ 3. $12.6 + {}^-8.6$ 4. $^-10.5 + 7.3$ 5. $^-16.0 + 8.2$

6. $\begin{array}{r} 126.4 \\ + \;{}^-18.3 \end{array}$
7. $\begin{array}{r} {}^-2.66 \\ + \;{}^-3.72 \end{array}$
8. $\begin{array}{r} {}^-8.09 \\ + \;\; 5.33 \end{array}$
9. $\begin{array}{r} 5.00 \\ + \;{}^-4.77 \end{array}$
10. $\begin{array}{r} {}^-0.746 \\ + \;{}^-0.285 \end{array}$

11. $\frac{1}{2} + {}^-1$ 12. $^-3\frac{1}{4} + \frac{3}{4}$ 13. $\frac{^-2}{3} + \frac{^-5}{3}$ 14. $\frac{5}{2} + \frac{^-7}{2}$ 15. $^-1\frac{1}{2} + \frac{^-1}{4}$

Find the differences.

16. $^-8.0 - 6.3$ 17. $3.2 - {}^-1.5$ 18. $4.5 - {}^-2.4$ 19. $7.1 - 9.2$ 20. $^-15.4 - {}^-20.0$

21. $\frac{1}{2} - 1$ 22. $\frac{^-3}{2} - \frac{1}{2}$ 23. $\frac{4}{3} - \frac{^-7}{3}$ 24. $\frac{3}{4} - 2\frac{1}{4}$ 25. $\frac{1}{8} - \frac{1}{2}$

1. The average daily temperature in Dawson, Yukon, in January is ⁻29°C. In Whitehorse it is ⁻18.9°C. How many degrees colder is it in Dawson?

2. Mt. Logan has an altitude of 6050 m and is the second highest mountain in North America. The lowest point in North America is Death Valley, California, with an altitude of ⁻89 m, or 89 m below sea level. How much higher is Mt. Logan than Death Valley?

3. During the Klondike Gold Rush of 1898 an estimated 35 000 people lived in Yukon Territory. The population is now about 21 800. About how many fewer people live in Yukon Territory today?

4. The coldest recorded temperature in the Yukon is ⁻62.8°C. The coldest Alaskan temperature is ⁻62.1°C. Which is the colder temperature? How much colder is it?

5. The normal low temperature in Whitehorse in January is ⁻22.8°C. The normal high temperature in January is 8.4°C higher. What is the normal high temperature in January?

6. The lowest Canadian temperature ever recorded was in the Yukon. It was ⁻62.8°C. The highest temperature in Canada was in Saskatchewan. This temperature was 45°C. How many degrees difference is there in the temperatures?

In each problem two of the digits have switched places. Switch them back so the problems are correct.

$$
\begin{array}{r}
5615 \\
+\ 2849 \\
\hline
8574
\end{array}
\qquad
\begin{array}{r}
6495 \\
-\ 4038 \\
\hline
1467
\end{array}
$$

Answers for Self-check   1. ⁻6   2. 7   3. 1   4. ⁻20   5. 13   6. >   7. <   8. >   9. >   10. 4
11. ⁻4   12. ⁻7   13. ⁻6   14. 5   15. ⁻5   16. ⁻13   17. 10   18. ⁻3   19. 12   20. ⁻10   21. ⁻1   22. 13
23. ⁻2   24. 8   25. 0   26. ⁻6   27. 4   28. 6

Self-check

Give the opposite of each number.

1. 6
2. $^-7$
3. $^-1$
4. 20
5. $^-13$

Give the correct symbol, > or <, for each ●.

6. $^-2$ ● $^-3$
7. $^-4$ ● 1
8. 12 ● $^-14$
9. $^-1$ ● $^-10$

Find the sums.

10. 8 + $^-4$
11. $^-7$ + 3
12. $^-2$ + $^-5$
13. 14 + $^-20$

14. 11 + $^-6$
15. $^-9$ + 4
16. $^-7$ + $^-6$
17. $^-3$ + 13

Find the differences.

18. 2 − 5
19. 8 − $^-4$
20. $^-3$ − 7
21. $^-4$ − $^-3$

22. 6 − $^-7$
23. $^-11$ − $^-9$
24. 17 − 9
25. $^-6$ − $^-6$

Add or subtract.

26. (3 + $^-7$) + $^-2$
27. (9 − $^-3$) − 8
28. ($^-3$ − $^-5$) − $^-4$

Answers for Self-check—page 257

Test

Give the opposite of each number.

1. 10
2. $^-2$
3. $^-14$
4. 11
5. $^-23$

Give the correct symbol, > or <, for each ●.

6. 0 ● $^-3$
7. $^-4$ ● $^-2$
8. 8 ● $^-9$
9. $^-1$ ● 1

Find the sums.

10. $^-2$ + 5
11. $^-9$ + $^-4$
12. 6 + $^-8$
13. 5 + $^-3$

14. 6 + $^-10$
15. 15 + $^-8$
16. $^-16$ + 9
17. 20 + $^-50$

Find the differences.

18. $^-2$ − 5
19. 6 − 12
20. 8 − $^-9$
21. $^-3$ − $^-8$

22. 10 − $^-7$
23. $^-14$ − $^-9$
24. 7 − $^-8$
25. 0 − $^-3$

Add or subtract.   26. ($^-5$ + 12) + $^-6$ 27. $^-13$ + ($^-2$ + 10)   28. ($^-7$ − 3) − $^-15$

Lucky Seven Integer Race

Number of players: 2

Mark the faces of a cube with the
integers 1, ⁻1, 2, ⁻2, 3, and ⁻3.

Use two counters.

Draw a number line with integers from ⁻7 to 7.

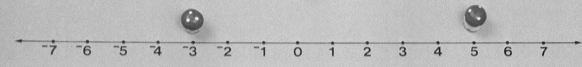

At the start of the game, the players place their
counters at 0 on the number line.

The players take turns tossing the cube and adding
the top number on the cube to the number marked by
their counter on the number line. Then they move
their counter to the sum on the number line.

The first player to land directly on 7 or ⁻7 wins
the game. If a toss would take a player beyond 7
or ⁻7, the turn is lost.

Variation: Play the game the same way, but subtract
the integer tossed on each turn.

Other Operations with Positive and Negative Numbers

Think of a **rise** in temperature as a **positive** number and a **drop** in temperature as a **negative** number.
Think of **hours from now** as a **positive** number and **hours ago** as a negative number.
Think of the temperature **now** as 0°C.

The temperature is dropping 2°C each hour. 4 hours from now the temperature will be ⁻8°C.

Equation: $4 \cdot {}^-2 = {}^-8$

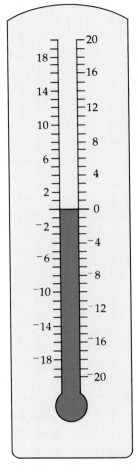

Give the missing number for each 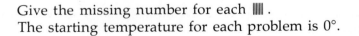.
The starting temperature for each problem is 0°.

1. The temperature is rising 2°C each hour. 4 hours ago the temperature was ▦.

    $^-4 \cdot 2 = $ ▦

2. The temperature is rising 2°C each hour. 4 hours from now the temperature will be ▦.

    $4 \cdot 2 = $ ▦

3. The temperature is dropping 2°C each hour. 4 hours ago the temperature was ▦.

    $^-4 \cdot {}^-2 = $ ▦

Give the missing integer for each 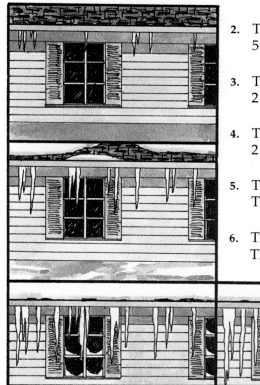 .
Then write a multiplication equation using integers for the problem.

The starting temperature for each problem is 0°C.

1. The temperature is rising 3°C each hour.
   5 hours ago the temperature was ▦ .

2. The temperature is dropping 3°C each hour.
   5 hours ago the temperature was ▦ .

3. The temperature is rising 6°C each hour.
   2 hours from now the temperature will be ▦ .

4. The temperature is dropping 6°C each hour.
   2 hours ago the temperature was ▦ .

5. The temperature is dropping 5°C each hour.
   The temperature 4 hours from now will be ▦ .

6. The temperature is rising 4°C each hour.
   The temperature 4 hours ago was ▦ .

Complete each sentence with **positive** or **negative**.

7. The product of two positive numbers is a ___?___ number.

8. The product of a positive number and a negative number is a ___?___ number.

9. The product of two negative numbers is a ___?___ number.

Find the products.

10. $^-3 \cdot 6$	11. $5 \cdot {}^-7$	12. $^-2 \cdot {}^-8$	13. $^-9 \cdot {}^-3$
14. $10 \cdot {}^-4$	15. $^-6 \cdot 5$	16. $^-3 \cdot {}^-3$	17. $6 \cdot {}^-9$
18. $^-2 \cdot {}^-1$	19. $^-9 \cdot 3$	20. $^-5 \cdot {}^-5$	21. $^-1 \cdot {}^-6$

✪ Basic principles for multiplication

One Principle	Commutative Principle
For each integer a, $a \cdot 1 = a$	For each pair of integers a and b, $a \cdot b = b \cdot a$

Associative Principle	Distributive Principle
For each three integers a, b, and c, $(a \cdot b) \cdot c = a \cdot (b \cdot c)$	For each three integers a, b, and c, $a \cdot (b + c) = (a \cdot b) + (a \cdot c)$ $(b + c) \cdot a = (b \cdot a) + (c \cdot a)$

The examples below show how the basic principles can be used to justify the rules used for multiplying positive and negative numbers.

Example 1: Show that $5 \cdot {}^-2 = {}^-10$.

$5 \cdot (2 + {}^-2) = 0$	$(2 + {}^-2) = 0$ because of the opposites principle, and $5 \cdot 0 = 0$
$(5 \cdot 2) + (5 \cdot {}^-2) = 0$	Distributive principle
$10 + (5 \cdot {}^-2) = 0$	$5 \cdot 2 = 10$
$(5 \cdot {}^-2)$ is the opposite of 10.	Definition of opposites
$5 \cdot {}^-2 = {}^-10$	The opposite of 10 is $^-10$.
$^-2 \cdot 5 = {}^-10$	Commutative principle

Example 2: Show that $^-5 \cdot {}^-2 = 10$.

$^-5 \cdot (2 + {}^-2) = 0$	$({}^-2 + 2) = 0$, $^-5 \cdot 0 = 0$
$({}^-5 \cdot 2) + ({}^-5 \cdot {}^-2) = 0$	Distributive principle
$^-10 + ({}^-5 \cdot {}^-2) = 0$	$^-5 \cdot 2 = {}^-10$, Example 1
$({}^-5 \cdot {}^-2)$ is the opposite of $^-10$.	Definition of opposites
$^-5 \cdot {}^-2 = 10$	The opposite of $^-10$ is 10.

Give the integer for n. Think about the basic principles.

1. $^-5 \cdot 1 = n$
2. $^-7 \cdot {}^-3 = {}^-3n$
3. $^-8(3 + {}^-2) = ({}^-8 \cdot 3) + ({}^-8n)$
4. $(4 \cdot {}^-3) \cdot 5 = 4 \cdot (n \cdot 5)$
5. $n \cdot 1 = {}^-10$
6. $^-4n = {}^-6 \cdot {}^-4$

Find the products.

1. $^-7 \cdot ^-6$
2. $3 \cdot ^-10$
3. $6 \cdot ^-8$
4. $^-8 \cdot ^-8$

5. $^-9 \cdot ^-3$
6. $4 \cdot ^-9$
7. $^-3 \cdot ^-3$
8. $7 \cdot 5$

9. $^-8 \cdot 6$
10. $^-6 \cdot ^-1$
11. $9 \cdot 0$
12. $^-4 \cdot ^-7$

13. $^-5 \cdot ^-5$
14. $^-3 \cdot ^-12$
15. $^-2 \cdot 15$
16. $8 \cdot ^-9$

17. $^-2 \cdot ^-50$
18. $4 \cdot ^-16$
19. $^-8 \cdot 15$
20. $^-10 \cdot ^-10$

21. $5 \cdot ^-3$
22. $^-8 \cdot ^-4$
23. $^-2 \cdot 4$
24. $^-1 \cdot 1$

25. $14 \cdot ^-2$
26. $^-9 \cdot 7$
27. $5 \cdot 9$
28. $^-10 \cdot ^-6$

29. $3 \cdot ^-40$
30. $^-60 \cdot ^-4$
31. $^-8 \cdot ^-6$
32. $12 \cdot ^-2$

Find the products.

33. $(^-2 \cdot ^-3) \cdot 4$
34. $^-5 \cdot (2 \cdot 5)$
35. $^-6 \cdot (^-1 \cdot ^-4)$

36. $8 \cdot 2 \cdot ^-2$
37. $^-3 \cdot ^-5 \cdot ^-2$
38. $^-1 \cdot ^-1 \cdot 9$

39. $^-6 \cdot ^-3 \cdot ^-1$
40. $^-2 \cdot ^-2 \cdot ^-3 \cdot ^-3$
41. $^-5 \cdot 2 \cdot ^-2 \cdot ^-5$

Find the integer for each power.

Example: $(2)^3 = 2 \cdot 2 \cdot 2 = 8$
$(^-2)^3 = ^-2 \cdot ^-2 \cdot ^-2 = ^-8$

42. $(^-3)^2$
43. $(^-4)^3$
44. $(^-10)^2$
45. $(2)^4$
46. $(^-1)^5$
47. $(3)^3$
48. $(^-2)^4$

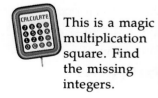

This is a magic multiplication square. Find the missing integers.

$^-8$	▥	$^-128$
256	16	▥
$^-2$	▥	▥

More practice, page 393, Set A

Dividing positive and negative numbers

You can check a division equation by using a related multiplication equation.

$$36 \div 9 = 4 \text{ because } 4 \cdot 9 = 36$$
$$12 \div 4 = 3 \text{ because } 3 \cdot 4 = 12$$
$$^-15 \div 3 = {}^-5 \text{ because } {}^-5 \cdot 3 = {}^-15$$
$$32 \div {}^-8 = {}^-4 \text{ because } {}^-4 \cdot {}^-8 = 32$$
$$^-40 \div {}^-5 = 8 \text{ because } 8 \cdot {}^-5 = {}^-40$$

Give a multiplication equation for each division equation.

1. $9 \div {}^-3 = {}^-3$
2. $^-10 \div 5 = {}^-2$
3. $^-12 \div {}^-2 = 6$

4. $20 \div 4 = 5$
5. $^-32 \div 4 = {}^-8$
6. $48 \div {}^-8 = {}^-6$

7. $^-7 \div {}^-7 = 1$
8. $^-18 \div 3 = {}^-6$
9. $^-35 \div {}^-5 = 7$

10. $8 \div {}^-1 = {}^-8$
11. $^-42 \div {}^-6 = 7$
12. $45 \div {}^-9 = {}^-5$

13. $^-56 \div {}^-8 = 7$
14. $81 \div {}^-9 = {}^-9$
15. $^-63 \div 7 = {}^-9$

Give the number for n.

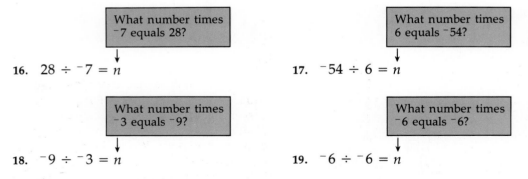

16. $28 \div {}^-7 = n$

17. $^-54 \div 6 = n$

18. $^-9 \div {}^-3 = n$

19. $^-6 \div {}^-6 = n$

Complete each sentence with **positive** or **negative**.

20. The quotient of two positive numbers is a ___?___ number.

21. The quotient of two negative numbers is a ___?___ number.

22. The quotient of a positive number and a negative number is a ___?___ number.

Find the quotients.

1. $18 \div {}^-9$ 2. ${}^-25 \div 5$ 3. ${}^-6 \div {}^-3$ 4. $14 \div {}^-2$

5. ${}^-24 \div {}^-3$ 6. $20 \div {}^-4$ 7. ${}^-24 \div {}^-6$ 8. $32 \div 8$

9. ${}^-15 \div 5$ 10. ${}^-9 \div {}^-3$ 11. ${}^-7 \div {}^-1$ 12. $28 \div {}^-4$

13. ${}^-30 \div 6$ 14. $72 \div {}^-9$ 15. ${}^-81 \div 9$ 16. ${}^-1 \div {}^-1$

17. ${}^-36 \div 9$ 18. $0 \div {}^-4$ 19. ${}^-40 \div {}^-10$ 20. $48 \div {}^-12$

21. ${}^-60 \div {}^-3$ 22. ${}^-84 \div 7$ 23. $100 \div {}^-25$ 24. ${}^-105 \div {}^-35$

Find the quotients.

Example: $\dfrac{{}^-10}{5} = {}^-10 \div 5 = {}^-2$

25. $\dfrac{{}^-24}{{}^-8}$ 26. $\dfrac{{}^-6}{{}^-3}$

27. $\dfrac{21}{{}^-7}$ 28. $\dfrac{{}^-30}{{}^-5}$ 29. $\dfrac{54}{6}$ 30. $\dfrac{81}{{}^-9}$

31. $\dfrac{{}^-8}{{}^-1}$ 32. $\dfrac{{}^-56}{{}^-7}$ 33. $\dfrac{42}{{}^-6}$ 34. $\dfrac{63}{{}^-9}$

35. $\dfrac{({}^-9 + {}^-3)}{{}^-4}$ 36. $\dfrac{({}^-4 \cdot {}^-8)}{2}$ 37. $\dfrac{(9 - 5)}{(5 - 9)}$ 38. $\dfrac{({}^-11 + 2)}{{}^-3}$

Calculator problems

39. $1764 \div {}^-36$

40. ${}^-5916 \div {}^-58$

41. ${}^-981\ 836 \div 389$

42. ${}^-1\ 299\ 144 \div {}^-616$

43. $10\ 717\ 707 \div {}^-1419$

44. ${}^-7\ 745\ 089 \div {}^-2783$

45. ${}^-17.48 \div 4.6$

46. ${}^-38.316 \div {}^-3.09$

47. $575.64 \div {}^-36.9$

48. $17.4557 \div 17.3$

Hexagonal cookies cost more than square cookies. Round cookies cost more than hexagonal cookies. Round cookies cost less than triangular cookies. Which kind of cookie costs the least? Which costs the most?

More practice, page 393, Set B

Combining operations with integers

What is the output for this flow chart?

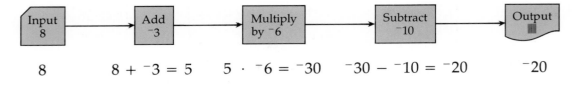

8   8 + ⁻3 = 5   5 · ⁻6 = ⁻30   ⁻30 − ⁻10 = ⁻20   ⁻20

The output number is ⁻20.

What is the output number for this flow chart?

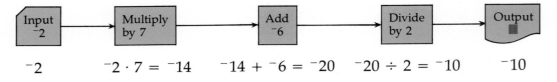

⁻2   ⁻2 · 7 = ⁻14   ⁻14 + ⁻6 = ⁻20   ⁻20 ÷ 2 = ⁻10   ⁻10

Give the output number.

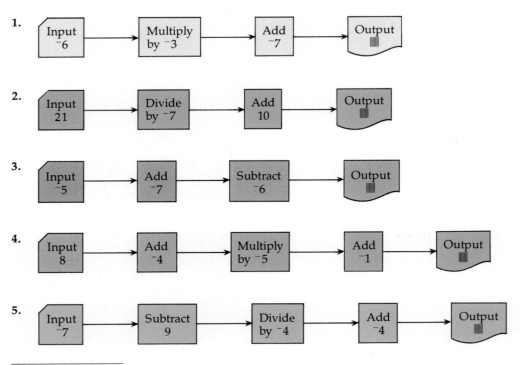

Find the output number for each flow chart.

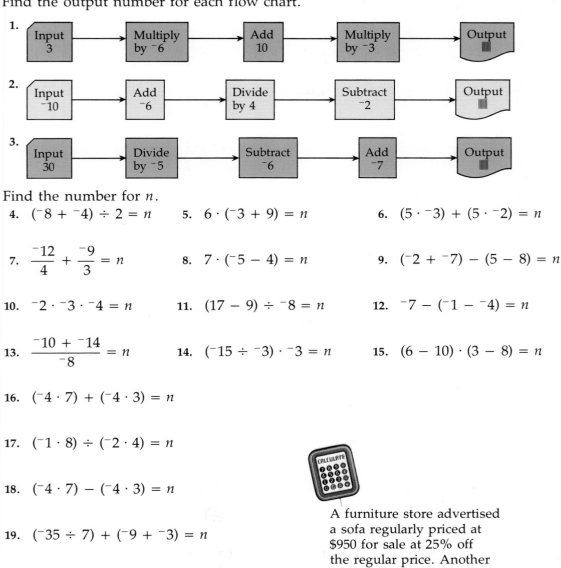

1. Input 3 → Multiply by $^-6$ → Add 10 → Multiply by $^-3$ → Output

2. Input $^-10$ → Add $^-6$ → Divide by 4 → Subtract $^-2$ → Output

3. Input 30 → Divide by $^-5$ → Subtract $^-6$ → Add $^-7$ → Output

Find the number for n.

4. $(^-8 + {^-4}) \div 2 = n$

5. $6 \cdot (^-3 + 9) = n$

6. $(5 \cdot {^-3}) + (5 \cdot {^-2}) = n$

7. $\dfrac{^-12}{4} + \dfrac{^-9}{3} = n$

8. $7 \cdot (^-5 - 4) = n$

9. $(^-2 + {^-7}) - (5 - 8) = n$

10. $^-2 \cdot {^-3} \cdot {^-4} = n$

11. $(17 - 9) \div {^-8} = n$

12. $^-7 - (^-1 - {^-4}) = n$

13. $\dfrac{^-10 + {^-14}}{^-8} = n$

14. $(^-15 \div {^-3}) \cdot {^-3} = n$

15. $(6 - 10) \cdot (3 - 8) = n$

16. $(^-4 \cdot 7) + (^-4 \cdot 3) = n$

17. $(^-1 \cdot 8) \div (^-2 \cdot 4) = n$

18. $(^-4 \cdot 7) - (^-4 \cdot 3) = n$

19. $(^-35 \div 7) + (^-9 + {^-3}) = n$

20. $15 - (^-7 - {^-4}) = n$

21. $(9 - 13) \cdot (9 + 13) = n$

A furniture store advertised a sofa regularly priced at $950 for sale at 25% off the regular price. Another store advertised the same sofa as regularly priced at $888 on sale at 20% off the regular price. Which sale price is less?

22. $^-3 \cdot [(^-26 + {^-19}) \div 9] - {^-7} = n$

23. $\dfrac{7 \cdot (^-18 - 52)}{(^-5 \cdot 5) + (^-5 \cdot 2)} = n$

✪ Absolute value

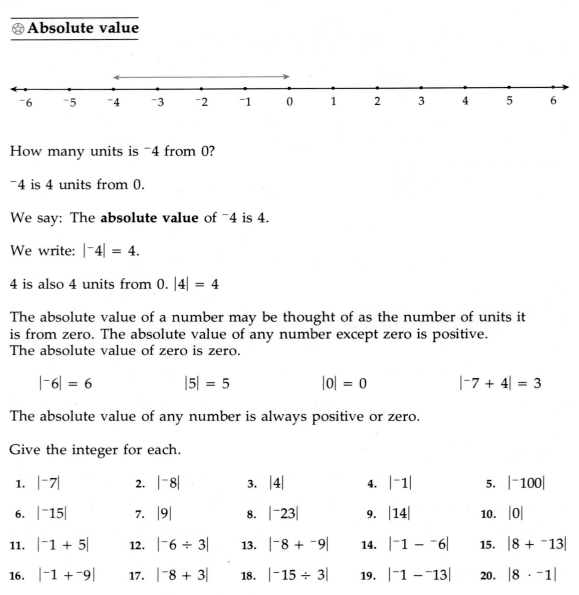

How many units is ⁻4 from 0?

⁻4 is 4 units from 0.

We say: The **absolute value** of ⁻4 is 4.

We write: $|^-4| = 4$.

4 is also 4 units from 0. $|4| = 4$

The absolute value of a number may be thought of as the number of units it is from zero. The absolute value of any number except zero is positive. The absolute value of zero is zero.

$$|^-6| = 6 \qquad |5| = 5 \qquad |0| = 0 \qquad |^-7 + 4| = 3$$

The absolute value of any number is always positive or zero.

Give the integer for each.

1. $|^-7|$ 2. $|^-8|$ 3. $|4|$ 4. $|^-1|$ 5. $|^-100|$

6. $|^-15|$ 7. $|9|$ 8. $|^-23|$ 9. $|14|$ 10. $|0|$

11. $|^-1 + 5|$ 12. $|^-6 \div 3|$ 13. $|^-8 + {}^-9|$ 14. $|^-1 - {}^-6|$ 15. $|8 + {}^-13|$

16. $|^-1 + {}^-9|$ 17. $|^-8 + 3|$ 18. $|^-15 \div 3|$ 19. $|^-1 - {}^-13|$ 20. $|8 \cdot {}^-1|$

21. $|13 - 15|$ 22. $|^-8 + 7|$ 23. $|^-9 + {}^-9|$ 24. $|3 \cdot {}^-5|$ 25. $|6 - {}^-7|$

Give the possible integers for x.
Example: If $|x| = 3$, then $x = 3$ or $x = {}^-3$.

26. $|x| = 7$ 27. $|x| = 10$ 28. $|x| = 0$ 29. $|x| = 4$ 30. $|x| = 1$

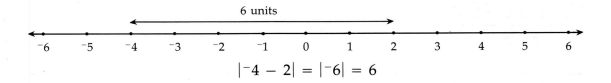

6 units

$$|^-4 - 2| = |^-6| = 6$$

The integers $^-4$ and 2 are 6 units apart on the number line.
The absolute value of the difference of two integers gives the number of units the two integers are apart.

$$|^-11 - {}^-18| = |7| = 7$$

$$|^-18 - {}^-11| = |^-7| = 7$$

$^-11$ and $^-18$ are 7 units apart on the number line.

Give the number of units the two integers are apart from each other.
Use absolute value.

1. $^-3, 2$ 2. $^-4, {}^-10$ 3. $^-16, {}^-9$ 4. $13, 7$ 5. $^-1, 1$

6. $4, {}^-11$ 7. $10, {}^-10$ 8. $13, {}^-8$ 9. $^-19, {}^-27$ 10. $0, {}^-8$

11. $^-7, {}^-14$ 12. $^-40, {}^-30$ 13. $7, {}^-6$ 14. $^-5, 15$ 15. $^-9, {}^-99$

Give the integer for each.

16. $|7 - {}^-3|$ 17. $|^-2 - {}^-4|$ 18. $|^-1 - 9|$ 19. $|10 - {}^-3|$ 20. $|14 - 9|$

21. $|9 - 14|$ 22. $|^-1 - {}^-11|$ 23. $|5 - {}^-16|$ 24. $|^-8 - 14|$ 25. $|0 - {}^-7|$

26. $|4 - 13|$ 27. $|^-4 - {}^-13|$ 28. $|^-6 - {}^-5|$ 29. $|19 - 7|$ 30. $|^-16 - 8|$

Give all the possible integers for x.

☆ 31. $|x - 2| = 6$

☆ 32. $|x - {}^-5| = 1$

☆ 33. $|8 - x| = 3$

 What is the largest 3-digit whole number whose cube is an 8-digit number?

Answers for Self-check 1. $^-27$ 2. $^-32$ 3. 18 4. $^-49$ 5. 6 6. $^-40$ 7. 36 8. $^-24$ 9. 72
10. $^-42$ 11. $^-3$ 12. $^-7$ 13. $^-5$ 14. 3 15. $^-5$ 16. $^-5$ 17. $^-5$ 18. $^-4$ 19. 8 20. $^-3$
21. $n = {}^-30$ 22. $n = {}^-6$ ☆ 23. 3 ☆ 24. 7 ☆ 25. 9 ☆ 26. 5

Self-check

Find the products.

1. $3 \cdot {}^-9$
2. ${}^-4 \cdot 8$
3. ${}^-9 \cdot {}^-2$
4. $7 \cdot {}^-7$
5. ${}^-6 \cdot {}^-1$

6. $5 \cdot {}^-8$
7. ${}^-6 \cdot {}^-6$
8. ${}^-2 \cdot 12$
9. ${}^-8 \cdot {}^-9$
10. ${}^-7 \cdot 6$

Find the quotients.

11. ${}^-18 \div 6$
12. $14 \div {}^-2$
13. ${}^-35 \div 7$
14. ${}^-3 \div {}^-1$
15. $10 \div {}^-2$

16. $\dfrac{{}^-40}{8}$
17. $\dfrac{{}^-20}{4}$
18. $\dfrac{32}{{}^-8}$
19. $\dfrac{{}^-56}{{}^-7}$
20. $\dfrac{{}^-27}{9}$

Find the number for n.

21. $6 \cdot (7 - 12) = n$

22. $({}^-2 \cdot {}^-7) - 20 = n$

Give the integer for each.

☆ 23. $|{}^-3|$
☆ 24. $|7|$

☆ 25. $|{}^-3 + {}^-6|$
☆ 26. $|4 - 9|$

Answers for Self-check—page 269

Test

Find the products.

1. ${}^-6 \cdot 4$
2. $3 \cdot {}^-7$
3. ${}^-5 \cdot {}^-7$
4. $6 \cdot 9$
5. ${}^-2 \cdot {}^-1$

6. ${}^-8 \cdot 8$
7. $4 \cdot {}^-9$
8. ${}^-10 \cdot {}^-8$
9. ${}^-12 \cdot 4$
10. ${}^-14 \cdot {}^-3$

Find the quotients.

11. $36 \div {}^-4$
12. ${}^-45 \div 9$
13. ${}^-16 \div {}^-4$
14. $18 \div {}^-6$
15. ${}^-72 \div {}^-9$

16. $\dfrac{{}^-20}{10}$
17. $\dfrac{64}{{}^-8}$
18. $\dfrac{{}^-21}{{}^-3}$
19. $\dfrac{30}{{}^-5}$
20. $\dfrac{{}^-63}{{}^-7}$

Find the number for n.

21. $({}^-3 - 5) \div {}^-2 = n$

22. $(3 \cdot {}^-6) + (3 \cdot {}^-4) = n$

Give the integer for each.

☆ 23. $|{}^-8|$
☆ 24. $|5|$

☆ 25. $|{}^-2 - 1|$
☆ 26. $|{}^-7 + 3|$

Math lab

An "Anti-Gravity Machine"

You can build a device that seems to defy the law of gravity and roll uphill. Here is how to make it.

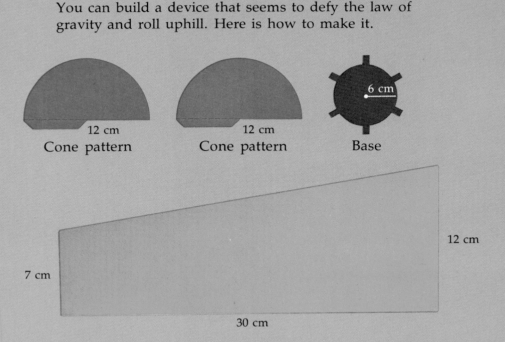

12 cm
Cone pattern

12 cm
Cone pattern

6 cm
Base

12 cm

7 cm

30 cm

Ramp pattern
Make two copies.

Draw copies of the patterns above on tagboard. Cut out the copies. Make the two cones, and tape the base on one of the cones. Then tape the other cone pattern onto the base to form a double cone as shown at the right.

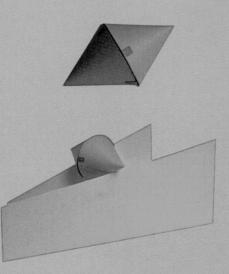

Tape the 7-cm edges of the ramp pattern together. Open up the high end of the ramp pattern to form a V-shape.

Place the double-ended cone on the low part of the ramp near the vertex of the V. The cone should roll uphill on the ramp.

Can you give an explanation of this anti-gravity device?

Equations

Make a spinner and 16 expression cards like the ones shown.

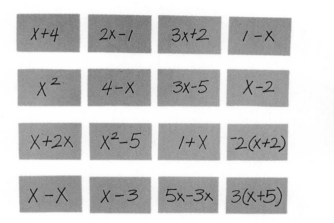 

Shuffle the cards and turn them facedown. Each person, in turn, spins the spinner and turns over the top card. The number on the spinner is then used to evaluate the expression. The person who gets the largest value for their expression is the winner.

Example:

expression card   spinner number

$1 - X$ $^-3$

Value of the expression: $1 - {}^-3 = 4$

Evaluate each expression card for a spinner number of $^-4$.

1. $3X+2$ 2. $4-X$ 3. $3(X+5)$ 4. $X-X$

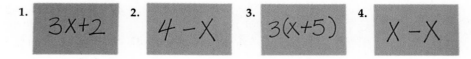

Try this game with one or more classmates.

Evaluate each expression.

1. $2x - 1$, when $x = 4$

2. $6n$, when $n = {}^-4$

3. $5 - x$, when $x = 11$

4. $h + {}^-10$, when $h = 6$

5. $4t + {}^-1$, when $t = 3$

6. $\dfrac{r}{{}^-6}$, when $r = 30$

7. $4(n + {}^-6)$, when $n = 2$

8. $x^2 - 3$, when $x = 50$

9. $\dfrac{h - 3}{{}^-4}$, when $h = 19$

10. $3 - k$, when $k = 10$

11. $2z + 4$, when $z = {}^-2$

12. $\dfrac{6v}{{}^-2}$, when $v = {}^-3$

13. $3y + 4y$, when $y = {}^-5$

14. $b^3 + 1$, when $b = {}^-2$

15. $^-8 + 5j$, when $j = 4$

16. $\dfrac{3w + 3}{6}$, when $w = {}^-9$

Copy and complete each table.

	x	$3x + 2$
	5	17
17.	3	
18.	1	
19.	0	
20.	$^-1$	
21.	$^-2$	
22.	$^-3$	
23.	$^-5$	
24.	$^-7$	

	y	$^-5y + 7$
	$^-4$	27
25.	$^-3$	
26.	$^-2$	
27.	$^-1$	
28.	0	
29.	1	
30.	2	
31.	3	
32.	4	

	z	$7z - 5z$
	6	12
33.	$^-4$	
34.	1	
35.	$^-5$	
36.	3	
37.	$^-1$	
38.	0	
39.	$^-10$	
40.	100	

Solving equations by adding or subtracting

Jack scored 10 points on a dartboard.
When he added these points to his
old score, the total was 5 points.
What was his old score?

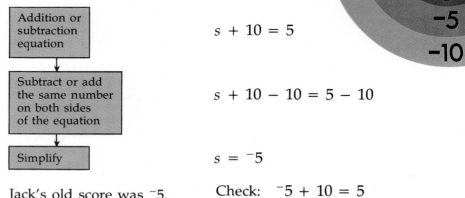

Let s = old score

Solve the equation: $s + 10 = 5$

Addition or subtraction equation

$$s + 10 = 5$$

Subtract or add the same number on both sides of the equation

$$s + 10 - 10 = 5 - 10$$

Simplify

$$s = {}^-5$$

Jack's old score was $^-5$.   Check: $^-5 + 10 = 5$

Other examples

$x - 7 = {}^-3$ $x - {}^-3 = {}^-9$

$x - 7 + 7 = {}^-3 + 7$ $x - {}^-3 + {}^-3 = {}^-9 + {}^-3$

$x = 4$ $x = {}^-12$

Check: $4 - 7 = {}^-3$ Check: $^-12 - {}^-3 = {}^-9$

Solve the equations.

1. $n + {}^-1 = 4$ 2. $x - 6 = {}^-2$ 3. $y + 7 = {}^-9$ 4. $z + {}^-4 = 5$

5. $r - {}^-2 = {}^-3$ 6. $a + 10 = 5$ 7. $s - 1 = {}^-1$ 8. $k - 5 = 8$

9. $h + {}^-4 = 4$ 10. $t + 15 = {}^-6$ 11. $b + {}^-9 = {}^-1$ 12. $m - 11 = {}^-3$

13. $c - {}^-10 = {}^-5$ 14. $g - 12 = 4$ 15. $p + {}^-16 = {}^-20$ 16. $q + 6 = {}^-13$

17. $j - 6 = {}^-7$ 18. $w + 17 = {}^-8$ 19. $d - 5 = 3$ 20. $f + 14 = {}^-8$

Solve the equations.

1. $d - 6 = {}^-5$
2. $f + {}^-5 = 10$
3. $g + 8 = {}^-6$

4. $t - {}^-2 = 7$
5. $r - 3 = {}^-8$
6. $x + 16 = 7$

7. $n + 6 = {}^-5$
8. $y + {}^-4 = {}^-7$
9. $j - 14 = 6$

10. $t + 7 = 0$
11. $a - 11 = {}^-6$
12. $h + 2 = {}^-12$

13. $m - {}^-5 = {}^-5$
14. $g + 14 = 3$
15. $p + {}^-7 = {}^-10$

16. $w - 13 = 1$
17. $z + {}^-2 = 3$
18. $c - 19 = {}^-5$

19. $e + 11 = {}^-9$
20. $s - 15 = {}^-7$
21. $u + {}^-17 = {}^-8$

22. $b - {}^-17 = 4$
23. $k + 20 = 11$
24. $q + {}^-12 = {}^-12$

25. $n + {}^-28 = 33$
26. $r - 43 = {}^-38$
27. $x - {}^-18 = 50$

28. $z + 55 = 33$
29. $t - 100 = {}^-66$
30. $y + {}^-46 = 31$

☆ 31. $(m + {}^-3) + 7 = {}^-9$
☆ 32. $(a - {}^-4) - {}^-2 = 2$

☆ 33. $(r - {}^-5) - 6 = {}^-7$
☆ 34. $(s + 7) - {}^-1 = 10$

☆ 35. $(x + 6) + {}^-8 = {}^-1$
☆ 36. $(h - 3) + {}^-6 = 3$

37. Markita scored ${}^-8$ points in a game. When she added this to her old score she had a total of 3 points. What was her old score?

38. Bill scored ${}^-5$ points in a game. When he added this to his old score he had a total of 7 points. What was his old score?

One box has 2 pennies.
Another box has 1 penny and 1 nickel.
A third box has 2 nickels.

However, no two coins are in a box with the correct label.

By looking at one coin from one box, you can tell what is in each box.

Which is the one box from which you can choose a coin to find the solution?

Solving equations by multiplying or dividing

The total of the numbers on the four cards is ⁻36. What is the average of the numbers?

Let a = average

Solve the equation $4a = ⁻36$.

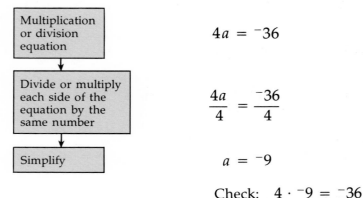

| Multiplication or division equation | $4a = ⁻36$ |

↓

| Divide or multiply each side of the equation by the same number | $\dfrac{4a}{4} = \dfrac{⁻36}{4}$ |

↓

| Simplify | $a = ⁻9$ |

Check: $4 \cdot ⁻9 = ⁻36$

The average of the numbers is ⁻9.

Other examples

$$⁻7k = 84$$

$$\frac{⁻7k}{⁻7} = \frac{84}{⁻7}$$

$$k = ⁻12$$

Check: $⁻7 \cdot ⁻12 = 84$

$$\frac{x}{⁻3} = 9$$

$$⁻3 \cdot \frac{x}{⁻3} = ⁻3 \cdot 9$$

$$x = ⁻27$$

Check: $\dfrac{⁻27}{⁻3} = 9$

$$\frac{t}{⁻7} = ⁻6$$

$$⁻7 \cdot \frac{t}{⁻7} = ⁻7 \cdot ⁻6$$

$$t = 42$$

Check: $\dfrac{42}{⁻7} = ⁻6$

Solve the equations.

1. $5n = ⁻30$

2. $⁻8y = ⁻48$

3. $10y = ⁻80$

4. $⁻12y = ⁻36$

5. $⁻2y = 38$

6. $3y = ⁻54$

7. $\dfrac{n}{8} = ⁻3$

8. $\dfrac{m}{10} = ⁻9$

9. $\dfrac{n}{⁻4} = ⁻11$

10. $\dfrac{x}{18} = ⁻2$

11. $\dfrac{u}{⁻9} = 0$

12. $\dfrac{z}{⁻2} = ⁻17$

Solve the equations.

1. $^-9n = {}^-27$ 2. $6t = {}^-18$ 3. $^-2n = {}^-10$ 4. $^-7x = 70$

5. $^-4k = {}^-44$ 6. $8w = 56$ 7. $10y = {}^-90$ 8. $^-3z = {}^-42$

9. $15s = {}^-60$ 10. $^-2y = 2$ 11. $14b = {}^-28$ 12. $^-5g = 75$

13. $\dfrac{a}{^-9} = {}^-4$ 14. $\dfrac{w}{^-7} = 3$ 15. $\dfrac{c}{^-1} = 12$ 16. $\dfrac{u}{16} = {}^-2$

17. $\dfrac{b}{^-12} = {}^-8$ 18. $\dfrac{m}{^-4} = 14$ 19. $\dfrac{v}{11} = 11$ 20. $\dfrac{e}{^-13} = {}^-4$

21. $\dfrac{j}{19} = {}^-7$ 22. $\dfrac{f}{^-5} = 60$ 23. $\dfrac{s}{25} = {}^-4$ 24. $\dfrac{x}{^-2} = {}^-19$

☆ 25. What is the average of the numbers on these cards?

Calculator problems

26. $\dfrac{r}{^-67} = {}^-176$ 27. $^-19t = 608$

28. $\dfrac{v}{2.7} = {}^-5.9$ 29. $^-76s = {}^-9652$

30. $\dfrac{b}{^-3.8} = 0.99$ 31. $^-111n = {}^-24\ 642$

32. $\dfrac{n}{^-60.4} = {}^-9.3$ 33. $3.7y = 71.78$

34. $\dfrac{n}{1.01} = {}^-17.6$ 35. $^-19.6c = {}^-656.6$

36. $\dfrac{x}{2.51} = 0.4$ 37. $32.5a = {}^-845$

1		2		3		4
8		7		6		5
9		10		11		12
16		15		14		13

Copy this puzzle.
Put a +, −, or = sign
in each blank square
so that the rows and
columns are correct
equations.

More practice, page 394, Set A

Module 11.3   **277**

✪ Solving equations using two operations

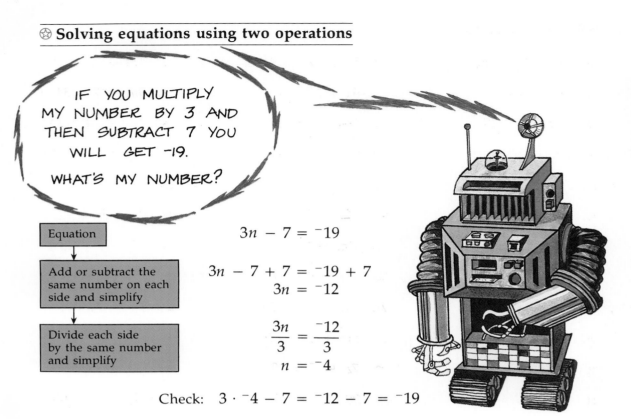

IF YOU MULTIPLY MY NUMBER BY 3 AND THEN SUBTRACT 7 YOU WILL GET ⁻19.

WHAT'S MY NUMBER?

| Equation | $3n - 7 = {}^-19$ |

| Add or subtract the same number on each side and simplify | $3n - 7 + 7 = {}^-19 + 7$
 $3n = {}^-12$ |

| Divide each side by the same number and simplify | $\dfrac{3n}{3} = \dfrac{{}^-12}{3}$
 $n = {}^-4$ |

Check: $3 \cdot {}^-4 - 7 = {}^-12 - 7 = {}^-19$

The unknown number is ⁻4.

Other examples

$$5y + {}^-7 = 8 \qquad\qquad {}^-2k - 9 = {}^-23$$

$$5y + {}^-7 - {}^-7 = 8 - {}^-7 \qquad {}^-2k - 9 + 9 = {}^-23 + 9$$

$$5y = 15 \qquad\qquad {}^-2k = {}^-14$$

$$\frac{5y}{5} = \frac{15}{5} \qquad\qquad \frac{{}^-2k}{{}^-2} = \frac{{}^-14}{{}^-2}$$

$$y = 3 \qquad\qquad k = 7$$

Check: $5 \cdot 3 + {}^-7 = 15 + {}^-7 = 8$ Check: ${}^-2 \cdot 7 - 9 = {}^-14 - 9 = {}^-23$

Solve the equations. Check the solutions.

1. $3t + 1 = {}^-8$
2. $6x - 4 = {}^-10$
3. $5k - {}^-7 = 17$
4. $9z + {}^-6 = 12$

5. $2c + 7 = {}^-3$
6. $8m + {}^-9 = 31$
7. ${}^-10n + 4 = 14$
8. ${}^-4s + 5 = 9$

9. $3b - 10 = {}^-25$
10. $7j - 6 = 36$
11. ${}^-4z - 8 = 12$
12. ${}^-6g + 5 = 29$

Solve the equations.

1. $4h - 7 = {}^-15$

2. $5r + {}^-9 = {}^-39$

3. ${}^-8t + {}^-11 = 13$

4. $3s - {}^-1 = 28$

5. $6x + 17 = 5$

6. $9n - {}^-7 = 34$

7. ${}^-7c - 6 = 29$

8. $10d + 7 = {}^-23$

9. ${}^-2z + 14 = 24$

10. ${}^-9r + {}^-7 = 38$

11. $5q - 6 = {}^-6$

12. $11p + {}^-9 = {}^-53$

13. $6k - {}^-10 = 46$

14. ${}^-3b + 19 = 1$

15. $8e + 15 = 23$

16. $12k - {}^-1 = 25$

17. ${}^-2x - 9 = 5$

18. $7n + 20 = {}^-29$

19. $9g - 15 = {}^-51$

20. $10w + {}^-8 = 42$

21. ${}^-4j - 9 = 23$

22. ${}^-5a + {}^-5 = {}^-40$

23. ${}^-8x + 9 = 57$

24. ${}^-5m + 14 = 4$

25. $3t + 7 = {}^-20$

26. ${}^-4x - 6 = {}^-26$

27. $3y + {}^-12 = 0$

28. ${}^-1r + 9 = {}^-6$

29. $11b + 1 = {}^-32$

30. $6k - 7 = {}^-1$

31. ${}^-5y + 10 = {}^-20$

32. $7z + {}^-3 = {}^-31$

33. ${}^-8v + 19 = {}^-5$

34. $9m + 17 = {}^-64$

35. $20c - 1 = 99$

36. ${}^-7j - {}^-7 = 63$

37. $11 = 2x + 7$

38. ${}^-21 = {}^-5n + {}^-6$

39. ${}^-71 = 10k - 1$

40. Lisa said, "If you multiply my number by 6 and add 21 you will get ${}^-3$." What is Lisa's number?

☆ 41. If a number is multiplied by 10 and ${}^-6$ is added to the product, the result is 34. What is the number?

☆ 42. When a number is multiplied by ${}^-7$ and 4 is subtracted from the product, the result is ${}^-46$. What is the number?

☆ 43. Write some equations using two operations. Use them to try a "Find My Number" game with a classmate.

2, 3, 5, 7, 11, 13, . . .

There are 25 prime numbers that are smaller than 100. What is the average of these prime numbers?

More practice, page 394, Set B

✪ Using the distributive principle to solve equations

Solve the equation $3x + 5x = {}^-48$.

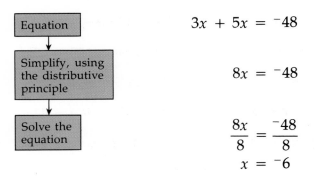

| Equation | $3x + 5x = {}^-48$ |

| Simplify, using the distributive principle | $8x = {}^-48$ |

| Solve the equation | $\dfrac{8x}{8} = \dfrac{{}^-48}{8}$ |
| | $x = {}^-6$ |

Check: $(3 \cdot {}^-6) + (5 \cdot {}^-6) = {}^-18 + {}^-30 = {}^-48$

Other examples

$6n - 2n = {}^-28$

$6n + {}^-2n = {}^-28$

$4n = {}^-28$

$\dfrac{4n}{4} = \dfrac{{}^-28}{4}$

$n = {}^-7$

Check: $(6 \cdot {}^-7) - (2 \cdot {}^-7) = {}^-42 - {}^-14$
$= {}^-28$

$5n + n = {}^-54$

$6n = {}^-54$

$\dfrac{6n}{6} = \dfrac{{}^-54}{6}$

$n = {}^-9$

Check: $(5 \cdot {}^-9) + {}^-9 = {}^-45 + {}^-9$
$= {}^-54$

Solve the equations. Check the solutions.

1. $4y + 3y = {}^-35$

2. ${}^-2x + 9x = 21$

3. $5k - 2k = {}^-15$

4. $8h + {}^-3h = 20$

5. $7n - {}^-5n = 36$

6. ${}^-6s + 9s = {}^-27$

7. $7b + 3b = 100$

8. $6j - 10j = {}^-32$

9. $11t + {}^-2t = 45$

10. $10d - {}^-5d = 60$

11. ${}^-12t + 6t = {}^-48$

12. $8t - 9t = {}^-1$

Solve the equations.

1. $7t + 3t = {}^-20$
2. $8x - 6x = 14$
3. $3h - 9h = 30$
4. $14n + {}^-6n = 24$
5. ${}^-3y + 7y = {}^-36$
6. $10s - 7s = {}^-3$
7. $9r - 2r = 49$
8. ${}^-4b + {}^-6b = 100$
9. $3j - {}^-4j = 77$
10. $5c + 4c = {}^-9$
11. $11w + {}^-4w = 28$
12. $2v + 2v = {}^-24$
13. $8u + 7u = 75$
14. $3q - 5q = {}^-16$
15. $13m + {}^-6m = {}^-56$
16. $5m + m = {}^-30$
17. $16d - 7d = 72$
18. $9z - 16z = 42$
19. ${}^-8b - 2b = 10$
20. $5e + {}^-11e = 54$
21. ${}^-17f + 9f = 40$
22. $6k - {}^-8k = 210$
23. ${}^-1k + 8k = 63$
24. $4p + 5p = {}^-81$
25. $(2k + 3k) + {}^-3 = 12$
26. $({}^-7n + {}^-3n) + {}^-4 = 26$
27. $(5t - 9t) - 6 = {}^-26$
28. $(4z - {}^-2z) - {}^-5 = {}^-19$
☆ 29. $8x + 7 + {}^-3x = {}^-3$
☆ 30. $\dfrac{9y + 7y}{4} = {}^-20$

Think What positive number squared is the same as that number plus 30?

Practicing your skills

1. $32.8 + 7.49 + 95.12 + 8.26$
2. $113.8 + 27.65 + 38.9 + 109.7$
3. $42.9 - 37.6$
4. $89 - 61.7$
5. $1.19 - 0.986$
6. $5.6 - 4.81$
7. $65.2 \cdot 3.8$
8. $5.01 \cdot 0.6$
9. $71.8 \cdot 0.41$
10. $9.8 \cdot 1.83$
11. $5.2\overline{)8.32}$
12. $0.86\overline{)3.05}$
13. $3\overline{)2}$
14. $8\overline{)7}$
15. $4\overline{)3}$
16. Find 25% of $840.
17. Find 45% of $1500.
18. What percent of 64 is 36?
19. What percent of 118 is 24?

✪ Writing and solving equations

Write and solve an equation
for this problem.

A certain number is multiplied
by 5, and 3 is added to the
product. If the sum is $^-17$,
what is the number?

Let n = the number

$$5n + 3 = {}^-17$$

$$5n + 3 - 3 = {}^-17 - 3$$

$$5n = {}^-20$$

$$\frac{5n}{5} = \frac{^-20}{5}$$

$$n = {}^-4$$

Check: $(5 \cdot {}^-4) + 3 = {}^-20 + 3 = {}^-17$

Other examples

A number is multiplied by 4,
and 2 is subtracted from the
product. If the result is $^-10$,
what is the number?

Let n = the number

$$4n - 2 = {}^-10$$

$$4n - 2 + 2 = {}^-10 + 2$$

$$4n = {}^-8$$

$$\frac{4n}{4} = \frac{^-8}{4}$$

$$n = {}^-2$$

Check: $(4 \cdot {}^-2) - 2 = {}^-8 - 2 = {}^-10$

3 times a certain number plus
4 times the same number is equal
to $^-35$. What is the number?

Let x = the number

$$3x + 4x = {}^-35$$

$$7x = {}^-35$$

$$\frac{7x}{7} = \frac{^-35}{7}$$

$$x = {}^-5$$

Check: $(3 \cdot {}^-5) + (4 \cdot {}^-5) = {}^-15 + {}^-20 = {}^-35$

Write and solve an equation for each problem.

1. If 9 is added to a certain number, the sum is ⁻5. What is the number?

2. A certain number is multiplied by 6, and 3 is added to the product. This gives a result of ⁻9. What is the number?

3. When a certain number is divided by ⁻6, the quotient is 3. What is the number?

4. 6 times a certain number plus 7 is equal to 1. What is the number?

5. A number is divided by 7. The quotient is ⁻12. What is the number?

6. If ⁻7 is added to 3 times a certain number, the sum is 8. What is the number?

7. 2 times a number plus 8 times the same number equals ⁻30. What is the number?

8. 3 times a number is added to 5 times the same number. The sum is ⁻56. What is the number?

9. A number is divided by 2 and ⁻8 is added to the quotient. The result is ⁻3. What is the number?

10. 8 times a certain number minus 5 times the same number is ⁻27. What is the number?

11. A number is multiplied by 3 and the product is divided by 2. The result is ⁻15. What is the number?

☆ 12. Rita sawed a board into 2 pieces of equal length. Then she cut 11 cm off one of the pieces. The remaining part was 38 cm long. How long was the board originally?

☆ 13. Gary had 3 nickels, 8 pennies, and several dimes. Altogether he had 93 cents. How many dimes did he have?

What number when doubled results in a number that is one less than the number itself?

Self-check

Evaluate each expression for the value given for the variable.

1. $2r + {}^-3$, when $r = 5$

2. $\dfrac{x - 5}{2}$, when $x = {}^-3$

3. $2t + 4t$, when $t = 7$

4. $1 - y$, when $y = 6$

Solve the equations.

5. $s - 7 = {}^-4$

6. $k + {}^-3 = 5$

7. $\dfrac{n}{{}^-2} = 5$

8. $4w = {}^-12$

9. $m + 10 = 7$

10. $d - {}^-2 = 7$

☆11. $2t + 1 = 9$

☆12. ${}^-4j - 3 = {}^-15$

☆13. $3h + {}^-1 = {}^-19$ ☆14. $3g + 4g = {}^-14$ ☆15. $9a + {}^-5a = 20$ ☆16. $11x - 8x = {}^-6$

Write and solve an equation for each problem.

☆17. A number is multiplied by ${}^-6$ and 10 is added to the product. The result is 22. What is the number?

☆18. A number is doubled and 14 is subtracted from the result. If the difference is ${}^-2$, what is the number?

Answers for Self-check—page 283

Test

Evaluate each expression for the value given for the variable.

1. $6n - 2$, when $n = 1$

2. $\dfrac{k + 7}{2}$, when $k = {}^-5$

3. $s - 6$, when $s = {}^-3$

4. $3c + 2c$, when $c = {}^-2$

Solve the equations.

5. $t + 2 = {}^-1$

6. $b - 6 = {}^-3$

7. ${}^-5h = 15$

8. $\dfrac{z}{6} = {}^-4$

9. $y - 15 = {}^-8$

10. $9w = {}^-63$

☆11. $4v + 3 = {}^-9$

☆12. $6q - 7 = {}^-1$

☆13. $5d - {}^-1 = 36$ ☆14. $7m + 3m = 40$ ☆15. ${}^-4x + 7x = {}^-21$ ☆16. $2p - 8p = 42$

Write and solve an equation for each problem.

☆17. A certain number is divided by 3, and 1 is added to the quotient. If the result is ${}^-4$, what is the number?

☆18. When ${}^-7$ is added to a number, and the sum is multiplied by ${}^-3$, the product is equal to 36. What is the number?

Puzzles from an Old Arithmetic Book

Puzzles have appeared in mathematics books for many years and have challenged generations of students. The puzzles below are from *Stoddard's American Intellectual Arithmetic*, published in 1866.

How many of the puzzles can you solve?

1. What is the difference between twice 25 and twice 5 and 20?

2. Place four 2's in such a manner that they shall exactly equal 23.

3. Write 12 in such a manner that you can show its half to be 7.

4. If from *six* you take IX, and from IX you take *ten*; and if *fifty* from *forty* be taken, then there will be just a half a dozen remain.

5. A man purchased a hat for $5 and handed the merchant a $50 bill to pay for it; the merchant being unable to make the change, sent the bill to a broker, got it changed, and then gave the man who bought the hat $45. The broker, after the purchaser of the hat had gone, discovered that the bill was counterfeit, and, therefore returned it to the merchant and received $50 good money. How much did the merchant lose by the operation?

6. A hound is in pursuit of a fox that is 10 rods ahead of him and, while the fox runs 1 rod, the hound runs 10 rods. How far will the hound run before he overtakes the fox?

7. Place ten pennies in a row, then carry one over two, leaving it upon the third, and continue doing this until the ten pennies occupy only five places, with two in each place.

8. "I am constrained to plant a grove
   To please the lady that I love,
   This ample grove is to compose
   Nineteen trees in nine straight rows:
   Five trees in each row I must place,
   Or I shall never see her face."

Coordinate Geometry

The location of point K is given by the **ordered pair** of integers ($^-$5, 3). To locate point K, start at the **origin** (0, 0). Move left 5 units on the horizontal, or x-axis. Then move up 3 units parallel to the vertical, or y-axis. The **coordinates** of point K are ($^-$5, 3).

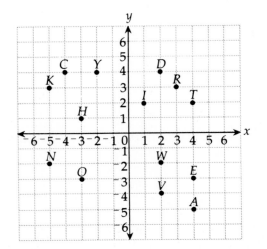

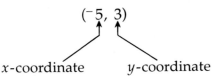

x-coordinate y-coordinate

Match the letters of the points on the graph with the coordinates listed below. The letters will spell out the answer to the riddle.

Riddle: Why do ducks and geese fly south for the winter?

Riddle answer:

___ ___ ___ ___   ___ ___ ___ ___
(4, 2) ($^-$3, 1) (4, $^-$3) ($^-$2, 4)   (2, 4) ($^-$3, $^-$3) ($^-$5, $^-$2) (4, 2)

___ ___ ___ ___   ___ ___ ___
($^-$5, 3) ($^-$5, $^-$2) ($^-$3, $^-$3) (2, $^-$2)   ($^-$3, 1) ($^-$3, $^-$3) (2, $^-$2)

___ ___   ___ ___ ___ ___ ___
(4, 2) ($^-$3, $^-$3)   (2, 4) (3, 3) (1, 2) (2, $^-$4) (4, $^-$3)

___   ___ ___ ___
(4, $^-$5)   ($^-$4, 4) (4, $^-$5) (3, 3)

Give the coordinates of each point.

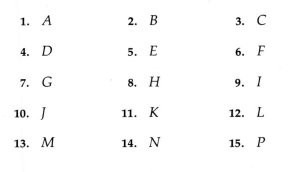

1. A
2. B
3. C
4. D
5. E
6. F
7. G
8. H
9. I
10. J
11. K
12. L
13. M
14. N
15. P

Draw and label x and y axes on graph paper.
Then graph the points for each ordered pair.

16. $A(^-2, ^-3)$
17. $B(4, ^-1)$
18. $C(6, 2)$
19. $D(^-1, ^-4)$
20. $E(0, 3)$

21. $F(^-4, 5)$
22. $G(^-5, ^-5)$
23. $H(6, ^-3)$
24. $I(^-4, 0)$
25. $J(5, ^-5)$

26. $K(0, ^-6)$
27. $L(^-2, ^-6)$
28. $M(3, 4)$
29. $N(1, ^-5)$
30. $O(0, 0)$

The x and y axes divide the coordinate plane into 4 regions or **quadrants**. The quadrants are numbered as shown at the right.

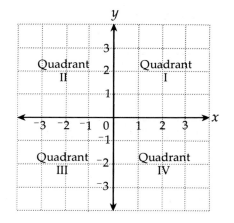

Give the number of the quadrant in which each point lies.

31. $(^-2, 1)$
32. $(4, 3)$
33. $(^-3, ^-2)$
34. $(4, ^-1)$
35. $(3, 2)$
36. $(^-2, ^-4)$
37. $(1, ^-3)$
38. $(^-1, 4)$
39. $(^-1, 1)$
40. $(^-2, ^-2)$

Points with rational number coordinates

The coordinates for the tips of the five-pointed star are ordered pairs of integers. To name the coordinates for points J, F, G, H, and I, rational number coordinates are needed.

An estimate of the coordinates of point J is $\left(\frac{-2}{3}, 2\right)$.

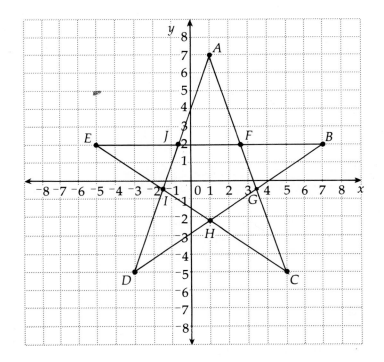

Name the point on the graph for each pair of coordinates or approximate coordinates.

1. $(5, \,^-5)$ 2. $\left(3\frac{1}{2}, \,^-\frac{1}{2}\right)$ 3. $(^-3, \,^-5)$ 4. $\left(2\frac{2}{3}, 2\right)$ 5. $\left(\frac{-2}{3}, 2\right)$

6. $(^-5, 2)$ 7. $(1, 7)$ 8. $\left(\frac{-3}{2}, \,^-\frac{1}{2}\right)$ 9. $\left(1, \,^-2\frac{1}{5}\right)$ 10. $(7, 2)$

Draw a coordinate grid on graph paper.
Graph each point.

11. $\left(^-3, \,^-4\frac{1}{2}\right)$ 12. $\left(3\frac{1}{2}, \,^-2\frac{1}{2}\right)$ 13. $\left(1, 5\frac{3}{4}\right)$ 14. $\left(6\frac{1}{2}, \,^-2\frac{1}{2}\right)$

15. $\left(^-\frac{1}{2}, \,^-2\frac{1}{2}\right)$ 16. $(2, 0)$ 17. $\left(^-3, \frac{3}{4}\right)$ 18. $\left(^-1, 4\frac{3}{4}\right)$

19. $\left(^-1, 1\frac{2}{3}\right)$ 20. $\left(4, 3\frac{1}{3}\right)$ 21. $\left(^-4\frac{1}{2}, 3\frac{1}{2}\right)$ 22. $\left(^-4\frac{1}{2}, \,^-2\frac{1}{2}\right)$

23. Which four points in exercises 11 to 22 seem to lie on a straight line?

Draw a coordinate grid on graph paper. Then graph each point.

1. $\left(2, \ ^-3\frac{1}{2}\right)$
2. $\left(^-3, \ \frac{1}{2}\right)$
3. $(^-5, \ ^-2.5)$
4. $\left(0, \ ^-5\frac{1}{3}\right)$

5. $\left(^-3\frac{1}{2}, \ 4\frac{1}{2}\right)$
6. $\left(^-6, \ 1\frac{2}{3}\right)$
7. $\left(2\frac{1}{2}, \ ^-2\frac{1}{2}\right)$
8. $\left(2\frac{1}{4}, \ 4\right)$

9. $(0, \ ^-3)$
10. $\left(^-\frac{1}{2}, \ 0\right)$
11. $\left(1, \ 3\frac{2}{3}\right)$
12. $(5.5, \ ^-3.5)$

13. $(^-6, \ ^-6)$
14. $(^-1.5, \ 3)$
15. $(2.5, \ ^-4.5)$
16. $(3.5, \ ^-3.5)$

Estimate the coordinates of each point to the nearest tenth.

Example: Point A (3.5, 2.2)

17. B
18. C
19. D

20. E
21. F
22. G

23. H
24. I
25. J

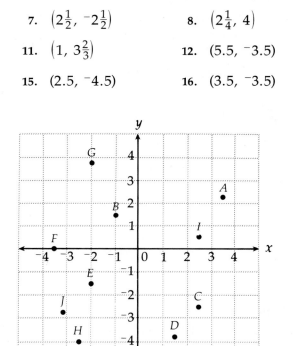

26. The x-coordinate in each pair is 2 more than the y-coordinate. Graph the point for each ordered pair.

(6, 4), (5, 3), (4, 2), (3, 1), (2, 0), (1, $^-1$), (0, $^-2$), ($^-1$, $^-3$), ($^-2$, $^-4$), ($^-3$, $^-5$) ($^-4$, $^-6$)

☆ 27. Make a list of 10 ordered pairs of numbers in which the y-coordinate is 3 more than the x-coordinate. Graph the points for the coordinates.

What are the coordinates of this point:

The x-coordinate is 3 times the y coordinate. The y-coordinate is 4 more than the x-coordinate.

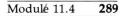

Graphing integer equations

Graph the equation $y = x - 2$.

For every value of x, there is a corresponding value of y. There are infinitely many ordered pairs of integers (x, y) for the equation. Usually, only a few pairs are found, and the points for those pairs are graphed.

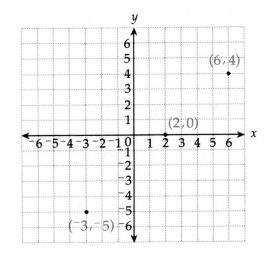

$y = x - 2$ (x, y)

If $x = 6$, $y = 6 - 2 = 4 \longrightarrow (6, 4)$

If $x = 2$, $y = 2 - 2 = 0 \longrightarrow (2, 0)$

If $x = {}^-3$, $y = {}^-3 - 2 = {}^-5 \longrightarrow ({}^-3, {}^-5)$

A **table of values** for x and y shows the ordered pairs of integers to be graphed.

1. Give the missing numbers in the table.

Equation: $y = x - 2$

x	6	2	$^-3$	4	3	0	$^-1$	$^-2$
y	4	0	$^-5$	▨	▨	▨	▨	▨

(handwritten above: -4 -5 2 -1 -3 -1 -7)
(handwritten below: -4 -5 7)

2. Complete the table of values for the equation $y = 2x - 1$.

Equation: $y = 2x - 1$

x	0	1	$^-1$	2	$^-2$	3	$^-3$	$^-5$
y	$^-1$	1	$^-3$	3	▨	▨	▨	▨

3. Complete the table of values for the equation $y = 3 - x$.

Equation: $y = 3 - x$

x	0	2	4	6	8	$^-2$	$^-4$	$^-6$
y	▨	▨	▨	▨	▨	▨	▨	▨

Copy and complete the tables for each equation.

1. $y = x + 4$

x	$^-4$	$^-3$	$^-2$	$^-1$	0	1	2	3
y	▦	▦	▦	▦	▦	▦	▦	▦

2. $y = x - 3$

x	4	3	2	0	$^-1$	$^-2$	$^-3$	$^-4$
y	▦	▦	▦	▦	▦	▦	▦	▦

3. $y = x$

x	$^-5$	$^-4$	$^-2$	0	1	2	4	5
y	▦	▦	▦	▦	▦	▦	▦	▦

4. $y = 3x$

x	$^-3$	$^-2$	$^-1$	0	1	2	3	4
y	▦	▦	▦	▦	▦	▦	▦	▦

5. $y = \frac{x}{2}$

x	6	4	2	0	$^-8$	$^-6$	$^-4$	$^-2$
y	▦	▦	▦	▦	▦	▦	▦	▦

6. $y = 2x + 1$

x	$^-3$	$^-2$	$^-1$	0	1	2	3	4
y	▦	▦	▦	▦	▦	▦	▦	▦

Graph these equations where x and y are integers. Use the tables from exercises 1–6.

7. $y = x + 4$

8. $y = x - 3$

9. $y = x$

10. $y = 3x$

11. $y = \frac{x}{2}$

12. $y = 2x + 1$

Make a table of values for each equation.
Then graph the equation.

13. $y = x + 5$

14. $y = 4 - x$

15. $y = 3x - 2$

16. $y = 2x + {}^-3$

17. $y = 2(x - 1)$

18. $y = {}^-x$

Think

Starting at (0, 0) and traveling in the counterclockwise spiral, the ordered pairs of integers for the first few points in order are (0, 0), (1, 0), (1, 1), (0, 1), ($^-1$, 1), ($^-1$, 0), ($^-1$, $^-1$), (0, $^-1$), (1, $^-1$), (2, $^-1$) . . .

What are the coordinates of the 100th point on this spiral?

Graphs of lines

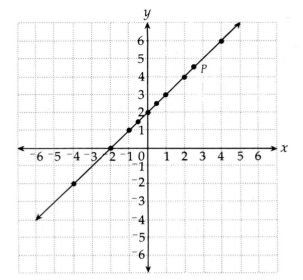

Graph the equation $y = x + 2$,
where x and y are rational numbers.

A   Make a table of values for x and y.

x	0	1	⁻1	0.5	⁻0.5	4	⁻4	2	⁻2
y	2	3	1	2.5	1.5	6	⁻2	4	0

B   Graph the coordinates (x, y) from the table.

C   All the points graphed seem to lie on a
straight line. Draw a line through the
points.

D   The coordinates (x, y) of any point on
the line will give a true statement when
they replace x and y in the equation $y = x + 2$.

Example: (2.5, 4.5) are the coordinates of point P on the line.

Replace x and y in the equation $y = x + 2$.

$4.5 = 2.5 + 2$

Replace x and y in the equation $y = x + 2$ with each pair of coordinates.
Then tell whether or not the coordinates are for a point on the line
for the equation.

1. (⁻3, ⁻1)   2. (2, 4)   3. (2.6, 4.6)   4. $\left(\frac{1}{3}, 2\frac{1}{3}\right)$ 5. (⁻5, 3)

6. (⁻5, ⁻3)   7. (⁻10, ⁻8)   8. (3.9, 5.1)   9. (⁻6, ⁻4)   10. (⁻7.2, ⁻5.2)

Copy and complete the tables for each equation.

1. $y = x - 1$

x	5	$3\frac{1}{2}$	1	0	$^-1$	$^-2\frac{1}{2}$	$^-4$	$^-5$
y	4	$2\frac{1}{2}$	▥	▥	▥	▥	▥	▥

2. $y = \frac{1}{2}x$

x	6	4	3	1	$^-1$	$^-4$	$^-5$	$^-6$
y	3	▥	▥	▥	▥	▥	▥	▥

3. $y = \frac{x}{4}$

x	8	5	3	0	$^-2$	$^-4$	$^-6$	$^-8$
y	▥	▥	▥	▥	▥	▥	▥	▥

4. $y = 2x + 0.5$

x	4	3	1.5	0.5	0	$^-0.5$	$^-2.5$	$^-4$
y	▥	▥	▥	▥	▥	▥	▥	▥

5. $y = 4x - 5$

x	0	$\frac{1}{4}$	$\frac{3}{4}$	1	2	$^-\frac{1}{4}$	$^-1$	$^-3$
y	▥	▥	▥	▥	▥	▥	▥	▥

6. $y = \frac{1}{3}x + 1$

x	$^-6$	$^-3$	$^-1$	0	1	2	3	6
y	▥	▥	▥	▥	▥	▥	▥	▥

Graph the equations for rational numbers x and y.
Use the tables from exercises 1–6.

7. $y = x - 1$

8. $y = \frac{1}{2}x$

9. $y = \frac{x}{4}$

10. $y = 2x + 0.5$

11. $y = 4x - 5$

12. $y = \frac{1}{3}x + 1$

☆ **13.** Complete the table of values for $y = x^2$.
Then graph the equation.

$y = x^2$

x	$^-3$	$^-2$	$^-1$	$^-\frac{1}{2}$	0	$\frac{1}{2}$	1	2	3
y	9	4	▥	▥	▥	▥	▥	▥	▥

☆ **14.** Graph the equation $y = |x|$.

A snowfall of 10 cm is equivalent to
0.81 cm of rainfall. A recent record
for snowfall in 24 hours was
187 cm at Silver Lake, Colorado.
What is the equivalent rainfall
for this amount of snow?

⭐ Graphing pairs of equations

Graph on the same coordinate grid
the pair of equations

$$y = x - 2$$

$$y = 4 - x$$

where x and y are rational numbers.

Find the point of intersection
of the graphs.

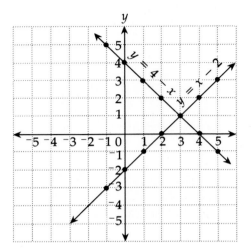

$y = x - 2$

x	5	4	3	2	1	0	⁻1
y	3	2	1	0	⁻1	⁻2	⁻3

$y = 4 - x$

x	5	4	3	2	1	0	⁻1
y	⁻1	0	1	2	3	4	5

Notice that the ordered pair (3, 1)
appears in both tables. The point
(3, 1) is the point of intersection
of the graphs.

1. The graphs of $y = x + 3$ and
   $y = {}^-2x$ intersect at point P.
   What are the coordinates of
   point P?

2. Substitute the x and y coordinates
   of point P in the equation
   $y = x + 3$. Do you get a true
   statement?

3. Substitute the x and y coordinates
   of point P in the equation
   $y = {}^-2x$. Do you get a true
   statement?

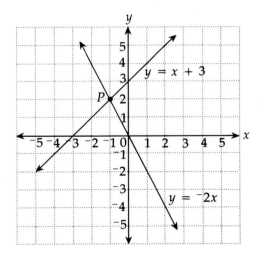

Copy and complete the tables for each pair of equations. Graph the equations. Then give the coordinates of the point of intersection.

1. $y = x - 1$

x	4	2	0	$^-2$	$^-4$
y					

$y = 5 - x$

x	5	3	1	$^-1$	$^-3$
y					

2. $y = x + 2$

x	$^-4$	$^-2$	$^-1$	0	2
y					

$y = 2x + 1$

x	0	1	$^-1$	2	$^-3$
y					

3. $y = 3x + 4$

x	$^-3$	$^-2$	$^-1$	0	1
y					

$y = ^-x$

x	5	3	0	$^-3$	$^-5$
y					

4. $y = x - 4$

x	5	4	1	0	$^-1$
y					

$y = 4 - x$

x	5	4	1	0	$^-1$
y					

5. $y = x + 1$

x	4	2	0	$^-2$	$^-4$
y					

$y = \frac{x}{2}$

x	6	4	0	$^-2$	$^-4$
y					

6. $y = x$

x	$^-4$	$^-2$	0	2	4
y					

$y = ^-x$

x	$^-2$	$^-1$	0	1	2
y	2				

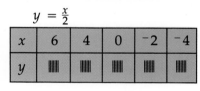

Make a table of values for the equation:

$$y = 1.8x + 0.72$$

Graph the equation.

⊛ Graphs of other equations

Draw the graph of $y = x^2 + 1$.

x	0	1	$^-1$	2	$^-2$	3	$^-3$	0.5	$^-0.5$
y	1	2	2	5	5	10	10	1.25	1.25

After the table has been
completed and the pairs
(x, y) have been graphed,
the points are joined to form
a smooth curve called
a **parabola**.

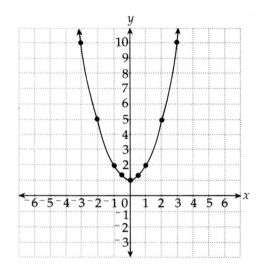

Draw the graph of $y = \frac{4}{x}$.

x	1	2	3	4	5	$^-1$	$^-2$	$^-3$	$^-4$	$^-5$
y	4	2	$\frac{4}{3}$	1	$\frac{4}{5}$	$^-4$	$^-2$	$^-\frac{4}{3}$	$^-1$	$^-\frac{4}{5}$

Notice that x cannot equal 0
since division by zero is not
possible. This means that the
graph of the equation has a
break in it at $x = 0$. The
graph has two distinct branches
and is called a **hyperbola**.

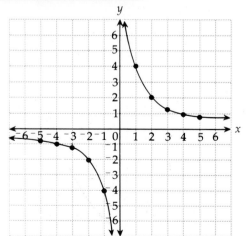

Copy and complete the table of values for each equation.
Then draw the graph of the equation.

1. $y = x^2 - 1$

x	3	2	1	$\frac{1}{2}$	0	$\frac{-1}{2}$	-1	-2	-3
y	8	3	▦	▦	▦	▦	▦	▦	▦

2. $y = \frac{x^2}{4}$

x	$^-4$	$^-2$	$^-1$	$\frac{-1}{2}$	0	$\frac{1}{2}$	1	3	4
y	▦	▦	▦	▦	▦	▦	▦	▦	▦

3. $y = \frac{8}{x}$

x	8	6	4	2	1	$^-1$	$^-2$	$^-4$	$^-8$
y	▦	▦	▦	▦	▦	▦	▦	▦	▦

4. $y = 4 - x^2$

x	3	2	1	$\frac{1}{2}$	0	$\frac{-1}{2}$	-1	-2	-3
y	▦	▦	▦	▦	▦	▦	▦	▦	▦

☆ **5.** $y = x^3$

x	2	$\frac{3}{2}$	1	$\frac{1}{2}$	0	$\frac{-1}{2}$	-1	$\frac{-3}{2}$	-2
y	▦	▦	▦	▦	▦	▦	▦	▦	▦

☆ **6.** $y = x^2 - 2x$

x	4	3	2	1	0	-1	-2	-3	-4
y	▦	▦	▦	▦	▦	▦	▦	▦	▦

☆ **7.** Draw the graphs of these two equations on the same coordinate grid. Find the points of intersection of the graphs.

$$y = x + 2$$

$$y = x^2$$

Think Change the position of one digit only to get a true statement.

$$102 + 1 = 101$$

Answers for Self-check **1.** $(^-2, 3)$ **2.** $\left(2, 3\frac{1}{2}\right)$ **3.** $\left(3, ^-1\frac{1}{2}\right)$ **4.** $(4,0)$ **5.** $(0, ^-2)$ **6.** $(^-4, 1)$
7. $(^-1, ^-3)$ **8.** $\left(^-2\frac{1}{2}, \frac{1}{2}\right)$

9.

x	$^-3$	$^-2$	$^-1$	0	1	2	3	4
y	$^-10$	$^-8$	$^-6$	$^-4$	$^-2$	0	2	4

11.

x	4	2.5	0.5	0	$^-0.5$	$^-2$	3.5	$^-4$
y	$^-3$	$^-1.5$	0.5	1	1.5	3	4.5	5

10.

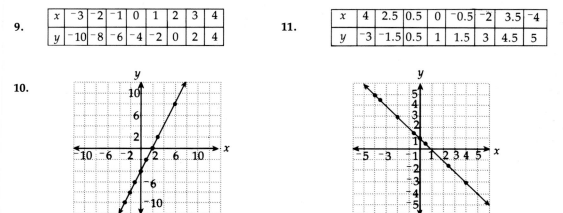

Self-check

Give the coordinates of each point.

1. *A* 2. *B* 3. *C* 4. *D*

5. *E* 6. *F* 7. *G* 8. *H*

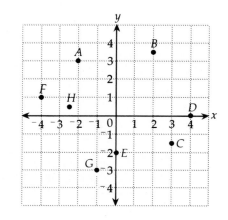

9. Copy and complete the table of values.

$y = 2x - 4$

x	-3	-2	-1	0	1	2	3	4
y								

10. Use the pairs (x, y) in the table for exercise 9 to graph the equation $y = 2x - 4$.

11. Copy and complete the table of values. Draw the graph of the equation $y = 1 - x$.

$y = 1 - x$

x	4	2.5	0.5	0	-0.5	-2	-3.5	-4
y								

Answers for Self-check—page 297

Test

Give the coordinates of each point.

1. *S* 2. *T* 3. *U* 4. *V*

5. *W* 6. *X* 7. *Y* 8. *Z*

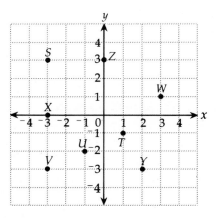

9. Copy and complete the table of values.

$y = 3x - 1$

x	3	2	1	0	-1	-2	-3	-4
y								

10. Use the pairs (x, y) in the table for exercise 9 to graph the equation $y = 3x - 1$.

11. Copy and complete the table of values. Draw the graph of the equation $y = \frac{x}{2} + 1$.

$y = \frac{x}{2} + 1$

x	6	5	4	2	0	-1	-2	-4
y								

Math lab

The Balancing Ruler Function

For this experiment you will need a centimeter ruler and 10 pennies.

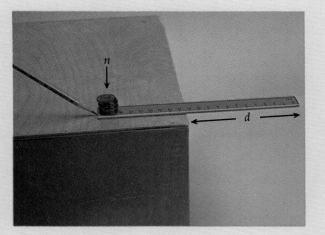

Place a ruler on the edge of a desk or table with the
end marked with zero extending over the edge. Place
one penny at the last mark on the other end of the ruler.
Use the point of a pencil to push the ruler toward the
edge until the ruler starts to tip over.

Record the distance (d) the ruler extends over the edge
to the nearest tenth of a centimeter and the number (n)
of pennies on the end of the ruler.

Repeat this experiment with different numbers of pennies,
and make a table of your findings.

n	1	2	3	4	5	6	7	8	9	10
d	▥	▥	▥	▥	▥	▥	▥	▥	▥	▥

Make a graph showing the
relationship between n and d.
Connect the points with a line
or curve. Different rulers will
give different graphs.

Symmetry and Transformations

A plane figure has **reflectional symmetry** when a line can be drawn through it so that one half can be flipped to fit exactly on the other half. The line is called **the line of reflectional symmetry**. Objects in nature may not be perfectly symmetric, but often appear to have reflectional symmetry. In manufactured objects, a more exact reflectional symmetry can be achieved.

Reflectional symmetry in nature

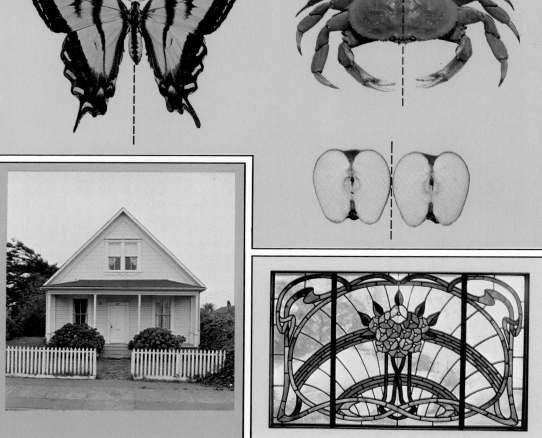

Reflectional symmetry in architecture   Reflectional symmetry in art

Find some pictures or objects that appear to have reflectional symmetry.

Here are two tests which can be used to see if a geometric figure or design has reflectional symmetry.

| **The fold test** | **The mirror test** |

  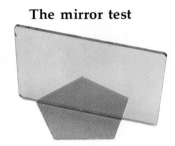

Trace the figure.   Fold the figure.   Place a mirror on the figure.

If the figure can be folded so that one half exactly matches the other, the figure has reflectional symmetry. The fold line is the line of reflectional symmetry.

If the mirror can be placed so that the part of the figure in front of it together with the reflection forms the original shape, the figure has reflectional symmetry.

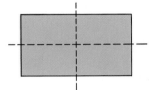

2 lines of symmetry   1 line of symmetry

Give the number of lines of reflectional symmetry for each figure.

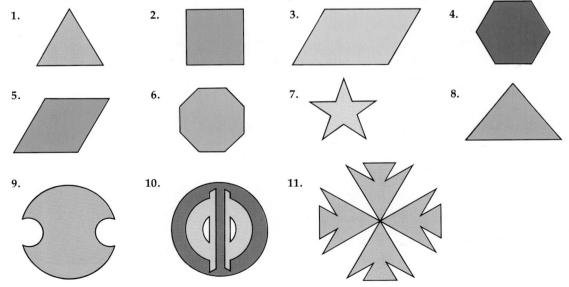

1.   2.   3.   4.

5.   6.   7.   8.

9.   10.   11.

Rotational symmetry

Rotational symmetry in nature   Rotational symmetry in art

A figure has **rotational symmetry** if it can be rotated about a center point through an angle less than 360° so that it appears to be in the same position as at the beginning.

Here is a test which can be used to determine whether or not a figure has rotational symmetry.

The trace and turn test

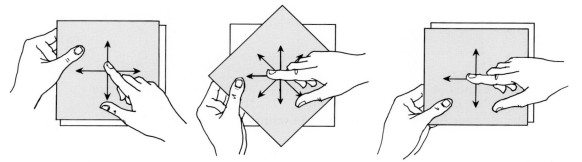

Trace the figure. Then hold your finger on the center point and turn the tracing. If the tracing fits exactly on the original figure before you have turned 360°, the figure has rotational symmetry. Since this figure fits back on itself after a 90° turn, it has **90° rotational symmetry**.

Which of these figures have 90° rotational symmetry?

1.   2.   3.   4.

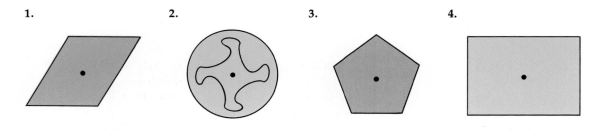

Give the number of degrees of rotational symmetry for each figure.

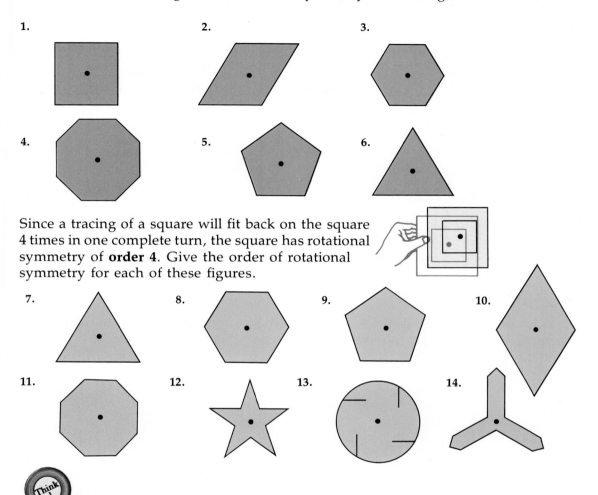

1.

2.

3.

4.

5.

6.

Since a tracing of a square will fit back on the square 4 times in one complete turn, the square has rotational symmetry of **order** 4. Give the order of rotational symmetry for each of these figures.

7.

8.

9.

10.

11.

12.

13.

14.

Think!

Three different types of axes of rotational symmetry for a cube are shown.

How many axes of rotational symmetry does a cube have?

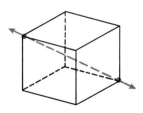

An axis of 120°
rotational
symmetry
through two
opposite vertices.

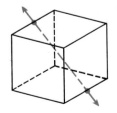

An axis of 180°
rotational
symmetry
through two
opposite edges.

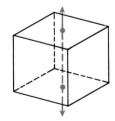

An axis of 90°
rotational
symmetry
through two
opposite faces.

Translational symmetry

A design has **translational symmetry** if the basic figure can be traced and repeatedly slid, or **translated**, without turns, to fit upon itself again.

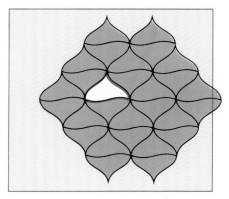

Trace the basic figure.

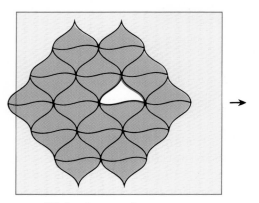

Slide the tracing.

Which of the following pictures have translational symmetry? Write **horizontally**, **vertically**, or **diagonally** to describe the direction the basic figure can be translated to fit upon itself.

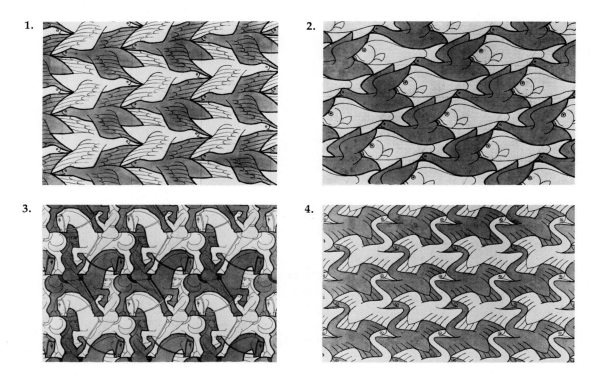

1.

2.

3.

4.

In each design, a basic figure has been chosen and outlined.
Using this basic figure, tell whether the design has translational symmetry.

1.

2.

3.

4.

5.

6.

Two different types of
planes of symmetry for
a cube are shown here.
How many different
planes of symmetry
does a cube have?

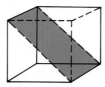

A plane of
symmetry
containing a
pair of opposite
edges of the
cube.

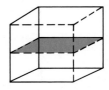

A plane of
symmetry that
is parallel to
a pair of
opposite faces
of the cube.

Finding reflection images

Problem   To find the reflection image of $\triangle ABC$ in $\overleftrightarrow{PQ}$.
Procedure

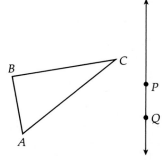

Step 1   Draw $\triangle ABC$ and $\overleftrightarrow{PQ}$.

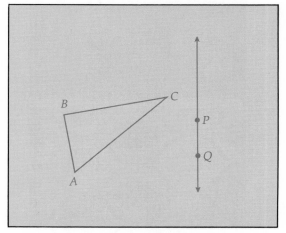

Step 2   Place tracing paper on the figure and trace $\triangle ABC$ and $\overleftrightarrow{PQ}$.

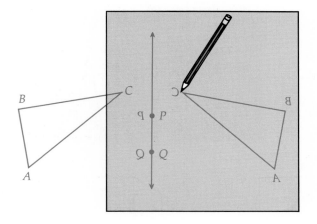

Step 3   Flip the tracing paper about $\overleftrightarrow{PQ}$, matching points P and Q. Mark points A', B', and C' by pushing a pencil point firmly on tracing paper points A, B, and C.

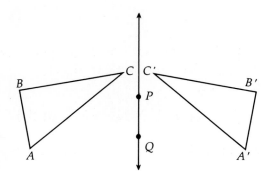

Step 4   Lift the tracing paper and draw $\triangle A'B'C'$. $\triangle A'B'C'$ is the reflection image of $\triangle ABC$ in $\overleftrightarrow{PQ}$.

Copy each of these figures and reflection lines. Use tracing paper to find the reflection image of each figure in the given line.

1.

2.

3.

4.

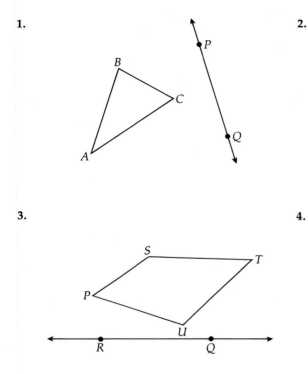

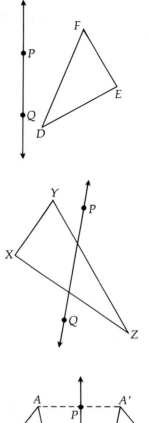

△A'B'C' is the reflection image of △ABC in $\overleftrightarrow{PQ}$. What can you say about the following?

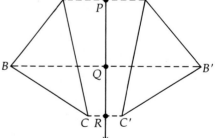

5. $\overline{AP}$ and $\overline{A'P}$ 6. $\overleftrightarrow{AA'}$ and $\overleftrightarrow{PQ}$

7. $\overline{AB}$ and $\overline{A'B'}$ 8. △ABC and △A'B'C'

☆ 9. △J'K'L' is the reflection image of △JKL after a reflection in line r. Trace the triangles. Construct the line r of reflection.

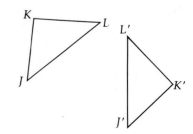

Finding rotation images

Problem   To find the rotation image of △ABC after a 90° clockwise rotation
around point O.

Procedure

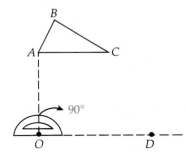

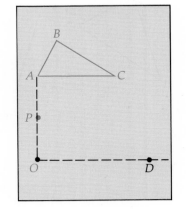

Step 1   Copy △ABC and point O.
Draw $\overline{OA}$. Construct $\overline{OD}$
so that ∠AOD is 90°.

Step 2   Trace △ABC, center
point O, and mark
guide point P.

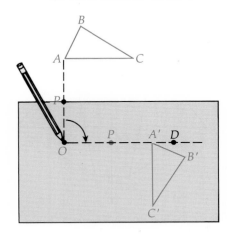

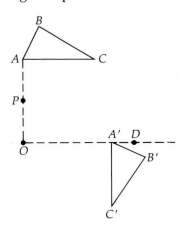

Step 3   Keep point O from
moving and turn the
tracing so that guide
point P goes through
an angle of 90°.

Step 4   Mark points A', B', and C'
by pushing a pencil point
firmly on tracing paper
points A, B, and C. Draw
△A'B'C'. △A'B'C' is
the image of △ABC after a
rotation of 90° about point O.

Copy each of these figures and their centers of rotation.
Use tracing paper to find the rotation images.

1. Find the 90° clockwise rotation image of △ABC around point R.

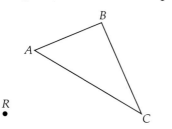

2. Find the 90° counterclockwise rotation image of △DEF around point R.

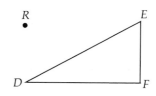

3. Find the 180° clockwise rotation image of quadrilateral JKLM around point R.

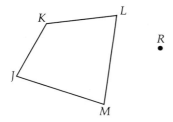

4. Find the 60° counterclockwise rotation image of parallelogram ABCD around point R.

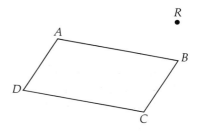

★ 5. Trace lines r and s and triangle ABC.

Find the reflection image, △A'B'C', of △ABC in line r. Then find the reflection image, △A"B"C", of △A'B'C' after a reflection in line s. Using tracing paper, show that △A"B"C" is the image of △ABC after a rotation around point P. Through how many degrees is this rotation?

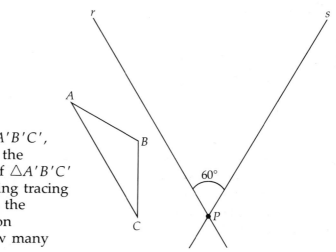

Finding translation images

Problem To find the translation image of $\triangle ABC$ after a translation in the direction and through the distance of arrow EF.

Procedure

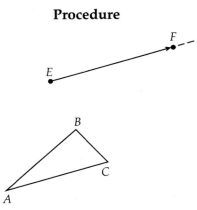

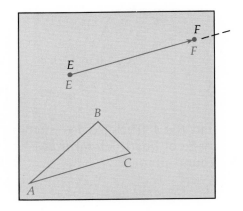

Step 1 Copy $\triangle ABC$ and arrow EF. Extend arrow EF.

Step 2 Trace $\triangle ABC$ and points E and F.

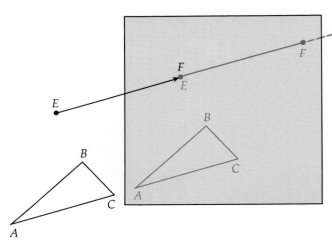

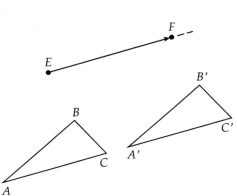

Step 3 Slide the tracing so that point E moves from E to F and point F stays on the arrow EF. Mark points A', B', and C' by pushing a pencil point firmly on tracing paper points A, B, and C.

Step 4 Draw $\triangle A'B'C'$. $\triangle A'B'C'$ is the translation image of $\triangle ABC$ in the direction and through the distance of arrow EF.

Copy each figure and the translation arrow.
Use tracing paper to find the translation image.

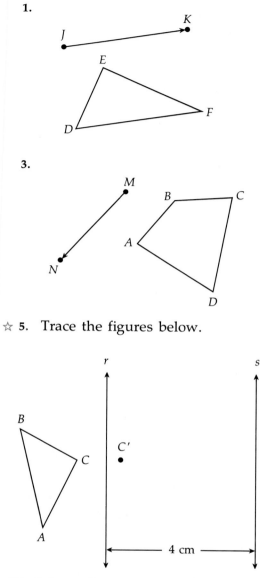

1.

2.

3.

4.

☆ 5. Trace the figures below.

Find the reflection image, $\triangle A'B'C'$, of $\triangle ABC$ in line r. Then find the reflection image of $\triangle A'B'C'$ in line s. Use tracing paper and show that $\triangle A''B''C''$ is the translation image of $\triangle ABC$. Through what distance is the translation?

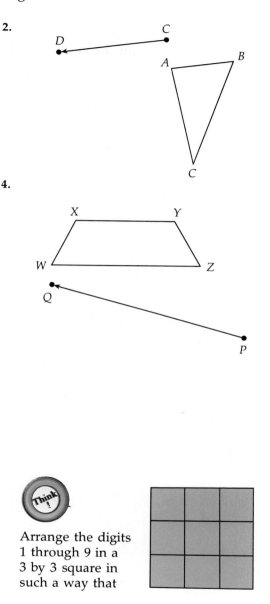

Think

Arrange the digits 1 through 9 in a 3 by 3 square in such a way that

1. the product of 2 times the 3-digit number in the first row is the number in the second row, and

2. the product of 3 times the number in the first row is the number in the third row.

✪ Graphing transformations

Reflections, rotations, and translations are called **transformations**. The results of these and other transformations can be shown by graphing a figure and its image after the transformation.

Problem   To graph a figure and its image after a translation.

Procedure

Step 1   Use a translation rule to make a table of key points and their images.

rule	
$(x, y) \rightarrow (x + 3, y + 5)$	
Point	**Image**
$A(1, 1)$	$\rightarrow$ $A'(4, 6)$
$B(2, {}^-1)$	$\rightarrow$ $B'(5, 4)$
$C({}^-2, {}^-1)$	$\rightarrow$ $C'(1, 4)$

Step 2   Graph the figure. Then graph its translation image.

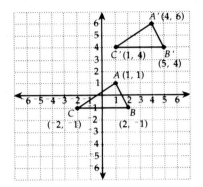

Complete each table and graph $\triangle ABC$ and its image. Then answer the questions.

A Translation

rule	
$(x, y) \rightarrow (x + 3, y + 0)$	
Point	**Image**
1. $A({}^-5, 2) \rightarrow A'(\blacksquare, \blacksquare)$	
2. $B({}^-3, 4) \rightarrow B'(\blacksquare, \blacksquare)$	
3. $C({}^-2, 3) \rightarrow C'(\blacksquare, \blacksquare)$	

4. In what direction is the translation?

5. Through how many units is the triangle translated?

A Reflection

rule	
$(x, y) \rightarrow ({}^-x, y)$	
Point	**Image**
6. $A({}^-2, 5) \rightarrow A'(\blacksquare, \blacksquare)$	
7. $B({}^-3, 2) \rightarrow B'(\blacksquare, \blacksquare)$	
8. $C({}^-4, 3) \rightarrow C'(\blacksquare, \blacksquare)$	

9. Describe the line of reflection for the transformation above.

A Rotation

rule	
$(x, y) \rightarrow ({}^-y, x)$	
Point	**Image**
10. $A(6, 0) \rightarrow A'(\blacksquare, \blacksquare)$	
11. $B(6, 3) \rightarrow B'(\blacksquare, \blacksquare)$	
12. $C(4, 1) \rightarrow C'(\blacksquare, \blacksquare)$	

13. What are the coordinates of the center of the rotation?

14. Through how many degrees is the rotation?

Complete each table and graph quadrilateral *ABCD* and its image.
Then answer the question.

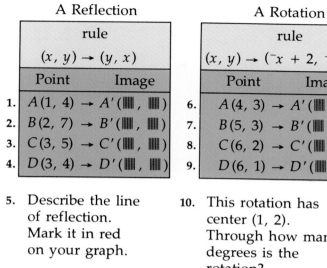

A Reflection

rule	
$(x, y) \rightarrow (y, x)$	
Point	Image
1. $A(1, 4) \rightarrow A'(\text{▥}, \text{▥})$	
2. $B(2, 7) \rightarrow B'(\text{▥}, \text{▥})$	
3. $C(3, 5) \rightarrow C'(\text{▥}, \text{▥})$	
4. $D(3, 4) \rightarrow D'(\text{▥}, \text{▥})$	

5. Describe the line of reflection. Mark it in red on your graph.

A Rotation

rule	
$(x, y) \rightarrow (^-x + 2, ^-y + 4)$	
Point	Image
6. $A(4, 3) \rightarrow A'(\text{▥}, \text{▥})$	
7. $B(5, 3) \rightarrow B'(\text{▥}, \text{▥})$	
8. $C(6, 2) \rightarrow C'(\text{▥}, \text{▥})$	
9. $D(6, 1) \rightarrow D'(\text{▥}, \text{▥})$	

10. This rotation has center (1, 2). Through how many degrees is the rotation?

A Magnification

rule	
$(x, y) \rightarrow (2x, 2y)$	
Point	Image
11. $A(1, 1) \rightarrow A'(\text{▥}, \text{▥})$	
12. $B(1, 3) \rightarrow B'(\text{▥}, \text{▥})$	
13. $C(3, 1) \rightarrow C'(\text{▥}, \text{▥})$	
14. $D(3, 3) \rightarrow D'(\text{▥}, \text{▥})$	

15. How do the lengths of the sides of $A'B'C'D'$ compare with the lengths of the sides of *ABCD*? How do the areas compare?

A Translation

rule	
$(x, y) \rightarrow (x - 3, y + 4)$	
Point	Image
16. $A(2, ^-4) \rightarrow A'(\text{▥}, \text{▥})$	
17. $B(3, ^-6) \rightarrow B'(\text{▥}, \text{▥})$	
18. $C(4, ^-4) \rightarrow C'(\text{▥}, \text{▥})$	
19. $D(5, ^-6) \rightarrow D'(\text{▥}, \text{▥})$	

20. Describe the translation by completing this phrase: "over ___, up ___."

☆ A Shear

rule	
$(x, y) \rightarrow (x + 2y, y)$	
Point	Image
21. $A(1, 2) \rightarrow A'(\text{▥}, \text{▥})$	
22. $B(1, 4) \rightarrow B'(\text{▥}, \text{▥})$	
23. $C(4, 4) \rightarrow C'(\text{▥}, \text{▥})$	
24. $D(4, 2) \rightarrow D'(\text{▥}, \text{▥})$	

25. How does the area of $A'B'C'D'$ compare with the area of *ABCD*?

☆ A Stretch

rule	
$(x, y) \rightarrow (\frac{1}{2}x, 2y)$	
Point	Image
26. $A(4, 4) \rightarrow A'(\text{▥}, \text{▥})$	
27. $B(6, 6) \rightarrow B'(\text{▥}, \text{▥})$	
28. $C(8, 6) \rightarrow C'(\text{▥}, \text{▥})$	
29. $D(10, 4) \rightarrow D'(\text{▥}, \text{▥})$	

30. Describe how the transformation changed the figure. How do the areas compare?

☆ 31. Make up some transformation rules and see how they change a figure. Give them to a classmate to graph.

Answers for Self-check   1. 2   2. 180°

Self-check

A

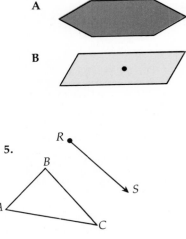

1. How many lines of symmetry does figure **A** have?

2. Give the number of degrees of rotational symmetry for figure **B**.

B

Copy each of these figures. Use tracing paper.

3.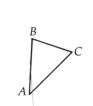

Find the reflection image.

4.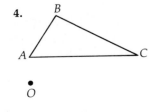

Find the 90° clockwise rotation image.

5.

Find the translation image.

Answers for Self-check—page 313

Test

1. Give the number of lines of symmetry for figure **C**.

2. Give the degrees of rotational symmetry for figure **C**.

Copy these figures on your paper.
Use tracing paper.

3. Find the reflection image of $\triangle ABC$ in line r.

4. Find the 60° clockwise rotation image of $\triangle ABC$ around point X.

5. Find the translation image of $\triangle ABC$ after the translation through $\overrightarrow{PQ}$.

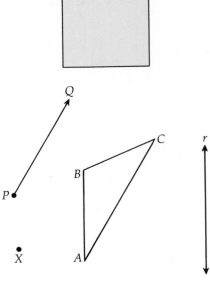

Math lab

Mirror Images

clear plastic

Try some activities using a clear piece of plastic.

1. Place the plastic on the dashed line. How do you explain what you see?

```
├─────────────────────┤
    FIRST CHOICE
```

Make another example like this.
"Choice" is a "reflection word".
Make as many reflection words as you can.

2. Is the sum correct? Place the plastic on the dashed line to check it.

$$3414$$
$$340$$
$$T4813$$
$$\overline{433T4813}$$

3. Place the plastic on the dashed line to decode this secret message.

Make a secret message like this and send it to a classmate.

4. Place the plastic on the dashed line to make the half word and the half numeral.

```
├─── DUD OUI ───┤
```

Make some half words and half numerals of your own.

5. Try these geometric activities using the plastic.

A Bisect a segment.

B Bisect an angle.

Unit 11 review

Find the sums.

1. $9 + {}^-5$
2. ${}^-2 + {}^-7$
3. ${}^-4 + 8$
4. ${}^-1 + {}^-9$

5. $16 + {}^-9$
6. ${}^-21 + {}^-14$
7. ${}^-6 + 18$
8. ${}^-17 + {}^-8$

Find the differences.

9. $10 - {}^-5$
10. ${}^-8 - {}^-12$
11. ${}^-7 - {}^-4$
12. ${}^-12 - 7$

13. ${}^-11 - {}^-4$
14. $15 - {}^-7$
15. ${}^-5 - {}^-3$
16. ${}^-21 - 6$

Add or subtract.

17. $(4 + {}^-8) - 2$
18. $({}^-12 - 4) + 4$
19. $(21 + {}^-2) + 12$

20. $(13 - {}^-5) + 9$
21. $7 + ({}^-9 - {}^-2)$
22. ${}^-11 - ({}^-20 - {}^-10)$

Find the products.

23. ${}^-5 \cdot 4$
24. ${}^-2 \cdot {}^-8$
25. $6 \cdot {}^-4$
26. ${}^-7 \cdot {}^-8$

27. $9 \cdot {}^-8$
28. $7 \cdot {}^-4$
29. ${}^-3 \cdot {}^-8$
30. ${}^-4 \cdot {}^-9$

Find the quotients.

31. $32 \div {}^-8$
32. ${}^-28 \div 4$
33. ${}^-27 \div {}^-3$
34. $81 \div 9$

35. $56 \div {}^-7$
36. ${}^-45 \div 9$
37. ${}^-40 \div 8$
38. ${}^-63 \div {}^-7$

Solve.

39. ${}^-3 \cdot ({}^-4 - {}^-8) = n$
40. $(2 + {}^-12) \cdot 5 = n$

41. $(64 \div {}^-8) + 8 = n$
42. $7 \cdot ({}^-63 \div 7) = n$

43. $(54 \div 6) + {}^-18 = n$
44. $({}^-32 \div {}^-4) \cdot {}^-6 = n$

45. $3x - 4 = {}^-13$
46. $\frac{x}{3} + 1 = {}^-2$
47. ${}^-4x + 3 = 15$

48. $2x + 5 = 1$
49. $3x + 5x = {}^-40$
50. $7x - 4x = {}^-18$

Unit **12**

Number Theory
Counting Problems
Probability
Statistics
Square Roots and Irrational Numbers

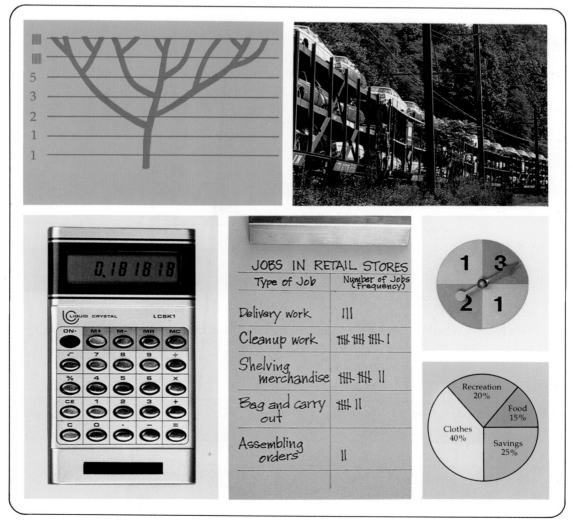

Number Theory

If a, b, and c are whole numbers and $a \cdot b = c$, then a and b are **factors** of c.

For example, 1, 2, 3, and 6 are all factors of 6 because

$1 \cdot 6 = 6$

$2 \cdot 3 = 6$

Whole number	Factors of the whole number
0	0, 1, 2, 3, 4, 5, 6, . . .
1	1
2	1, 2
3	1, 3
4	1, 2, 4
5	1, 5
6	1, 2, 3, 6
7	1, 7
8	1, 2, 4, 8
9	1, 3, 9
10	1, 2, 5, 10
11	1, 11
12	1, 2, 3, 4, 6, 12
.	.
.	.
.	.

1. What whole number has an unlimited number of factors?

2. What whole number has exactly one factor?

3. List the whole numbers less than 20 that have exactly 2 factors.

4. List the non-zero whole numbers less than 20 that have 3 or more factors.

> The whole numbers that have exactly 2 factors are the **prime numbers**.

> The non-zero whole numbers that have 3 or more factors are the **composite numbers**.

5. Which two whole numbers are neither prime nor composite?

6. Complete each set of numbers.

Prime numbers less than 100	2, 3, 5, 7, 11, . . .

Composite numbers less than 100	4, 6, 8, 9, 10, 12, . . .

This table gives the first 249 prime numbers.

1. How many composite numbers are between 7 and 11?

2. How many composite numbers are between 89 and 97?

3. How many composite numbers are between 953 and 967?

4. Which two primes have no composite numbers between them?

5. Primes that have just one composite number between them are called **twin primes**. For example: 11 and 13 are twin primes. List the other pairs of twin primes less than 100.

The First 249 Primes									
	0	1	2	3	4	5	6	7	8
0		2	3	5	7	11	13	17	19	23
1	29	31	37	41	43	47	53	59	61	67
2	71	73	79	83	89	97	101	103	107	109
3	113	127	131	137	139	149	151	157	163	167
4	173	179	181	191	193	197	199	211	223	227
5	229	233	239	241	251	257	263	269	271	277
6	281	283	293	307	311	313	317	331	337	347
7	349	353	359	367	373	379	383	389	397	401
8	409	419	421	431	433	439	443	449	457	461
9	463	467	479	487	491	499	503	509	521	523
10	541	547	557	563	569	571	577	587	593	599
11	601	607	613	617	619	631	641	643	647	653
12	659	661	673	677	683	691	701	709	719	727
13	733	739	743	751	757	761	769	773	787	797
14	809	811	821	823	827	829	839	853	857	859
15	863	877	881	883	887	907	911	919	929	937
16	941	947	953	967	971	977	983	991	997	1009
17	1013	1019	1021	1031	1033	1039	1049	1051	1061	1063
18	1069	1087	1091	1093	1097	1103	1109	1117	1123	1129
19	1151	1153	1163	1171	1181	1187	1193	1201	1213	1217
20	1223	1229	1231	1237	1249	1259	1277	1279	1283	1289
21	1291	1297	1301	1303	1307	1319	1321	1327	1361	1367
22	1373	1381	1399	1409	1423	1427	1429	1433	1439	1447
23	1451	1453	1459	1471	1481	1483	1487	1489	1493	1499
24	1511	1523	1531	1543	1549	1553	1559	1567	1571	1579

6. The prime 313 is the 65th prime. It is in the 6th row and under the column headed by 5. Find these primes: 83rd, 92nd, 124th, 191st, 235th.

7. What is the one hundredth prime?

☆ 8. Show that 1581 is not the 250th prime.

☆ 9. Find the 250th prime.

☆ 10. The three consecutive primes 11, 13, and 17 have the form n, $n + 2$ and $n + 6$. Find three other primes that have this form.

The formula, $n^2 - n + 11$, is called a prime-rich formula.

What is the first whole number for which $n^2 - n + 11$ is **not** a prime number?

...tion

...**ctorization** of a number is the number expressed as the product ...umbers.

$$60 = 2 \cdot 2 \cdot 3 \cdot 5$$

Prime factorization of 60

> ### Unique Factorization Theorem
>
> Each composite number can be expressed as a product of prime numbers in exactly one way, except for the order of the factors.

A factor tree can be used to give the prime factorization of a composite number. The top row of the factor tree gives the prime factorization of the number at the bottom.

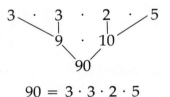

$$90 = 3 \cdot 3 \cdot 2 \cdot 5$$

Copy and complete each factor tree. Then give the prime factorization of the number.

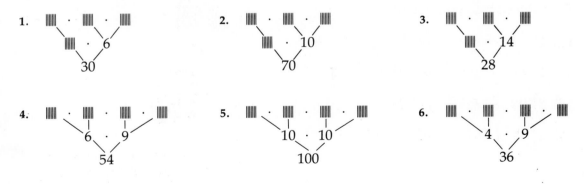

1.
30

2.
70

3.
28

4.
54

5.
100

6.
36

Exponents can be used to express the prime factorization of a number.

Prime factorization of 72

$72 = 2 \cdot 2 \cdot 2 \cdot 3 \cdot 3$

Using exponents

$72 = 2^3 \cdot 3^2$

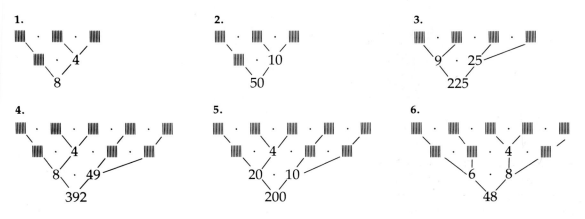

Copy and complete each factor tree.
Then give the prime factorization using exponents.

1.

$\cdots \cdot \cdots \cdot \cdots$
$\cdots \cdot 4$
8

2.

$\cdots \cdot \cdots \cdot \cdots$
$\cdots \cdot 10$
50

3.

$\cdots \cdot \cdots \cdot \cdots \cdot \cdots$
$9 \cdot 25$
225

4.

$\cdots \cdot \cdots \cdot \cdots \cdot \cdots \cdot \cdots$
$\cdots \cdot 4 \cdot \cdots \cdot \cdots$
$8 \cdot 49$
392

5.

$\cdots \cdot \cdots \cdot \cdots \cdot \cdots \cdot \cdots$
$\cdots \cdot 4 \cdot \cdots \cdot \cdots$
$20 \cdot 10$
200

6.

$\cdots \cdot \cdots \cdot \cdots \cdot \cdots \cdot \cdots$
$\cdots \cdot \cdots \cdot 4 \cdot \cdots$
$6 \cdot 8$
48

Give each prime factorization using exponents.

7. $1323 = 3 \cdot 3 \cdot 3 \cdot 7 \cdot 7$

8. $8575 = 5 \cdot 5 \cdot 7 \cdot 7 \cdot 7$

9. $176 = 2 \cdot 2 \cdot 2 \cdot 2 \cdot 11$

10. $9604 = 2 \cdot 2 \cdot 7 \cdot 7 \cdot 7 \cdot 7$

11. $180 = 2 \cdot 2 \cdot 3 \cdot 3 \cdot 5$

12. $900 = 2 \cdot 2 \cdot 3 \cdot 3 \cdot 5 \cdot 5$

Find the missing number.

13. $2^2 \cdot 3^4 = $ ▥

14. $3^2 \cdot 5^2 \cdot 7 = $ ▥

15. $2^3 \cdot 5^2 = $ ▥

16. $2^3 \cdot 5^3 = $ ▥

17. $3^3 \cdot 5^2 = $ ▥

18. $2^5 \cdot 5^5 = $ ▥

19. $2^5 \cdot 7 = $ ▥

20. $2^6 \cdot 5^6 = $ ▥

CALCULATE

Find the smallest number
that has 8 different
primes in its prime
factorization.

Some rules for divisibility

If a first number can be divided by a second number with a zero remainder, the first number is **divisible** by the second number.

$$51 \div 3 = 17 \qquad\qquad 134 \div 7 = 19 \text{ R1}$$

51 is divisible by 3.   134 is not divisible by 7.

Rules of divisibility can be used to determine if one number is divisible by another without actually dividing to find out.

The even numbers {0, 2, 4, 6, 8, 10, 12 . . .} are multiples of 2.

> **Divisibility by 2**
>
> Rule: A number is divisible by 2 if the last digit is 0, 2, 4, 6, or 8.

Which of these numbers are divisible by 2?

1. 36
2. 447
3. 148
4. 250
5. 681

6. 3764
7. 1732
8. 5623
9. 3648
10. 5275

> **Divisibility by 3**
>
> Rule: A number is divisible by 3 if the sum of the digits of the number is divisible by 3.

Examples: $2673 \longrightarrow 2 + 6 + 7 + 3 = 18$

Since 18 is divisible by 3, so is 2673.

$4238 \longrightarrow 4 + 2 + 3 + 8 = 17$

Since 17 is not divisible by 3, neither is 4238.

Which of these numbers are divisible by 3?

11. 237
12. 456
13. 517
14. 6214
15. 7280

16. 35 271
17. 46 234
18. 62 832
19. 87 969
20. 23 640

> **Divisibility by 4**
>
> Rule: A number is divisible by 4 if the 2-digit number in the tens' and ones' place is divisible by 4.

Examples: 3256 is divisible by 4 because 56 is divisible by 4.

3257 is not divisible by 4 because 57 is not divisible by 4.

Also, since $4 \cdot 25 = 100$, every multiple of 100 is divisible by 4.

Which of these numbers are divisible by 4?

1. 324	**2.** 500	**3.** 1358	**4.** 7604	**5.** 2332
6. 2450	**7.** 27 526	**8.** 28 668	**9.** 32 000	**10.** 48 286

The multiples of 5, {0, 5, 10, 15, 20, 25, . . .}, all end in 0 or 5.

> **Divisibility by 5**
>
> Rule: A number is divisible by 5 if it ends in 0 or 5.

Which of these numbers are divisible by 5?

11. 38	**12.** 35	**13.** 65	**14.** 64	**15.** 70
16. 320	**17.** 685	**18.** 1276	**19.** 3400	**20.** 28 145

> **Divisibility by 9**
>
> Rule: A number is divisible by 9 if the sum of the digits of the number is divisible by 9.

Examples: $7362 \longrightarrow 7 + 3 + 6 + 2 = 18$

18 is divisible by 9, so 7362 is divisible by 9.

$4623 \longrightarrow 4 + 6 + 2 + 3 = 15$

15 is not divisible by 9, so neither is 4623.

Which of these numbers are divisible by 9?

21. 3843	**22.** 9684	**23.** 2567	**24.** 3105	**25.** 7767
26. 84 870	**27.** 68 237	**28.** 59 679	**29.** 88 695	**30.** 61 317

✪ More rules for divisibility

Some divisibility rules require several steps.

> **Divisibility by 6**
> Rule: A number is divisible by 6 if it
> is divisible by **both** 2 and 3.

Example: Is 324 divisible by 6?
    324 is divisible by 2 because it ends in 4.
    324 is divisible by 3 because $3 + 2 + 4 = 9$ and $9 \div 3 = 3$.

Since 324 is divisible by both 2 and 3, it is divisible by 6.

Which of these numbers are divisible by 6?

1. 423
2. 432
3. 234
4. 567
5. 765

6. 2385
7. 3258
8. 8523
9. 5382
10. 7642

> **Divisibility by 7**
> Rule: Double the last digit and subtract
> the sum from the other digits.
> Continue until you can tell whether
> or not the difference is divisible
> by 7. If it is, the original
> number is also divisible by 7.

Example: Is 54 838 divisible by 7?

$$
\begin{array}{rl}
5483|8 & \text{double and subtract} \\
-16 & \\
\hline
546|7 & \text{double and subtract} \\
-14 & \\
\hline
53|2 & \text{double and subtract} \\
-4 & \\
\hline
49 & \text{Since 49 is divisible by 7, so is 54 838.}
\end{array}
$$

Which of these numbers are divisible by 7?

11. 1981
12. 2492
13. 2991
14. 1344
15. 5905

16. 53 760
17. 19 509
18. 32 418
19. 38 052
20. 63 175

Example: 37 256 is divisible by 8 because 256 is divisible by 8.
37 257 is not divisible by 8 because 257 is not divisible by 8.

Also, since $8 \cdot 125 = 1000$, every multiple of 1000 is divisible by 8.

Which of these numbers are divisible by 8?

1. 5848
2. 7480
3. 3320
4. 6410
5. 8648
6. 12 416
7. 36 720
8. 58 626
9. 72 800
10. 93 400

Example: 92 818 $9 + 8 + 8 = 25, 2 + 1 = 3$ $25 - 3 = 22$
22 is divisible by 11, so 92 818 is divisible by 11.

652 814 $6 + 2 + 1 = 9, 5 + 8 + 4 = 17$ $17 - 9 = 8$
8 is not divisible by 11, so 652 814 is not divisible by 11.

Which of these numbers are divisible by 11?

11. 74 514
12. 814
13. 9163
14. 3862
15. 5753
16. 486 937
17. 60 705
18. 57 642
19. 725 043
20. 81 917

Use the divisibility rules to help you write the complete factorization of each number.

21. 105
22. 462
23. 385
24. 1155
25. 714
26. 1015
27. 2415
28. 5670

You know that $12 = 4 \cdot 3$. Write a rule for divisibility by 12. Test your rule on these numbers.

1. 2724
2. 62 736
3. 53 446
4. 16 568
5. 16 250
6. 486 492

✪ Sequences

A **sequence** is a set of numbers given in a specific order, usually according to some rule or pattern.

Sequence of Odd Numbers

Terms	1st	2nd	3rd	4th	5th . . .	nth . . .
Numbers	1	3	5	7	9 . . .	$2n - 1$ . . .

The rule for this sequence is

$$n\text{th term} = 2n - 1$$

For example,

the   5th term $= 2 \cdot 5 - 1 = 9$
the 19th term $= 2 \cdot 19 - 1 = 37$
the 83rd term $= 2 \cdot 83 - 1 = 165$

Give the next three terms of each sequence.

$2n-1$

1. nth term $= 4n - 3$

1st	2nd	3rd	4th	5th	6th
$4 \cdot 1 - 3$	$4 \cdot 2 - 3$	$4 \cdot 3 - 3$	$4 \cdot 4 - 3$	$4 \cdot 5 - 3$	$4 \cdot 6 - 3$
1	5	9	▒	▒	▒

2. nth term $= n^2$

1st	2nd	3rd	4th	5th	6th
1	4	9	▒	▒	▒

3. nth term $= n^2 - n$

1st	2nd	3rd	4th	5th	6th
0	2	6	▒	▒	▒

4. Give the 17th term for each sequence above.

Give the 5th, 6th and 7th term for each sequence.

1. 6, 11, 16, 21, ▥, ▥, ▥, . . ., $5n + 1$, . . .

2. 1, 7, 13, 19, ▥, ▥, ▥, . . ., $6n - 5$, . . .

3. 7, 10, 13, 16, ▥, ▥, ▥, . . ., $3n + 4$, . . .

4. 3, 6, 9, 12, ▥, ▥, ▥, . . ., $4n - n$, . . .

5. 3, 8, 15, 24, ▥, ▥, ▥, . . ., $n(n + 2)$, . . .

6. 2, 8, 18, 32, ▥, ▥, ▥, . . ., $2n^2$, . . .

Give the first six terms for each of the following.

7. $3n - 2$

8. $n^3 - 1$

9. $3n^2 + 1$

10. $7n + 3$

11. $n(n + n)$

12. $2n^2 + 3n + 1$

Give the rule for the nth term for each sequence.

☆ 13. 4, 8, 12, 16, 20, 24, 28, . . .

☆ 14. 5, 6, 7, 8, 9, 10, 11, . . .

☆ 15. 1, 4, 9, 16, 25, 36, 49, . . .

☆ 16. 4, 7, 12, 19, 28, 39, 52, . . .

☆ 17. 9, 11, 13, 15, 17, 19, 21, . . .

☆ 18. 3, 8, 13, 18, 23, 28, 33, . . .

Every whole number is in one of these sequences.

A {0, 3, 6, 9, 12, 15, 18, . . .}

B {1, 4, 7, 10, 13, 16, 19, . . .}

C {2, 5, 8, 11, 14, 17, 20, . . .}

In which sequence is each of the following numbers?

1. 5 677 429

2. 2 684 286

3. 8 270 531

4. 5 053 126

✪ Some special number patterns

This triangular pattern of numbers is called **Pascal's Triangle.**

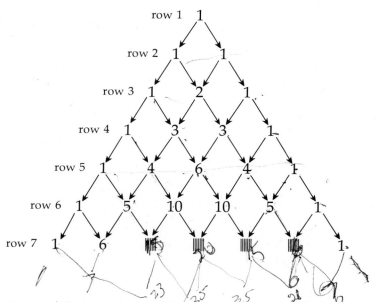

1. Study the pattern of the numbers. Give the missing numbers in row 7.

2. Make a Pascal's Triangle that has 10 rows.

3. Find the sum of all the numbers in each row for the first 10 rows.

sum row 1	sum row 2	sum row 3	sum row 4	sum row 5		sum row 10
1	2	4	8			

4. Study the pattern for the sequence of sums above. Without extending your triangle give the sums for rows 11 through 15.

This sequence of numbers is called the Fibonacci (Fi-bon-nach'-ee) sequence. Each number after the first two numbers is the sum of the two preceding numbers.

Fibonacci sequence: 1, 1, 2, 3, 5, 8, 13, . . .

The Fibonacci sequence is named for Leonardo of Pisa (1175–1230) who was also known as Fibonacci. This sequence of numbers can be found in patterns in nature. For example, the branches on some plants grow in the Fibonacci pattern. Start at the bottom red line and count intersected branches. What are the numbers for the top two lines?

1. List all the Fibonacci numbers less than 100.

2. There are just five Fibonacci numbers between 100 and 1000. Find them.

3. The Fibonacci numbers can be found also in Pascal's Triangle. Find the sums for the rising diagonal rows of Pascal's Triangle.

4. Give the sums for rising diagonal rows 8, 9, and 10.

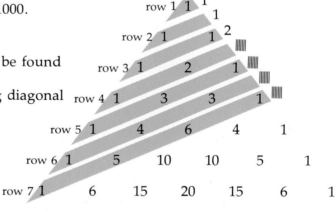

 The numbers 317 811 and 514 229 are consecutive Fibonacci numbers. Give the next five Fibonacci numbers after these two.

Self-check

Write **P** for each prime number. For each composite number, give the prime factorization using exponents.

1. 49   **2.** 43   **3.** 161   **4.** 157   **5.** 36   **6.** 144

Give the product.

7. $2^3 \cdot 5^2$ **8.** $3^2 \cdot 5^2$ **9.** $2^2 \cdot 3^2 \cdot 5$ **10.** $3 \cdot 5^2$

In each row find the number that is

11. divisible by 2: 37, 43, 58   ☆ **15.** Give the third row of Pascal's Triangle.

12. divisible by 3: 236, 4785, 3421

13. divisible by 9: 8645, 3279, 8379

☆ **14.** divisible by 7: 1779, 4606, 4839

Give the first six numbers of each sequence.

☆ **16.** nth term: $n + 5$ ☆ **17.** nth term: $2n - 1$ ☆ **18.** nth term: $2n^2$

Answers for Self-check—page 329

Test

Write **P** for each prime number. For each composite number, give the prime factorization using exponents.

1. 37   **2.** 77   **3.** 45   **4.** 207   **5.** 100   **6.** 223

Give the product.

7. $2^3 \cdot 3^2 \cdot 5$ **8.** 3^4 **9.** $2 \cdot 3 \cdot 5^2 \cdot 7$ **10.** $3^2 \cdot 5^3$

In each row find the number that is

11. divisible by 3: 287, 4562, 3429   ☆ **15.** Give the fourth row of Pascal's Triangle.

12. divisible by 5: 4623, 3280, 1523

13. divisible by 9: 2769, 3716, 4824

☆ **14.** divisible by 11: 4269, 83 246, 95 876

Give the first six numbers of each sequence.

☆ **16.** nth term: $n + 3$ ☆ **17.** nth term: $4n - 3$ ☆ **18.** nth term: $n^2 + 1$

Math lab

The Fibonacci Sequence

The sequence of numbers

    1, 1, 2, 3, 5, 8, 13, 21, 34, 55, . . .

is called the Fibonacci Sequence. Each number in the sequence is called a Fibonacci number.

There is a simple pattern in the sequence. Try to find it, then write the next ten Fibonacci Sequence numbers.

Examples of Fibonacci numbers can often be found in nature. Many varieties of flowers have a Fibonacci number of petals.

Count the petals on each variety of flower shown below.

Find some other flowers. Count the petals. Is the number a Fibonacci number?

Counting Problems

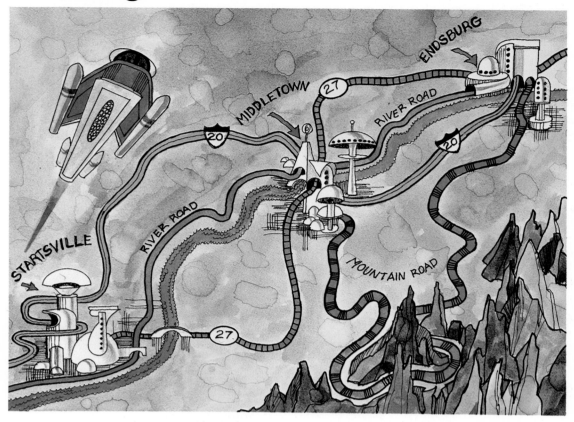

There are three roads from Startsville to Middletown.

Interstate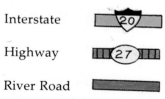

Highway

River Road

There are four roads from Middletown to Endsburg.

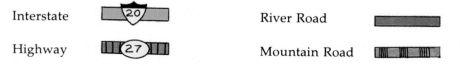

Interstate   River Road

Highway   Mountain Road

How many ways can you find to go from Startsville to Endsburg?

Carol drew a simple diagram of the problem. Then she reasoned,

"There are 3 ways to get from Startsville to Middletown. For each of these 3 ways there are 4 ways to get from Middletown to Endsburg. Therefore there are 3 · 4 or 12 ways to go from Startsville to Endsburg."

Carol applied the **Basic Counting Principle**.

> If one thing can be done in n ways and a second thing can be done in m ways then the two things can be done together in $n \cdot m$ or nm ways.

Other examples

A John has 4 shirts and 2 pairs of slacks. He has 4 · 2 or 8 shirt-slack outfits.

B A menu offers ice cream sundaes with a choice of 6 kinds of ice cream and 3 kinds of topping. How many different sundaes are possible? There are 6 · 3 or 18 choices of sundaes.

Solve each problem.

1. How many 2-letter words can be formed using one of the vowels i or a, followed by one of the consonants n, t or s? Write all the words.

2. There are 5 roads from city A to city B. There are 3 roads from city B to city C. How many routes are there from city A to city C, passing through city B?

3. Melissa has 6 blouses and 4 skirts. How many skirt-blouse outfits can be formed?

4. A tire manufacturer makes 4 different grades of tires in 15 different sizes. How many different type tires does the manufacturer make?

5. Flying from New York to Chicago Karen could fly on any 1 of 4 airlines. From Chicago to San Francisco, she could fly on any 1 of 3 airlines. On how many different combinations of airlines could Karen fly from New York to Chicago to San Francisco?

6. Linda plays 3 kinds of musical instruments. Todd also plays 3 kinds of instruments. How many different ways can they use the instruments to play a duet?

Factorials

How many different ways can this triangle be named?

You can list all the ways:

$\triangle ABC$ $\qquad$ $\triangle BAC$ $\qquad$ $\triangle CAB$ $\qquad$ $\triangle ACB$ $\qquad$ $\triangle BCA$ $\qquad$ $\triangle CBA$

Or you can apply the Basic Counting Principle.

There are 3 choices for the first letter.

There are 2 choices for the second letter.

There is 1 choice for the third letter.

Altogether there are $1 \cdot 2 \cdot 3 = 6$ ways of naming the triangle.

The product $1 \cdot 2 \cdot 3$ can be written as 3! We read 3! as **three factorial**.

$3! = 6$

$1 \cdot 2 \cdot 3 \cdot 4 = 4! = 24$

The product of all the whole numbers from 1 to n is called n factorial.

$1 \cdot 2 \cdot 3 \cdot 4 \cdot 5 \cdot \ldots \cdot (n - 1) \cdot n = n!$

Copy and complete the table.

$n!$	Factors	Product
1!	1	1
2!	$1 \cdot 2$	2
3!	$1 \cdot 2 \cdot 3$	6
4!	$1 \cdot 2 \cdot 3 \cdot 4$	▨
5!		▨
6!		▨
7!		▨
8!		▨
9!		▨
10!		▨

Compute.

1. $2! \cdot 3!$
2. $5! - 3!$
3. $\dfrac{4!}{2!}$
4. $\dfrac{5!}{4!}$

5. $5 \cdot 4!$
6. $2! + 3!$
7. $(2 + 3)!$
8. $6! - 4!$

9. $(6 - 4)!$
10. $\dfrac{6!}{120}$
11. $(8 - 3 + 1)!$
12. $\dfrac{5040}{7!}$

13. $\dfrac{5!}{(5 - 3)!}$
14. $\dfrac{6!}{(6 - 2)!}$
15. $7! \cdot 8$
16. $\dfrac{10!}{(10 - 4)! \cdot 4!}$

Solve the equations. Express the answers in factorial notation when possible.

Example: Solve $\dfrac{6!}{6} = n$ $\dfrac{6!}{6} = \dfrac{1 \cdot 2 \cdot 3 \cdot 4 \cdot 5 \cdot 6}{6} = 1 \cdot 2 \cdot 3 \cdot 4 \cdot 5 = 5!, n = 5!$

17. $5! \cdot 6 = n$
18. $n \cdot 8 = 8!$
19. $\dfrac{1 \cdot 2 \cdot 3 \cdot 4}{n} = 4$

20. $n \cdot 10 = 10!$
21. $\dfrac{n}{3!} = 4 \cdot 5$
22. $n \cdot 6 \cdot 7 = 7!$

23. $\dfrac{7!}{5!} = n$
24. $\dfrac{(n + 1)!}{n!} = 8$
25. $\dfrac{n!}{(n - 1)!} = 6$

26. There are 4! ways of arranging the four blocks in a row. Compute 4! to find the number of ways.

☆ 27. List the ways the four letters a, e, t, and s can be arranged on a line. How many sensible 4-letter words are formed?

Which expression below has the same value as

$1^5 \cdot 2^4 \cdot 3^3 \cdot 4^2 \cdot 5^1$

A 5!
B 6!
C $1! \cdot 2! \cdot 3! \cdot 4! \cdot 5!$
D 8!

⊛ Permutations

Tank car

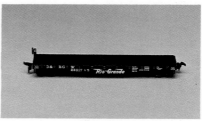

Flat car

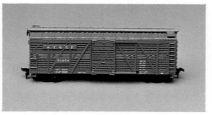

Stock car

Box car

There are 4 kinds of railroad cars available for use. 3 of the 4 cars are to be hooked to an engine one behind the other. How many arrangements of 3 cars are possible?

An arrangement of a group of objects in a certain order is called a **permutation** of the objects. The Basic Counting Principle can be used to find the number of permutations.

Number of permutations = P =   4 · 3 · 2   = 24

choices	choices	choices
for the	for the	for the
first car	second car	third car

There are 24 arrangements or permutations using 3 of the 4 cars.

Other examples

There are 5 railroad cars available for use. 4 of the 5 cars are to be hooked up to an engine. How many different arrangements or permutations are possible?

Number of permutations = P =   5 · 4 · 3 · 2   = 120

choices	choices	choices	choices
for the	for the	for the	for the
first car	second car	third car	fourth car

There are 120 permutations of the 5 cars, using 4 at a time.

Solve.

1. 6 railroad cars are pulled by a switch engine. How many permutations of the 6 cars are possible?

2. 8 railroad cars are to be pulled by an engine. How many choices are there for the first 2 cars behind the engine?

3. 5 people are in line to buy tickets for a commuter train. How many different ways can the 5 people line up for tickets?

4. 9 people get on the train, one at a time. How many permutations or orders of getting on the train are possible for the 9 people?

5. There are 4 empty seats in a row in a commuter car. 2 people enter and sit down. How many ways can they choose 2 of the 4 seats? (Hint: The first person to sit down has 4 choices of a seat. The second has 3 choices.)

6. There are 6 empty seats in a row in a commuter car. 4 people enter and sit down. How many ways can they choose 4 of the 6 seats?

7. The average freight train has about 70 cars. Express the number of permutations of the cars in factorial notation.

8. A train is composed of 8 cars plus an engine and a caboose. How many ways can the train be made up if the engine must come first and the caboose must come at the end?

☆ 9. A 2-level automobile carrier can carry 12 compact autos. How many permutations of the 12 cars are there? Write the answer as a standard numeral.

 A deck of 52 cards is shuffled and the top 4 cards are laid out in a row. How many different possible arrangements of the 4 cards are there?

✪ Selections or combinations

The selection of a group of objects from a set of objects, without regard to the order of selection, is called a **combination**, C, of the objects.

Maria has read 5 books. She has to write a book report on any 3 of the 5 books. She can use any combination of 3 books from the 5 books. How many combinations are there?

A set of 3 books from a set of 5 are to be selected but the order of selection does not matter.

Number of permutations
of 3 books from 5 books: $5 \cdot 4 \cdot 3 = 60$

Number of permutations
of 3 books from 3 books: $3 \cdot 2 \cdot 1 = 6$

Total number of combinations: $C = \dfrac{60}{6} = 10$

There are 10 combinations of books from which she can make her reports.

Other examples

From a set of 6 books, 2 books must be selected. How many combinations, C, are possible?

From a set of 10 cards, 4 cards are selected. How many different 4 card selections are possible?

$$C = \frac{6 \cdot 5}{2!} = \frac{30}{2} = 15$$

$$C = \frac{10 \cdot 9 \cdot 8 \cdot 7}{4!} = \frac{10 \cdot 9 \cdot 8 \cdot 7}{1 \cdot 2 \cdot 3 \cdot 4} = 210$$

1. From a list of 8 books, 2 are to be selected. How many combinations are possible?

2. A librarian received 10 new books and wants to display 3 of them. How many selections of 3 out of the 10 books are possible?

3. Choose 3 books from this list:
   The Mystery of Misty Isle
   All About Whales
   Adventures with Rusty
   Improve Your Memory
   How many choices of combinations do you have?

4. Mike has 5 library books checked out. 2 of the books are overdue. How many combinations of books could be overdue?

5. From a list of 3 books, 1 book is to be chosen. How many choices are possible?

6. From a list of 7 books, 7 books are to be chosen. How many choices are possible?

7. Choose 2 books from this list:
   History book
   Math book
   Social Studies book
   How many combinations are there?

8. 3 students each chose 1 book from a group of 9 books. How many different combinations of the remaining 6 books are possible?

9. A 10-item True-False quiz has 4 true answers. How many combinations of the true items are possible?

☆ 10. Estimate or find out how many books are in your school library. Compute the number of ways you could select 3 library books.

How many different 5 card combinations are possible from a deck of 52 cards?

Answers for Self-check   1. 6!   2. 10!   3. 5!   4. 12!   5. 20   6. 5! or 120   7. 6! or 720

☆ 8. 40!   ☆ 9. $\dfrac{6 \cdot 5 \cdot 4 \cdot 3}{1 \cdot 2 \cdot 3 \cdot 4} = 15$ ☆ 10. $\dfrac{10 \cdot 9}{1 \cdot 2} = 45$

Self-check

Write in factorial notation.

1. $1 \cdot 2 \cdot 3 \cdot 4 \cdot 5 \cdot 6$ 2. $9! \cdot 10$ 3. $\dfrac{7!}{6 \cdot 7}$ 4. $10! \cdot 11 \cdot 12$

Solve.

5. Dave has 5 shirts and 4 pairs of slacks. How many shirt-slack outfits does he have?

6. How many 5 digit numerals can be formed using 1, 2, 3, 4, and 5 with no digit repeated?

7. 6 students are in a cafeteria line. How many different ways could they stand in line?

☆ 8. A freight engine is pulling 40 cars. Express the number of permutations of the cars in factorial notation.

☆ 9. From a set of 6 books, 4 books are selected. How many selections of 4 books are possible?

☆ 10. 2 numbers are selected from 10 different numbers. How many selections are possible?

Answers for Self-check—page 339

Test

Write in factorial notation.

1. $1 \cdot 2 \cdot 3 \cdot 4 \cdot 5 \cdot 6 \cdot 7 \cdot 8$ 2. $3! \cdot 4 \cdot 5$ 3. $\dfrac{10!}{8 \cdot 9 \cdot 10}$ 4. $1 \cdot 2 \cdot 3 \cdot 4$

Solve.

5. Pamela has 6 sweaters and 3 skirts. How many sweater-skirt outfits can she make?

6. A bakery makes 10 kinds of cakes with 5 kinds of icing. How many different varieties of cake are possible?

7. How many ways can a penny, dime, nickel, and a quarter be arranged in a line?

☆ 8. There are 32 students in a class. The students come into the room one at a time. How many different arrangements of the students are possible? Express the answer in factorial notation.

☆ 9. From a set of 8 books, 3 books are selected. How many selections are possible?

☆ 10. 3 letters from the 26 letters of the alphabet are selected. How many selections are possible?

Math lab

Ordered Cubes Game

This is a game for two or more players. Write the numeral 1 on all the faces of one cube, 2 on the faces of a second cube, 3 on a third, and 4 on a fourth.

Each player, in turn, picks up all four cubes and shakes them. Without looking, the player drops the cubes one at a time, and then records the order in which the cubes are dropped. The object of the game is to drop the cubes in the order 1, 2, 3, 4. The player scores one point for each cube dropped in the correct order.

Samples:

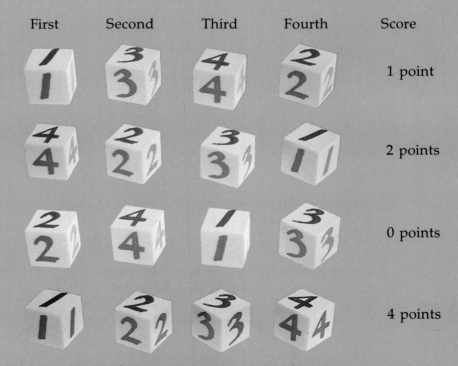

First	Second	Third	Fourth	Score
1	3	4	2	1 point
4	2	3	1	2 points
2	4	1	3	0 points
1	2	3	4	4 points

The first player to get a total of 10 or more points wins the game.

Probability

Label 3 faces of a small cube with the letter A,
2 faces with the letter B, and 1 face with the
letter C.

Estimate how many times each letter will come up
when the cube is tossed 60 times.

Toss the cube 60 times.

Keep a tally of the letters that come up on top.
Compare the results with your estimate.

When the cube is tossed, each face of the cube has the same chance of appearing on top.

The result of each toss is called an **outcome**.

There are 3 chances in 6 of tossing an A.

The **probability**, P, of tossing an A is $\frac{3}{6}$ or $\frac{1}{2}$.

We write this as $P(A) = \frac{3}{6} = \frac{1}{2}$

$$P(B) = \frac{2}{6} = \frac{1}{3}$$

$$P(C) = \frac{1}{6}$$

The probability of an outcome $= \dfrac{\text{Number of ways the outcome can happen}}{\text{Total number of outcomes}}$

Give the probability of each outcome.

1. Toss a penny.

   A $P(\text{tails}) = $ |||||
   B $P(\text{heads}) = $ |||||

2. Spin the spinner.

   A $P(1) = $ |||||
   B $P(2) = $ |||||
   C $P(3) = $ |||||

3. Draw 1 marble.

   A $P(\text{red marble}) = $ |||||
   B $P(\text{blue marble}) = $ |||||

4. Toss a die.

   A $P(\boxdot) = $ ||||| **D** $P(\boxed{::}) = $ |||||
   B $P(\boxed{\cdot\cdot}) = $ ||||| **E** $P(\boxed{:\cdot:}) = $ |||||
   C $P(\boxed{\cdot\cdot\cdot}) = $ ||||| **F** $P(\boxed{:::}) = $ |||||

5. Spin the spinner.

   A $P(\text{even number}) = $ |||||
   B $P(\text{odd number}) = $ |||||

6. Draw one card.

   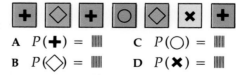

   A $P(\boldsymbol{+}) = $ ||||| **C** $P(\bigcirc) = $ |||||
   B $P(\Diamond) = $ ||||| **D** $P(\boldsymbol{\times}) = $ |||||

Expected number of occurrences

A coin is tossed 100 times.

About how many times would you expect the coin to come up heads?

$$P(H) = \frac{1}{2}$$

You would expect the coin to come up heads about $\frac{1}{2}$ of the number of trials.

$$\underset{\substack{\uparrow \\ \text{Number of} \\ \text{trials}}}{100} \cdot \underset{\substack{\uparrow \\ P(H)}}{\frac{1}{2}} = \underset{\substack{\uparrow \\ \text{Expected} \\ \text{number of} \\ \text{occurrences}}}{50}$$

You would **expect** the coin to come up heads **about** 50 times in 100 tosses. Notice the word **about**. If you actually tossed a coin 100 times, it would be surprising if you got **exactly** 50 heads.

Other examples

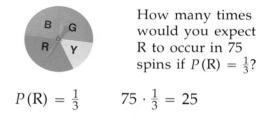

How many times would you expect R to occur in 75 spins if $P(R) = \frac{1}{3}$?

$$P(R) = \frac{1}{3} \qquad 75 \cdot \frac{1}{3} = 25$$

How many times would you expect to draw a card with a B in 50 trials?

$$P(B) = \frac{2}{5} \qquad 50 \cdot \frac{2}{5} = 20$$

Find the expected number of occurrences.

1.

$$P(3) = \frac{1}{10}$$

How many times would you expect an outcome of 3 in 40 spins?

2.

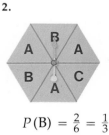

$$P(B) = \frac{2}{6} = \frac{1}{3}$$

How many times would you expect an outcome of B in 60 spins?

3.

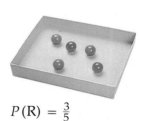

$$P(R) = \frac{3}{5}$$

How many times would you expect to draw a red marble in 30 draws?

Find the expected number of occurrences.

1.

$P(R) = \frac{1}{3}$

Number of trials: 120

About how many times will red occur?

2.

$P(6) = \frac{1}{6}$

Number of trials: 84

About how many times will 6 appear on top?

3.

$P(X) = \frac{3}{6}$

Number of trials: 48

About how many X's will occur?

4.

$P(3 \text{ heads}) = \frac{1}{8}$

3 coins at a time.
Number of tosses: 200
About how many times will 3 heads come up?

5.

$P(\text{sum of } 7) = \frac{1}{6}$

Number of tosses: 60
About how many sums of 7 will occur?

6.

$P(A) = \frac{2}{5}$

Number of trials: 125
About how many A's will occur?

7. $P(T) = 0.3$

Number of trials: 80
About how many T's will occur?

8. $P(X) = \frac{3}{4}$

Number of trials: 160
About how many X's will occur?

9. $P(Z) = 0.9$

Number of trials: 50
About how many Z's will occur?

10. $P(K) = 0.07$

Number of trials: 500
About how many K's will occur?

11. $P(M) = \frac{3}{8}$

Number of trials: 72
About how many M's will occur?

12. $P(J) = 0.44$

Number of trials: 225
About how many J's will occur?

13. Suppose the probability of rain on any day in April is 0.4. About how many days in the 30 days should have rain?

☆ **14.** Suppose the probability of the letter *e* occurring in written English is 0.12. About how many times would the letter *e* be expected to occur in 100 letters? Count off 100 letters in some sentences. Count the number of *e*'s.

Probability of ordered-pair outcomes

What is the probability
of getting **Win** on
each spinner?

Outcome:
← (1, 4)

There are 4 equally likely outcomes for the first spinner.

There are 5 equally likely outcomes for the second spinner.

Using the Basic Counting Principle, there are 4 · 5 or 20 outcomes for the two spinners. One of the 20 outcomes is (Win, Win).

$P(\text{Win, Win}) = \frac{1}{20}$

Each outcome for spinning the two spinners can be denoted by an **ordered pair**.

1. List all 20 ordered pair outcomes.

2. How many ordered pair outcomes have the same first and second members?

3. What is the probability of getting the same result on both spinners?

4. How many ordered pair outcomes have Win as either the first or second member?

5. What is the probability of getting at least one of the spinners to stop on Win?

6. What is the probability of getting a pair of numbers with a sum of 6?

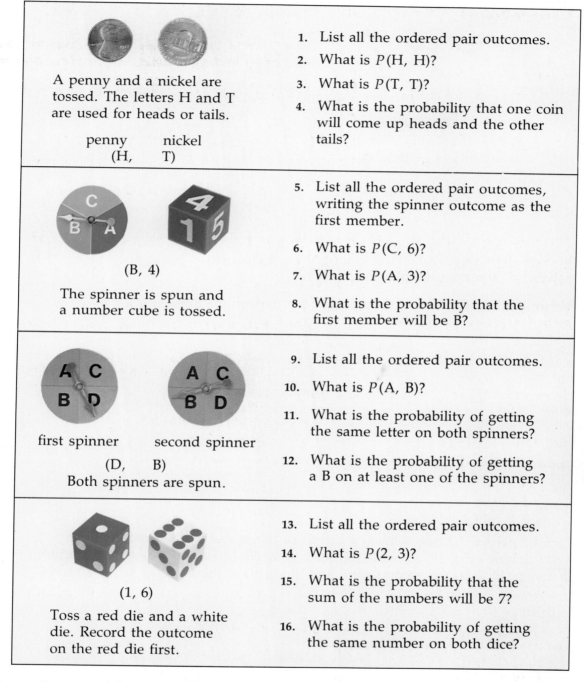

A penny and a nickel are tossed. The letters H and T are used for heads or tails.

penny   nickel
(H,   T)

1. List all the ordered pair outcomes.
2. What is $P(H, H)$?
3. What is $P(T, T)$?
4. What is the probability that one coin will come up heads and the other tails?

(B, 4)

The spinner is spun and a number cube is tossed.

5. List all the ordered pair outcomes, writing the spinner outcome as the first member.
6. What is $P(C, 6)$?
7. What is $P(A, 3)$?
8. What is the probability that the first member will be B?

first spinner   second spinner

(D,   B)
Both spinners are spun.

9. List all the ordered pair outcomes.
10. What is $P(A, B)$?
11. What is the probability of getting the same letter on both spinners?
12. What is the probability of getting a B on at least one of the spinners?

(1, 6)

Toss a red die and a white die. Record the outcome on the red die first.

13. List all the ordered pair outcomes.
14. What is $P(2, 3)$?
15. What is the probability that the sum of the numbers will be 7?
16. What is the probability of getting the same number on both dice?

☆ 17. Try one of the probability experiments on this page. Repeat the experiment for many trials. Keep a tally of the outcomes. Find the ratio of the number of **each** outcome to the total number of trials. Compare their ratios with the probability of each outcome.

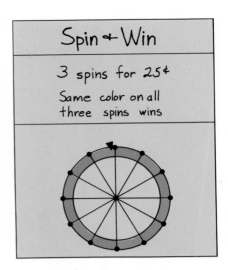

A SPIN & WIN wheel was used at the school fair. What is the probability of getting blue on all 3 spins?

On each spin the probability of getting the red color (R) is $\frac{1}{2}$, and the probability of getting the blue color (B) is $\frac{1}{2}$.

The **probability tree** below shows what can happen for three spins.

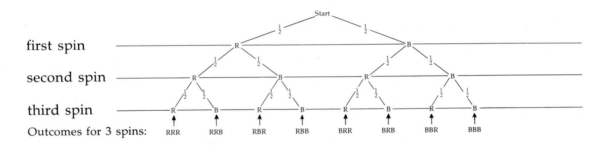

first spin

second spin

third spin

Outcomes for 3 spins: RRR RRB RBR RBB BRR BRB BBR BBB

Each branch of the tree is labeled $\frac{1}{2}$ because the probability of getting either a red or blue outcome for each spin is $\frac{1}{2}$. A symbol like BBB means blue on the first spin, blue on the second spin, and blue on the third spin.

$$P(\text{BBB}) = P(\text{B}) \cdot P(\text{B}) \cdot P(\text{B}) = \frac{1}{2} \cdot \frac{1}{2} \cdot \frac{1}{2} = \frac{1}{8}$$

The probability of getting 3 blues is $\frac{1}{8}$.

1. What is $P(\text{BRR})$?

2. What is $P(\text{RBR})$?

3. What is the probability of getting exactly 2 red spins out of 3 spins?

4. What is the probability of getting the same color on all 3 spins?

The probability tree for two tosses of a number cube is shown below.

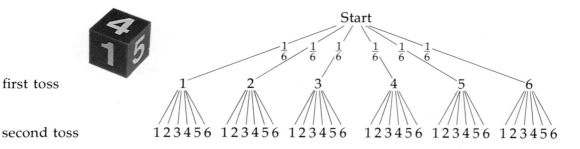

first toss

second toss

1. How many different outcomes are possible for two tosses?
2. The symbol (2, 5) means a 2 on the first toss and a 5 on the second toss. What is $P(2, 5)$?

Give the probability of each outcome.

3. (3, 4)   4. (6, 4)   5. (4, 6)   6. (1, 1)

7. The sum of the numbers in 2 tosses is 7.

8. The two numbers tossed are the same.

9. The two numbers tossed are not the same.

10. The two numbers tossed are both even numbers.

11. The product of the two numbers tossed is 6.

12. The first number tossed is less than the second number tossed.

13. The first number is 2 more than the second number.

☆ 14. Suppose a die is tossed 3 times in succession. What is $P(1, 1, 1)$?

☆ 15. Toss a die two times and make a tally showing when both numbers are the same or different. Repeat the pairs of tosses 100 times. How many times did you get the same number on both tosses? Compare the results.

Two rows of cards numbered 1 through 13 are laid out in two rows.

| 1 | 2 | 3 | 4 | 5 | 6 | 7 | 8 | 9 | 10 | 11 | 12 | 13 |
| 1 | 2 | 3 | 4 | 5 | 6 | 7 | 8 | 9 | 10 | 11 | 12 | 13 |

Moving only the cards in the second row, arrange them so that the sum of any two cards above and below each other is a square number.

| Same number on both tosses | ‖ |
| Different number | ⫙⫙ ⫙⫙ ‖‖‖ |

⊛ Finding probabilities by experiment

Kelly used a paper clip to perform
a probability experiment. She bent
one end of the paper clip up as
shown. Then she dropped the paper
clip on the floor several times.
She kept a tally of the number of
times the paper clip landed pointing
up or down. The outcomes did not
seem to be equally likely.

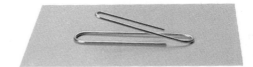

Down   Up   Tally

Up	|||
Down	卌 卌 ||

Kelly dropped the bent paper clip 15 times.

$$\frac{\text{Number Up}}{\text{Number of trials}} = \frac{3}{15} = \frac{1}{5} \qquad \frac{\text{Number Down}}{\text{Number of trials}} = \frac{12}{15} = \frac{4}{5}$$

Experimental probabilities: $P(U) = \frac{1}{5}$ $\qquad P(D) = \frac{4}{5}$

Find the experimental probabilities.

Student	Outcomes		Number of	$P(U)$	$P(D)$
	U	D	trials		
1. Anne	4	21	25		
2. Jack	3	7	10		
3. Diane	2	18			
4. Bob	6	18			
5. Carol	4	17			

6. Combine the trials of all five students in the table and find $P(U)$ and $P(D)$.

7. Do the outcomes of this experiment appear to be equally likely?

Experiment A

A paper fastener is dropped on a desk top.
It lands facing either up or down.

Up

Down

Find the experimental probabilities.

	Student	Outcomes		Number of trials	$P(U)$	$P(D)$
		U	D			
1.	Mike	11	9			
2.	Joan	10	10			
3.	Michele	9	11			
4.	Larry	12	8			
5.	Kevin	6	14			

6. Combine the trials of all five students in the table.
   Find $P(U)$ and $P(D)$ for all the trials.

Experiment B

A small thumb tack is dropped on a desk top.
It lands either with the point up or down.

Find the experimental probabilities.

	Student	Outcomes		Number of trials	$P(U)$	$P(D)$
		U	D			
7.	Barbara	11	14			
8.	Susan	7	18			
9.	Bill	10	15			
10.	Brad	9	16			

11. Combine the trials of all four students in the table.
    Find $P(U)$ and $P(D)$ for all the trials.

☆ 12. Try one of the probability experiments in this lesson. Repeat the experiment
    for at least 50 trials. Combine your trials with your classmates and find
    the experimental probabilities of the outcomes.

✪ Using combinations to find probabilities

A box has 3 red marbles and 1 blue marble.

If you were to draw 2 marbles from the box without looking, what is the probability that both marbles would be red?

First we must find the number of different outcomes when 2 marbles are drawn from 4 marbles, regardless of color.

Let C_1 = number of combinations of 4 marbles taken 2 at a time

$$C_1 = \frac{4 \cdot 3}{2!} = 6$$

Next we must find how many of the 2-marble draws contain 2 red marbles. This is the number of combinations of 3 red marbles taken 2 at a time.

Let C_2 = number of combinations of 3 red marbles taken 2 at a time

$$C_2 = \frac{3 \cdot 2}{2!} = 3$$

The probability of drawing two red marbles is $\frac{C_2}{C_1}$.

$$P(2 \text{ red marbles}) = \frac{C_2}{C_1} = \frac{3}{6} = \frac{1}{2}$$

Draw 2 marbles.

Draw 3 marbles.

1. How many ways can 2 marbles be selected from 5 marbles?

2. How many ways can 2 red marbles be selected from 3 red marbles?

3. $P(2 \text{ red marbles}) = $ ▦

4. How many ways can 3 marbles be selected from 6 marbles?

5. How many ways can 3 red marbles be selected from 3 red marbles?

6. $P(3 \text{ red marbles}) = $ ▦

Find the probabilities.

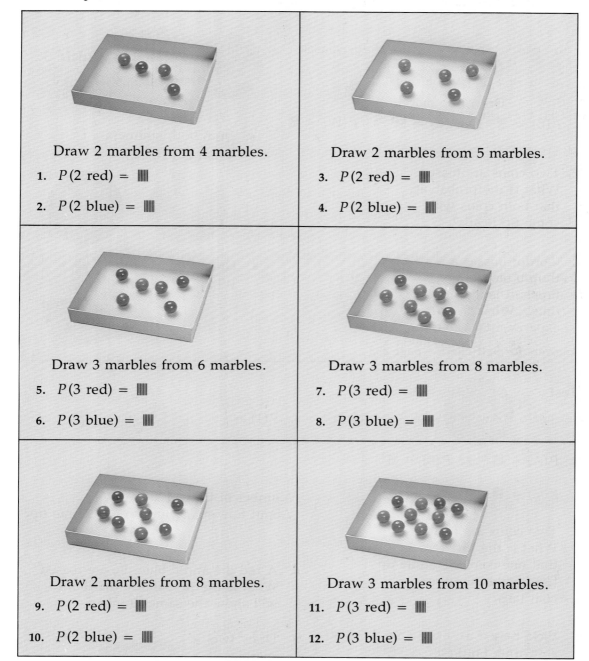

Draw 2 marbles from 4 marbles.

1. $P(2\ \text{red}) =$ ▓

2. $P(2\ \text{blue}) =$ ▓

Draw 2 marbles from 5 marbles.

3. $P(2\ \text{red}) =$ ▓

4. $P(2\ \text{blue}) =$ ▓

Draw 3 marbles from 6 marbles.

5. $P(3\ \text{red}) =$ ▓

6. $P(3\ \text{blue}) =$ ▓

Draw 3 marbles from 8 marbles.

7. $P(3\ \text{red}) =$ ▓

8. $P(3\ \text{blue}) =$ ▓

Draw 2 marbles from 8 marbles.

9. $P(2\ \text{red}) =$ ▓

10. $P(2\ \text{blue}) =$ ▓

Draw 3 marbles from 10 marbles.

11. $P(3\ \text{red}) =$ ▓

12. $P(3\ \text{blue}) =$ ▓

☆ 13. Try one or more of the marble experiments. Work with a classmate. Compare the experimental probability with the computed probability.

Answers for Self-check 1. $\frac{3}{6}$ or $\frac{1}{2}$ 2. $\frac{2}{6}$ or $\frac{1}{3}$ 3. $\frac{1}{6}$ 4. About 9 5. $\frac{1}{4}$ 6. $\frac{1}{12}$ 7. $\frac{10}{24}$ or $\frac{5}{12}$ 8. $\frac{1}{3}$

Self-check

Draw one marble.

1. $P(B) = $ ▥ 2. $P(R) = $ ▥ 3. $P(W) = $ ▥

4.

$P(Y) = \frac{1}{4}$

Number of trials: 36

About how many Y's will occur?

5. Two coins are tossed. What is the probability that both coins will come up heads?

6. Spin both spinners. What is $P(B, 2)$?

7. Gordon tosses a thumb tack 24 times. It landed up 10 times. What is the experimental value for $P(U)$?

☆ 8. Draw 2 marbles. What is $P(2 \text{ red})$?

Answers for Self-check—page 353

Test

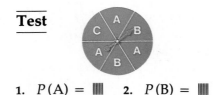

1. $P(A) = $ ▥ 2. $P(B) = $ ▥

3. $P(C) = $ ▥

4. $P(1) = \frac{1}{6}$

Number of trials: 120
About how many times will 1 come up?

5. Two coins are tossed. What is the probability that one coin will come up heads and the other coin tails?

6. A red die and a blue die are tossed. What is the probability that both will show the same number?

7. Vicki tossed a soft drink bottle cap 30 times. It landed down 12 times. What is the experimental value for $P(\text{Down})$?

☆ 8. Draw two marbles from 6 marbles.

What is $P(2 \text{ blue})$?

Math lab

The Birthday Problem

If you were in a group of 25 people, would you be surprised to find that 2 people in the group shared the same birthday?

The following list of the birthdays of famous Americans was randomly selected from the *Encyclopedia of American Biography*. Do any of the birthdays fall on the same day and month (not necessarily the same year)?

Randomly selected list from *Encyclopedia of American Biography*

Anne Newport Royall *June 11, 1769*

Oliver Wendell Holmes *March 8, 1841*

Lydia Marie Francis Child *February 11, 1802*

Henry D. Lloyd *May 1, 1847*

Henry Barnard *January 24, 1811*

Justin Smith Morrill *April 14, 1810*

Susan B. Anthony *February 15, 1820*

Isabella Stewart Gardner *April 14, 1840*

Salmon Portland Chase *January 13, 1808*

Edmund Randolph *August 10, 1753*

Helen M. Jackson *October 15, 1830*

Ulysses S. Grant *April 27, 1822*

Daniel Drake *October 20, 1785*

Ruth Fulton Benedict *June 5, 1887*

Richard Buckminster Fuller *July 12, 1895*

George Eastman *July 12, 1854*

William Christopher Handy *November 16, 1873*

Ann Lee *February 29, 1736*

Samuel Bowless III *February 9, 1826*

Mary Harris Jones *May 1, 1830*

Daniel Louis Armstrong *July 4, 1900*

John Pierpont Morgan *September 7, 1867*

Margaret Higgins Sanger *September 14, 1883*

Bruce Barton *August 5, 1886*

Josephus Daniels *May 18, 1862*

The probability that two birthdays will fall on the same day is over $\frac{1}{2}$ for 23 birthdays and nearly $\frac{3}{4}$ for 30 birthdays.

Check the birthdays in your own class. Do any 2 people have the same birthday?

Number of people	Probability of at least 2 people with the same birthday
10	0.117
20	0.411
23	0.507
30	0.706
40	0.891
60	0.994

Statistics

A group of students wanted to know what jobs were available during the summer. To find out, they took a survey in their town. The results from retail stores are shown by a **frequency distribution** and **bar graph**.

JOBS IN RETAIL STORES

Type of Job	Number of Jobs (frequency)
Delivery work	III
Cleanup work	IIII IIII IIII I
Shelving merchandise	IIII IIII II
Bag and carry out	IIII II
Assembling orders	II

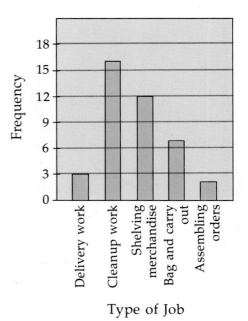

1. How many jobs were found by the survey?

2. What type of work had the greatest frequency?

3. What type of work had the least frequency?

4. What percent of the jobs are cleanup work?

5. What percent of the jobs are assembling orders?

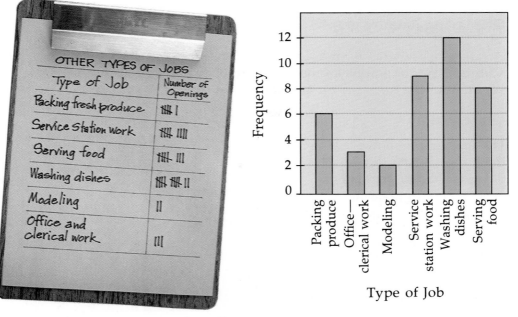

OTHER TYPES OF JOBS

Type of Job	Number of Openings
Packing fresh produce	ⅢⅠ I
Service Station work	ⅢⅠ IIII
Serving food	ⅢⅠ III
Washing dishes	ⅢⅠ ⅢⅠ II
Modeling	II
Office and clerical work	III

1. How many job openings were found?
2. What type of job had the most openings available?
3. For what type of work were eight openings found?
4. What percent of the jobs were serving food?
5. What percent of the jobs were restaurant type jobs?

Make a bar graph to show the data in the frequency table below.

STUDENT JOB PREFERENCES

Type of Job	Number of Students
Grocery work	ⅢⅠ ⅢⅠ
Modeling	ⅢⅠ IIII
Service station	ⅢⅠ ⅢⅠ
Food services	ⅢⅠ ⅢⅠ II
Office work	ⅢⅠ ⅢⅠ

6. What is the largest number you will need to show on your graph?

7. How many different types of jobs do you have to show?

8. How many students are represented in the frequency table?

9. What percent of the students prefer office work?

10. What percent prefer food services?

Displaying data by graphs

Various types of graphs are used here to display data related to student summer jobs.

Grocery store

The **line graph** shows that between the hours of 10 a.m. and 11 a.m. the store had 17 customers.

1. Give the number of customers during each of the other time periods of that day.

2. What were the two busiest hours?

3. A total of 160 people shopped that day. If the average number of bags of groceries per person was 2.25, how many bags were used that day?

4. If the average cost of each bag of groceries was $12.75, how much money was taken in by the store that day?

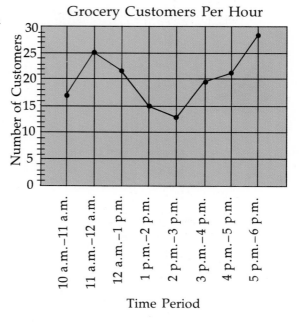

Grocery Customers Per Hour

Number of Customers

Time Period

Office mailroom

The **pictograph** shows that on Monday, 225 letters were sorted and delivered.

5. Estimate the number of letters that were sorted and delivered each of the other 4 days.

6. There were 950 letters sorted and delivered during the week. It has been estimated that the average business letter costs a company $6.50 to produce. At that rate, what did the 950 letters cost?

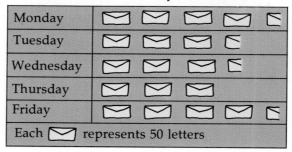

Number of Letters Sorted and Delivered Each Day for a Week

Monday	
Tuesday	
Wednesday	
Thursday	
Friday	
Each represents 50 letters	

The circle graph shows a student's budget. The full circle represents $200 of earnings from a summer job.

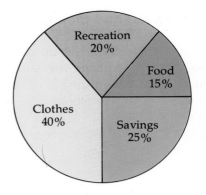

1. The circle graph shows that 25% of the $200 is budgeted for savings. How much is this?
2. How much is budgeted for clothes?
3. How much is budgeted for recreation?
4. How much is budgeted for food?

5. Make a pictograph to show this data.

Ice Cream Cones Sold (= 10 cones)

Monday ЖЖЖЖЖ
Tuesday Ж ЖЖЖ
Wednesday ЖЖЖЖЖЖЖ
Thursday ЖЖЖЖЖЖ
Friday ЖЖЖЖ

6. Make a circle graph to show this data.

Hours in the Stockroom
4 hours unpacking
2 hours wrapping purchases
1 hour counting stock
1 hour cleaning

7. Make a line graph to show this data.

Money Earned in 6 Weeks
1st week	$27.50
2nd week	$36.25
3rd week	$22.00
4th week	$40.75
5th week	$38.50
6th week	$45.20

Copy and complete 10 rows of this pattern.

$$1 \longrightarrow 1 = 1^3$$
$$3 + 5 \longrightarrow 8 = 2^3$$
$$7 + 9 + 11 \longrightarrow 27 = 3^3$$
$$13 + 15 + 17 + 19 \longrightarrow 64 = 4^3$$
$$21 + 23 + 25 + 27 + 29 \longrightarrow \text{▥} = 5^3$$
$$31 + 33 + 35 + 37 + 39 + 41 \longrightarrow \text{▥} = 6^3$$

Mean, median, and mode

One group of students set up a car washing business during the summer. The chart shows the number of cars they washed the first week.

What was the **mean** or average number of cars washed per day?

First Week

Day	Number of cars
Monday	17
Tuesday	22
Wednesday	20
Thursday	25
Friday	30
Saturday	38

Finding the answer

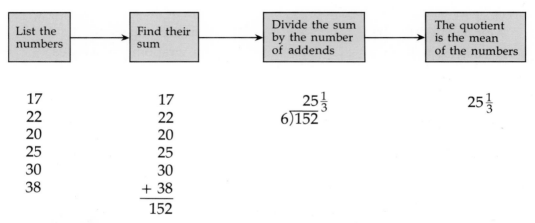

List the numbers	Find their sum	Divide the sum by the number of addends	The quotient is the mean of the numbers

$$
\begin{array}{c}
17 \\
22 \\
20 \\
25 \\
30 \\
38
\end{array}
\qquad
\begin{array}{r}
17 \\
22 \\
20 \\
25 \\
30 \\
+\ 38 \\
\hline
152
\end{array}
\qquad
6)\overline{152}\ \ 25\tfrac{1}{3}
\qquad
25\tfrac{1}{3}
$$

The **mean** number of cars washed per day was 25.

Find the mean number of cars washed per day for each 6-day week.

Second Week

1.

Day	Number of cars
Monday	22
Tuesday	24
Wednesday	22
Thursday	19
Friday	31
Saturday	42

Third Week

2.

Day	Number of cars
Monday	18
Tuesday	15
Wednesday	0 (holiday)
Thursday	26
Friday	35
Saturday	41

Fourth Week

3.

Day	Number of cars
Monday	29
Tuesday	36
Wednesday	28
Thursday	22
Friday	34
Saturday	40

The following list shows the daily numbers of cars washed.
This list can be used to find the median and the mode.

0, 15, 18, 19, 22, 22, 22, 24, 26, 28, 29, 31, 34, 35, 36, 40, 41, 42

| The **mode** is the number or numbers that occur most often. A set may not have a mode. For this set, the mode is 22. | The **median** is the middle number or the average of the two middle numbers. For this set, the median is 27, the average of 26 and 28. |

Find the mean to the nearest tenth, the median, and the mode for each set of numbers. Some sets of numbers may have no mode or more than one mode.

Example: 48, 49, 52, 52, 52, 55, 56, 56, 59, 63, 64, 70

$$676 \div 12 = 56.3 \qquad 52 \qquad 55.5$$
       Mean   Mode Median

1. 11, 13, 14, 14, 14, 15, 17, 19, 21, 21, 23, 27, 31

2. 28, 29, 31, 31, 31, 32, 33, 35, 36, 36, 36, 36

3. 307, 309, 309, 312, 314, 315, 321

4. 275, 276, 279, 281, 283, 287, 287, 290, 295

5. 4283, 4286, 4287, 4290, 4295, 4300

6. 6.8, 6.9, 7.1, 7.1, 7.3, 7.5, 7.6, 7.6, 7.8, 8.1, 8.4

7. 23.4, 23.6, 25.1, 25.7, 28.5, 29.0, 30.1, 31.7

8. 75.2, 76.1, 76.8, 77.3, 78.0, 78.3, 79.1

☆ 9. Collect data for one of the following. Find the mean, median, and mode (if there is one) for your data.

    A   The height, mass, or age of the players on one of your favorite sports teams

    B   The cost of one item from as many different stores as you can find

    C   Data of your own choosing

In a recent year, a fast food chain advertised that over 20 billion hamburgers had been sold in Canada and the United States.

If the population of the United States was 220 356 000 and the population of Canada was 22 998 000, how many hamburgers were sold per person?

✪ Mean variation and range

The chart shows some hourly wages for student summer jobs. The last column shows the difference between the hourly wage and the mean hourly wage. The average of these differences is called the **mean variation** from the mean. What is the mean variation from the mean hourly wage?

Job	Hourly wage	Mean hourly wage	Difference
Packing fresh produce	$1.85	$1.73	$0.12
Delivery work	$1.40	$1.73	$0.33
Office work	$1.75	$1.73	$0.02
Grocery work	$1.95	$1.73	$0.22
Shelving merchandise	$1.20	$1.73	$0.53
Sales clerk	$2.20	$1.73	$0.47

Finding the answer

Find the mean hourly wage to the nearest cent	→	Find the absolute difference between each wage and the mean wage	→	Find the mean of these differences

$ 1.85
1.40 $1.73 (to the
1.75 6)$10.35 nearest
1.95   cent)
1.20
+ 2.20
$10.35

$0.12, $0.33, $0.02,
$0.22, $0.53, $0.47

$ 0.12
0.33 $0.28 (to the
0.02 6)$1.69 nearest
0.22   cent)
0.53
+ 0.47
$ 1.69

The mean variation is $0.28.

This chart shows hourly wages for jobs around the house. Copy and complete the chart. Then find the mean variation from the mean hourly wage.

	Job	Hourly wage	Mean hourly wage	Difference
1.	Cutting grass	$2.50	▥	▥
2.	Painting	$2.75	▥	▥
3.	Gardening	$2.25	▥	▥
4.	Cleaning	$2.95	▥	▥
5.	Baby-sitting	$2.00	▥	▥

The **range** of a set of numbers is the difference between the smallest number and the largest number in that set.

For each set of data, give the range, the mean, and the mean variation from the mean.

1.

Student	Number of hours worked per week at summer job
Jason Alberts	24
Todd Johnson	35
Elaine Knowlton	28
Tom White	30
Susan Berg	40
Delasandra Sanchez	35

2.

Class	Number of students with summer jobs
Room 9A	15
Room 9B	18
Room 9C	16
Room 10A	22
Room 10B	23
Room 10C	20

3.

Student	Total summer earnings
Jason Alberts	$532.80
Todd Johnson	$588.00
Elaine Knowlton	$739.20
Tom White	$630.00
Susan Berg	$576.00
Delasandra Sanchez	$819.00

4.

Day	Average number of hours worked per day
Monday	5
Tuesday	4
Wednesday	6
Thursday	3
Friday	6
Saturday	6

☆ 5. If each student worked a total of 12 weeks, which students in charts 1 and 3 had which jobs from the chart on the top of page 362?

☆ 6. Find how your height in centimeters compares to the average height in your class.

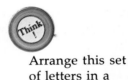

Arrange this set of letters in a line so that

AA
BB
CC
DD

1. the A's are separated by 1 letter,

2. the B's are separated by 2 letters,

3. the C's are separated by 3 letters, and

4. the D's are separated by 4 letters.

⊛ Sample statistics and predictions

The chart shows how 50 students, chosen at random from Washington School, responded to this question:

"Of the kinds of summer jobs listed on the chart, which would you prefer?"

Type of work	Number chosen
Garden work	卌
Sales work	卌 卌
Baby-sitting	卌 卌 卌 l
Office work	卌 ll
Delivery	卌 卌 ll

These 50 students are a **sample** of the total number of students attending Washington School. Since the 50 students were chosen at random, they can be used to **predict** things about the total school population.

What percent of the 50 students preferred each kind of work?

1. garden work   2. sales work   3. baby-sitting

4. office work   5. delivery

Out of 500 students, how many do you predict would prefer each kind of work?

6. garden work   7. sales work   8. baby-sitting

9. office work   10. delivery

This chart shows how people from 40 homes, selected at random in a community, responded to the question above.

"Could you use the help of a teenager for work around your house this summer?"

| Could use help | ⫿⫿⫿ ⫿⫿⫿ II |
| Could not use help | ⫿⫿⫿ ⫿⫿⫿ ⫿⫿⫿ ⫿⫿⫿ ⫿⫿⫿ III |

1. What percent of the people responding could use teenage help for the summer?

2. There are an estimated 7500 homes in the community surveyed. Predict the number of homes that could use teenage help for the summer.

In another community, a survey found 60 homes that wanted to hire teenagers. These are the types of jobs they wanted done. Assume each home wanted only one job done.

Type of job	Homes wanting work done
Lawn care	⫿⫿⫿ ⫿⫿⫿ ⫿⫿⫿ I
Inside cleaning	⫿⫿⫿ III
Outside cleaning	⫿⫿⫿ ⫿⫿⫿ II
Baby-sitting	⫿⫿⫿ ⫿⫿⫿ ⫿⫿⫿
Miscellaneous	⫿⫿⫿ IIII

3. How many total jobs are represented in the chart?

4. Give the percent of the total for each type of job (to nearest tenth of a percent).

5. If 1200 homes in this community want teenage summer help, how many baby-sitting jobs would you predict?

6. Predict the number of lawn care jobs for the 1200 homes.

7. Predict the number of cleaning jobs, inside and outside, for the 1200 homes.

☆ 8. Survey a random sample of students in your own school and then make predictions about the total school population.

Possible questions: A Favorite TV program

B Kind of job they prefer for summer work

C Favorite school subject

D Career choice

⊛ Scattergrams

The chart shows the maximum hourly wage earned by a number of students of different ages during the summer.

Name	Age	Hourly wage	Name	Age	Hourly wage
Ann	15	$2.20	Michael	14	$1.50
Jennifer	16	$2.00	Sonja	$15\frac{1}{2}$	$2.40
Eric	13	$1.75	Karen	$13\frac{1}{2}$	$1.75
Alan	$14\frac{1}{2}$	$1.90	Loren	$16\frac{1}{2}$	$2.50
Stephen	$16\frac{1}{2}$	$2.40	Betty	$14\frac{1}{2}$	$2.00
Kathy	14	$1.80	John	13	$1.50
Don	$15\frac{1}{2}$	$1.75	Alison	16	$2.25
Edgar	$16\frac{1}{2}$	$2.10	June	$15\frac{1}{2}$	$2.10
Rebecca	$13\frac{1}{2}$	$1.65	Martin	14	$2.00
Lynn	15	$1.95	Roberta	17	$2.30
Mark	17	$2.75	Tracy	$14\frac{1}{2}$	$1.70
Sandra	16	$2.40	Larry	15	$1.80

The graph below shows the relation between age and hourly wage. Such a graph is called a **scattergram**. Each dot represents a student, showing their age and wage.

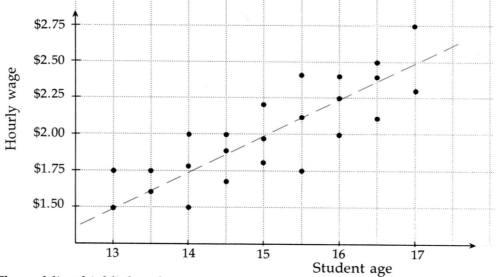

The red line highlights the pattern.

1. Is there a relation between a student's age and the hourly wage?

2. If you were $13\frac{1}{2}$ years old, about what hourly wage would you expect to earn, according to the scattergram?

3. If you were $16\frac{1}{2}$, about what wage could you expect?

The charts below give the heights and masses of the same group of students.

	Height (cm)	Mass (kg)
Ann	168	52
Jennifer	140	63
Eric	150	46
Alan	163	59
Stephen	178	77
Kathy	147	37
Don	174	63
Edgar	182	64

	Height (cm)	Mass (kg)
Rebecca	142	33
Lynn	160	55
Mark	184	78
Sandra	173	71
Michael	153	38
Sonja	165	55
Karen	148	39
Loren	172	58

	Height (cm)	Mass (kg)
Betty	152	42
John	160	45
Alison	183	69
June	158	57
Martin	145	34
Roberta	183	73
Tracy	154	71
Larry	163	50

Draw a graph with a range from 30 kg to 80 kg on the horizontal axis and a range from 140 cm to 190 cm on the vertical axis.

Use the data in the charts to construct a scattergram.

Draw a line that shows about as many dots above the line as below.

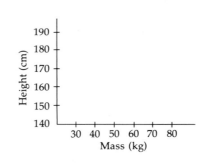

1. Is there a relation between height and mass?

2. According to your graph, teenagers who are 160 cm tall would have about what mass?

3. Use your scattergram to estimate the height of a teenager whose mass is 65.

4. Mark your measurements on the scattergram. Are you very close to the line?

☆ 5. Make a scattergram for the heights and masses of your own class.

Answers for Self-check   1. delivery   2. 1.5 h   3. mean: 14.1 years; median: 14.25 years; mode: 13 years   ☆ 4. 1.0   ☆ 5. 45   ☆ 6. 25% or 30

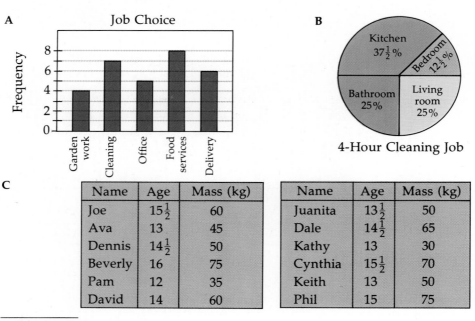

A — Job Choice

B — 4-Hour Cleaning Job

Kitchen 37½% · Bedroom 12½% · Bathroom 25% · Living room 25%

C

Name	Age	Mass (kg)
Joe	$15\frac{1}{2}$	60
Ava	13	45
Dennis	$14\frac{1}{2}$	50
Beverly	16	75
Pam	12	35
David	14	60

Name	Age	Mass (kg)
Juanita	$13\frac{1}{2}$	50
Dale	$14\frac{1}{2}$	65
Kathy	13	30
Cynthia	$15\frac{1}{2}$	70
Keith	13	50
Phil	15	75

Self-check

1. Graph **A**: What type of work was chosen by 6 students?
2. Graph **B**: How much time was spent cleaning the kitchen?
3. Chart **C**: Find the mean (to the nearest tenth), median, and mode of the students' ages.
☆ 4. Chart **C**: Find the mean variation (to the nearest tenth) from the mean age.
☆ 5. Chart **C**: What is the range of the masses?
☆ 6. Chart **C**: These 12 students are a random sample from 120 students. About how many of the 120 would you expect would be 13 years old?

Answers for Self-check—page 367

Test

1. Graph **A**: What type of work was chosen by 5 students?
2. Graph **B**: How much time was spent cleaning the bedroom?
3. Chart **C**: Find the mean (to the nearest tenth), median, and mode of the students' masses.
☆ 4. Chart **C**: Find the mean variation from the mean mass.
☆ 5. Chart **C**: What is the range of the students' ages?
☆ 6. Chart **C**: These 12 students are a random sample from 120 students. About how many of the 120 would you expect would have a mass of about 50 kg?

Math lab

Frequency of Letters

The graph shows the average percent of occurrence for each letter of the alphabet in a written article. The letter *L* occurs about 3.5% of the time, while the letter *S* occurs about 6% of the time. Notice that several letters occur less than 1% of the time.

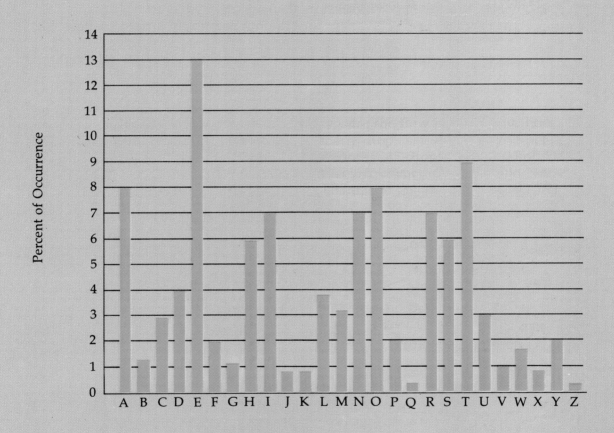

Choose a written article. Find the percent of occurrence of each letter in the article. Compare your percents with the percents shown on the graph.

Square Roots and Irrational Numbers

In a right triangle the two perpendicular sides are called the **legs** of the triangle. The third side is the **hypotenuse**.

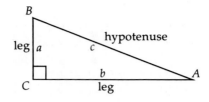

Over 2000 years ago the famous Greek mathematician, Pythagoras, discovered an important relation between the legs and the hypotenuse of a right triangle.

You may discover this relationship by completing the table below for each right triangle.

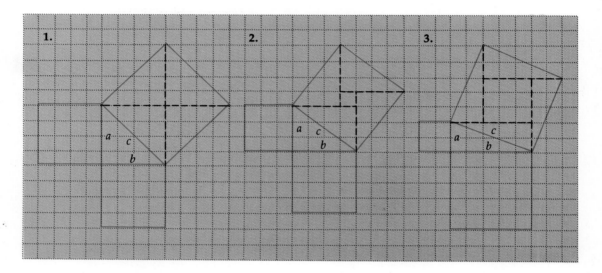

	Figure	Area of the square on side a a^2	Area of the square on side b b^2	Area of the square on side c c^2
1.	1			
2.	2			
3.	3			

4. For each figure find the sum $a^2 + b^2$.

5. How does this sum compare to c^2?

The relation between the legs and the hypotenuse of any right triangle is called the Pythagorean Theorem.

> **The Pythagorean Theorem**
>
> In a right triangle the sum of the areas of the squares on the legs is equal to the area of the square on the hypotenuse.

The Pythgorean Theorem can be written as the formula

$$a^2 + b^2 = c^2$$

where a and b are the legs and c is the hypotenuse of a right triangle.

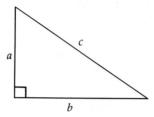

Example: Find the length of the hypotenuse of a right triangle with legs $a = 3$ units and $b = 4$ units.

$$a^2 + b^2 = c^2$$
$$3^2 + 4^2 = c^2$$
$$25 = c^2$$
Since $25 = 5^2 = c^2$,
$$c = 5$$

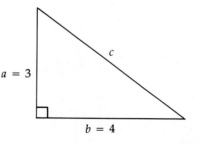

Find the length of the hypotenuse c of each right triangle whose legs are a and b.

1.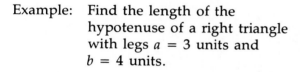
   $a = 6$, $b = 8$

2. $a = 8$, $b = 15$

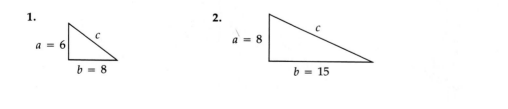

3. $a = 5$ units
    $b = 12$ units

4. $a = 9$ units
    $b = 12$ units

5. $a = 7$ units
    $b = 24$ units

Square roots

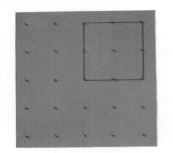

The area of the square is

$$2 \cdot 2 = 4$$

The length of one side can be written as $\sqrt{4}$. We read $\sqrt{4}$ as "the square root of 4." The symbol "$\sqrt{}$" is called a **radical** sign.

$\sqrt{9} = 3$ because $3^2 = 9$ $\sqrt{4} = 2$ because $2 \cdot 2 = 4$

$\sqrt{16} = 4$ because $4^2 = 16$

$\sqrt{n} =$ the positive number whose square is n.

Give a whole number for each square root.

Example: $\sqrt{25} = 5$

1. $\sqrt{16}$ 2. $\sqrt{9}$ 3. $\sqrt{49}$ 4. $\sqrt{100}$

5. $\sqrt{1}$ 6. $\sqrt{4}$ 7. $\sqrt{36}$ 8. $\sqrt{81}$ 9. $\sqrt{64}$

10. $\sqrt{25}$ 11. $\sqrt{121}$ 12. $\sqrt{144}$ 13. $\sqrt{400}$ 14. $\sqrt{225}$

15. $\sqrt{900}$ 16. $\sqrt{625}$ 17. $\sqrt{1600}$ 18. $\sqrt{4900}$ 19. $\sqrt{2500}$

Use the squares in the table to write a decimal for each square root.

Example: $\sqrt{7.29} = 2.7$

20. $\sqrt{50.41}$ 21. $\sqrt{3.61}$ 22. $\sqrt{4.41}$

23. $\sqrt{20.25}$ 24. $\sqrt{1.44}$ 25. $\sqrt{12.96}$

26. $\sqrt{33.64}$ 27. $\sqrt{2.25}$ 28. $\sqrt{5.29}$

Find the square root of each rational number.

Example: $\sqrt{\frac{25}{36}} = \frac{5}{6}$ because $\left(\frac{5}{6}\right)^2 = \frac{25}{36}$

29. $\sqrt{\frac{1}{4}}$ 30. $\sqrt{\frac{4}{9}}$ 31. $\sqrt{\frac{16}{25}}$

Squares of selected decimals
$(1.2)^2 = 1.44$
$(1.5)^2 = 2.25$
$(1.9)^2 = 3.61$
$(2.1)^2 = 4.41$
$(2.3)^2 = 5.29$
$(2.7)^2 = 7.29$
$(3.6)^2 = 12.96$
$(4.5)^2 = 20.25$
$(5.8)^2 = 33.64$
$(7.1)^2 = 50.41$

Some square roots of whole numbers are whole numbers.

Examples: $\sqrt{100} = 10$ and $\sqrt{16} = 4$.

Some square roots of whole numbers can only be approximated by decimals.

Example: Find $\sqrt{2}$ to the
nearest tenth.

Computation:

$$\begin{array}{cc} 1.4 & 1.5 \\ \times\,1.4 & \times\,1.5 \\ \hline 1.96 & 2.25 \end{array}$$

$(1.4)^2$ is
nearer to 2.

Answer:

$\sqrt{2} = 1.4$ to
the nearest
tenth

The flow chart gives a method for finding the square
root of a number.

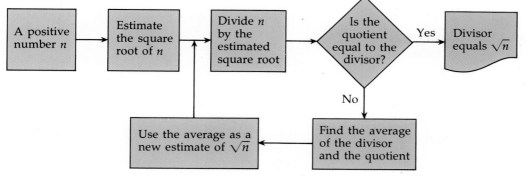

Example: Find $\sqrt{87}$ to the nearest tenth.

A Estimate of $\sqrt{87}$: 9.5

B $\begin{array}{r} 9.1 \dots \\ 9.5\overline{)87.0\wedge 0} \end{array}$

C Average of 9.5 and 9.1 $= \dfrac{9.5 + 9.1}{2} = \dfrac{18.6}{2} = 9.3$

D $\begin{array}{r} 9.3 \dots \\ 9.3\overline{)87.0\wedge 0} \end{array}$ The quotient to tenths
is the same as the divisor.

E $\sqrt{87} = 9.3$ to the nearest tenth.

Use the flow chart method to find each square root to the nearest tenth.

1. $\sqrt{75}$ 2. $\sqrt{38}$ 3. $\sqrt{17}$ 4. $\sqrt{93}$ 5. $\sqrt{50}$

6. $\sqrt{120}$ 7. $\sqrt{200}$ 8. $\sqrt{313}$ 9. $\sqrt{433}$ 10. $\sqrt{529}$

✪ Using a square root table

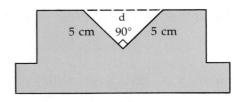

An inspector must check the distance across the V-shaped groove in the machine part shown. What is distance d to the nearest tenth of a centimeter?

$$d^2 = 5^2 + 5^2$$
$$d^2 = 50$$
$$d = \sqrt{50}$$

Since $50 = 10 \cdot 5$, find $\sqrt{50}$ under the $\sqrt{10 \cdot n}$ column in the row where $n = 5$.

$$d = \sqrt{50} = 7.071 \ldots$$
$$d = 7.07 \text{ cm to the nearest}$$
$$\text{hundredth}$$

Use the table to find decimal approximations for the following square roots.

1. $\sqrt{15}$ 2. $\sqrt{7}$ 3. $\sqrt{10}$

4. $\sqrt{14}$ 5. $\sqrt{22}$ 6. $\sqrt{29}$

7. $\sqrt{18}$ 8. $\sqrt{3}$ 9. $\sqrt{19}$

10. $\sqrt{24}$ 11. $\sqrt{40}$ 12. $\sqrt{60}$

13. $\sqrt{110}$ 14. $\sqrt{150}$ 15. $\sqrt{230}$

16. $\sqrt{290}$ 17. $\sqrt{2}$ 18. $\sqrt{160}$

19. $\sqrt{12}$ 20. $\sqrt{90}$ 21. $\sqrt{23}$

A Short Table of Squares and Square Roots			
Number n	Square n^2	Square root $\sqrt{n}$	Square root of 10 times n $\sqrt{10 \cdot n}$
1	1	1.000	3.162
2	4	1.414	4.472
3	9	1.732	5.477
4	16	2.000	6.325
5	25	2.236	7.071
6	36	2.449	7.746
7	49	2.646	8.367
8	64	2.828	8.944
9	81	3.000	9.487
10	100	3.162	10.000
11	121	3.317	10.488
12	144	3.464	10.954
13	169	3.606	11.402
14	196	3.742	11.832
15	226	3.873	12.247
16	256	4.000	12.649
17	289	4.123	13.038
18	324	4.243	13.416
19	361	4.359	13.784
20	400	4.472	14.142
21	441	4.583	14.491
22	484	4.690	14.832
23	529	4.796	15.166
24	576	4.899	15.492
25	625	5.000	15.811
26	676	5.099	16.125
27	729	5.196	16.432
28	784	5.292	16.733
29	841	5.385	17.029
30	900	5.477	17.321

Solve the problems. Give square root approximations to the nearest hundredth.

1. 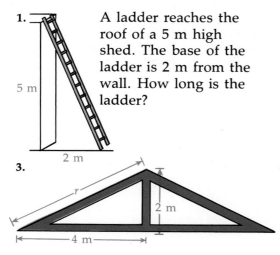 A ladder reaches the roof of a 5 m high shed. The base of the ladder is 2 m from the wall. How long is the ladder?

5 m

2 m

2. A small machine part was shaped like a right triangle with legs 7 cm and 4 cm. How long is the third side of the part?

4 cm

7 cm

3.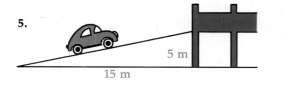

r

2 m

4 m

Use the distances on the rafters of the roof of the building in the diagram. How long is rafter r?

4. It is 10 km along the road from the grocery store to the beach. It is 6 km along the road from the beach to the boat dock. How far is it across the lake from the dock to the store?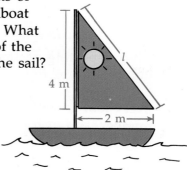

Grocery store

10 km

Lake

6 km   Boat dock

Beach

5.

5 m

15 m

A ramp to a bridge is 15 m along the ground and 5 m above the ground at the bridge. How long is the ramp?

6. The dimensions of a sail on a sailboat are as shown. What is the length of the third side of the sail?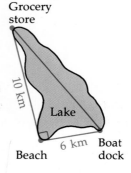

4 m

2 m

Guess a number that would be a solution to this equation:

$$n^3 = 12\ 167$$
$$n \cdot n \cdot n = 12\ 167$$

Try your guess, then try again.
Can you find the number in less than 5 tries?

Find n for each.

1. $n^3 = 4913$ **2.** $n^3 = 175\ 616$ **3.** $n^3 = 39\ 304$

⊛ Rational and irrational numbers

When the numerator of a fraction is divided by the denominator, part of the **repeating decimal** for that fractional number is displayed on the calculator.

Example: For $\frac{2}{11}$, divide 2 by 11.
The repeating decimal is 0.181818 . . .
We write: $0.\overline{18}$

Some calculators display a key marked $\sqrt{x}$. When a whole number that is not a square is entered and the $\sqrt{x}$ key is pushed, part of a non-repeating decimal for the square root is displayed.

Example: For $\sqrt{2}$, the part of a non-repeating decimal shown is 1.4142135.

Every **repeating decimal** represents a **rational number** and every rational number can be represented by a repeating decimal or terminating decimal.

Every **non-repeating** and non-terminating decimal represents an **irrational number**, and every irrational number has a non-repeating decimal.

Some of the decimals below have an obvious pattern and some do not. If you see a pattern, extend the decimal 5 more places. Tell whether each decimal represents a rational or irrational number.

1. 0.3423423 . . .

2. 7.9999 . . .

3. 0.040040004 . . .

4. 6.01301301 . . .

5. 5.474747 . . .

6. 4.1598376 . . .

7. 0.142857142 . . .

8. 0.1234567 . . .

9. 0.01020304 . . .

10. 0.250000 . . .

Calculator problems

Find a repeating decimal for each of these fractional numbers.

1. $\frac{2}{3}$　　2. $\frac{4}{7}$　　3. $\frac{5}{6}$　　4. $\frac{1}{7}$　　5. $\frac{5}{9}$　　6. $\frac{3}{11}$

7. $\frac{7}{27}$　　8. $\frac{9}{37}$　　9. $\frac{7}{9}$　　10. $\frac{7}{99}$　　11. $\frac{7}{999}$　　12. $\frac{7}{9999}$

13. $\frac{5}{11}$　　14. $\frac{5}{111}$　　15. $\frac{5}{1111}$　　16. $\frac{7}{12}$　　17. $\frac{3}{36}$　　18. $\frac{3}{74}$

Find the non-repeating decimal to as many places as you can for each of the following irrational numbers.

19. $\sqrt{3}$　　20. $\sqrt{5}$　　21. $\sqrt{7}$　　22. $\sqrt{6}$　　23. $\sqrt{8}$　　24. $\sqrt{10}$

25. $\sqrt{12}$　　26. $\sqrt{11}$　　27. $\sqrt{13}$　　28. $\sqrt{14}$　　29. $\sqrt{15}$　　30. $\sqrt{18}$

31. $\sqrt{17}$　　32. $\sqrt{19}$　　33. $\sqrt{28}$　　34. $\sqrt{23}$　　35. $\sqrt{24}$　　36. $\sqrt{21}$

37. A rectangle in which the ratio
of the length to the width is
$\dfrac{1 + \sqrt{5}}{2}$ is said to be most pleasing
to the eye. This ratio is called
the **Golden Ratio**.
Find a part of the non-repeating
decimal for the Golden Ratio
(to as many places as possible).

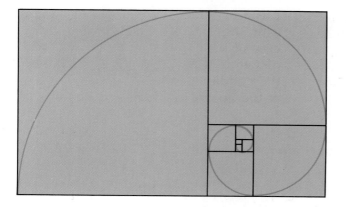

The number π is an irrational
number which has been computed
to thousands of decimal places.
Here is an approximation of π
to 24 places.

3.141592653589793238462643

Which of these rational numbers
is closest to π?

A $\frac{22}{7}$　　B $\frac{179}{57}$　　C $\frac{355}{113}$

Can you give a rational number that
is closer to π? (Hint: Use a
denominator that is a power of ten.)

Self-check

Use the Pythagorean theorem to solve these problems. Use the square root table on page 374 to give approximations of square roots to the nearest hundredth.

1. The pole is 3 units high. The stake is 4 units from the base of the pole. How long is the wire?

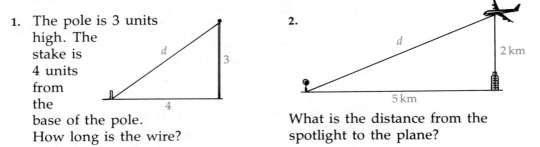

2.

   What is the distance from the spotlight to the plane?

3. Use these squares to give the decimal approximation, to the nearest tenth, for $\sqrt{14}$.

   $(3.7)^2 = 13.69$
   $(3.8)^2 = 14.44$

4. Use the square root table to give $\sqrt{270}$ to the nearest hundredth.

5. A repeating decimal represents a/an (irrational, rational) __?__ number.

Answers for Self-check—page 377

Test

Use the Pythagorean theorem to solve these problems. Give square roots to the nearest hundredth.

1.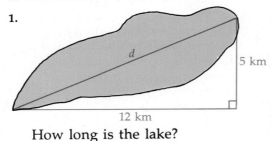

   How long is the lake?

2. An A-frame house is 9 m high. It is 3 m from the base of the roof to the middle of the door. How long is the roof?

   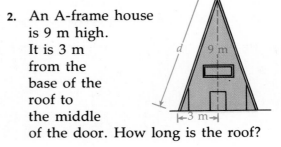

3. Use these squares to give the decimal approximation, to the nearest tenth, for $\sqrt{23}$.

   $(4.7)^2 = 22.09$
   $(4.8)^2 = 23.04$

4. Use the square root table to give $\sqrt{120}$ to the nearest hundredth.

5. A non-repeating decimal represents a/an (rational, irrational) __?__ number.

Math lab

A π Experiment

π is the ratio of the circumference of a circle to the diameter of a circle.

$\pi = 3.14159265358979323846$ (to 20 decimal places).

A French naturalist, Comte de Buffon (1707–1788), claimed that the following method, based on probability, can be used to give an **approximate** value for π. Try it.

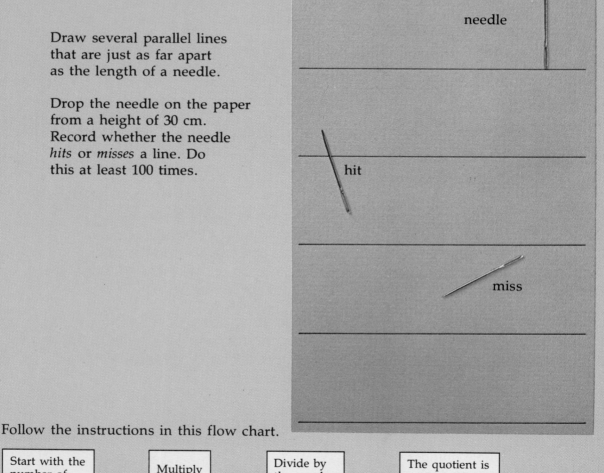

Draw several parallel lines that are just as far apart as the length of a needle.

Drop the needle on the paper from a height of 30 cm. Record whether the needle *hits* or *misses* a line. Do this at least 100 times.

Follow the instructions in this flow chart.

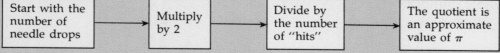

Start with the number of needle drops → Multiply by 2 → Divide by the number of "hits" → The quotient is an approximate value of π

How close did you come to the value of π?

Now total the number of "needle drops" and "hits" for your class. Using this total, do you get a closer approximation for π?

Unit 12 review

Give the prime factorization using exponents.

1. 56   2. 108   3. 121   4. 42   5. 36

Give the first six numbers of each sequence.

6. nth term: $n^2 + 1$ 7. nth term: $2n + 3$ 8. nth term: $4n - 1$

Write in factorial notation.

9. $1 \cdot 2 \cdot 3 \cdot 4 \cdot 5$ 10. $10! \cdot 11$ 11. $7! \cdot 8 \cdot 9$

Solve.

12. Susan has 4 skirts and 6 sweaters. How many skirt-sweater outfits does she have?

13. 4 people are waiting for a bus. In how many different ways can they line up to board the bus?

14. There are 4 routes from city A to city B and 5 routes from city B to city C. How many different routes are there from city A to city C, going through city B?

15. A train engine is going to pull 3 passenger cars and a caboose. How many arrangements of the passenger cars in front of the caboose can be made?

16. A penny and a nickel are tossed. What is the probability of getting two heads?

17. A penny is tossed 60 times. About how many times will tails occur?

Give a whole number for each square root.

18. 4   19. 81

20. 36   21. 25

Give the square root to the nearest tenth.

22. $\sqrt{10}$ 23. $\sqrt{34}$

24. $\sqrt{125}$ 25. $\sqrt{260}$

Appendix

Add.

1.	46.21 + 64.39	**2.**	38.5 + 29.7	**3.**	0.847 + 0.728	**4.**	653.2 + 295.9	**5.**	57.6 + 48.2
6.	295.66 + 704.39	**7.**	0.648 + 3.281	**8.**	5.043 + 7.209	**9.**	84.96 + 65.99	**10.**	482.71 + 738.68
11.	7.65 4.32 + 2.63	**12.**	64.3 57.8 + 36.2	**13.**	284.3 572.6 + 487.1	**14.**	8.741 3.026 + 5.845	**15.**	49.271 6.439 + 28.05
16.	25.26 58.34 81.57 + 30.02	**17.**	0.856 2.784 0.601 + 7.523	**18.**	81.205 7.316 3.714 + 22.601	**19.**	4.071 0.642 0.951 + 7.014	**20.**	6.052 28.371 14.681 + 9.708

Set B   For use after page 35

Subtract.

1.	4.03 − 2.71	**2.**	7.402 − 3.265	**3.**	24.36 − 15.84	**4.**	51.06 − 28.47	**5.**	32.14 − 18.27
6.	76.401 − 8.219	**7.**	84.22 − 17.48	**8.**	3.089 − 0.915	**9.**	60.413 − 28.065	**10.**	413.26 − 132.48
11.	52.00 − 36.34	**12.**	704.3 − 486.2	**13.**	20.504 − 3.689	**14.**	42.100 − 9.748	**15.**	0.8043 − 0.2674
16.	31.041 − 25.728	**17.**	5.4030 − 4.7605	**18.**	764.22 − 39.74	**19.**	925.41 − 367.28	**20.**	51.34 − 12.76
21.	0.8401 − 0.3682	**22.**	6.32 − 4.681	**23.**	47.312 − 28.637	**24.**	37.021 − 24.376	**25.**	725.09 − 648.33

Multiply.

1. 28.7 $\times$ 0.4	2. 5.74 $\times$ 0.8	3. 0.96 $\times$ 0.5	4. 7.6 $\times$ 0.28	5. 3.06 $\times$ 3.6
6. 425 $\times$ 0.31	7. 68.3 $\times$ 44	8. 196.3 $\times$ 0.8	9. 50.03 $\times$ 0.26	10. 7.421 $\times$ 0.8
11. 8.47 $\times$ 3.2	12. 27.39 $\times$ 5.1	13. 0.64 $\times$ 0.73	14. 224 $\times$ 0.09	15. 0.54 $\times$ 8.5
16. 6.48 $\times$ 0.31	17. 47.6 $\times$ 72	18. 5.64 $\times$ 6.4	19. 0.93 $\times$ 2.7	20. 0.39 $\times$ 0.93
21. 3.021 $\times$ 0.56	22. 83.24 $\times$ 6.58	23. 0.751 $\times$ 0.282	24. 6.031 $\times$ 0.94	25. 4.87 $\times$ 22.9
26. 5.63 $\times$ 68.4	27. 0.3241 $\times$ 0.59	28. 0.832 $\times$ 2.61	29. 2.89 $\times$ 70.4	30. 6.51 $\times$ 0.483

Divide.

1. $7\overline{)16.8}$ 2. $9\overline{)4.05}$ 3. $13\overline{)59.8}$ 4. $15\overline{)10.8}$ 5. $45\overline{)544.5}$

6. $26\overline{)137.8}$ 7. $8\overline{)209.6}$ 8. $52\overline{)192.4}$ 9. $47\overline{)29.61}$ 10. $68\overline{)190.4}$

11. $91\overline{)283.01}$ 12. $32\overline{)26.24}$ 13. $65\overline{)38.35}$ 14. $126\overline{)113.4}$ 15. $217\overline{)99.82}$

Find the quotients to the nearest hundredth.

16. $0.6\overline{)5.2}$ 17. $2.5\overline{)3.26}$ 18. $0.03\overline{)4.7}$ 19. $5.13\overline{)2.68}$ 20. $0.009\overline{)6.5}$

21. $0.73\overline{)4}$ 22. $0.63\overline{)24}$ 23. $8.7\overline{)36.4}$ 24. $0.006\overline{)0.05}$ 25. $0.07\overline{)0.5}$

26. $4.8\overline{)2.93}$ 27. $51.3\overline{)2.54}$ 28. $7.31\overline{)84.2}$ 29. $0.92\overline{)0.93}$ 30. $0.34\overline{)6.5}$

31. $0.04\overline{)0.29}$ 32. $6.1\overline{)38.2}$ 33. $0.84\overline{)9.1}$ 34. $0.052\overline{)7.25}$ 35. $2.93\overline{)7.2}$

Write a decimal for each fraction.

1. $\frac{3}{8}$ 2. $\frac{4}{5}$ 3. $\frac{7}{16}$ 4. $\frac{5}{8}$ 5. $\frac{1}{4}$ 6. $\frac{3}{5}$

7. $\frac{9}{4}$ 8. $\frac{7}{2}$ 9. $\frac{7}{8}$ 10. $\frac{3}{16}$ 11. $\frac{11}{8}$ 12. $\frac{7}{10}$

13. $\frac{5}{16}$ 14. $\frac{3}{4}$ 15. $\frac{19}{50}$ 16. $\frac{17}{20}$ 17. $\frac{15}{4}$ 18. $\frac{27}{50}$

19. $\frac{7}{20}$ 20. $\frac{3}{2}$ 21. $\frac{13}{25}$ 22. $\frac{8}{5}$ 23. $\frac{9}{10}$ 24. $\frac{19}{20}$

25. $\frac{11}{25}$ 26. $\frac{13}{50}$ 27. $\frac{1}{20}$ 28. $\frac{17}{4}$ 29. $\frac{15}{8}$ 30. $\frac{13}{16}$

Write a mixed decimal in hundredths for each fraction.

31. $\frac{3}{7}$ 32. $\frac{2}{9}$ 33. $\frac{5}{8}$ 34. $\frac{7}{15}$ 35. $\frac{13}{9}$ 36. $\frac{11}{3}$

37. $\frac{1}{6}$ 38. $\frac{6}{13}$ 39. $\frac{4}{7}$ 40. $\frac{10}{9}$ 41. $\frac{4}{15}$ 42. $\frac{12}{7}$

43. $\frac{7}{8}$ 44. $\frac{9}{7}$ 45. $\frac{5}{16}$ 46. $\frac{4}{11}$ 47. $\frac{13}{8}$ 48. $\frac{4}{9}$

49. $\frac{3}{16}$ 50. $\frac{2}{11}$ 51. $\frac{7}{9}$ 52. $\frac{8}{3}$ 53. $\frac{6}{7}$ 54. $\frac{7}{15}$

55. $\frac{5}{3}$ 56. $\frac{7}{6}$ 57. $\frac{8}{15}$ 58. $\frac{7}{12}$ 59. $\frac{11}{16}$ 60. $\frac{11}{6}$

Write a lowest-terms fraction for each decimal.

1. 0.8   2. 0.45   3. 0.36   4. 0.04   5. 0.6   6. 0.625

7. 0.375   8. 0.26   9. 0.02   10. 0.74   11. 0.4375   12. 0.48

13. 0.8125   14. 0.875   15. 0.34   16. 0.3125   17. 0.38   18. 0.065

19. $0.1\overline{5}$ 20. $0.\overline{36}$ 21. $0.\overline{27}$ 22. $0.\overline{8}$ 23. $0.\overline{93}$ 24. $0.\overline{45}$

25. $0.\overline{2}$ 26. $0.\overline{21}$ 27. $0.\overline{81}$ 28. $0.\overline{18}$ 29. $0.\overline{7}$ 30. $0.\overline{72}$

Set A For use after page 145

Add.

1. $\frac{3}{4}$
$+\frac{5}{6}$

2. $\frac{2}{3}$
$+\frac{1}{2}$

3. $\frac{5}{6}$
$+\frac{2}{5}$

4. $\frac{1}{6}$
$+\frac{5}{8}$

5. $\frac{3}{10}$
$+\frac{3}{4}$

6. $\frac{3}{8}$
$+\frac{1}{4}$

7. $9\frac{2}{3}$
$+6\frac{3}{4}$

8. $7\frac{3}{8}$
$+2\frac{1}{2}$

9. $4\frac{3}{8}$
$+8\frac{1}{6}$

10. $5\frac{7}{8}$
$+7\frac{3}{4}$

11. $3\frac{4}{5}$
$+9\frac{1}{6}$

12. $8\frac{1}{2}$
$+7\frac{5}{6}$

13. $54\frac{3}{4}$
$+32\frac{1}{5}$

14. $47\frac{1}{6}$
$+74\frac{1}{4}$

15. $19\frac{1}{2}$
$+56\frac{3}{4}$

16. $28\frac{1}{5}$
$+44\frac{3}{10}$

17. $86\frac{1}{3}$
$+12\frac{1}{2}$

18. $65\frac{1}{9}$
$+29\frac{2}{3}$

19. $9\frac{1}{2}$
$4\frac{2}{3}$
$+3\frac{1}{6}$

20. $6\frac{5}{8}$
$2\frac{1}{4}$
$+2\frac{1}{2}$

21. $12\frac{3}{4}$
$14\frac{1}{3}$
$+26\frac{1}{6}$

22. $34\frac{1}{2}$
$23\frac{1}{4}$
$+58\frac{2}{5}$

23. $51\frac{5}{6}$
$68\frac{3}{8}$
$+39\frac{1}{4}$

24. $43\frac{1}{8}$
$56\frac{2}{3}$
$+72\frac{1}{2}$

Set B For use after page 147

Subtract.

1. $\frac{3}{4}$
$-\frac{1}{8}$

2. $\frac{2}{3}$
$-\frac{1}{6}$

3. $\frac{3}{5}$
$-\frac{1}{2}$

4. $\frac{3}{4}$
$-\frac{2}{3}$

5. $\frac{5}{6}$
$-\frac{1}{4}$

6. $\frac{3}{4}$
$-\frac{1}{5}$

7. $\frac{4}{5}$
$-\frac{2}{3}$

8. $\frac{3}{4}$
$-\frac{1}{2}$

9. $\frac{1}{2}$
$-\frac{1}{8}$

10. $\frac{7}{8}$
$-\frac{5}{6}$

11. $\frac{5}{6}$
$-\frac{5}{12}$

12. $\frac{5}{8}$
$-\frac{1}{3}$

13. 7
$-3\frac{3}{4}$

14. $5\frac{3}{4}$
$-2\frac{3}{8}$

15. $9\frac{1}{3}$
$-4\frac{1}{6}$

16. $6\frac{1}{4}$
$-1\frac{1}{2}$

17. $8\frac{1}{4}$
$-3\frac{2}{3}$

18. $4\frac{1}{10}$
$-2\frac{1}{5}$

19. $35\frac{1}{8}$
$-18\frac{3}{4}$

20. $54\frac{1}{6}$
$-27\frac{3}{8}$

21. $68\frac{1}{3}$
$-13\frac{3}{4}$

22. $28\frac{1}{5}$
$-9\frac{3}{4}$

23. $47\frac{1}{8}$
$-36\frac{2}{3}$

24. $71\frac{1}{3}$
$-45\frac{2}{7}$

25. $74\frac{1}{10}$
$-48\frac{3}{4}$

26. $82\frac{1}{2}$
$-19\frac{3}{4}$

27. $52\frac{3}{8}$
$-34\frac{5}{6}$

28. $96\frac{1}{10}$
$-87\frac{2}{3}$

29. $65\frac{1}{2}$
$-45\frac{5}{6}$

30. $31\frac{1}{5}$
$-29\frac{2}{3}$

Find the products.

1. $\frac{1}{2} \cdot \frac{4}{5} = a$

2. $\frac{1}{8} \cdot \frac{2}{3} = d$

3. $\frac{6}{7} \cdot \frac{1}{3} = f$

4. $\frac{1}{9} \cdot \frac{3}{4} = x$

5. $\frac{3}{8} \cdot \frac{8}{9} = k$

6. $\frac{4}{5} \cdot \frac{3}{10} = m$

7. $\frac{2}{15} \cdot \frac{5}{8} = e$

8. $\frac{1}{8} \cdot \frac{1}{9} = b$

9. $\frac{9}{10} \cdot \frac{1}{6} = g$

10. $\frac{2}{3} \cdot \frac{4}{5} = j$

11. $\frac{3}{7} \cdot \frac{7}{8} = z$

12. $\frac{9}{10} \cdot \frac{2}{3} = c$

13. $\frac{1}{12} \cdot \frac{4}{5} = n$

14. $\frac{2}{5} \cdot \frac{1}{8} = p$

15. $\frac{6}{7} \cdot \frac{7}{9} = r$

16. $\frac{3}{8} \cdot \frac{4}{5} = h$

17. $\frac{2}{9} \cdot \frac{7}{8} = q$

18. $\frac{1}{24} \cdot \frac{6}{7} = s$

19. $\frac{9}{10} \cdot \frac{5}{9} = v$

20. $\frac{4}{7} \cdot \frac{1}{2} = x$

21. $2\frac{1}{5} \cdot 3\frac{1}{3} = w$

22. $1\frac{1}{4} \cdot 1\frac{1}{10} = z$

23. $3\frac{1}{8} \cdot 1\frac{2}{5} = b$

24. $\frac{1}{7} \cdot 4\frac{2}{3} = u$

25. $\frac{5}{7} \cdot 4\frac{1}{5} = e$

26. $\frac{5}{8} \cdot 5\frac{1}{3} = h$

27. $2\frac{2}{3} \cdot 3\frac{1}{4} = c$

28. $6\frac{3}{4} \cdot \frac{2}{9} = y$

29. $2\frac{2}{7} \cdot 4\frac{2}{3} = t$

30. $1\frac{1}{5} \cdot \frac{1}{12} = a$

31. $1\frac{1}{3} \cdot \frac{3}{16} = k$

32. $1\frac{7}{8} \cdot \frac{4}{5} = w$

Find the quotients.

1. $\frac{5}{9} \div \frac{2}{3} = w$

2. $\frac{3}{4} \div \frac{5}{12} = c$

3. $\frac{9}{10} \div \frac{3}{5} = r$

4. $\frac{7}{10} \div \frac{1}{2} = a$

5. $\frac{3}{8} \div \frac{1}{4} = x$

6. $\frac{1}{10} \div \frac{7}{10} = a$

7. $\frac{1}{8} \div \frac{3}{16} = f$

8. $\frac{1}{12} \div \frac{1}{6} = n$

9. $\frac{6}{7} \div \frac{2}{7} = d$

10. $\frac{2}{3} \div \frac{1}{6} = j$

11. $\frac{5}{12} \div \frac{3}{8} = e$

12. $\frac{1}{15} \div \frac{2}{3} = k$

13. $\frac{3}{8} \div \frac{3}{4} = b$

14. $\frac{1}{4} \div \frac{7}{24} = m$

15. $\frac{5}{6} \div \frac{4}{9} = g$

16. $\frac{1}{15} \div \frac{2}{5} = p$

17. $\frac{1}{9} \div \frac{7}{12} = h$

18. $\frac{5}{8} \div \frac{3}{8} = r$

19. $\frac{3}{7} \div \frac{1}{14} = x$

20. $\frac{5}{24} \div \frac{3}{8} = w$

21. $3\frac{1}{3} \div \frac{2}{9} = c$

22. $1\frac{1}{5} \div 1\frac{1}{3} = e$

23. $\frac{2}{7} \div 1\frac{3}{7} = h$

24. $1\frac{5}{8} \div 1\frac{3}{4} = n$

25. $7\frac{1}{3} \div 2 = p$

26. $\frac{5}{6} \div 2\frac{2}{5} = a$

27. $2\frac{1}{4} \div 5\frac{1}{4} = r$

28. $5\frac{5}{6} \div 4\frac{2}{3} = s$

29. $6 \div 2\frac{1}{2} = v$

30. $3\frac{1}{9} \div 4\frac{2}{3} = w$

31. $4\frac{1}{4} \div 1\frac{3}{8} = k$

32. $3\frac{3}{7} \div 1\frac{1}{5} = d$

Set A For use after page 161

Solve each proportion.

1. $\frac{2}{5} = \frac{n}{20}$ 2. $\frac{4}{7} = \frac{12}{n}$ 3. $\frac{1}{2} = \frac{n}{72}$ 4. $\frac{6}{9} = \frac{14}{n}$ 5. $\frac{3}{8} = \frac{n}{36}$

6. $\frac{12}{15} = \frac{36}{n}$ 7. $\frac{2}{3} = \frac{n}{63}$ 8. $\frac{7}{8} = \frac{n}{56}$ 9. $\frac{9}{21} = \frac{15}{n}$ 10. $\frac{6}{10} = \frac{n}{25}$

11. $\frac{3}{4} = \frac{n}{56}$ 12. $\frac{2}{7} = \frac{26}{n}$ 13. $\frac{4}{5} = \frac{n}{70}$ 14. $\frac{3}{15} = \frac{n}{45}$ 15. $\frac{4}{6} = \frac{18}{n}$

16. $\frac{9}{15} = \frac{n}{20}$ 17. $\frac{5}{6} = \frac{12}{n}$ 18. $\frac{3}{12} = \frac{8}{n}$ 19. $\frac{6}{8} = \frac{n}{96}$ 20. $\frac{1}{5} = \frac{n}{65}$

21. $\frac{10}{12} = \frac{35}{n}$ 22. $\frac{3}{9} = \frac{n}{72}$ 23. $\frac{3}{7} = \frac{n}{91}$ 24. $\frac{2}{10} = \frac{18}{n}$ 25. $\frac{2}{6} = \frac{28}{n}$

26. $\frac{3}{6} = \frac{36}{n}$ 27. $\frac{5}{8} = \frac{12}{n}$ 28. $\frac{9}{12} = \frac{n}{32}$ 29. $\frac{2}{4} = \frac{31}{n}$ 30. $\frac{8}{10} = \frac{28}{n}$

31. $\frac{4}{12} = \frac{32}{n}$ 32. $\frac{6}{7} = \frac{15}{n}$ 33. $\frac{5}{10} = \frac{30}{n}$ 34. $\frac{3}{5} = \frac{51}{n}$ 35. $\frac{6}{21} = \frac{10}{n}$

36. $\frac{5}{7} = \frac{21}{n}$ 37. $\frac{2}{12} = \frac{n}{72}$ 38. $\frac{2}{8} = \frac{5}{n}$ 39. $\frac{4}{8} = \frac{27}{n}$ 40. $\frac{2}{14} = \frac{n}{63}$

Set B For use after page 193

Write each decimal as a percent.

1. 0.23   2. 0.08   3. 0.46   4. 0.88   5. 0.09

6. 0.034   7. 0.501   8. 0.725   9. 0.091   10. 0.206

11. 2.03   12. 4.7   13. 6.27   14. 8.04   15. 1.76

16. 0.516   17. 0.39   18. 2.75   19. 0.74   20. 4.21

21. 8.2   22. 0.652   23. 9.33   24. 1.07   25. 0.8

26. 3.15   27. 0.72   28. 0.048   29. 5.6   30. 0.01

31. 6.04   32. 0.057   33. 0.68   34. 0.306   35. 2.5

36. 0.98   37. 0.018   38. 7.2   39. 3.26   40. 0.468

Find a percent for each fraction. Round each percent to the nearest tenth of a percent.

1. $\frac{2}{7}$ 2. $\frac{1}{6}$ 3. $\frac{8}{9}$ 4. $\frac{5}{8}$ 5. $\frac{6}{11}$

6. $\frac{5}{12}$ 7. $\frac{3}{23}$ 8. $\frac{13}{32}$ 9. $\frac{9}{13}$ 10. $\frac{4}{41}$

11. $\frac{7}{34}$ 12. $\frac{5}{19}$ 13. $\frac{7}{15}$ 14. $\frac{1}{3}$ 15. $\frac{15}{16}$

16. $\frac{7}{11}$ 17. $\frac{12}{13}$ 18. $\frac{6}{7}$ 19. $\frac{16}{35}$ 20. $\frac{11}{15}$

21. $\frac{31}{45}$ 22. $\frac{7}{8}$ 23. $\frac{17}{30}$ 24. $\frac{5}{27}$ 25. $\frac{9}{17}$

26. $\frac{13}{24}$ 27. $\frac{4}{29}$ 28. $\frac{2}{15}$ 29. $\frac{9}{11}$ 30. $\frac{12}{19}$

31. $\frac{15}{17}$ 32. $\frac{3}{16}$ 33. $\frac{8}{19}$ 34. $\frac{10}{21}$ 35. $\frac{13}{18}$

Write each percent as a lowest-terms fraction.

1. 10%   2. 65%   3. 70%   4. 90%   5. 38%

6. 22%   7. 30%   8. 15%   9. 42%   10. 6.2%

11. 34%   12. 4.8%   13. 85%   14. 6.75%   15. 9.6%

16. 4.25%   17. 8.35%   18. 25%   19. 3.5%   20. 1.5%

21. 8.4%   22. 0.64%   23. 40%   24. 26.2%   25. 0.8%

26. 0.75%   27. 5.2%   28. 0.4%   29. 0.72%   30. 0.82%

31. 3.6%   32. 26.5%   33. 9.5%   34. 0.45%   35. 8.5%

36. 44%   37. 9.2%   38. 0.68%   39. 0.2%   40. 3.2%

Set A For use after page 205

Find the percent of each number.

1. 22% of 52	**2.** 36% of 72	**3.** 52% of 88	**4.** 9% of 320
5. 5.7% of 26.22	**6.** 45% of 82.6	**7.** 72% of 235	**8.** 83% of 715
9. 91% of 406	**10.** 23% of 68.2	**11.** 3.9% of 54.02	**12.** 65% of 254
13. 60% of 562	**14.** 86% of 73	**15.** 74% of 420	**16.** 4.3% of 180.6
17. 15% of 75	**18.** 41% of 645	**19.** 2.8% of 61.54	**20.** 59% of 86
21. 55% of 18.6	**22.** 9.5% of 15.74	**23.** 7% of 152.6	**24.** 90% of 890
25. 37% of 500	**26.** 64% of 81	**27.** 85% of 418	**28.** 42% of 53
29. 87% of 347	**30.** 53% of 50	**31.** 38% of 150	**32.** 25% of 91
33. 44% of 78.9	**34.** 7.4% of 400	**35.** 12% of 935	**36.** 120% of 300

Set B For use after page 207

1. What percent of 85 is 34?	**2.** What percent of 70 is 21?
3. What percent of 35 is 7?	**4.** What percent of 250 is 15?
5. What percent of 75 is 6?	**6.** What percent of 48 is 24?
7. What percent of 50 is 30?	**8.** What percent of 60 is 9?
9. What percent of 20 is 1?	**10.** What percent of 120 is 114?
11. What percent of 350 is 119?	**12.** What percent of 45 is 17?
13. What percent of 55 is 22?	**14.** What percent of 30 is 14?
15. What percent of 90 is 72?	**16.** What percent of 50 is 43?
17. What percent of 60 is 21?	**18.** What percent of 240 is 156?
19. What percent of 56 is 14?	**20.** What percent of 400 is 16?
21. What percent of 60 is 45?	**22.** What percent of 62 is 31?
23. What percent of 70 is 42?	**24.** What percent of 25 is 9?
25. What percent of 45 is 18?	**26.** What percent of 1200 is 660?

Write and solve an equation for each.

1. 40% of a number is 14.
    What is the number?

2. 6% of a number is 3.
    What is the number?

3. 18% of a number is 9.
    What is the number?

4. 20% of a number is 13.
    What is the number?

5. 35% of a number is 14.
    What is the number?

6. 95% of a number is 76.
    What is the number?

7. 60% of a number is 42.
    What is the number?

8. 16% of a number is 22.40.
    What is the number?

9. 4% of a number is 1.80.
    What is the number?

10. 25% of a number is 57.50.
    What is the number?

11. 48% of a number is 44.64.
    What is the number?

12. 56% of a number is 28.
    What is the number?

13. 75% of a number is 18.
    What is the number?

14. 5% of a number is 4.
    What is the number?

15. 12% of a number is 9.
    What is the number?

16. 84% of a number is 42.
    What is the number?

Solve.

1. $35\% \cdot 26 = n$

2. $45\% \cdot 51 = n$

3. $9\% \cdot 365 = n$

4. $15\% \cdot 434 = n$

5. $28\% \cdot 640 = n$

6. $74\% \cdot 165 = n$

7. $81\% \cdot 209 = n$

8. $95\% \cdot 184 = n$

9. $62\% \cdot 12.6 = n$

10. What percent of 65 is 26?

11. What percent of 45 is 9?

12. What percent of 15 is 12?

13. What percent of 40 is 28?

14. What percent of 62 is 31?

15. What percent of 80 is 76?

16. $15\% \cdot n = 6$

17. $40\% \cdot n = 14$

18. $90\% \cdot n = 63$

19. $8\% \cdot n = 2$

20. $65\% \cdot n = 13$

21. $10\% \cdot n = 8$

22. $20\% \cdot n = 13$

23. $5\% \cdot n = 4$

24. $50\% \cdot n = 21$

Find the discount and sale price for each.

1. Regular price: $26.00
   Discount rate: 10%

2. Regular price: $15.50
   Discount rate: 20%

3. Regular price: $72.00
   Discount rate: 15%

4. Regular price: $50.00
   Discount rate: 40%

5. Regular price: $9.45
   Discount rate: 20%

6. Regular price: $42.00
   Discount rate: 10.5%

7. Regular price: $60.40
   Discount rate: 15%

8. Regular price: $84.00
   Discount rate: $33\frac{1}{3}\%$

9. Regular price: $11.00
   Discount rate: 45%

10. Regular price: $38.00
    Discount rate: 25%

Set B For use after page 221

Find the interest.

1. $P = \$500$
   $r = 3\%$
   $t = 5$ years

2. $P = \$750$
   $r = 4\%$
   $t = 4$ years

3. $P = \$15.00$
   $r = 2\%$
   $t = \frac{1}{2}$ year

4. $P = \$2000$
   $r = 3\%$
   $t = 3$ years

5. $P = \$850$
   $r = 5\%$
   $t = 4$ years

6. $P = \$7200$
   $r = 4\%$
   $t = 2$ years

7. $P = \$12\ 000$
   $r = 10\%$
   $t = 15$ years

8. $P = \$900$
   $r = 12\%$
   $t = \frac{1}{2}$ year

9. $P = \$30\ 000$
   $r = 7\%$
   $t = 20$ years

10. $P = \$8000$
    $r = 8\%$
    $t = 3$ years

11. $P = \$24\ 000$
    $r = 9.5\%$
    $t = 10$ years

12. $P = \$450$
    $r = 15\%$
    $t = \frac{1}{2}$ year

13. $P = \$1000$
    $r = 5\%$
    $t = 2$ years

14. $P = \$6400$
    $r = 7.5\%$
    $t = 3$ years

15. $P = \$700$
    $r = 8\%$
    $t = \frac{1}{2}$ year

Find the sums.

1. $\begin{array}{r} 7 \\ +\ ^-9 \\ \hline \end{array}$	**2.** $\begin{array}{r} ^-4 \\ +\ ^-6 \\ \hline \end{array}$	**3.** $\begin{array}{r} ^-2 \\ +\ 8 \\ \hline \end{array}$	**4.** $\begin{array}{r} ^-5 \\ +\ 3 \\ \hline \end{array}$	**5.** $\begin{array}{r} ^-6 \\ +\ ^-9 \\ \hline \end{array}$	**6.** $\begin{array}{r} 3 \\ +\ ^-7 \\ \hline \end{array}$
7. $\begin{array}{r} ^-3 \\ +\ 6 \\ \hline \end{array}$	**8.** $\begin{array}{r} ^-8 \\ +\ 6 \\ \hline \end{array}$	**9.** $\begin{array}{r} ^-7 \\ +\ ^-5 \\ \hline \end{array}$	**10.** $\begin{array}{r} ^-3 \\ +\ 4 \\ \hline \end{array}$	**11.** $\begin{array}{r} 2 \\ +\ ^-7 \\ \hline \end{array}$	**12.** $\begin{array}{r} 8 \\ +\ ^-4 \\ \hline \end{array}$
13. $\begin{array}{r} ^-10 \\ +\ 2 \\ \hline \end{array}$	**14.** $\begin{array}{r} ^-11 \\ +\ 16 \\ \hline \end{array}$	**15.** $\begin{array}{r} ^-3 \\ +\ 9 \\ \hline \end{array}$	**16.** $\begin{array}{r} ^-13 \\ +\ 10 \\ \hline \end{array}$	**17.** $\begin{array}{r} 15 \\ +\ ^-18 \\ \hline \end{array}$	**18.** $\begin{array}{r} 15 \\ +\ ^-9 \\ \hline \end{array}$
19. $\begin{array}{r} ^-2 \\ +\ 11 \\ \hline \end{array}$	**20.** $\begin{array}{r} 8 \\ +\ ^-12 \\ \hline \end{array}$	**21.** $\begin{array}{r} 13 \\ +\ ^-6 \\ \hline \end{array}$	**22.** $\begin{array}{r} ^-8 \\ +\ 16 \\ \hline \end{array}$	**23.** $\begin{array}{r} ^-14 \\ +\ 8 \\ \hline \end{array}$	**24.** $\begin{array}{r} ^-5 \\ +\ 10 \\ \hline \end{array}$
25. $\begin{array}{r} ^-3 \\ 7 \\ ^-5 \\ +\ 2 \\ \hline \end{array}$	**26.** $\begin{array}{r} 9 \\ ^-2 \\ ^-1 \\ +\ ^-3 \\ \hline \end{array}$	**27.** $\begin{array}{r} 7 \\ ^-10 \\ 4 \\ +\ 8 \\ \hline \end{array}$	**28.** $\begin{array}{r} 6 \\ ^-8 \\ ^-7 \\ +\ 1 \\ \hline \end{array}$	**29.** $\begin{array}{r} ^-4 \\ ^-7 \\ 12 \\ +\ ^-2 \\ \hline \end{array}$	**30.** $\begin{array}{r} 8 \\ ^-3 \\ 2 \\ +\ ^-5 \\ \hline \end{array}$

Find the differences.

1. $\begin{array}{r} ^-3 \\ -\ 2 \\ \hline \end{array}$	**2.** $\begin{array}{r} 6 \\ -\ ^-2 \\ \hline \end{array}$	**3.** $\begin{array}{r} ^-2 \\ -\ 5 \\ \hline \end{array}$	**4.** $\begin{array}{r} ^-4 \\ -\ ^-8 \\ \hline \end{array}$	**5.** $\begin{array}{r} 4 \\ -\ ^-4 \\ \hline \end{array}$	**6.** $\begin{array}{r} 5 \\ -\ 7 \\ \hline \end{array}$
7. $\begin{array}{r} ^-14 \\ -\ ^-6 \\ \hline \end{array}$	**8.** $\begin{array}{r} 3 \\ -\ 9 \\ \hline \end{array}$	**9.** $\begin{array}{r} 5 \\ -\ ^-12 \\ \hline \end{array}$	**10.** $\begin{array}{r} ^-10 \\ -\ 7 \\ \hline \end{array}$	**11.** $\begin{array}{r} ^-6 \\ -\ ^-5 \\ \hline \end{array}$	**12.** $\begin{array}{r} ^-7 \\ -\ 8 \\ \hline \end{array}$
13. $\begin{array}{r} 7 \\ -\ 16 \\ \hline \end{array}$	**14.** $\begin{array}{r} ^-14 \\ -\ 0 \\ \hline \end{array}$	**15.** $\begin{array}{r} 8 \\ -\ ^-4 \\ \hline \end{array}$	**16.** $\begin{array}{r} ^-6 \\ -\ 3 \\ \hline \end{array}$	**17.** $\begin{array}{r} ^-2 \\ -\ ^-8 \\ \hline \end{array}$	**18.** $\begin{array}{r} ^-3 \\ -\ ^-4 \\ \hline \end{array}$
19. $\begin{array}{r} ^-8 \\ -\ 5 \\ \hline \end{array}$	**20.** $\begin{array}{r} ^-6 \\ -\ ^-7 \\ \hline \end{array}$	**21.** $\begin{array}{r} 5 \\ -\ 11 \\ \hline \end{array}$	**22.** $\begin{array}{r} ^-9 \\ -\ ^-5 \\ \hline \end{array}$	**23.** $\begin{array}{r} 4 \\ -\ ^-7 \\ \hline \end{array}$	**24.** $\begin{array}{r} 8 \\ -\ ^-12 \\ \hline \end{array}$
25. $\begin{array}{r} ^-3 \\ -\ 9 \\ \hline \end{array}$	**26.** $\begin{array}{r} ^-4 \\ -\ 2 \\ \hline \end{array}$	**27.** $\begin{array}{r} 5 \\ -\ ^-15 \\ \hline \end{array}$	**28.** $\begin{array}{r} ^-13 \\ -\ ^-6 \\ \hline \end{array}$	**29.** $\begin{array}{r} 20 \\ -\ ^-30 \\ \hline \end{array}$	**30.** $\begin{array}{r} 8 \\ -\ ^-9 \\ \hline \end{array}$

Find the products.

1. $^-4 \cdot 5$	2. $8 \cdot {}^-3$	3. $^-6 \cdot {}^-7$	4. $9 \cdot {}^-6$
5. $7 \cdot {}^-2$	6. $6 \cdot 5$	7. $^-4 \cdot 8$	8. $^-3 \cdot 10$
9. $^-5 \cdot {}^-9$	10. $^-4 \cdot 7$	11. $12 \cdot {}^-4$	12. $^-7 \cdot 3$
13. $13 \cdot {}^-3$	14. $^-4 \cdot {}^-4$	15. $^-6 \cdot 8$	16. $5 \cdot {}^-5$
17. $2 \cdot 0$	18. $^-5 \cdot 8$	19. $^-9 \cdot 7$	20. $^-40 \cdot 6$
21. $^-7 \cdot {}^-7$	22. $20 \cdot {}^-2$	23. $^-6 \cdot 3$	24. $8 \cdot {}^-9$
25. $11 \cdot {}^-5$	26. $^-3 \cdot {}^-9$	27. $^-5 \cdot 7$	28. $6 \cdot {}^-12$
29. $^-4 \cdot {}^-6$	30. $3 \cdot {}^-15$	31. $^-8 \cdot 30$	32. $14 \cdot {}^-2$
33. $14 \cdot {}^-4$	34. $8 \cdot {}^-11$	35. $9 \cdot {}^-4$	36. $^-8 \cdot {}^-1$

Find the quotients.

1. $24 \div {}^-3$	2. $^-12 \div {}^-4$	3. $^-20 \div 5$	4. $^-14 \div 2$
5. $9 \div {}^-1$	6. $^-32 \div 8$	7. $^-15 \div {}^-3$	8. $10 \div {}^-5$
9. $^-21 \div 7$	10. $40 \div 8$	11. $^-24 \div 6$	12. $^-18 \div 3$
13. $48 \div {}^-8$	14. $^-30 \div {}^-6$	15. $56 \div {}^-8$	16. $^-42 \div 7$
17. $16 \div {}^-4$	18. $72 \div {}^-9$	19. $25 \div {}^-5$	20. $36 \div {}^-4$
21. $54 \div {}^-6$	22. $^-49 \div {}^-7$	23. $^-28 \div 4$	24. $63 \div {}^-7$
25. $^-35 \div {}^-7$	26. $48 \div {}^-6$	27. $100 \div {}^-50$	28. $^-60 \div {}^-10$
29. $40 \div {}^-2$	30. $^-36 \div 12$	31. $45 \div {}^-9$	32. $^-70 \div 5$
33. $^-80 \div 4$	34. $120 \div {}^-30$	35. $^-81 \div {}^-9$	36. $^-52 \div 4$

Solve the equations.

1. $n + {}^-3 = 2$ 2. $a - 4 = {}^-6$ 3. $z - 10 = 5$ 4. $y + {}^-6 = {}^-9$

5. $w - {}^-2 = 10$ 6. $b + 5 = {}^-1$ 7. $e - 9 = {}^-11$ 8. $c - 8 = {}^-2$

9. $k + {}^-6 = 13$ 10. $r - 9 = {}^-12$ 11. $t + 9 = 17$ 12. $f - {}^-3 = {}^-7$

13. $m - 12 = {}^-8$ 14. $x + 8 = 3$ 15. $s - {}^-6 = {}^-7$ 16. $y + {}^-12 = {}^-3$

17. $7n = {}^-28$ 18. ${}^-3y = {}^-18$ 19. ${}^-8a = 40$ 20. $4x = {}^-20$

21. ${}^-9c = 54$ 22. ${}^-5d = 15$ 23. ${}^-6e = 42$ 24. $5f = {}^-40$

25. $\dfrac{r}{7} = {}^-3$ 26. $\dfrac{t}{{}^-6} = 8$ 27. $\dfrac{n}{{}^-2} = 13$ 28. $\dfrac{x}{{}^-5} = 5$

29. $\dfrac{s}{{}^-7} = 8$ 30. $\dfrac{m}{{}^-10} = {}^-6$ 31. $\dfrac{v}{{}^-8} = 9$ 32. $\dfrac{w}{{}^-5} = {}^-7$

Solve the equations.

1. $4r + 2 = {}^-6$ 2. $3s - 6 = {}^-18$ 3. $8a + {}^-5 = 11$

4. ${}^-5w + 3 = {}^-12$ 5. $2x - 3 = {}^-13$ 6. ${}^-3t - 8 = 10$

7. $2m - 9 = {}^-1$ 8. $6b - 2 = {}^-14$ 9. $2k - 5 = 1$

10. $3d + 16 = {}^-8$ 11. ${}^-5g + {}^-3 = 7$ 12. $4e + 12 = {}^-4$

13. ${}^-6h + 10 = {}^-20$ 14. ${}^-2c - 5 = 7$ 15. $3j - {}^-4 = 25$

16. ${}^-8n - 5 = 3$ 17. $6p + 2 = 20$ 18. $5u + 2 = 32$

19. $2f + {}^-1 = {}^-11$ 20. $6v + {}^-8 = 16$ 21. ${}^-2w - 4 = {}^-20$

22. $10a + {}^-6 = 24$ 23. ${}^-2y + {}^-8 = 18$ 24. ${}^-3z - 5 = 7$

25. ${}^-4x - 8 = {}^-44$ 26. $2e - {}^-7 = 19$ 27. $5x + 14 = {}^-21$

28. ${}^-9c - 15 = 12$ 29. $15d + {}^-14 = 16$ 30. ${}^-8h - 29 = 11$

Problem 1 (For use after page 15)

Tanya collects coins. Last month she collected 50 coins. When her mother asked her how much money she had, she said $1.00. What combination of coins could Tanya have collected? (Hint: Guess and check. Use this table to organize your guesses.)

Pennies $0.01	Nickels $0.05	Dimes $0.10	Quarters $0.25	Half-dollars $0.50	Total number of coins	Total value
45						

Problem 2 (For use after page 25)

Jersey numbers	Number of digits	Total digits
1–9	1 each	9
10–19	2 each	

Julio spray-painted numbers on the shirts of the people running in a marathon. Each number had to be painted separately. He started at 1 and painted the numbers consecutively. Julio painted 192 digits altogether. How many people were in the marathon? (Hint: Complete this table.)

Problem 3 (For use after page 37)

In the holiday basketball tournament, each team played each of the other teams once. Altogether, 28 games were played. How many teams were in the tournament? (Hint: Try 2 teams. Try 3 teams. Look for a pattern in the number of games played.)

Problem 4   (For use after page 65)

Al Pine cut down 100 trees in 5 days.
Each day he cut down 6 more trees
than the previous day. How many
trees did he cut down on each day?
(Hint: Pick a number for the first day
and try it.)

Problem 5   (For use after page 79)

	First week	Second week	Third week	Fourth week
Arnold				
Kenji				
Frank				
Dick				

Arnold, Kenji, Frank, and Dick each
went on 4 dates with 4 different girls
on 4 consecutive weeks. On the
second week, Arnold dated Eileen and
Frank dated Luisa. The third week
Kenji dated Heidi and Dick dated
Gloria. The fourth week Frank dated
Gloria and Dick dated Luisa. Which
girl and boy dated each of the 4
weeks? (Hint: Use this table to help
you organize what you know.)

Problem 6   (For use after page 91)

Rhonda Rumor told a secret to 4
friends on Monday. On Tuesday, each
of the 4 friends told the secret to 4
more friends. On Wednesday, each
person told 4 more people. If this
pattern continues, how many people
will have heard the secret by the end
of Saturday? (Hint: Complete this
picture; look for a pattern.)

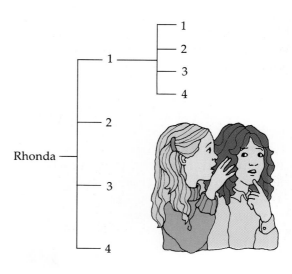

Problem 7 (For use after page 123)

On Wednesday, Steve, Donna, and Anna picked some apples. They divided the apples evenly among themselves. On Thursday, each child ate 4 apples. Then the total number of apples left was the same as the amount each child had on Wednesday. How many apples did they pick altogether? (Hint: Guess how many were left and try it.)

Problem 8 (For use after page 139)

Jennie saw some gulls and some dogs on the beach. There were 36 animals and a total of 100 legs. How many gulls and how many dogs did Jennie see on the beach? (Hint: Try 20 gulls and 16 dogs. Find the number of legs. Guess and check again if necessary.)

Problem 9 (For use after page 155)

Find the average monthly rainfall in Waterville. (Hint: Try this one on your own.)

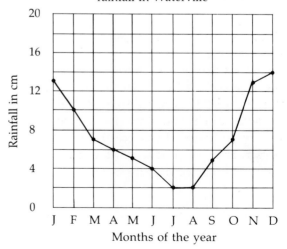

Average monthly rainfall in Waterville

Problem 10 (For use after page 167)

There are 20 doodles. All noodles are doodles. All doodles are poodles. There are 12 noodles. There are 30 poodles. How many poodles are not doodles or noodles? (Hint: Use this picture to help you find the answer.)

Problem 11 (For use after page 185)

Some children are seated at a large round table. They pass around a box of candy containing 25 pieces. Jan takes the first piece. Each child takes a piece as the box is passed around. Jan also gets the last piece of candy. She may have had more than the first and last pieces. How many children could be seated around the table? (Hint: Try 2 people at the table, then 3, then 4, then 5, and so on. Look for a pattern.)

Problem 12 (For use after page 199)

The Grims always try to steal the Grins's high spirits. The Grins are only safe when there is an equal number of Grins and Grims together, or if there are more Grins than Grims. Three Grins and 3 Grims were traveling through the woods when they came to a river. The only boat available carries 2 people at a time. How can the Grins and Grims get across the river safely? (Hint: A person can row back if necessary.)

Problem 13   (For use after page 209)

Mr. Jenkins lost the second page of his telephone bill. The page showed three amounts—the 4% state tax on the base rate and on intrastate calls; the 6% federal tax on the base rate, intrastate calls, and interstate calls; and the total bill. What was Mr. Jenkins's total bill? (Hint: You will need multiplication and addition to solve this.)

TELEPHONE BILL

Base Rate -------- $ 9.17

Long Distance ---- $ 4.50
(Intrastate)

Long Distance ---- $10.75
(Interstate)

Page 1

Problem 14   (For use after page 239)

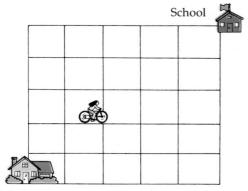

School

Keiko's house

Every day Keiko rides her bike to school. Each day she wants to ride a different way to school. There are 180 school days this year. Can she travel a different route every day? How many routes are there? (Hint: Find how many ways there are to get to each intersection. Then look for a pattern.)

Problem 15   (For use after page 257)

Ernie Thompson has been offered a job as a secretary to his old math teacher. The pay scale is $0.01 for the first week, $0.02 for the second week, $0.04 for the third week, and so on. Ernie does not know how much money he will make with this pay scale. How much will Ernie earn if he works for 20 weeks? (Hint: Complete this table and look for a pattern.)

Week	Earnings	Total
1	$0.01	$0.01
2	$0.02	$0.03
3	$0.04	$0.07
4		
5		

Problem 16 (For use after page 269)

If Erin's checking account balance falls below $500, she has to pay $0.25 for each check she writes. How much should she deposit on August 13 to avoid paying for each check? (Hint: *Withdrawing* money is the same as subtracting money.)

DATE	AMOUNT	BALANCE
		$1072.70
8/2	- - - -	$ 268.98
8/3	WITHDREW	$ 125.00
8/10	WITHDREW	$ 722.69
8/11	DEPOSITED	$1240.50
8/12	WITHDREW	$?
8/13	DEPOSIT	

Problem 17 (For use after page 283)

On Jim's first day of work at a local stationery store, 3 boxes were delivered. They were labeled, "Pencils," "Erasers," and "Pencils/Erasers." Each label was incorrect. Jim selected 1 item from 1 box. Then he labeled each box correctly. How did he do this? (Hint: Use this table to help you decide what Jim did.)

Box label	Actual Contents
Pencils	Erasers or Pencils/Erasers
Erasers	Pencils or Pencils/Erasers
Pencils/Erasers	All Pencils or all Erasers

Problem 18 (For use after page 297)

At the Randolph's family reunion, every nephew was also a cousin. Half of all uncles were cousins. Half of all cousins were nephews. There were 40 nephews and 20 uncles. No uncle was a nephew. How many cousins were neither nephews nor uncles? (Hint: Remember the *Doodles*, *Poodles* and *Noodles* in Problem 10?)

Problem 19   (For use after page 313)

Alejandro, Bonnie, Carrie, Denise, and Earl ran for president, vice-president, secretary, treasurer, and historian of the school. How many different ways could these offices be filled? (Hint: Suppose there were 2 offices and 2 people. How many ways? Try 3 offices and 3 people. Look for a pattern.)

Problem 20   (For use after page 329)

Nurse Thompson must give a patient 1000 cc of medication intravenously over a 10-h period. She can check the flow of the medication by counting the number of drops per minute. To be sure the flow is consistent, how many drops should she count per minute if 15 drops = 1 cc? (Hint: How many cc of medication should Nurse Thompson give her patient in 1 h?)

Problem 21   (For use after page 339)

Every Blip is a Blop. Half of all Bleeps are Blops. Half of all Blops are Blips. There are 30 Bleeps and 20 Blips. No Bleep is a Blip. How many Blops are neither Blips nor Bleeps? (Hint: Draw a Venn diagram.)

Problem 22 (For use after page 353)

Franklin School has 1000 lockers and 1000 students. One day, all 1000 students participated in a math project. The first student opened all 1000 lockers. The second student closed every locker that was a multiple of 2. The third student *changed* every locker that was a multiple of 3—*change* means open it if it is closed, or close it if it is open. The fourth student changed every fourth locker, and so forth until all 1000 students took a turn. Which lockers were open after all 1000 students finished? (Hint: Suppose there were 25 students and 25 lockers. Which lockers would remain open?)

Problem 23 (For use after page 363)

Five players on the Big Red Basketball Team are Dave, Paul, Ed, Jerry, and Steve.
– 2 wear white shoes and 3 wear red shoes.
– 3 are forwards and 2 are guards.
– Dave and Jerry wear the same color of shoes.
– Steve and Ed wear different colors of shoes.
– Paul and Ed play the same position.
– Jerry and Steve play different positions.
– The guard who wears white shoes is the leading scorer on the team. Who is this person? (Hint: Find which boys wear red shoes and which boys are forwards.)

Table of Measures

<table>
<tr><td colspan="2" align="center">**Metric System**</td><td colspan="2" align="center">**U.S. Customary Units**</td></tr>
</table>

———————————————————————— **Length** ————————————————————————

Metric		U.S. Customary	
1 millimeter (mm)	{0.1 centimeter (cm) {0.001 meter (m)	1 foot (ft)	{12 inches (in.)
1 centimeter (cm)	{10 millimeters (mm)	1 yard (yd)	{36 inches (in.) {3 feet (ft)
1 decimeter (dm)	{100 millimeters (mm) {10 centimeters (cm)	1 mile (mi)	{5280 feet (ft) {1760 yards (yd)
1 meter (m)	{1000 millimeters (mm) {100 centimeters (cm) {10 decimeters (dm)	1 nautical mile	{6076 feet (ft) {1852 meters (m)
1 kilometer (km)	{1000 meters (m)		

———————————————————————— **Area** ————————————————————————

Metric		U.S. Customary	
1 square meter (m²)	{100 square decimeters (dm²) {10 000 square centimeters (cm²)	1 square foot	{144 square inches (in.²)
1 hectare (ha)	{0.01 square kilometer (km²) {10 000 square meters (m²)	1 square yard (yd²)	{9 square feet (ft²) {1296 square inches (in.²)
1 square kilometer (km²)	{1 000 000 square meters (m²) {100 hectares (ha)	1 acre (A)	{43 560 square feet (ft²) {4 840 square yards (yd²)
		1 square mile (mi²)	{640 acres (A)

———————————————————————— **Volume** ————————————————————————

Metric		U.S. Customary	
1 cubic decimeter (dm³)	{0.001 cubic meter (m³) {1000 cubic centimeters (cm³) {1 liter (L)	1 cubic foot (ft³)	{1728 cubic inches (in.³)
1 cubic meter (m³)	{1 000 000 cubic centimeters (cm³) {1 000 cubic decimeters (dm³)	1 cubic yard (yd³)	{27 cubic feet (ft³) {46 656 cubic inches (in.³)

———————————————————————— **Capacity** ————————————————————————

Metric		U.S. Customary	
1 teaspoon	{5 milliliters (mL)	1 cup (c)	{8 fluid ounces (fl oz)
1 tablespoon	{12.5 milliliters (mL)	1 pint (pt)	{16 fluid ounces (fl oz) {2 cups (c)
1 liter (L)	{1000 milliliters (mL) {1000 cubic centimeters (cm³) {1 cubic decimeter (dm³) {4 metric cups	1 quart (qt)	{32 fluid ounces (fl oz) {4 cups (c) {2 pints (pt)
1 kiloliter (kL)	{1000 liters (L)	1 gallon (gal)	{128 fluid ounces (fl oz) {16 cups (c) {8 pints (pt) {4 quarts (qt)

———————————————————————— **Mass** ————————————————————————

Metric		U.S. Customary	
1 gram (g)	{1000 milligrams (mg)	1 pound (lb)	{16 ounces (oz)
1 kilogram (kg)	{1000 grams (g)	1 ton (T)	{2000 pounds (lbs)
1 metric ton (t)	{1000 kilograms (kg)		

Mathematical Symbols

$=$	Is equal to	$\overleftrightarrow{AB}$	Line through points A and B
$\neq$	Is not equal to	$\overrightarrow{AB}$	Ray AB
$>$	Is greater than	$\overline{AB}$	Segment with endpoints A and B
$<$	Is less than	$\angle ABC$	Angle ABC
$\leq$	Is less than or equal to	$m(\angle ABC)$	Measure of angle ABC
$\approx$	Is approximately equal to	$m(\overline{AB})$	Measure, or length, of segment AB
$\cong$	Is congruent to	$\triangle ABC$	Triangle ABC
$\sim$	Is similar to	$\overparen{RS}$	Arc with endpoints R and S
$\%$	Percent	$35°$	Thirty-five *degrees,*
π	Pi	$14'$	fourteen *minutes,*
$\sqrt{}$	Square root	$20''$	twenty *seconds*

Metric System Prefixes

tera	T	one trillion	deci	d	one tenth
giga	G	one billion	centi	c	one hundredth
mega	M	one million	milli	m	one thousandth
kilo	k	one thousand	micro	μ	one millionth
hecto	h	one hundred	nano	n	one billionth
deka	da	ten	pico	p	one trillionth

Formulas

$P = a + b + c$	Perimeter of triangle	$C = \pi \cdot d$	Circumference of circle
$P = 2(l + w)$	Perimeter of rectangle	$A = \pi \cdot r^2$	Area of circle
$A = l \cdot w$	Area of rectangle	$V = \frac{4}{3} \cdot \pi \cdot r^3$	Volume of sphere
$A = b \cdot h$	Area of parallelogram	$V = \pi \cdot r^2 \cdot h$	Volume of cylinder
$A = \frac{1}{2} \cdot h \cdot (B+b)$	Area of trapezoid	$V = \frac{1}{3} \cdot \pi \cdot r^2 h$	Volume of cone
$A = \frac{1}{2} \cdot b \cdot h$	Area of triangle	$V = B \cdot h$	Volume of prism
$a^2 + b^2 = c^2$	Pythagorean Theorem		$(B = \text{base area})$
$V = l \cdot w \cdot h$	Volume of rectangular solid	$V = \frac{1}{3} \cdot B \cdot h$	Volume of pyramid

Glossary

absolute value   The distance from a point on the number line to the origin. The absolute value of a number is never negative. We denote absolute value by vertical lines: $|^-5| = 5$; $|5| = 5$; $|0| = 0$.

accuracy   The *more accurate* of two measures is the measure with the smaller relative error.

acute angle   An angle smaller than a right angle.

addend   Any one member of a set of numbers to be added. In the equation $7 + 9 = 16$, 7 and 9 are addends.

additive inverse   Each of two numbers whose sum is zero is said to be the additive inverse of the other.

adjacent angles   Two angles with a common vertex, a common side, and no common interior points. In the figure, $\angle 1$ and $\angle 2$ are adjacent angles.

adjacent sides   Two sides of a polygon with a common vertex.

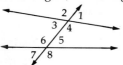

algorithm (algorism)   A computational procedure. For example, the algorithm for finding the quotient of two numbers.

alternate exterior angles   A transversal of two lines forms eight angles as shown. Angles 1, 2, 7, and 8 are exterior angles. Angles 1 and 7, on alternate sides of the transversal, are a pair of alternate exterior angles, as are angles 2 and 8.

alternate interior angles   Two of the four interior angles (3, 4, 5, and 6) shown above which are on alternate sides of the transversal. Angles 3 and 5 form such a pair, as do angles 4 and 6.

altitude (of a triangle)   The segment from any vertex perpendicular to the opposite side. Also, see *height*.

$\overline{BD}$ is the altitude. $\overline{AC}$ is the base.

angle   Two rays which have a common vertex (endpoint).

$\angle ABC$

angle bisector   The ray which divides an angle into two congruent angles. In the figure $\overrightarrow{DB}$ bisects $\angle ADC$.

approximation   A number that is suitably "close" to another number. For example, a decimal approximation for $\frac{2}{9}$ is 0.22. The symbol "$\approx$" denotes "is approximately"; for example $\pi \approx 3.14$.

arc   A part of a circle. Note that three points, instead of two, are used to denote a specific arc since $\overset{\frown}{AB}$ could denote a *minor* arc $\overset{\frown}{ACB}$ or a *major* arc $\overset{\frown}{ADB}$.

area   The measure of a plane region in terms of a chosen unit, usually a square.

arithmetic mean   The sum of a list of numbers divided by the number of addends in the list. (Often called the "average")

associative (grouping) principle   The principle which states that the sum (or product) of three or more numbers is the same regardless of grouping:
$(a + b) + c = a + (b + c)$
or $(a \cdot b) \cdot c = a \cdot (b \cdot c)$

average   See *arithmetic mean*.

base (of numeration)   The term "base" refers to the type of grouping involved in a system of numeration. For example, in base eight: $25_{(8)}$ means 2 eights and 5, and $346_{(8)}$ means 3 sixty-fours, 4 eights, and 6.

base (of a polygon)   Any side of a polygon may be referred to as a base. See figure for *altitude of a triangle*.

base (of a space figure)   See examples below.

Bases of a cylinder   Base of a cone   Base of a pyramid

bisect   To divide into two congruent parts.

center   A (fixed) point of symmetry for a geometric figure. See the figure for *circle*.

centi- A prefix meaning *one hundredth*.

centimeter A unit of length that is $\frac{1}{100}$ of a meter.

central angle An angle with its vertex at the center of the circle.

chord A segment with both endpoints on a circle.

circle The set of all points in a plane which are a specified distance from a fixed point called the *center*.

circumference The distance around a circle. For each circle, the number is the product of its diameter and the number π. The formula is $C = \pi d$.

circumscribed circle A circle drawn through the vertices of a polygon. A circle can be circumscribed about any triangle but only about certain other polygons.

circumscribed polygon If the sides of a polygon are tangent to a circle, then the polygon is circumscribed about the circle. Also, see *inscribed circle*.

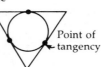

Point of tangency

combination A selection of a group of objects from a set without regard to order. The number of combinations of 2 objects from a set of 3 objects, say {A,B,C} is 3; namely {A,B}, {A,C}, {B,C}.

common factor A number that is a factor of each of two or more given numbers. For example, 3 is a common factor of 6 and 9.

common multiple A number that is a multiple of each of two or more given numbers. For example, 18 is a common multiple of 2, 3, and 9.

commutative (order) principle The principle which states that the sum (or product) of any two numbers is the same regardless of the order in which they are added (or multiplied): $a + b = b + a$ or $a \cdot b = b \cdot a$

complementary angles Two angles whose measures have a sum of 90°.

composite number Any whole number greater than 1 which is not prime. Composite numbers have more than two different factors.

concave figure A non-convex figure.

concentric circles Two or more circles that have the same center.

cone A space figure formed by a closed plane curve and all line segments from a point not in the plane of the curve to all the points of the curve.

congruent angles Angles which have the same measure.

congruent polygons Two figures are congruent if they can be matched so that corresponding angles are congruent and corresponding sides are congruent.

congruent segments Segments which have the same length. We write $\overline{AB} \cong \overline{CD}$.

convex figure A figure is convex if every segment joining any two points on the boundary of the figure contains only points on the figure or in its interior.

coordinate axes Two intersecting perpendicular number lines used for graphing ordered number pairs (*coordinates*).

•(2, 3)

coordinates An ordered number pair matched with a point in the coordinate plane. See the figure for *coordinate axes*.

correspondence A matching of elements in one set with those of another set.

corresponding segments Two segments matched by any one-to-one correspondence between segments of two figures.

cross products In the equation $\frac{a}{b} = \frac{c}{d}$, the products ad and bc are called cross products. Two ratios $\frac{a}{b}$ and $\frac{c}{d}$ are equal if and only if $ad = bc$.

cross section The intersection of a space figure and a plane.

cube (geometry) A regular polyhedron each of whose six faces are squares.

cube (numeration) A number raised to the third power. 8 is the cube of 2 because $2^3 = 8$. Also, to raise a number to the third power.

cylinder The space figure formed by two congruent curves in parallel planes and the

parallel segments connecting corresponding points of the curves.

decagon A 10-sided polygon.

deci- A prefix meaning *one tenth*.

decimeter A unit of length that is $\frac{1}{10}$ of a meter, or 10 centimeters.

decimal (numeral) Any base-ten numeral written using a decimal point.

decimal point The dot that is used in a decimal numeral.

decimal system of numeration A system of numeration in which powers of ten and place value are used.

degree A unit angle that is $\frac{1}{90}$ of a right angle.

deka- A prefix meaning *ten*.

dekameter A unit of length that is 10 meters.

denominator For each fraction $\frac{a}{b}$, b is the denominator.

diagonal A segment connecting two nonconsecutive vertices of a polygon.

diameter Any chord that contains the center of a circle.

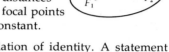

difference The number resulting from subtraction.

digits The basic symbols used in a place-value system of numeration. In base ten, the symbols are 0, 1, 2, 3, 4, 5, 6, 7, 8, and 9.

distributive principle The fundamental principle connecting addition and multiplication. $a \cdot (b + c) = a \cdot b + a \cdot c$.

dividend The number to be divided in a division problem.

```
          3  ← Quotient
      5)17    ← Dividend
         15
Divisor   2  ← Remainder
```

divisible A given number is divisible by a second number if the remainder is zero. If $a = b \cdot c$ with $b \neq 0$ and $c \neq 0$, then a is divisible by either b or c.

division The inverse of the operation of multiplication.

$$\begin{array}{ccc} F & F & P \\ 3 \cdot 4 & = & 12 \end{array} \qquad \begin{array}{ccc} P & F & F \\ 12 \div 4 & = & 3 \\ 12 \div 3 & = & 4 \end{array}$$

divisor See *dividend*.

dodecahedron A polyhedron which has 12 faces. A regular dodecahedron has 12 congruent pentagonal faces.

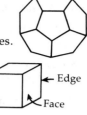

edge A segment that is a side of any face of a space figure. A cube has 12 edges.

element Any member of a set.

ellipse A closed plane curve generated by a point (P) moving in such a way that the sum of the distances from two fixed focal points (F_1 and F_2) is constant.

equality The relation of identity. A statement of equality asserts that two symbols name the same object or number.

equally likely outcomes Outcomes or results that have the same chance of occurring.

equation A mathematical sentence using the equality symbol (=) $7 + n = 9$ is an equation.

equiangular triangle A triangle all of whose angles have the same measure.

equilateral triangle A triangle having all sides the same length.

equivalent decimals Decimals which represent the same number. For example, 0.5, 0.50, and 0.500 are equivalent decimals.

equivalent fractions Fractions which represent the same number such as $\frac{1}{2}$, $\frac{5}{10}$, and $\frac{50}{100}$.

equivalent ratios Two ratios which represent the same fractional number. For example, the ratio 5:10 is the same as 1:2. $\frac{5}{10} = \frac{1}{2}$

estimate An approximation for a given number. Often used in the sense of a rough calculation.

even number A whole-number multiple of 2. The set of even numbers is {0, 2, 4, 6, . . .}.

expanded notation A representation of a number as a sum of powers of ten such as: $3425 = 3 \cdot 10^3 + 4 \cdot 10^2 + 2 \cdot 10^1 + 5 \cdot 10^0$.

exponent A numeral written above and to the right of a mathematical expression to indicate how many times a number is to be used as a factor. For example, in the expression 5^4, the 4 indicates that 5 is to be used as a factor 4 times: $5 \cdot 5 \cdot 5 \cdot 5 = 5^4$

extremes The first and last terms in a proportion written in the form $a:b = c:d$. The numbers a and d are extremes and b and c are called the *means*.

face Any one of the bounding polygonal regions of a space figure. See the figure for *edge*.

factor Any one member of a set of numbers to be multiplied. In the equation $5 \cdot 7 = 35$, 5 and 7 are factors.

factorial If n is a positive whole number, factorial n denoted by $n!$, is defined to be $n! = 1 \cdot 2 \cdot 3 \cdot 4 \cdot \ldots \cdot (n - 2) \cdot (n - 1) \cdot n$. $0!$ is defined to be 1.

factor tree A diagram suggestive of a tree showing the prime factorization of a number.

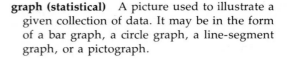

flow chart A diagram which gives instructions in a logical order.

formula A general fact or rule expressed by using symbols. For example, the area of any parallelogram with base b and height h is given by $b \cdot h$. The formula is usually presented with the equation $A = b \cdot h$.

fraction A symbol for a fractional number of the form $\frac{a}{b}$ such that $b \neq 0$.

fractional number The set of non-negative rational numbers.

frequency The number of times an outcome occurs in a probability experiment or the number of times a bit of data occurs in a collection of data.

frequency distribution A set of data in tabular or graphical form which is classified so that the frequency of each class is given.

function A correspondence that associates each element in a first set with a unique element of a second set. Different elements in a first set may possibly be matched with the same element of the second set.

gram A unit of mass. The mass of a one cubic centimeter of water at 4°C.

graph A set of points associated with a given set of numbers or number pairs showing a relation or function.

Graph of $y = 2 \cdot x$

graph (statistical) A picture used to illustrate a given collection of data. It may be in the form of a bar graph, a circle graph, a line-segment graph, or a pictograph.

greatest common factor (GCF) The largest, or greatest, number that is a factor of each of a set of numbers.

greatest possible error Half of the basic unit in which a measurement is given. For example, if a length is given as 18 centimeters to the nearest centimeter, then the basic unit is the centimeter and the greatest possible error is 0.5 centimeter.

hectare A unit of area that is 10 000 square meters.

hecto- A prefix meaning *one hundred*.

height (of a prism) The perpendicular distance between the planes of the parallel faces.

hexagon A 6-sided polygon.

hyperbola The intersection of right circular cone and a plane parallel to the axis of the cone. The curve consists of two non-intersecting branches.

hypotenuse The side of a right triangle opposite the right angle.

icosahedron A polyhedron of 20 faces. A regular icosahedron has equilateral triangles for its faces.

identity element For addition, zero is the identity element since $a + 0 = a$ for any number a. Similarly, for multiplication, 1 is the identity element since $a \cdot 1 = a$.

identity principles For any number a, $a + 0 = a$ and $a \cdot 1 = a$.

improper fraction A fraction whose numerator is greater than or equal to its denominator.

inequality A mathematical statement using either of the symbols $<$ or $>$ such as $\frac{3}{4} < \frac{7}{8}$.

inscribed angle An angle that contains three points of the circle and has its vertex on the circle.

inscribed polygon See *circumscribed circle*.

integers The set consisting of the natural numbers {1, 2, 3, . . .}, the negatives of the natural numbers {⁻1, ⁻2, ⁻3, . . .}, and zero.

intersecting lines Two lines which have a common point.

inverse (operation) Operations which are opposite in effect such as addition and subtraction or multiplication and division.

irrational number A real number that cannot be expressed as the quotient of two integers; a non-rational number. Irrational numbers have infinite nonrepeating decimal representations.

isosceles triangle A triangle with at least two congruent sides.

kilo- A prefix meaning *one thousand*.

kilogram The basic unit of mass in the metric system. 1000 grams.

kilometer A unit of length that is 1000 meters.

least common denominator The least common multiple of the denominators of two or more fractions. For example, the least common denominator of $\frac{5}{6}$ and $\frac{3}{4}$ is 12.

least common multiple (LCM) The smallest non-zero number that is a multiple of each of two or more given numbers. The LCM of 4 and 6 is 12.

legs (of a right triangle)
The perpendicular sides of a right triangle.

length The measure of a segment (or curve) in terms of a chosen unit.

line segment A set of points consisting of two points A and B and all points between them. The symbol $\overline{AB}$ is used to denote a segment.

liter (cubic decimeter) The basic unit of capacity in the metric system. 1000 cubic centimeters.

lowest-terms (simplest) fraction A fraction is in lowest terms if the numerator and denominator of the fraction have no common factor other than 1.

mean See *arithmetic mean*.

means The second and third terms in a proportion written in the form $a:b = c:d$. See *extremes*.

median (of a set) The middle number of a set containing an odd number of elements that are arranged in order. If a set contains an even number of elements, the average of the two middle numbers is the median.

median (of a triangle) The segment from the vertex to the midpoint of the opposite side of a triangle.

meter The basic unit of length in the metric system approximately 1 650 763.73 times the wave length of the orange-red spectral emission line of krypton-86.

midpoint (middle point) A point which divides a segment into two congruent segments.

milli- A prefix meaning *one thousandth*.

minute A unit of angular measure that is $\frac{1}{60}$ of a degree.

mixed decimal numeral A combination of a decimal and a fraction such as $0.4\frac{1}{3}$ and read as "four and one-third tenths."

mixed numeral A numeral such as $4\frac{2}{3}$ indicating the sum of a whole number and a fractional number; $4\frac{2}{3} = 4 + \frac{2}{3}$.

mode The most frequently occurring element of a set. There may be more than one mode of a set.

multiple A first number is a multiple of a second number if there is a whole number that multiplies by the second number to give the first number. For example, 24 is a multiple of 4 and 6 since $4 \times 6 = 24$.

multiplication An operation that combines a first number (*factor*) and a second number (*factor*) to give another number (this result is called the *product* of the two factors).

multiplicative inverse See *reciprocal*.

natural numbers The set of numbers {1, 2, 3, . . .}.

negative integers The set of numbers {⁻1, ⁻2, ⁻3, . . .}.

number pair An ordered pair of numbers such as (3, 4), often coordinates of a point in a plane.

numeral   A symbol for a number.

numerator   For each fraction $\frac{a}{b}$, a is the numerator.

obtuse angle   An angle greater than a right angle and smaller than a straight angle.

octagon   An 8-sided polygon.

octahedron   A polyhedron having eight faces. Each face of a regular octahedron is an equilateral triangle.

odd number   Any number in the set {1, 3, 5, 7, . . .}.

one principle   For any number a, $a \cdot 1 = a$. See *identity principle* for multiplication.

operation   A binary operation like "multiplication" associates each ordered pair of numbers with one number. Usually we speak of the four fundamental operations: addition, subtraction, multiplication, and division.

opposites principle   For any integer a, $a + {}^{-}a = 0$.

origin   The intersection of the coordinate axes; the point associated with the number pair $(0, 0)$.

outcome   A possible result in a probability experiment.

parabola   The intersection of a right circular cone and a plane parallel to an element of the cone.

parallel lines   Lines in the same plane which do not intersect.

parallelogram   A quadrilateral whose opposite sides are parallel.

pentagon   A 5-sided polygon.

percent (%)   Literally means "per hundred." A symbol such as 3% is an abbreviation for "3 per 100" or 0.03.

perimeter   The sum of the lengths of the sides of a polygon.

period   In writing numerals, each set of three digits separated by a space is called a period.

permutation   An ordered selection of a group of objects from a given set. For example, six permutations of 2 objects can be formed from any set of 3 objects.
$$\{A, B, C\} \rightarrow \{A, B\}, \{B, A\}, \{A, C\}, \{C, A\},$$
$$\{B, C\}, \{C, B\}$$

perpendicular bisector
A line which bisects a segment as well as being perpendicular to it.

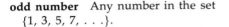

$m \perp$ bis $\overline{AB}$

perpendicular lines   Two intersecting lines that form right angles.

pi (π)   The ratio of the circumference of a circle to its diameter. $\pi \approx 3.14$.

place value   A system used for writing numerals for numbers, using only a definite number of symbols or digits. In the decimal system of numeration each place of a numeral has ten times the value of the place to its right.

plane figure   A set of points in one plane.

point of tangency   If a line and circle intersect in just one point, the intersection is the point of tangency.

polygon   A closed plane figure whose boundary is made up of segments.

polyhedron   A space figure each of whose faces is a polygonal region.

positive integer   Any number in the set {1, 2, 3, . . .}.

power   In the statement $a = b^n$, a is the nth power of b. For example, for $1000 = 10^3$, 1000 is the third power of 10.

prime factorization   An expression of a composite number as a product of prime factors.

prime number   A whole number greater than 1 whose only factors are itself and 1.

prism   A 3-dimensional (space) figure whose bases are congruent polygonal regions in parallel planes and whose faces are parallelograms.

probability   The ratio of the number of times a certain outcome can occur to the number of total possible outcomes.

product   The number $a \cdot b$ which results from applying the multiplication operation to the numbers a and b.

proportion An equation stating that two ratios are equal: $a:b = c:d$ or $\dfrac{a}{b} = \dfrac{c}{d}$.

protractor An instrument for measuring angles.

pyramid A 3-dimensional (space) figure with a polygonal base and triangular lateral faces.

Pythagorean Theorem In any right triangle, the sum of the areas of the squares on the legs is equal to the area of the square on the hypotenuse.

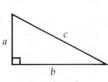

$$a^2 + b^2 = c^2$$

quadrilateral A 4-sided polygon.

quotient The number $a \div b$ (or $b \div a$) which results from applying the division operation to the numbers a and b.

radius Any segment from the center of a circle to a point on the circle.

Radius OA

ratio The ratio of two numbers a and b is their quotient, $\dfrac{a}{b}$.

rational number The quotient of two integers, the divisor not being zero.

ray A half-line together with the point determining it (endpoint).

Ray AB or $\overrightarrow{AB}$

reciprocal If $a \cdot b = 1$, each of the numbers a and b is the reciprocal (multiplicative inverse) of the other. Each non-zero real number has a unique reciprocal. Zero has no reciprocal.

rectangle A parallelogram with four right angles.

reflection A rigid motion that maps the points of a plane onto itself. If point P is reflected in a line with a reflection image P_1, then the line is the perpendicular bisector of $\overline{PP_1}$.

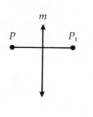

region All the points in the part of a plane bounded by a simple closed curve. The interior of this curve is a region.

regular polygon A polygon that is equiangular and equilateral; for example, a square.

remainder In whole-number division, if dividend D is divided by divisor d and the relation $D = (q \cdot d) + r$ is obtained where $0 < r < d$, then r is called the remainder. Note that $r = 0$ if d is a factor of D (see *dividend*). Also, the difference in a subtraction problem.

repeating decimal A decimal whose digits from some point on repeat periodically. Examples: 6.2835835 . . . and 0.3333333 . . . .. These examples may also be written $6.28\overline{35}$ and $0.\overline{3}$ respectively.

rhombus An equilateral parallelogram which is not a square.

right angle An angle whose measure is 90°.

right triangle A triangle that has one right angle.

rigid motion A transformation of the points of the plane that preserves all distances.

Roman numerals The numerals I, V, X, L, C, D, M, and combinations of these numerals used in the Roman numeration system.

rotation A rigid motion in which the points of the plane are turned about a fixed point.

rounding A process of replacing a number by an approximation (another number) with fewer significant digits. For example, 456 789 rounded to the nearest thousand would be 457 000.

scale drawing A drawing of an object made so that distances in the drawing are proportional to actual distances. A scale of 1:10 indicates that distances in the drawing are $\frac{1}{10}$ of the actual distances.

scalene triangle A triangle with no pair of congruent sides.

scattergram A graph of distinct points representing data in order to analyze whether or not the data can be related by some formula or function.

scientific notation A notation used for writing any number as the product of a power of ten and a number between 1 and 10 (including 1).

second A unit of angular measure that is $\frac{1}{60}$ of a minute.

segment A set of points consisting of two points A and B and all points between them.

A ●————————● B

Segment AB or $\overline{AB}$

semicircle An arc that is exactly half a circle. One of two arcs cut off by a diameter.

set A group or collection of objects.

similar polygons Two figures are similar if they can be matched so that corresponding angles are congruent and corresponding sides have the same ratio.

skew lines Lines that are not in the same plane. They do not intersect, yet they are not parallel.

space The set of all points. This term usually denotes a 3-dimensional quality. We also refer to a plane as 2-dimensional space and a line as a 1-dimensional space.

space figure A geometric figure whose points are not all in the same plane.

sphere The set of all points in space at a fixed distance from a given point.

square root If $x^2 = y$, then x is the square root of y. $\sqrt{4} = 2$

statistics The science of analyzing numerical information.

straightedge An unmarked ruler.

subtend Literally means "to be opposite to." For example, central angles and inscribed angles in a circle are said to subtend the arcs they cut off. Also, chords and arcs in a circle subtend the angles of a circle.

$\overarc{AB}$ subtends $\angle AOB$ or $\overline{AB}$ is subtended by $\angle AOB$

subtraction The operation that is the inverse of the addition operation.

A	A	S		S	A	A
				11	− 5	= 6
5	+ 6	= 11		11	− 6	= 5

sum The number $a + b$ which results when the operation of addition is applied to the numbers a and b.

supplementary angles Two angles whose measures have a sum of 180°.

surface area The total area of the polygonal regions (faces) of a polyhedron.

symmetric figure A plane figure which can be divided into two congruent parts by a line (of symmetry).

tangent A line which intersects a circle in just one point.

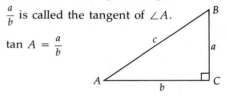

$\overrightarrow{AB}$ is a tangent to circle O at point A.

tangent ratio In right triangle ABC the ratio $\frac{a}{b}$ is called the tangent of $\angle A$.

$$\tan A = \frac{a}{b}$$

terminating decimal A decimal such as 0.5, 1.0, 1.24, 0.0307, and so on, that represents the quotient of a whole number and a power of 10.
$$0.5 = \frac{5}{10}, \; 1.24 = \frac{124}{10^2}, \; 0.0307 = \frac{307}{10^4}$$

tessellation A repeated pattern of geometric figures which will completely "cover a plane" without any gaps or overlapping.

tetrahedron A polyhedron having 4 faces.

translation A rigid motion in which each point of the plane is moved the same distance and in the same direction.

transversal A line which intersects two or more lines.

trapezoid A quadrilateral with one pair of parallel sides.

bases, or parallel sides

triangle A 3-sided polygon.

unit The object adopted as a standard of measurement. For length, we choose a *unit* segment; for area, we choose a *unit square*; and for volume, a *cube*.

variable A symbol, usually a letter, used to represent any number in a given set. For example, we may say: "If x is a whole number, then $2 \cdot x$ is an even number."

vertex A point that two rays of an angle have in common. Also, the common point of any two sides of a polygon.

vertical angles Two pairs of angles formed by two intersecting lines. Angles 1 and 3 (and 2 and 4) are vertical angles.

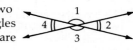

volume The measure of a space figure in terms of a chosen unit.

whole numbers Any number in the set $\{0, 1, 2, 3, \ldots\}$.

zero principle The principle which states that for any number a, $a + 0 = a$. Also, see *identity element* for addition.

Selected Answers For

Mathematics
In Our World

7.1 The Decimal System

Page 3
5. 35 000 000 000   **7.** 206 000 000 000
9. 537 000

Page 4
1. 38 000   **3.** 3 943 000   **5.** 36 000
7. 10 000

Page 5
1. 900   **3.** 92 400   **5.** 437 000
6. 8000   **9.** 58 000   **11.** 83 800
13. 580 000   **15.** 760 000   **17.** 840 000
19. 100 000   **21.** 950 000
23. 6 960 000   **25.** 500   **27.** 4000
29. 50 000   **31.** 840 000   **33.** 3000

Page 6
1. 2 tenths, 8 hundredths, 1 thousandth
3. 0 tenths, 7 hundredths, 5 thousandths
5. 0 tenths, 4 hundredths, 0 thousandths

Page 7
1. 4 tenths   **3.** 8 hundredths
5. 1 tenth   **7.** 1 ten thousandth
9. 0 hundredths   **11.** 6 ten thousandths
13. 6 hundredths   **15.** 4 ten thousandths

Page 8
1. <   **3.** >   **5.** <   **7.** <   **9.** >
11. <   **13.** >   **15.** <

Page 9
1. A   **3.** A   **5.** C   **7.** A

Page 10
1. 13.3   **3.** 5.9   **5.** 386.1   **7.** 16.1

Page 11
1. 8.26   **3.** 8.51   **5.** 53.66   **7.** 2.97
13. 9.144   **15.** 5.031   **17.** 1.915
19. 7.348   **25.** 28   **27.** 88   **33.** 7
35. 0.4

Page 12
1. $8 \cdot 10^6$ **3.** $3 \cdot 10^9$ **5.** $6 \cdot 10^8$
7. $7 \cdot 10^{10}$ **9.** $9 \cdot 10^{11}$ **11.** $2 \cdot 10^{13}$

Page 13
1. $(3 \cdot 10^7) + (6 \cdot 10^6)$
3. $(5 \cdot 10^5) + (2 \cdot 10^4)$
5. $(1 \cdot 10^6) + (9 \cdot 10^5) + (7 \cdot 10^3) +$
$(4 \cdot 10^2) + (2 \cdot 10)$ **7.** $(4 \cdot 10^5) +$
$(5 \cdot 10^4) + (2 \cdot 10^3) + (1 \cdot 10^2) + (9 \cdot 10)$

Page 15
1. $3.1 \cdot 10^3$ **3.** $5.53 \cdot 10^5$
9. $4.6 \cdot 10^7$ **11.** $3.814 \cdot 10^8$
13. $2.5 \cdot 10^9$ **15.** $3.02 \cdot 10^7$
17. $8 \cdot 10^2$

7.2 Operations and Expressions

Page 19
1. 2   **3.** 9   **5.** 64   **7.** 66   **9.** 24
11. 6

Page 20
1. 56   **3.** 2   **5.** 2

Page 21
1. 17   **3.** 7   **5.** 16   **17.** 72
19. 7   **21.** 210

Page 23
1. 72   **3.** 30   **5.** 10   **17.** 19
19. 13   **21.** 2   **29.** 3   **35.** 5
41. 11

Page 25
1. 60   **3.** 40   **5.** 1800   **13.** 12
19. 40

7.3 Addition and Subtraction

Page 28
1. true   **3.** true   **7.** true   **9.** false
13. commutative   **15.** associative

Page 29
1. 127   **3.** 821   **5.** 1223   **7.** 12 185
13. 1536   **15.** 18 575   **17.** 24 398

Page 30
1. 225.1   3. 3.921

Page 31
1. 173.20   3. 194.05   5. 144.19
7. 179.5   9. 210.2   17. 97.52
19. 47.675   21. 74.955

Page 32
1. 358   3. 408   5. 1338

Page 33
1. 1517   3. 3982   5. 2239   7. 3242
9. 6049   11. 1342   13. 6457
15. 567

Page 34
1. 4.76   3. 35.77

Page 35
1. 484   3. 1.59   5. 5035   7. 2894
9. 7322   11. 6.369   13. 63.36
15. 3.407   25. 15.65   27. 3.862

Page 36
1. $n = 36$ 3. $c = 69$ 5. $r = 84$
7. $y = 656$ 9. $b = 1000$
11. $x = 29.80$ 13. $y = 7070$
15. $m = 61.97$

Page 37
1. $c = 4$ 3. $y = 8.8$ 5. $t = 0.75$
7. $b = 37$ 9. $n = 3.2$ 11. $x = 451$
13. $d = 3834$ 15. $n = 8$

7.4 Using Your Skills

Page 41
1. 1.8kg 3. height, 5 cm; mass, 2.4kg

Page 42
1. Estimate: $900; exact: $893
3. Estimate: $500; exact: $545

Page 43
9. Estimate: $500; exact: $496
13. Estimate: $600; exact: $575
17. Estimate: $6000, exact: $6005

Page 44
1. Estimate: $2.00; exact: $1.94
3. Estimate: $1.00; exact: $0.97
5. Estimate: $2.50; exact: $2.46

Page 45
1. Estimate: $3.00; exact: $2.63
5. Estimate: $13.00; exact: $12.57

Page 46
1. $5.20   3. $11.39   5. $4.57
7. $13.94   9. $8.27   11. $6.75
13. $2.34   15. $9.57

Page 47
1. $5.74; $5.97   3. $15.61; $16.23
5. $19.06; $19.82   7. $12.93

Pages 48–49
1. 138 km   3. 82 km   5. 209 km
9. Route B by 42 km

7.5 Geometry—Construction and Measurement

Page 53
3. F, e 5. C, b 9. trapezoid

Page 59
1. $x = 80°$ 3. $x = 90°$ 7. 57°

Page 61
5. $\angle 3, \angle 5, \angle 7$

Page 62
1. 8   3. $m(\angle 2) = 180° - m(\angle 1)$,
$180° - 45° = 135°$

Page 63
1. $m(\angle 1) = 120°$, $m(\angle 2) = 60°$
5. central angle: 36°; vertex angle: 144°
7. central angle: 24°; vertex angle: 156°

Page 64
1. central angle: 30°; inscribed angle: 15°
3. central angle: 60°; inscribed angle: 30°

Page 65
1. $\angle B = 23°$ 3. $\angle B = 80°$ 7. 106°

8.1   Multiplication

Page 70
1. commutative principle of multiplication
3. false   5. false   7. false

Page 71
1. 40   3. 800   5. 170   17. 560
19. 240   21. 600   27. 12 000
29. 56 000   31. 640   37. $5x$ 39. t
41. $9q$ 43. $18r$ 45. $10n$

Page 72
1. 432   3. 27 468   5. 49 425
7. 474 804   9. 2 183 586

Page 73
1. 117   3. 1925   5. 2146   7. 44 826
9. 18 000   23. 4025   25. 10 304
27. 12 551

Page 74
1. 0.08   3. 0.35   5. 0.36   7. 0.25

Page 75
5. 0.42   7. 0.16   9. 0.0001
11. 0.012   13. 0.021   15. 0.18
17. 0.81   19. 0.0021   21. 0.09
23. 0.006   25. 0.24

Page 76
1. 15.04   3. 15.04   5. 0.1504
7. 3.8874   9. 12.768

Page 77
1. 3.04   3. 4.14   5. 1.38   7. 0.2656
9. 43.848   11. 2.752   33. 49.58888
35. 22.61884

Page 78
1. $n = 30$ 3. $c = 88$ 5. $r = 21$
7. $y = 24$ 9. $n = 3.6$ 11. $c = 1.0$

Page 79
1. $n = 30$ 3. $y = 180$ 5. $d = 160$
7. $r = 54$ 9. $a = 150$ 11. $d = 50$
13. $x = 16.32$ 15. $y = 15.7$
17. $s = 700.8$ 19. $c = 44.145$
21. $u = 9.24$

8.2   Division

Page 82
1. 9   3. 4   5. 2   7. 5   9. 3
11. 8   13. 7   15. 9

Page 83
31. 50   33. 100   35. 6   37. 3
39. 600   41. 500

Page 84
1. 43 R16   3. 206 R14   5. 27 R103
7. 70 R426

Page 85
1. 64 R21   3. 76 R1   5. 23 R18
7. 84   9. 326 R13   11. 147
13. 309 R70   15. 408   17. 28 R127

Page 86
1. 3.75   3. 5.375   5. 0.4375
7. 0.47

Page 87
1. 7.75   3. 4.7   5. 0.49   7. 75.6
9. 1.5   11. 3.62   13. 7.83   15. 0.28
17. 0.01

Page 88
1. 4.24   3. 21.75   5. 0.12   7. 21.23

Page 89
1. 15.7   3. 56.1   5. 1266.7   7. 0.9
9. 5.3   11. 36.5   17. 8.62   19. 6.28
21. 180.56   23. 2.77   25. 7.78
27. 0.25

Page 90
1. $x = 6$ 3. $n = 10$ 5. $y = 8$
7. $t = 10$ 9. $b = 7$ 11. $z = 0.02$
13. $r = 700$ 15. $t = 7$

Page 91
1. $x = 80$ 3. $d = 6$ 5. $r = 2$
7. $x = 10$ 9. $b = 5$ 11. $t = 80$
13. $r = 0.5$ 15. $x = 0.45$ 17. $y = 7.3$
25. $x = 78$ 27. $x = 26\ 692$

8.3   Using Your Skills

Page 95
1. B

Page 96
1. C   3. D   5. F   7. E

Page 97
1. $r + 12$ 5. $n + 4$ 7. $7n$
9. $n - 10$ 11. $n + 8$ 13. $15 + n$

Page 98
1. $n + 5 = 32, n = 27$
3. $8n = 72, n = 9$ 5. $7n = 63, n = 9$

Page 99
1. $n + 8 = 28, n = 20$ 3. $n + 3 = 12$,
$n = 9$ 5. $\frac{n}{12} = 8, n = 96$

Page 100
1. 45   3. It is necessary to know either
the number of student tickets sold or the
number of adult tickets sold.

Page 101
1. 155   3. A more complete list of
homeroom class enrollment is needed.
5. 27

Page 102
1. **B**; $83 \cdot 19 = d, d = 1577$ km

Page 103
1. Estimate: 90 km/h; $r \cdot 6 = 546$,
$r = 91$ km/h

Page 104
1. $n = 2$ 3. $a = 6$ 5. $s = 4$

Page 105
1. $c = 5$ 3. $p = 5$ 5. $x = 9$
7. $s = 2$ 9. $a = 5$ 11. $n = 6$
13. $p = 10$ 15. $n = 9$

Pages 106–107
1. $5x + 5 = 45; x = 8$
3. $2n + 80 = 274; n = 97$
5. $19b + 17 = 701; b = 36$
7. $s = 0.25$

8.4   Measurement Concepts

Page 111
1. cm   3. m   5. cm   11. 10
13. 1000   15. 100

Page 112
1. 138.4 cm   3. 1.384 m   5. 642.8 cm
7. 742   9. 45   11. 0.268   13. 320
15. 2.37

Page 113
1. 7658.9   5. 4.37   7. 3246   13. cm
17. dam

Page 114
1. m^2 3. cm^2

Page 115
1. $A = 1000$ m^2 3. $A = 10$ hectares

Page 116
1. $V = 108$ m^3

Page 117
1. 40 560 cm³, 40 560 mL, 40.56 L
5. $V = 18$ cm³, 0.018 L

Page 118
1. kg   3. g   5. t   7. kg
9. mg

Page 119
1. 7 384 000   3. 8000   5. 645
7. 1   9. 5768   15. dag   17. g
25. 250 g

Page 120
1. B 35°C   3. B 220°C   5. A 5°C
7. A 130°C

Page 121
1. 3600   3. 1   5. 319
11. 5 h 13.5 min

Page 122
1. 1.53 cm   5. 0.05 cm   9. 29.3 cm

Page 123
1. 2   3. 4   7. 235 mm²

Page 126
1. 0.1   3. 1.0   7. 35.81
11. $4.72 \cdot 10^8$ 15. 4200
19. $a = 12\ 203$ 21. $z = 3506$
23. $r = 2175$ 33. $g = 6.37$ rounded to
nearest hundredth   35. $n = 5.54$

Page 131
1. $0.\overline{6}$ 3. $0.\overline{27}$ 5. $1.8\overline{3}$ 7. $1.2\overline{27}$
13. $0.83\frac{1}{3}$ 15. $1.66\frac{2}{3}$

Page 132
1. yes   3. yes   5. yes   7. no
11. yes   13. yes

Page 133
1. $\frac{3}{4}$ 3. $\frac{3}{8}$ 5. $\frac{4}{5}$ 7. $\frac{4}{5}$ 9. $\frac{5}{6}$
11. $\frac{5}{6}$ 13. $\frac{2}{3}$ 15. $\frac{4}{5}$

Page 134
1. $\frac{7}{20}$ 3. $\frac{3}{25}$ 5. $\frac{11}{20}$ 7. $\frac{1}{8}$ 9. $\frac{1}{2}$
11. $\frac{1}{50}$ 13. $\frac{2}{25}$ 15. $\frac{7}{50}$

Page 135
1. $\frac{2}{3}$ 3. $\frac{4}{9}$ 5. $\frac{10}{33}$ 7. $\frac{6}{11}$
9. $\frac{2}{11}$ 11. $\frac{3}{11}$

Page 136
1. $8\frac{1}{3}$ 3. $6\frac{1}{6}$ 5. $8\frac{2}{5}$ 7. $8\frac{2}{4} = 8\frac{1}{2}$
9. $5\frac{6}{8} = 5\frac{3}{4}$ 11. 8

Page 137
1. $\frac{43}{8}$ 3. $\frac{13}{8}$ 5. $\frac{11}{4}$ 7. $\frac{38}{5}$
9. $\frac{23}{4}$ 11. $\frac{27}{10}$ 27. $1\frac{1}{3}$

Page 139
1. $<$ 3. $<$ 5. $>$ 7. $<$ 9. $<$
11. $<$ 13. $>$ 15. $>$ 25. $>$
27. $<$

9.1   Fractional Numbers

Page 128
1. $\frac{1}{3}$ 3. $\frac{1}{5}$ 5. $\frac{3}{4}$

Page 129
1. $\frac{2}{3}$ 3. $\frac{2}{4}$ 5. $\frac{1}{3}$

Page 130
1. 0.25   3. 0.35   5. 0.3125
7. 0.4   9. 1.5   11. 0.7   13. 0.34
15. 1.25

9.2   Computing with Fractions

Page 144
1. $\frac{7}{8}$ 3. $\frac{22}{24} = \frac{11}{12}$ 5. $\frac{23}{30}$
7. $\frac{25}{24} = 1\frac{1}{24}$ 9. $\frac{19}{24}$

Page 145
1. $15\frac{5}{8}$ 3. $16\frac{1}{3}$ 5. $10\frac{7}{12}$
7. $111\frac{8}{6} = 112\frac{1}{3}$ 9. $84\frac{3}{8}$ 11. $127\frac{1}{4}$

Page 146
1. $\frac{3}{8}$ 3. $\frac{1}{6}$ 5. $\frac{7}{12}$ 7. $7\frac{1}{4}$
9. $4\frac{13}{24}$

Page 147
1. $\frac{1}{6}$　3. $\frac{5}{12}$　5. $\frac{1}{15}$　7. $\frac{3}{8}$　9. $\frac{8}{15}$
11. $\frac{3}{10}$　13. $6\frac{13}{24}$　15. $2\frac{19}{24}$

Page 148
1. $e = \frac{1}{3}$　3. $h = \frac{1}{2}$　5. $i = \frac{5}{12}$
7. $a = \frac{1}{2}$　9. $c = \frac{7}{12}$

Page 149
1. $g = \frac{1}{5}$　3. $m = \frac{7}{16}$　5. $r = \frac{7}{12}$
7. $s = \frac{1}{20}$　9. $i = 4\frac{1}{6}$　21. $\frac{4}{3}$ or $1\frac{1}{3}$
23. $\frac{2}{7}$

Page 150
1. $e = 4$　3. $i = 1\frac{1}{15}$　5. $k = 1\frac{1}{9}$
7. $a = 1$　9. $b = 2$　11. $g = \frac{1}{2}$

Page 151
1. $c = 1\frac{7}{11}$　3. $i = 2\frac{4}{5}$　5. $m = 1\frac{19}{32}$
7. $a = 2\frac{3}{4}$　9. $g = 1\frac{3}{5}$

Page 153
1. $6\frac{7}{12}$ cans　3. $2\frac{5}{8}$ cans of white paint
5. $1\frac{2}{3}$ cans of red paint and $7\frac{1}{2}$ cans of yellow;
$9\frac{1}{6}$ cans of orange were made

Pages 154–155
1. $\frac{3}{4} \cdot 16 = 12$ liters　5. 55 liters
9. $60\frac{1}{2}$ liters

9.3　Ratio and Proportion

Page 158
1. 4:1 or $\frac{4}{1}$　3. 4:8 or $\frac{4}{8}$　5. 4:4 or $\frac{4}{4}$

Page 159
Answers may vary. Sample answers given.
1. $\frac{4}{1} = \frac{8}{2} = \frac{12}{3} = \frac{16}{4}$　5. $\frac{4}{5} = \frac{8}{10} = \frac{12}{15} = \frac{16}{20}$
7. $\frac{4}{4} = \frac{8}{8} = \frac{12}{12} = \frac{16}{16}$　11. $\frac{12}{16} = \frac{21}{28}$

Page 160
1. $n = 15$　3. $n = 26$　5. $n = 51$
7. $n = 21.6$

Page 161
1. $\frac{5}{4} = \frac{n}{60}$, $n = 75$ swings per minute; $\frac{5}{4} = \frac{1}{n}$,
$n = 0.8$, period is 0.8 second　3. $\frac{3}{4} = \frac{1}{n}$,
$n = 1.33$, period is 1.33 seconds　5. $\frac{6}{2} = \frac{1}{n}$,
$n = 0.33$, period is 0.33 second

Page 162
1. 23¢　3. 12¢　5. 39¢　7. 19.6¢
9. 9.5¢

Page 163
1. 25¢, 3 baskets for 69¢ (23¢ each) is lower
in price.　3. 1.4 kg for $1.19 (85¢ per kg)
is lower in price, 85.5¢ per kg

Pages 164–165
1. $\frac{15}{2} = \frac{x}{26}$, $x = 195$　3. $\frac{3}{8} = \frac{x}{120}$, $x = 45$

Page 166
1. $\frac{1}{95} = \frac{6.2}{x}$, $x = 589$ km

Page 167
Note: Degree of measurement accuracy will
cause answers to vary.　1. $12 \cdot 1.2 = 14.4$ m
3. $7.4 \cdot 1.2 = 8.88$ m

9.4　Congruent and Similar Triangles

Page 171
1. $\overline{AB} \cong \overline{ED}$, $\overline{BC} \cong \overline{EF}$, $\overline{AC} \cong \overline{DF}$, $\angle B \cong \angle E$,
$\angle A \cong \angle D$, $\angle C \cong \angle F$　5. $\overline{HG} \cong \overline{PQ}$,
$\overline{GI} \cong \overline{PR}$, $\overline{HI} \cong \overline{QR}$, $\angle G \cong \angle P$, $\angle I \cong \angle R$,
$\angle H \cong \angle Q$

Page 173
1. not congruent　3. $\triangle MNO \cong \triangle TPS$

Page 175
1. $\triangle ABC \cong \triangle DEF$　5. not congruent

Page 177
1. $\triangle ABC \cong \triangle DEF$　5. SAS　7. ASA

Page 178
1. $\triangle ABC \sim \triangle DEF$, $\frac{2}{6} = \frac{3}{9} = \frac{4}{12}$
3. not similar

Page 179
1. $\frac{8}{16} = \frac{12}{t}$, $t = 24$ 5. $\frac{5}{6} = \frac{h}{50}$, $h = 41\frac{2}{3}$

Page 180
1. $\frac{h}{3} = \frac{23}{4.5}$, $h = 15.\overline{3}$ m

Page 181
1. $\frac{d}{12} = \frac{21}{14}$, $d = 18$ m

Page 182
1. $\tan 43° \approx 0.9$

Page 183
1. $a = 50.4$ cm   5. $b = 44.0$ m

Page 184
1. 0.532   3. 1.000   9. 53°
11. 67°

Page 185
1. $h = 5.32$ m   5. 26°

Page 188
1. 0.6   3. 0.125   7. $\frac{3}{4}$ 11. $2\frac{2}{3}$
17. $\frac{25}{4}$ 21. $<$ 25. $\frac{9}{8} = 1\frac{1}{8}$ 31. $\frac{1}{2}$
35. $n = 12$

10.1 Percent Concepts

Page 190
1. 6%   3. 32%   5. 17%

Page 191
1. 33%   3. 9%   5. 19%   9. 0.59, 59%   11. $\frac{16}{100}$, 16%

Page 192
1. 0.08   3. 0.66   5. 0.83
7. 0.031   9. 0.674   11. 0.042

Page 193
1. 16%   3. 38%   5. 83%
7. 18.7%   9. 1.8%   11. 138%
13. 109%

Page 194
1. 50%   3. 30%   5. 70%
7. $16\frac{2}{3}\%$ 9. $58\frac{1}{3}\%$ 11. $31\frac{1}{4}\%$

Page 195
1. 66.7%   3. 53.3%   5. 51.9%
7. 63.3%   9. 42.9%   11. 54.2%

Page 196
1. $\frac{1}{8}$ 3. $\frac{1}{3}$ 5. $\frac{2}{3}$ 7. $\frac{1}{6}$ 9. $\frac{3}{80}$
11. $\frac{7}{8}$

Page 197
1. $\frac{1}{5}$ 3. $\frac{3}{5}$ 5. $\frac{4}{5}$ 7. $\frac{3}{4}$ 9. $\frac{17}{200}$

Page 198
1. 112%   3. 101%   5. 300%
7. 110%   9. 120%   11. 225%
13. 240%   15. 165%

Page 199
1. 1.25   3. 1.08   5. 1.50   7. 5.00
9. 1.77   21. $1\frac{4}{5}$ 23. $1\frac{1}{4}$ 25. $1\frac{1}{10}$

Page 201
1. 80%   3. 20%

10.2 Types of Percent Problems

Page 203
1. 60 ml   3. $\frac{1}{4}$

Page 204
1. 120   3. 7.5   5. 15   7. 5
9. 5.775

Page 205
1. 75　3. 72　5. 14　7. 66
13. 63.46　17. $x = 15$　19. $x = 374.4$
21. $x = 89.7$

Page 206
1. 20%　3. $16\frac{2}{3}\%$　5. $56\frac{1}{4}\%$　7. 90%

Page 207
1. 25%　3. 20%　5. 80%　7. 7%

Page 208
1. 240　3. 15

Page 209
1. $n = 90$　3. $n = 58$　5. $n = 170$
11. $0.25n = 10$, $n = 40$　13. $0.04n = 20$, $n = 500$

Page 220
1. $I = \$140.00$　3. $I = \$20.00$
5. $I = \$204.60$

Page 221
1. $300, $1300　3. $45, $295
5. $24 000, $44 000

Page 222
1. Unpaid balance: $215.50, Interest: $3.23, New balance: $218.73　3. Unpaid balance: $111.66, Interest: $1.67, New balance: $113.33

Page 223
1. $100, $1.50, $101.50　3. $78.45, $1.18, $79.63　5. $301.92, $4.53, $306.45
7. $28.44, $0.43, $28.87　9. $144.22, $2.16, $146.38

10.3　Using Your Skills

Page 214
1. C 40¢　3. A $12.00
Estimates may vary.
7. $40　9. $30　11. $10

Page 215
1. C 50%
Estimates may vary.
5. 25%　7. 50%　9. 20%

Page 216
1. 47 g, 94%

Page 217
1. 43 g, 86%　3. 48 g, 96%
5. 36 g, 36%

Page 218
1. Discount: $3.50, Sale price: $31.50
3. Discount: $42.00, Sale price: $42.00

Page 219
1. $63.71　3. $10.36

10.4　Measurement Formulas

Page 227
1. $9.42 \approx 9$ cm　3. $18.84 \approx 20$ cm
5. $12.56 \approx 10$ cm　7. $75.36 \approx 75$ cm
9. $38.622 \approx 38.6$ m

Page 228
Each answer is rounded to the appropriate significant digits.　1. 60 m²
3. 108.64 m² ≈ 110 m²
5. 63.92 m² ≈ 64 m²　9. 621 m² ≈ 620 m²
11. 232 cm² ≈ 200 cm²

Page 229
Each answer is rounded to the appropriate significant digits.　1. 24 m² ≈ 20 m²
3. 29.16 m² ≈ 29 m²　7. 910 m²
9. 1050 m² ≈ 1100 m²　15. $220.41

Page 230
Each answer is rounded to the appropriate significant digits.　1. 45 cm² ≈ 50 cm²
3. 1053 m² ≈ 1100 m²　5. 2.12625 cm² ≈ 2.1 cm²　7. 157.035 cm² ≈ 160 cm²

Page 231
1. 80.5 cm² ≈ 80 cm²
3. 32.4 cm² ≈ 32 cm²
5. 42.4656 m² ≈ 42.5 m²

Page 232
1. 50.24 cm² ≈ 50 cm²
3. 40.6944 m² ≈ 41 m²
5. 78.5 cm² ≈ 80 cm²
7. 452.16 m² ≈ 450 m²

Page 233
1. Area of table top ≈ 0.5024 m²,
area of rug ≈ 2.0096 m². The area of the
rug is 4 times the area of the table top.

Page 234
1. Area of each square = 36 cm²
Surface area = 216 cm² ≈ 200 cm²
3. Area of square = 144 cm²
Area of each triangle = 62.4 cm²
Surface area = 393.6 cm² ≈ 390 cm²

Page 235
1. 1807.6 cm²   3. 61.8 m²   5. 6280 m²

Page 236
1. 128. cm² ≈ 100 cm²
3. 417.6 cm³ ≈ 420 cm³
5. 2520 cm³ ≈ 2500 cm³

Page 237
1. 162 cm³ ≈ 200 cm³
3. 168 cm³ ≈ 170 cm³
5. 57 375 cm³ ≈ 57 000 m³
7. 102 808.33 m³ ≈ 100 000 m³

Page 238
1. 2411.52 cm³ ≈ 2000 cm³
3. 129.368 cm³ ≈ 130 cm³
5. 1256 cm³ ≈ 1000 cm³

Page 239
Answers are rounded to nearest hundredth.
1. 19 625 m³ ≈ 20 000 m³
3. 104.06 cm³ ≈ 100 cm³
5. 4.51 m³ ≈ 4.5 m³

Page 242
1. 75%   3. 33%   5. 5%   17. $\frac{1}{8}$
19. $\frac{1}{5}$ 21. 172.8   23. 49.8
31. 31.8%   33. 10%
37. $0.35n = 189$, $n = 540$

11.1 Adding and Subtracting Positive and Negative Numbers

Page 245
1. ⁻7   3. ⁻13   5. ⁻10   7. 9
17. $n = 0$ 19. $n = 5$ 21. $n = 0$

Page 246
1. ⁻3   3. ⁻16   5. ⁻84   9. ⁻6
11. 2

Page 247
1. <   3. >   5. >   7. <   9. <
17. ⁻7 < ⁻1 < 4 or 4 > ⁻1 > ⁻7
19. ⁻20 < ⁻11 < ⁻10 or ⁻10 > ⁻11 > ⁻20

Page 248
1. 4   3. 4   5. ⁻3   7. ⁻7
9. 10   11. ⁻3   13. ⁻7   15. ⁻3

Page 249
1. ⁻5   3. 1   5. ⁻4   7. ⁻9
9. 4   11. 2   13. ⁻4   15. ⁻9
33. $n = $⁻6   35. $n = 7$ 37. $n = $⁻4
39. $n = $⁻10

Page 251
1. 1   3. ⁻11   5. 4   7. ⁻2
13. ⁻14   15. ⁻9   17. 1   25. ⁻7
27. 1   35. ⁻4   37. ⁻6   39. ⁻5

Page 252
1. 7 + ⁻2 = 5   3. 14 + ⁻6 = 8
5. ⁻2 + 10 = 8   7. ⁻10 + 6 = ⁻4
9. 8 + ⁻4 = 4

Page 253
1. $n = {}^-2$ 3. $n = 9$ 5. $n = {}^-6$
7. $n = {}^-3$ 9. $n = 1$ 11. $n = {}^-8$
13. $n = 9$ 15. $n = 13$ 33. ${}^-10$
35. 11   45. 13   47. ${}^-4$ 49. ${}^-8$
51. ${}^-10$

Page 254
1. $6 + {}^-2 = 4$ 3. $5 + 7 = 12$
5. $3 + {}^-10 = {}^-7$ 7. ${}^-5 + 2 = {}^-3$
9. $9 + 4 = 13$ 11. ${}^-15 + 9 = {}^-6$

Page 255
1. 7   3. ${}^-4$ 5. ${}^-11$ 7. ${}^-2$
9. 1   11. 35   13. 1   15. ${}^-10$
45. $n = {}^-9$ 47. $n = 4$ 49. $n = 15$

Page 256
1. 2.2   3. 4.0   5. ${}^-7.8$ 7. ${}^-6.38$
9. 0.23   11. ${}^-\frac{1}{2}$ 13. ${}^-2\frac{1}{3}$ 17. 4.7
19. ${}^-2.1$

Page 257
1. 10.1°C   3. 13 200   5. ${}^-14.4$°C

11.2   Other Operations with Positive and Negative Numbers

Page 261
1. ${}^-15$°C, ${}^-5 \cdot 3 = {}^-15$ 3. 12°C, $6 \cdot 2 = 12$
11. ${}^-35$ 13. 27   15. ${}^-30$ 17. ${}^-54$

Page 262
1. $n = {}^-5$ 3. $n = {}^-2$ 5. $n = {}^-10$

Page 263
1. 42   3. ${}^-48$ 5. 27   7. 9
9. ${}^-48$ 11. 0   33. 24   35. ${}^-24$
37. ${}^-30$ 43. ${}^-64$ 45. 16

Page 264
1. ${}^-3 \cdot {}^-3 = 9$ 3. $6 \cdot {}^-2 = {}^-12$
5. ${}^-8 \cdot 4 = {}^-32$ 7. $1 \cdot {}^-7 = {}^-7$
9. $7 \cdot {}^-5 = {}^-35$

Page 265
1. ${}^-2$ 3. 2   5. 8   7. 4   9. ${}^-3$
11. 7   27. $21 \div {}^-7 = {}^-3$ 29. $54 \div 6 = 9$
39. ${}^-49$ 41. ${}^-2524$ 43. ${}^-7553$

Page 266
1. 11   3. ${}^-6$ 5. 0

Page 267
1. 24   3. ${}^-7$ 5. $n = 36$ 7. $n = {}^-6$
9. $n = {}^-6$ 17. $n = 1$

Page 268
1. 7   3. 4   5. 100   7. 9   9. 14
11. 4   13. 17   27. $x = 10$ or $x = {}^-10$
29. $x = {}^-4$ or $x = 4$

Page 269
1. 5   3. 7   5. 2   7. 20   9. 8
17. 2   19. 13   21. 5

11.3   Equations

Page 273
1. 7   3. ${}^-6$ 5. 11   7. ${}^-16$
9. ${}^-4$

Page 274
1. $n = 5$ 3. $y = {}^-16$ 5. $r = {}^-5$
7. $s = 0$ 9. $h = 8$ 11. $b = 8$

Page 275
1. $d = 1$ 3. $g = {}^-14$ 5. $r = {}^-5$
7. $n = {}^-11$ 9. $j = 20$ 11. $a = 5$
13. $m = {}^-10$ 15. $p = {}^-3$

Page 276
1. $n = {}^-6$ 3. $y = {}^-8$ 5. $y = {}^-19$
7. $n = {}^-24$

Page 277
1. $n = 3$ 3. $n = 5$ 5. $k = 11$
7. $y = {}^-9$ 9. $s = {}^-4$ 11. $b = {}^-2$
27. $t = {}^-32$ 29. $s = 127$

Page 278
1. $t = {}^-3$ 3. $k = 2$ 5. $c = {}^-5$
7. $n = {}^-1$ 9. $b = {}^-5$

Page 279
1. $h = {}^-2$ 3. $t = {}^-3$ 5. $x = {}^-2$
7. $c = {}^-5$ 9. $z = {}^-5$ 11. $q = 0$
13. $k = 6$ 15. $e = 1$

Page 280
1. $y = {}^-5$ 3. $k = {}^-5$ 5. $n = 3$
7. $b = 10$

Page 281
1. $t = {}^-2$ 3. $h = {}^-5$ 5. $y = {}^-9$
7. $r = 7$ 9. $j = 11$ 11. $w = 4$
13. $u = 5$ 15. $m = {}^-8$ 25. $k = 3$
Practicing your skills: 1.   143.67   3.   5.3
5.   0.204   7.   247.76   9.   29.438
11.   1.6

Page 283
1. $n + 9 = {}^-5, n = {}^-14$ 3. $\frac{n}{6} = 3, n = {}^-18$
9. $\frac{n}{2} + {}^-8 = {}^-3, n = 10$

Page 285
1. The intended interpretation is:
$(2 \cdot 25) - (2 \cdot 5 + 20) = 50 - 30 = 20$

11.4   Coordinate Geometry

Page 287
1. $(4,3)$ 3. $(3,{}^-2)$ 5. $({}^-5,{}^-2)$
7. $(0,4)$ 9. $(5,{}^-1)$

Page 288
1. C 3. D 5. J

Page 289
18. C $(2\frac{1}{2},{}^-2\frac{1}{2})$ 20. E $({}^-2,{}^-1\frac{1}{2})$
22. G $({}^-2,3\frac{3}{4})$

Page 292
1. yes   3. yes   5. no

Page 294
1. $({}^-1,2)$ 3. yes

Page 295
1. $(3,2)$ 3. $({}^-1,1)$

11.5   Symmetry and Transformations

Page 301
1. 3   3. 0   5. 2   7. 5

Page 302
1. 180° rotational symmetry
3. 72° rotational symmetry

Page 303
1. 90°   3. 60°   5. 72°   7. order 3

Page 304
1. horizontally or vertically

Page 305
1. yes   3. yes   5. no

Page 312
1. A' $({}^-2,2)$ 3. C' $(1,3)$ 5. 3

Page 313
1. $(4,1)$ 3. $(5,3)$
5. The line containing the
points $(0,0)$, $(2,2)$, $({}^-2,{}^-2)$, etc.
11. $(2,2)$ 13. $(6,2)$
15. The sides of $A'B'C'D'$ are twice as long.
The area of $A'B'C'D'$ is 4 times that of $ABCD$.

Page 316
1. 4   3. 4   9. 15   11. $^-3$
17. $^-6$ 19. 31   23. $^-20$ 25. $^-24$
31. $^-4$ 33. 9   39. $n = {}^-12$
41. $n = 0$

12.1   Number Theory

Page 318
3.   2, 3, 5, 7, 11, 13, 17, 19

Page 319
1.   3   3.   13   7.   541

Page 320
1. $30 = 2 \cdot 3 \cdot 5$ 3. $28 = 2 \cdot 2 \cdot 7$
5. $100 = 2 \cdot 2 \cdot 5 \cdot 5$

Page 321
1. 2^3 3. $3^2 \cdot 5^2$ 5. $2^3 \cdot 5^2$
7. $3^3 \cdot 7^2$ 13.   324

Page 322
Exercises **1** and **3** are divisible by 2.
Exercise **5** is not. Exercise **11** is divisible by 3.
Exercise **13** is not.

Page 323
Exercise **1** is divisible by 4. Ex. **3** is *not*.
Ex. **11** is *not* divisible by 5, Ex. **13** is.
Ex. **21** is divisible by 9. Ex. **23** is *not*.

Page 324
Ex. **1** is *not* divisible by 6. Ex. **3** is.
Ex. **11** is divisible by 7. Ex. **13** is *not*.

Page 325
Ex. **1** and **3** are divisible by 8. Ex. **4** is *not*.
Ex. **11** is divisible by 11. Ex. **17** is *not*.
21. $3 \cdot 7 \cdot 5$ 23. $5 \cdot 7 \cdot 11$
25. $2 \cdot 3 \cdot 7 \cdot 17$

Page 326
1.   13, 17, 21

Page 327
1.   26, 31, 36   3.   19, 22, 25
7.   1, 4, 7, 10, 13, 16
9.   4, 13, 28, 49, 76, 109

Page 328
1.   15, 20, 15, 6

Page 329
1.   1, 1, 2, 3, 5, 8, 13, 21, 34, 55, 89

12.2   Counting Problems

Page 333
1.   6 (at, as, in, is, it, an)   3.   24

Page 335
1.   12   3.   12   5.   120   7.   120
9.   2   17. $n = 6!$ 19. $n = 3!$
21. $n = 5!$

Page 337
1. $6! = 720$ 3. $5! = 120$ 7. $70!$

Page 339
1. $C = 28$ 3. $C = 4$ 7. $C = 3$

12.3   Probability

Page 343
1.   P(tails) = $\frac{1}{2}$, P(heads) = $\frac{1}{2}$
3.   P(red marble) = $\frac{3}{5}$, P(blue marble) = $\frac{2}{5}$

Page 344
1. $40 \cdot \frac{1}{10} = 4$

Page 345
1. $\frac{1}{3} \cdot 120 = 40$ 3. $\frac{3}{6} \cdot 48 = 24$
7. $0.3 \cdot 80 = 24$

Page 346
1. (1,1), (1,2), (1,3), (1,4), (1,win), (2,1), (2,2), (2,3), (2,4), (2,win), (3,1), (3,2), (3,3), (3,4), (3,win), (win,1), (win,2), (win,3), (win,4), (win,win)   3. $\frac{4}{20}$ or $\frac{1}{5}$

Page 347
1. (H,H), (T,T), (H,T), (T,H)   3. $\frac{1}{4}$
5. (A,1), (A,2), (A,3), (A,4), (A,5), (A,6), (B,1), (B,2), (B,3), (B,4), (B,5), (B,6), (C,1), (C,2), (C,3), (C,4), (C,5), (C,6)   7. $\frac{1}{18}$

Page 348
1. $\frac{1}{8}$ 3. $\frac{3}{8}$

Page 349
1. 36   3. $\frac{1}{36}$ 5. $\frac{1}{36}$ 7. $\frac{6}{36}$ or $\frac{1}{6}$
9. $\frac{30}{36}$ or $\frac{5}{6}$

Page 350
1. $\frac{4}{25}$, $\frac{21}{25}$ 3. $\frac{2}{20}$ or $\frac{1}{10}$, $\frac{18}{20}$ or $\frac{9}{10}$

Page 351
1. 20, $\frac{11}{20}$, $\frac{9}{20}$ 3. 20, $\frac{9}{20}$, $\frac{11}{20}$
5. 20, $\frac{6}{20}$ or $\frac{3}{10}$, $\frac{14}{20}$ or $\frac{7}{10}$ 7. 25, $\frac{11}{25}$, $\frac{14}{25}$

Page 352
1. 10   3. $\frac{3}{10}$ 5. 1

Page 353
1. $P(2 \text{ red}) = \frac{1}{6}$ 3. $P(2 \text{ red}) = \frac{6}{10}$
5. $P(3 \text{ red}) = \frac{1}{20}$

12.4 Statistics

Page 356
1. 40   3. Assembling orders   5. 5%

Page 357
1. 40   3. Serving food   7. 5

Page 358
1. 11–12 a.m.: 25, 12 a.m.–1 p.m.: 22, 1–2 p.m.: 15, 2–3 p.m.: 13, 3–4 p.m.: 19, 4–5 p.m.: 21, 5–6 p.m.: 28   3. 360

Page 359
1. $50   3. $40

Page 360
1. $26\frac{2}{3} \approx 27$

Page 361
1. mean: 18.5, mode: 14, median: 17
3. mean: 312.4, mode: 309, median: 312
5. mean: 4290.2, median: 4288.5

Page 362
1. $2.49, $0.01   3. $2.49, $0.24

Page 363
1. range: 16, mean: 32, mean variation: $4.\overline{6}$

Page 364
1. 10%   3. 32%   7. 100   9. 70

Page 365
1. 30%   3. 60

Page 366
1. In general, the older the student the higher the wage.

Page 367
1. yes   3. about 170 cm

12.5 Square Roots and Irrational Numbers

Page 370
1. 16, 16, 32

Page 371
1. $c = 10$ units   3. $c = 13$ units

Page 372
1. 4   3. 7   5. 1   7. 6   9. 8
11. 11   21. 1.9   23. 4.5   25. 3.6
29. $\frac{1}{2}$

Page 373
1. 8.7   3. 4.1   5. 7.1   7. 14.1

Page 374
1. 3.873   3. 3.162   5. 4.690
7. 4.243   9. 4.359

Page 375
1. 5.39 m   3. 4.47 m

Page 376
1. 42342 rational   3. 00004 irrational
5. 47474 rational

Page 377
1. $0.\overline{6}$ 3. $0.8\overline{3}$ 5. $0.\overline{5}$ 7. $0.\overline{259}$
9. $0.\overline{7}$ 11. $0.\overline{007}$ 19. 1.732
21. 2.646   23. 2.828   25. 3.464

Page 380
1. $2^3 \cdot 7$ 3. 11^2 7. 5, 7, 9, 11, 13, 15
9. 5!   13. 4! or 24

More Practice

Page 382
Set A: 1. 110.60   3. 1.575   5. 105.8
7. 3.929   9. 150.95   11. 14.60
13. 1344.0
Set B: 1. 1.32   3. 8.52   5. 13.87
7. 66.74   9. 32.348   11. 15.66

Page 383
Set A: 1. 11.48   3. 0.480   5. 11.016
7. 3005.2   9. 13.0078   11. 27.104
Set B: 1. 2.4   3. 4.6   5. 12.1
7. 26.2   9. 0.63   17. 1.304
19. 0.52   21. 5.48   23. 4.18

Page 384
Set A: 1. 0.375   3. 0.4375   5. 0.25
7. 2.25   9. 0.875   31. $0.42\frac{6}{7}$
33. $0.62\frac{1}{2}$ 35. $1.44\frac{4}{9}$ 37. $0.16\frac{2}{3}$
39. $0.57\frac{1}{7}$
Set B: 1. $\frac{4}{5}$ 3. $\frac{9}{25}$ 5. $\frac{3}{5}$ 7. $\frac{3}{8}$
9. $\frac{1}{50}$ 11. $\frac{7}{16}$

Page 385
Set A: 1. $1\frac{7}{12}$ 3. $1\frac{7}{30}$ 5. $1\frac{1}{20}$
7. $16\frac{5}{12}$ 9. $12\frac{13}{24}$ 11. $12\frac{29}{30}$
Set B: 1. $\frac{5}{8}$ 3. $\frac{1}{10}$ 5. $\frac{7}{12}$ 7. $\frac{2}{15}$
9. $\frac{3}{8}$ 11. $\frac{5}{12}$

Page 386
Set A: 1. $a = \frac{2}{5}$ 3. $f = \frac{2}{7}$ 5. $k = \frac{1}{3}$
7. $e = \frac{1}{12}$ 9. $g = \frac{3}{20}$ 11. $z = \frac{3}{8}$
Set B: 1. $w = \frac{5}{6}$ 3. $r = 1\frac{1}{2}$ 5. $x = 1\frac{1}{2}$
7. $f = \frac{2}{3}$ 9. $d = 3$ 11. $e = 1\frac{1}{9}$

Page 387
Set A: 1. $n = 8$ 3. $n = 36$
5. $n = 13\frac{1}{2}$ 7. $n = 42$ 9. $n = 35$
11. $n = 42$ 13. $n = 56$ 15. $n = 27$
Set B: 1. 23%   3. 46%   5. 9%
7. 50.1%   9. 9.1%   11. 203%
13. 627%   15. 176%

Page 388
Set A: 1. 28.6%   3. 88.9%   5. 54.5%
7. 13.0%   9. 69.2%   11. 20.6%
13. 46.7%   15. 93.8%
Set B: 1. $\frac{1}{10}$ 3. $\frac{7}{10}$ 5. $\frac{19}{50}$ 7. $\frac{3}{10}$
9. $\frac{21}{50}$ 11. $\frac{17}{50}$ 13. $\frac{17}{20}$ 15. $\frac{12}{125}$

Page 389
Set A: 1. 11.44   3. 45.76
5. 1.49454   7. 169.2   9. 369.46
11. 2.10678   13. 337.2   15. 310.8
Set B: 1. 40%   3. 20%   5. 8%
7. 60%   9. 5%   11. 34%   13. 40%
15. 80%

Page 390

Set A: 1. $0.40n = 14$, $n = 35$
3. $0.18n = 9$, $n = 50$
5. $0.35n = 14$, $n = 40$
7. $0.60n = 42$, $n = 70$
9. $0.04n = 1.80$, $n = 45$
Set B: 1. $n = 9.1$ 3. $n = 32.85$
5. $n = 179.2$ 11. 20%   13. 70%
17. $n = 35$ 19. $n = 25$

Page 391

Set A: 1. Discount: \$2.60, Sale price: \$23.40
3. Discount: \$10.80, Sale price: \$61.20
5. Discount: \$1.89, Sale price: \$7.56
Set B: 1. $I = \$75.00$ 3. $I = \$0.15$
5. $I = \$170.00$ 7. $I = \$18\,000.00$
9. $I = \$42\,000.00$

Page 392

Set A: 1. $^-2$ 3. 6   5. $^-15$ 7. 3
9. $^-12$ 11. $^-5$ 13. $^-8$ 15. 6
Set B: 1. $^-5$ 3. $^-7$ 5. 8   7. $^-8$
9. 17   11. $^-1$ 13. $^-9$ 15. 12

Page 393

Set A: 1. $^-20$ 3. 42   5. $^-14$
7. $^-32$ 9. 45   11. $^-48$ 13. $^-39$
15. $^-48$
Set B: 1. $^-8$ 3. $^-4$ 5. $^-9$ 7. 5
9. $^-3$ 11. $^-4$ 13. $^-6$ 15. $^-7$

Page 394

Set A: 1. $n = 5$ 3. $z = 15$ 5. $w = 8$
7. $e = ^-2$ 9. $k = 19$ 11. $t = 8$
13. $m = 4$ 15. $s = ^-13$
Set B: 1. $r = ^-2$ 3. $a = 2$ 5. $x = ^-5$
7. $m = 4$ 9. $k = 3$ 11. $g = ^-2$
13. $h = 5$ 15. $j = 7$